THE ENCYCLOPEDIA OF
ANCIENT EGYPT

THE ENCYCLOPEDIA OF
ANCIENT EGYPT

MARGARET BUNSON

GRAMERCY BOOKS
NEW YORK

This 1999 edition is published by Gramercy Books, an imprint of Random House Value Publishing, a division of Random House, Inc., New York, by arrangement with Facts on File, Inc., New York.

Gramercy is a registered trademark and the colophon is a trademark of Random House, Inc.

Random House
New York • Toronto • London • Sydney • Auckland
www.randomhouse.com

Printed and bound in the United States of America

Library of Congress Cataloging-in-Publication Data

Bunson, Margaret.
 The encyclopedia of ancient Egypt / Margaret Bunson.
   p. cm.
 Originally published : New York : Facts on File Publications, c1991.
 Include bibliographical references and index.
 ISBN 0-517-20380-4
 1. Egypt—Civilization—To 332 B.C.—Dictionaries. 2. Egypt—Antiquities—Dictionaries. I. Title.
 DT58.D96 1999
 932'.003—dc21   99-11512
                  CIP

8 7 6

Dedicated to the memory of Dr. Rafael Zamora of Aguadilla, Puerto Rico, *sine qua non*, and with sincere gratitude to Deirdre Mullane for her unstinting support

CONTENTS

HOW TO USE THIS BOOK

The Encyclopedia of Ancient Egypt has been prepared to offer diverse information about that nation from the predynastic period to the close of the New Kingdom (1070 B.C.). Specific topics are keyed to historical eras or designed to provide details about particular customs, practices or traditions. Major subjects, such as agriculture, gods and goddesses, mortuary rituals, the military, pharaohs, queens, and religion, span the different dynasties in order to offer an overview of the evolution of such matters.

Sites and personalities from the various eras are included, with reference to their importance or their role in the development of the nation. The dates of these individuals are provided, and the Greek name is included in many cases, especially if that version of the name is familiar to modern studies. In all instances the kings are recorded with their prenomens ("first cartouche" or throne names) given in parentheses.

Anyone wishing to begin learning about this period of ancient Egyptian history should read EGYPT, an entry that provides geographical and historical material about the nation. Charts provided at the front of the book will also give information concerning Egypt's development and relationship to other lands.

If interested in a particular subject, begin with that entry and then read the cross-referenced entries concerning the same subject matter. For instance, if the reader is interested in the 18th Dynasty and Tut'ankhamun, the section on EGYPT, HISTORICAL PERIODS will place that royal line and that king in the proper chronological and political setting. Tut'ankhamun is listed separately, and in the entry concerning his life one will discover other relatives or issues of significance to his reign.

If interested in the religious life of the ancient Egyptians, the reader can start with the entry on religion and then read the cross-references to the gods and goddesses, temples, priests, mortuary rituals, cosmogony, and eternity. Additional entries on the Per-Ankh (House of Life), solar cults, barks of the gods and cult centers will offer further details and new avenues of exploration on the subject.

If the reader is interested in pyramids, the entry on that subject will lead to others, such as mastabas, sarcophagi, cartonnage (coffins), offerings, liturgies, the Judgment Hall of Osiris, valley temples, and mummies (which are discussed in detail in the entry on mortuary rituals).

Once the book has become familiar to the reader, he or she can begin to explore unique aspects of Egyptian life that have survived over the centuries in the various art forms and in the stunning architecture found along the Nile. Individuals are included alongside customs or traditions so that the spirit of the various eras can come to life. Other entries on literature, art and architecture, astronomy, and women will add details about the various aspects of day-to-day existence so many centuries ago. Art work (adaptations of reliefs, paintings or statues) has been included, with maps to provide clarification of the geographic aspects of Egypt.

PREHISTORIC ERAS

Upper Egypt	
Badarian	c. 4500–4000 B.C.
Naqada I (Amratian)	c. 4000–3500 B.C.
Naqada II (Gerzean)	c. 3500–3000 B.C.
Lower Egypt	
Faiyum A	c. 4400–3900 B.C.
Merimde	c. 4300–3700 B.C.
El Omari	c. 3700–3400 B.C.
Ma'adi	c. 3400–3000 B.C.

HISTORICAL PERIODS

PERIOD	DYNASTY	ACHIEVEMENTS
LATE PREDYNASTIC PERIOD c. 3000 B.C.		Under Na'rmer and other kings, Egypt slowly becomes a nation, with territories subdued and a form of government beginning.
EARLY DYNASTIC PERIOD (ARCHAIC) 2920–2575 B.C.	1st Dynasty 2920–2770 B.C.	Upper and Lower Egypt possibly united, probably still in separate confederations. Trade with Mediterranean cities. Development of calendar and writing. Expeditions to Nubia. Royal tombs at Abydos and Saqqara. Memphis founded.
	2nd Dynasty 2770–2649 B.C.	Rebellions and wars continue. Kha'sekhemwy finishes unification process of nation. Medical treatises in use by priests. Stone used in buildings and statues. Work in faience, gems, wood and ivory. Furniture created with style. Osirian cult popular.
	3rd Dynasty 2649–2575 B.C.	Step Pyramid built at Saqqara. Northern Nubia under Egyptian domination.
OLD KINGDOM PERIOD 2575–2134 B.C.	4th Dynasty 2575–2465 B.C.	Navy put into use. Pyramids built at Giza. Bent Pyramid built at Dashur. Nubian and Libyan campaigns conducted. Copper mines in operation in Sinai. Wood brought from Lebanon. Heliopolis and cult of Re' popular.
	5th Dynasty 2465–2323 B.C.	Expeditions sent to Punt. Pyramid Texts adorn walls of royal tombs. Art and architecture flower.
	6th Dynasty 2323–2150 B.C.	Nubian expeditions increased. Mercenaries used in battles. Military stance altered against Libya and the Sinai. Unrest develops in various nomes. Long reign of Pepi II.
	7th Dynasty 2150 B.C.	Memphite dynasty.
	8th Dynasty 2150–2134 B.C.	Brief period of territorial rule.

PERIOD	DYNASTY	ACHIEVEMENTS
FIRST INTERMEDIATE PERIOD 2134–2040 B.C.	9th/10th Dynasties 2134–2040 B.C.	Herakleopolitan clan campaigns to unite nation. Coffin texts used in noble tombs. Kings use nome allies in battles. Eloquent Peasant preaches to king. *Instructions* written for Merikare'.
	11th Dynasty (Theban) 2134–2040 B.C.	Inyotef clan rules as contemporaries of Herakleopolitan kings. Thebans begin war to regain all of Egypt.
MIDDLE KINGDOM 2040–1640 B.C.	11th Dynasty (All of Egypt) 2040–1991 B.C.	Mentuhotpe II defeats kings from Herakleopolis. Deir el-Bahri site of mortuary shrine. Art and architecture revived.
	12th Dynasty 1991–1783 B.C.	Amenemhet I assumes throne. *Instructions* dictated. Tale of *Sinuhe the Sailor* written. Faiyum restored with hydraulics. Copper and gold mines in operation. Forts built to Third Cataract of Nile. Canal rebuilt at First Cataract. Cultural renaissance takes place. Amon becomes important deity. Wall of Prince erected on borders.
	13th Dynasty 1783–after 1640 B.C.	Attempts made to restore unity. Nomes become independent. Asiatic (Hyksos) infiltrations take place.
	14th Dynasty	Xois line of kings, probably contemporaries of 13th or 15th Dynasties.
SECOND INTERMEDIATE PERIOD 1640–1532 B.C.	15th Dynasty 1640–1532 B.C.	Hyksos royal house in eastern Delta makes Avaris its capital. Horse, chariots, *shaduf* and weapons of bronze introduced.
	16th Dynasty	Minor Hyksos kings as contemporaries of 15th Dynasty.
	17th Dynasty 1640–1550 B.C.	Theban kings ruling over Upper Egypt. New musical instruments introduced. War begins against Hyksos. Nubian mercenaries used in army.
NEW KINGDOM 1550–1070 B.C.	18th Dynasty 1550–1307 B.C.	Hyksos withdraw from Egypt. Upper and Lower Egypt united. Tuthmosis I reaches Euphrates. Amenhotep I opens Valley of Kings. Tuthmosis III carves out empire. Amon chief deity of Egypt. Thebes becomes capital. Akhenaten abandons Thebes for 'Amarna and god Aten. Horemhab takes throne and begins road to empire again. Karnak and Luxor temples extended.
	19th Dynasty 1307–1196 B.C.	Ramessids regain lost lands but clash with Hittites. Abu Simbel and Per-Ramesses constructed. Treaty with Hittites. Hypostyle hall built at Karnak.
	20th Dynasty 1196–1070 B.C.	Pirates and other invaders defeated. Ramesses III repels Sea Peoples and Libyans. Empire starts to collapse in face of Hittite demands and evolving nations. Medinet Habu erected. Tomb robberies discovered at Thebes and trial ensues. Priests of Amon work to usurp throne.

(continued)

PERIOD	DYNASTY	ACHIEVEMENTS
	LATER PERIODS*	
THIRD INTERMEDIATE PERIOD 1070–712 B.C.	21st Dynasty 1070–945 B.C.	
	22nd Dynasty 945–712 B.C.	
	23rd Dynasty c. 828–712 B.C.	
	24th Dynasty 724–712 B.C. (Saite)	
	25th Dynasty 770–712 B.C. (Nubian and Theban)	
LATE PERIOD 712–332 B.C.	25th Dynasty 712–657 B.C. (All of Egypt)	
	26th Dynasty 664–525 B.C.	
	27th Dynasty 525–404 B.C. (Persian)	
	28th Dynasty 404–399 B.C.	
	29th Dynasty 399–380 B.C.	
	30th Dynasty 380–343 B.C.	
	2nd Persian Period 343–332 B.C.	
GRECO-ROMAN PERIOD 332 B.C.–A.D. 395	Macedonian Dynasty 332–304 B.C.	
	Ptolemaic Dynasty 304–c.30 B.C.	
	Roman Emperors c.30 B.C.–A.D. 395	

*The Encyclopedia of Ancient Egypt covers the period from the unification to the fall of the New Kingdom. Though not discussed in detail in this volume, the later periods are mentioned briefly in the entry EGYPT, HISTORICAL PERIODS to provide the reader with a concise summary of later events sometimes referred to by scholars.

REGIONAL TIME CHART FOR EGYPT

PERIOD	EGYPT	MESOPOTAMIA AND MEDITERRANEAN
3000 B.C.	Egyptian military leaders begin process of unification.	Sumerian city states flourishing, with Uruk and Lagash gaining prominence.
2900 B.C.	First kings rule in Memphis. Towns flourishing. Trade set with Mediterranean. Expeditions sent to Nubia. Royal tombs at Abydos and Saqqara. Calendar and paper in use. Medical lore written by priests.	Troy settled and towns develop in Syria and in Palestine. Megalithic temples erected on Malta.
2700 B.C.	Kha'sekhemwy completes unification of Egypt. Stone used in buildings, statues, and work is done in faience, gems, wood and ivory. Furniture becomes stylish.	Gilgamesh rules in Uruk. Minoans on Crete establish trade routes at sea.
2600 B.C.	Step Pyramid raised at Saqqara. Northern Nubia under Egyptian domination.	

PERIOD	EGYPT	MESOPOTAMIA AND MEDITERRANEAN
2500 B.C.	Pyramids erected at Giza. Bent Pyramid built at Dashur. Copper mines in operation on Sinai. Wood brought from Lebanon. Heliopolis and cult of Re'flourishes.	First dynasty begins at Ur. Megaliths appear in Europe.
2400 B.C.	Expeditions sent to Punt. Pyramid Texts used in royal tombs. Art and architecture flower.	Sumer unified by Umma king. Sargon of Akkad conquers Elam, Syria and southeastern Asia Minor.
2300/2100 B.C.	Nubian expeditions increased. Military activities broadened. Unrest develops in parts of Egypt. Pepi II's reign lasts almost a century. Memphite dynasty tries to unite Egypt. Territorial rule becomes only form of government. Herakleopolitans try to conquer lands. Coffin texts used in tombs. Mentuhotpe of Thebes begins war of unification.	Famed ziggurat built at Sumer.
2000 B.C.	Mentuhotpe II unifies Egypt. Deir el-Bahri becomes shrine. Art and architecture flower.	Sumer is invaded by Mesopotamian tribes; Ur is destroyed. Babylon become a cultural pinnacle.
1900 B.C.	Amenemhet I assumes throne. *Instructions for Merikare'* written. Faiyum reclaimed with hydraulics. Wall of Prince erected on borders.	Minoans build palaces on Crete. Cyprus begins copper trade.
1800/1700 B.C.	Copper and gold mines in operation. Forts built to Third Cataract on Nile. Canal built at First Cataract. Cultural renaissance evident. Amon becomes important deity. Egypt begins to disintegrate into separate territories. Asiatic infiltrations begin.	Hammurabi gives famous laws in Babylon.
1600 B.C.	Hyksos build capital at Avaris. Theban dynasty rules in Upper Egypt. Opposition mounts against Asiatics.	Knossos palace destroyed on Crete.
1500 B.C.	Thebans make war on Avaris. Hyksos routed from Delta. Tuthmosis I reaches Euphrates. Valley of the Kings started as royal burial site.	Hittites destroy Babylon. Santorini-Thera erupts in Mediterranean. Minoan culture collapses. Assyria becomes vassal state of the Mitanni Empire.
1400 B.C.	Hatshepsut rules Eygpt as Queen-Pharaoh. Tuthmosis III carves out Egyptian empire. Tuthmosis IV restores Sphinx at Giza.	Suppliliuma I founds Hittite Empire. Assyria becomes empire again. Mitanni power crushed.
1300 B.C.	Amenhotep III rules vast empire from Thebes. Akhenaten moves capital to 'Amarna, with worship of god Aten. Smenkhkare' and Tut'ankhamun succeed him. Horemhab takes throne. Ramesses I starts new dynasty.	Assyrians begin occupation of Babylon. Hittites clash with Egyptians.
1200/1000 B.C.	Ramesses II wars against Hittites, signs treaty. Libyans try to invade Delta area, stopped by Merneptah. Sea Peoples defeated and enslaved. Powers of king weaken after Ramesses III. Abu Simbel and Per-Ramesses constructed. Hypostyle hall built at Karnak. Medinet Habu erected. Priests of Amon usurp powers and throne.	Babylon restored by Nebuchadnezzar. Sea Peoples assault Hittite domains. Assyria wars on neighboring lands. Phoenicia devastated by Sea Peoples and pirates.

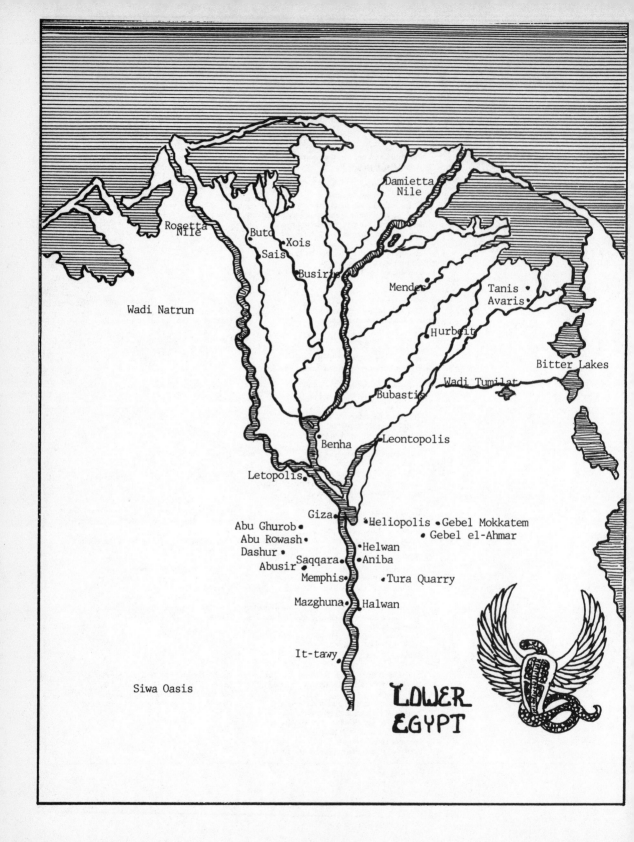

Damietta
Nile

Rosetta
Nile

Buto
Xois
Sais

Busiris

Wadi Natrun

Mendes

Tanis
Avaris

Hurbeit

Bitter Lakes

Wadi Tumilat

Bubastis

Benha

Leontopolis

Letopolis

Giza

Heliopolis

Gebel Mokkatem

Abu Ghurob

Gebel el-Ahmar

Abu Rowash

Dashur

Helwan

Saqqara

Aniba

Abusir

Memphis

Tura Quarry

Mazghuna

Halwan

It-tawy

Siwa Oasis

LOWER
EGYPT

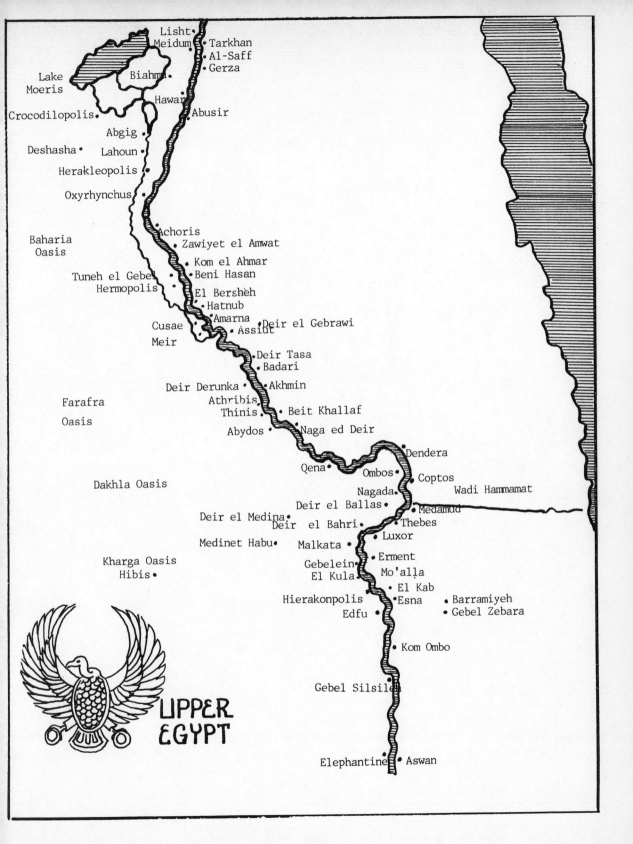

Lisht
Meidum • Tarkhan
• Al-Saff
• Gerza

Lake
Moeris
Biahmu •
Hawara •
Abusir •
Crocodilopolis •
Abgig •
Deshasha • Lahoun •
Herakleopolis •
Oxyrhynchus •

Baharia
Oasis
Achoris •
• Zawiyet el Amwat
• Kom el Ahmar
Tuneh el Gebel • Beni Hasan
Hermopolis • El Bersheh
• Hatnub
• Amarna
Cusae • • Deir el Gebrawi
Meir • Assiut
• Deir Tasa
• Badari

Farafra
Oasis
Deir Derunka • • Akhmin
Athribis •
Thinis • • Beit Khallaf
Abydos • • Naga ed Deir
• Dendera
Qena • Ombos • • Coptos
Dakhla Oasis Nagada • Wadi Hammamat
Deir el Ballas • • Medamud
Deir el Medina • • Thebes
Deir el Bahri •
Medinet Habu • Luxor •
Malkata • Erment
Kharga Oasis Gebelein • Mo'alla
Hibis • El Kula • • El Kab
Hierakonpolis • Esna • Barramiyeh
Edfu • Gebel Zebara

• Kom Ombo

Gebel Silsileh

UPPER
EGYPT

Elephantine • Aswan

A'ah the ancient Egyptian name for the moon, representing the god THOTH.

A'a-Nefer the name for the sacred bull at ERMENT (Hermonthis), which was originally dedicated to the god MONT. In time this animal played a part in the cultic ceremonies of other deities. (See APIS, BUCHIS and MNEVIS.)

A'aru, Field of a paradise that Egyptians believed awaited them after death. The Field of A'aru was a garden located in the region known as AMENTI, the West, traditionally the site of death and the grave in Egyptian religious texts. A'aru was situated near water and was "blessed with breezes," two critical attributes of any edenic landscape in the Egyptian mortuary texts. (See ETERNITY and MORTUARY RITUALS.)

A'at a queen of the 12th Dynasty, a lesser ranked wife of AMENEMHET III (1844–1797 B.C.). A'at was recorded as having died at the age of thirty-five. She was buried in a granite sarcophagus at DASHUR, near the king.

ab the name given the human heart in religious documents. As a physical or anatomical organ, the heart was called *hat*.

Abbott Papyrus a Ramessid document dating to the 20th Dynasty (c. 1160 B.C.). The papyrus is valued for its account of the investigation of serious grave robberies during that era. High-ranking officials were involved in the investigation, which was dramatic and prolonged, and a trial ensued. The Abbott Papyrus is 17 inches high and contains columns that give an account of the proceedings. The document is now in the British Museum, where it is prized for its detailed analysis of the closing decades of the New

The *ab*, or heart, amulet, normally made out of green jasper or some other green stone.

Kingdom. (See AMHERST PAPYRUS and TOMB ROBBERY TRIAL.)

Abgig a region of the FAIYUM near HAWARA where ruling families of the local inhabitants maintained estates and influence. All that remains of ancient Abgig in modern times is a relic of the 12th Dynasty (c. 1991–1783 B.C.), a large stela of SENWOSRET I.

Abisko a site not far from the First Cataract of the Nile, where Middle Kingdom inscriptions were discovered. These inscriptions date to the reign of MENTUHOTPE II of the 11th Dynasty (2061–2010 B.C.) and commemorate his Nubian military campaign.

Abu the ancient Egyptian name for ELEPHANTINE Island at Aswan.

Abu Ghurob a site at the edge of the desert near GIZA, where IZI (Neuserre') built his sun temple c.

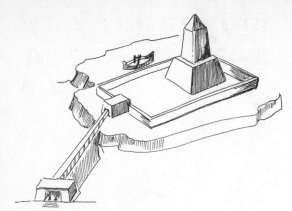

Sun temple of Izi (Neuserre') as reconstructed.

2400 B.C. The shrine contained a covered causeway that led to a VALLEY TEMPLE and a rectangular podium, supported by a squat obelisk in the style of HELIOPOLIS' religious structures. The corridors of the temple were decorated with reliefs depicting the seasons of the year. A solar bark, designed to transport the king's spirit into eternity, measuring more than 97 feet in length and fashioned out of bricks, once graced the temple complex. The local inhabitants call the complex the Pyramid of Righa.

Abu Rowash a site near the flat-topped hills of GIZA, an extension of the Old Kingdom cemetery of MEMPHIS. Various dynastic tomb complexes were discovered there, including the unfinished pyramid of RA'DJEDEF of the 4th Dynasty (2575–2465 B.C.).

Abu Simbel site, south of Aswan near the Second Cataract of the Nile, of the temple of RAMESSES II of the 19th Dynasty (1290–1224 B.C.). This shrine was dedicated to the gods AMON and Re'-Horakthy, and to the memory of Ramesses himself. A court and terrace were designed to emphasize the striking facade's primary feature, four colossal seated statues of Ramesses among several smaller figures. The colossal statues measure approximately 65 feet in height. Inscriptions added to the structure identify it as Ramesses' mortuary shrine. Within the temple is a hall that measures more than 58 feet by 54 feet, with elaborate pillars, vestibules and reliefs. This hall is surrounded by other chambers and by a set of royal apartments, no doubt prepared for the king's convenience and that of his retinue and harem.

A second rock-hewn temple on the site was erected in honor of the goddess HATHOR. Colossal statues at this shrine include one of Queen NEFERTARI, one of Ramesses' consorts. The underground portions of

this temple include a square hall, vestibules and chambers set aside for religious rituals in honor of the goddess. The temples of Abu Simbel were hubs of activity during the Ramessid era, ceremonial centers maintaining a large staff of priests and workers. Some records indicate that there was an earthquake in the region shortly after the shrine was completed. Repairs were conducted over a period of time to restore the complex to its original beauty. Because the flood level of the Nile was altered by the construction of the Aswan High Dam, the temples of Abu Simbel were removed from the original site and rebuilt on a higher level, away from the river, in 1968. The cost of the four-year project was estimated at $40 million.

ABU SIMBEL   a colossal statue from the shrine of Ramesses II.

Abusir an ancient site, located between GIZA and SAQQARA, where tomb complexes of the 5th Dynasty were discovered. The PYRAMIDS of SAHURE' (2458–2446 B.C.), KAKAI (2446–2426 B.C.) and IZI (Neuserre') (2416–2392 B.C.) are considerably smaller than the pyramids at Giza but their design and construction reveal a maturity and a sophistication of style and skill among Egyptian tomb artisans. Elegant, and adorned with papyrus columns, the pyramids at Abusir were once covered in fine limestone. The floors were fashioned of hewn basalt, and Sahure''s complex contained a copper drain pipe measuring 330 yards in length. Reliefs and paintings in the interiors of the pyramids and their adjoining temples document a stable period, a time when the natural resources of Egypt were being successfully exploited, international trade was fostered and artistic values exchanged. (See ART AND ARCHITECTURE.)

Abydos a city north of DENDERA, capital of the eighth NOME, or district, called the Thinite nome. Abydos was considered the greatest of all cemeteries and the home of the god OSIRIS. The necropolis area of the city was in use from the earliest times and benefited from royal patronage throughout its history.

Of the royal monuments, the temple of SETI I of the 19th Dynasty (1306–1290 B.C.) is the largest, built of fine white limestone and containing splendid reliefs. The first two courts of the temple and the portico were probably completed by RAMESSES II (1290–1224 B.C.), his successor, after Seti's death. One scene in the temple depicts Ramesses adoring the gods ISIS and Osiris as well as Seti deified. Ramesses is also credited with the decorations in the first hypostyle hall of the temple, which has seven doors leading to chapels beyond a second hypostyle hall. The second hypostyle hall serves as a vestibule for the seven chapels incorporated into its west wall. False vaults cover the chapels, and all have reliefs. The chapels honored six gods and deified Seti I.

A KING LIST was discovered in a gallery in the shrine, showing Seti I and Ramesses II as a prince offering honors to their royal predecessors. Beside the Gallery of Lists there are halls for the preservation of the barks of the gods, butchers' quarters and magazines. Immediately behind the temple is an area called the OSIREION, actually a cenotaph, or false tomb, built by Seti I but probably completed by MERNEPTAH, his grandson. A feature of this shrine is an island, formed by canals of water that were kept filled at all times, upon which the sarcophagus and canopic chest were maintained.

The temple of Ramesses II, located to the northeast of the shrine of Seti I, is noted for its delicate reliefs, which provide a depiction of the Battle of KADESH, carved into limestone. A red granite doorway leads to a pillared open court, and more reliefs depict a procession of offerings for the king. A portico on the west side of the temple opens onto small chapels honoring Seti I and various deities. Some of the deities have been provided with suites of rooms, and

Abydos, the cult center of Osiris, depicted here in a typical shrine.

there is a humanoid Djed Pillar in one of the apartment chambers. Granite statues honor Ramesses II, Seti I, the god Amon and two other goddesses. The temple of Osiris in Abydos is located to the northeast of Ramesses II's temple. Originally called Kom el-Sultan, the area has only a few remains of a limestone portico and ramparts. Cenotaphs dedicated to individuals were buried in the area.

The SHUNET EL-ZBIB, or Storehouse of Dates, the enclosure dating to the 2nd Dynasty (2770–2649 B.C.), is in the northwestern desert. Two actual complexes, with massive inner walls and outer mud-brick walls, had main ramparts. The cenotaphs of the royal personages are located farther out in the desert, at a site known as UMM EL-GA'AB, the "Mother of Pots," because of the large numbers of vessels discovered on the surface—jars used for the funerary offerings of the graves. To the south, cenotaphs of the Middle Kingdom and early New Kingdom were also discovered. A temple of SENWOSRET III (1878–1841? B.C.) stands at the edge of the desert. The king's cenotaph lays near the face of the nearby cliffs. A pyramid, possibly that of 'AHMOSE I of the 18th Dynasty (1550–

1525 B.C.), is located south of the temple. A mortuary complex of Queen TETISHERI, the grandmother of Ahmose, is also in the area.

Abydos, as the seat of the Osirian cult, was a large city and was revered during all eras of ancient Egypt. The city's original deity was apparently a black, dog-headed creature known as "Chief of the Dwellers of the West," a title assumed by Osiris when his cult grew popular along the Nile. The West, AMENTI, was always the territory of death in the nation's religious and mythological texts. Osiris' head was believed to have rested in Abydos, according to the mythological texts. In time, however, the tomb of DJER of the 1st Dynasty, the second king (c. 2900 B.C.), was named the true grave of Osiris by his priests. The grave thus became involved in the annual celebration of Osiris' death and resurrection.

Two stelae were discovered in Abydos. One, measuring 6 feet by 3 feet, was from the 13th Dynasty, placed there by NEFERHOTEP I (c. 1741–1730 B.C.). The second records the plans of TUTHMOSIS I of the 18th Dynasty (1504–1492 B.C.) to honor Osiris by endowing the god's temple with gifts.

Abydos List   See KING LISTS.

Achoris   a site located just south of the FAIYUM, named Tinha by its modern inhabitants. Achoris was used as a necropolis by the powerful NOMARCHS of the 5th Dynasty era (2465–2323 B.C.). Rock-carved tombs were discovered there.

'Adjib   the fifth king of the 1st Dynasty at MEMPHIS (c. 2700 B.C.). He is reported to have ruled about 14 years, in an era of change and turmoil, when the NOME clans offered resistance to unity. He used the title King of Upper and Lower Egypt, but there is no evidence that he had control of the entire area.

His queen was Tarset or Betrest, a Memphite heiress who perhaps added legitimacy to his claim as a unifier of Egypt. She is listed as the mother of his successor, SEMERKHET.

Admonitions of Ipuwer   a text recording the observations and adages of a sage who described conditions in Egypt at the end of the Old or the Middle Kingdom. The *Admonitions* offer a remarkably pessimistic view of Egyptian society and the state of affairs at the time, something not seen frequently in Egyptian writings. The text was discovered in the Papyrus Leiden 344, having been copied by 19th Dynasty scribes (c. 1200 B.C.). The *Admonitions* address an unidentified king with vivid images of invading tribesmen from the desert wastes and other problems confronting Egypt at the time.

afnet   a head covering shown on the goddesses SELKET and ISIS and on one statue of TUT'ANKHAMUN (1333–1323 B.C.), discovered in his tomb. The *afnet* resembled the NEMES, the royal headdress, but was not striped and lacked the front panels. Its use was probably restricted to royalty.

Afnet, the head covering used by Egyptian royalty and in depictions of the gods.

agate   a semiprecious stone, a variety of quartz, found in the Egyptian quarry at WADI HAMMAMAT.

agriculture   the science and practice of the ancient Egyptians from predynastic times that enabled them to transform an expanse of semiarid land into rich fields after each inundation of the Nile. Agriculture in Egypt always depended upon the pooling of resources and labor so that the mineral-rich waters of the Nile could be introduced inland for the fertilization of lands to be cultivated.

Early farmers dug trenches from the Nile shore to the farmlands, using draw wells and then the SHADUF, a primitive machine that allowed them to raise levels of water from the Nile into canals. The *shaduf* was introduced into Egypt by the HYKSOS, or Asiatics (c. 1600/1500 B.C.). Fields thus irrigated produced abundant annual crops.

From the predynastic times agriculture was the mainstay of the Egyptian economy. Most Egyptians were employed in agricultural labors, either on their own lands or on the estates of the temples or nobles. Control of irrigation became a major concern, and provincial officials were held responsible for the reg-

Shaduf, the Hyksos invention that greatly aided the Egyptians in their agricultural endeavors.

ulation of water. Storage of crops occurred at the local level and at the royal granaries in the capital. Assessors were sent from the capital to the provinces to collect taxes in the form of grain. The local temples of the gods also had vast fields with their own irrigation needs. The temples had storage units, and were subject to taxes in most eras, unless exempted for a particular reason or favor.

Agriculture began in the FAIYUM and in the DELTA regions well before the start of the dynastic period. Normally the Egyptians plowed the fields with oxen, and teams of two men each worked to form shallow furrows for the seeds. One man guided the plow and

A pastoral scene of cattle and the plow from the Old Kingdom.

the other led the oxen through the designated pattern. Some tomb reliefs depict the activity and show a second plow being dragged behind the first one. The second implement turned up the earth between the furrows. If the farmers wanted only the top layer of soil tilled in any given season, they used lighter plows, normally pushed by the farm staff. In either case the furrows had to be broken up after the initial plowing. Men and women entered the fields with simple wooden hoes to break up the clumps of earth.

The sowing of the fields was a two-part activity in most areas. The farmers put the seeds into the earth and then drove herds of sheep or swine into the fields to trample the seeds deep into the furrows. Normally crops were harvested with sickles.

Barley, emmer and other crops were gathered with such tools and taken to the local threshing areas, where again animals were employed. The harvest was carried on the backs of donkeys or asses, and at the storge area the crops were ground by oxen.

The first fruits of each harvest were reserved for the local gods and the temples. The deity Min, popular throughout Egypt, was offered praise for each crop drawn from the earth. Altars were sometimes erected to provide adequate ceremony, and granary officials, priests or government representatives, were on hand for all harvests; they measured the crops for tax assessments. These celebrations were attended by entire districts, and the people gave thanks to the Nile and to the agricultural patrons for the abundance of another year.

Egyptian Crops and Products

The Egyptians used the main cereal crops of their fields for the staples of their daily diets: emmer (*Triticum dicoccum*) for bread and barley for beer. Wheat was not known along the Nile until the Ptolemaic Period (304–30 B.C.). Early Egyptians also raised chickpeas and lentils, pomegranates, lettuce (of various varieties), onions, carob, garlic and plants used for oils, such as sesame. Honey collected from hives was used as a sweetener and there were condiments and spices, although these are presently unidentified.

Most commoners did not enjoy the luxury of meat as part of their daily meals. Herds of cattle were large in many eras, however, and the Egyptians liked beef, mutton, pork and goat. It is also probable that certain species of wild antelope supplemented diets.

The Nile provided a variety of fish for the table, and the Egyptians became skilled at catching them. Fish were netted or caught in baskets. Spearfishing and angling were done from small rafts made of papyrus. There appear to have been some religious

HYDRAULIC SYSTEMS IN THE FAIYUM

One of the first necessities for the evolving Egyptian nation was to control the Nile River, which inundated the land throughout its valley each year with vast desposits of silt and mud. In the Faiyum, where predynastic inhabitants had discovered the ease with which they could turn to agricultural pursuits, efforts were made to channel the water coming through the Bahr Yusef into the region. Dikes, canals and ditches were dug in the Old Kingdom (2575–2134 B.C.) but the major work was accomplished by the kings of the 12th Dynasty, especially by AMENEMHET III (1844–1797 B.C.).

The purpose of the irrigation systems and hydraulic projects was to extend the time during which the Nile waters could be made available to fields in the western Delta and the Faiyum. The Nile had formed Lake Moeris there in predynastic eras, and the Egyptians started building a retaining wall some 27 miles long, a construction which provided them with 27,000 acres of farmland. During the flood period, the Nile provided new water for the lake, and the water was carefully channeled into depressions that were dug from the soil by hand. Regulators, such as matted covers and wooden slats, provided control over the flow of the water. It has been estimated that Lake Moeris doubled in size during inundations, and most of its water was directed into other depressions or into channels that led to a vast irrigation-ditch complex.

Sluices and narrow ravines were devised for regulating irrigation, and gullies were cut into the natural banks or placed in the retaining walls at various points so that the water could be stored or used as the seasons and the crops demanded. These sluices were covered with the same reed mats and kept under constant supervision by a unit of trained irrigation experts. The mats were lowered or raised according to the requirements of distant fields, which were connected to the water reserve by channels. All of the hydraulic system required constant vigilance and repairs, and both were carried out throughout the year.

When the *shaduf* was introduced into Egypt by the HYKSOS in the Second Intermediate Period (1640–1532 B.C.), the movement of water was greatly improved. Crops could be rotated and an additional growing season could be coaxed from the Faiyum because of the ability of crews to transfer water efficiently.

Though the Egyptians had a skillfully designed hydraulic system, they did not have earth-moving equipment. Hundreds of able-bodied men came into an area and simply dug out the ground in a desired region. The earth was put into baskets, which were carried away to a particular point where a wall was needed or where mounds would protect various crops or estates. The assembly line of diggers, basket carriers and mound builders worked ceaselessly until the new reservoir was completed and filled. Such a feat was accomplished in the reign of AMENHOTEP III (1391–1353 B.C.) of the 18th Dynasty. The king built a vast royal resort, MALKATA, on the western shore of the Nile at THEBES, including a lake for the royal barges dug out of the ground by crews of workmen who had accomplished the king's will in just over two weeks.

restrictions regarding the eating of at least one type of fish in particular districts. This custom was observed by priests and by the upper classes, while commoners gathered whatever came their way and ate with relish.

The Nile also provided a variety of waterfowl, which were caught in clap-nets and taken to poultry yards for slaughter. The two halves of the net were spread over an area and then snapped shut to ensnare the fowl. These fowl, however, were probably reserved for the upper classes. Pigeons were as common in ancient times in Egypt as now and were used as a food source, perhaps even raised for that purpose. Ducks and geese were also plentiful, and during the New Kingdom, chickens were introduced into the Nile Valley.

Grapes were grown in the western delta and in the oases, one of which became famous for its quality wines. The Egyptians drank both red and whtie wines, and the vineyards labeled them according to quality and variety. The favorite beverage of both rich and poor alike, however, was barley beer, made everywhere and kept in vats. Pomegranate and date wines were also available. Other useful crops were the PAPYRUS, date palm and flax. Such plants provided sources of fibers and other materials.

'Aha   first king of the 1st Dynasty at MEMPHIS (2920 B.C.), probably the legendary MENES because the name *Men* was among his royal titles. 'Aha, unlike the fabled Menes, was not the unifier of Egypt but did begin the great dynastic era of the nation. Legends credit him as the founder of the city of MEMPHIS, having built a dike to reroute a branch of the Nile so that a flat plain could be formed. Memphis was just one of the important political centers of Egypt at the time, but 'Aha made it his capital. During his reign, the land around the First Cataract appears to have come under Egyptian domination, and 'Aha commemorated the event. BERENIB was his queen, and his mother was probably Neithotpe. Aha's son and heir, DJER, was born to a lesser ranked wife, HENT.

Two legends grew in later eras about 'Aha. One was that he was killed by a hippopotamus, the other that he was attacked by wild dogs and saved by a crocodile in the FAIYUM. He is credited with founding the city of CROCODILOPOLIS as a result. 'Aha is listed as having conducted a campaign against the Nubians, perhaps on the occasion of Egypt's southern expansion to the First Cataract. He was buried at SAQQARA, the necropolis of Memphis, but he built a second mortuary complex near ABYDOS. He is supposed to have ruled until his death at the age of sixty-three. (See BAHR LIBEINI and EGYPT, HISTORICAL PERIODS.)

Cartonnage mask of Queen Ahhotep (I), discovered in Thebes.

Ahhotep (I)   a queen of the 17th Dynasty, the daughter of Sekenenre'-TA'O and Queen TETISHERI. Ahhotep married her brother, Sekenenre'-TA'O II (c. 1560 B.C.). He died in the war against the HYKSOS. Ahhotep gave birth to two sons, KAMOSE and 'AHMOSE, who succeeded their father in the military campaigns and in the rule of Egypt. Sekenenre'-Ta'o II had been king only of Upper Egypt, but his sons united the land once again and assumed full powers. Kamose died before the Hyksos could be defeated, but 'Ahmose ruled as Pharaoh. He honored Ahhotep, who lived to the age of 90. She was buried beside Kamose at Thebes. (See AX OF AHHOTEP.)

Ahhotep (II)   a queen of the 18th Dynasty, the daughter of AHMOSE I and Queen AHMOSE-NEFERTARI and the wife of AMENHOTEP I (1525–1504 B.C.). One of the vital queens of the early eras of the New Kingdom, Ahhotep was the sister of Amenhotep and his ranking consort throughout her life. The royal records listed her as "King's Daughter, King's Wife, King's Mother," although Amenhotep I died without an heir to succeed him. The mystery was solved in 1918, when the body of a baby boy was discovered at Deir el-Bahri on the western shore of Thebes. Insignias on his mummified form identified the baby as the son of Amenhotep I and Queen Ahhotep. His name was Prince AMUNEMHAT. The baby had died in his first or second year and was buried. The priests of the 20th Dynasty, discovering his original tomb violated, buried him again, near the body of his aunt, Princess Ahmose Merytamon. Queen Ahhotep was buried in the royal necropolis at Thebes.

'Ahmose I (Nebpehtire')   the first king of the 18th Dynasty in the New Kingdom (1550–1525 B.C.) 'Ahmose succeeded his brother, Wadj-Kheperre KAMOSE, who was the last king of the 17th Dynasty at Thebes. Both were sons of Sekenenre'-TA'O II and Queen AHHOTEP (I), Kamose being the elder. When Kamose died of natural causes or in the course of battle while

Statue of 'Ahmose I of the 18th Dynasty as a prince, found in Thebes.

campaigning against the HYKSOS, who held lands in the north, 'Ahmose became the head of the Theban royal line. He started his reign by taking up the war that had claimed the lives of his father and brother, and drove the Asiatic enemy back to their capital of AVARIS, which he promptly put under siege. Avaris was located at QANTIR in the Delta (the region chosen by the Ramessids in a later era as a new capital for Egypt).

'Ahmose and the Egyptians used the natural advantages provided to them while dealing with the Hyksos. Avaris was located on one of the eastern branches of the Nile, thus 'Ahmose was able to use ships and land forces against the foe. The assault on Avaris was interrupted by a rebellion in the Theban territories in Upper Egypt, and 'Ahmose had to leave the siege in the hands of his military commanders in order to assault the NOMES rising in defense of the Asiatics. Kamose had been ferocious in avenging what he deemed to be acts of treachery by any Egyptian who viewed the Asiatics as allies. Perhaps

some Egyptians feared that 'Ahmose would retaliate in a similar manner if he managed to overcome Avaris. An army and a small fleet aided the king in putting down the rebellion, and 'Ahmose returned to Avaris, where negotiations were apparently taking place between the two sides.

The Asiatics were attempting to gain some advantage, asking to be allowed to withdraw from Egypt gracefully. 'Ahmose saw the surrender of that city in c. 1532 B.C. The remaining Hyksos nobles fled to Sharuhen, in southern Palestine, with the Egyptians in hot pursuit. The siege and surrender of the city of Avaris was recorded in the funerary inscriptions of a private person, 'AHMOSE, SON OF EBANA. Information from the tomb of another private person, 'AHMOSE PEN-NEKHEBET, offered additional details.

Sharuhen was put under siege by 'Ahmose and fell after three years. The fleeing Hyksos were pursued once again into Syrian territories. 'Ahmose relinquished command of the troops there, however, to return to the Nile. The Nubians had started their own revolt in territories staked out by the Egyptians of former dynasties. 'Ahmose sailed to a region in NUBIA called Wawat and then continued to the island of SAI, near the Third Cataract, and was victorious in all of his confrontations with the local tribesmen there. When the campaign ended, 'Ahmose established the viceroyalty of Nubia at Aswan and at ELEPHANTINE. 'AHMOSE SITAYET, a trusted agent, was stationed there to conduct the royal affairs on the southern boundaries.

'Ahmose returned to Nubia a second time to face rebels, but he was able to concentrate most of his energies on Egypt's internal affairs, in the areas of the royal courts and in the realms of the nome chieftains and their allegiances. He set about restoring the government, an institution sorely in need of revitalization after the Hyksos domination and the division of Upper and Lower Egypt.

He no doubt began rebuilding the government's authority by placing those loyal to him in key positions up and down the Nile. Land grants were made to Egyptians by the king, but there is no evidence that such a policy was widespread. 'Ahmose also had to rebuild canals, dikes and irrigation systems, and had to reorganize the assessment and tax systems. He encouraged trade to obtain raw materials from outside Egypt and fostered a renaissance in art and architecture.

'Ahmose conducted another campaign in Nubia and one in the Levant, but little is documented about their cause or outcome. As an act of gratitude for his victory, however, he endowed the temple of AMON with precious gifts. This generosity set a precedent for the temple at KARNAK and began Amon's ascendancy over Egypt's other time-honored deities.

Throughout his reign, 'Ahmose lived with three dynamic royal women. His principal queen was 'AHMOSE-NEFERTIRY, his sister. His grandmother, TETISHERI, remained vigorous for years after the war, and Ahhotep, his mother, lived with him in the palace. 'Ahmose also married INHAPI and an untitled woman named Kasmut.

Ruler of Egypt for almost twenty-five years, he built his tomb at Thebes and a mortuary complex at Abydos. Mortuary rituals honoring him were conducted at his tomb for a considerable period after his death. 'Ahmose's mummy was discovered wreathed in pale blue delphiniums. He appears to have been of average height, thin, with excellent teeth and a prominent chin. His remains show indications of arthritis and scoliosis, and apparently he was not circumcised, although circumcision was an Egyptian custom.

'Ahmose a queen of the 18th Dynasty, the wife of TUTHMOSIS I (1504–1492 B.C.). She was the daughter of 'AHMOSE I and probably a lesser-ranked wife and was the sister of AMENHOTEP I, Tuthmosis' predecessor, given in marriage by him to Tuthmosis. Queen 'Ahmose gave birth to four royal children and was celebrated in the reliefs of DEIR EL-BAHRI as a consort of the god AMON. These inscriptions were placed on the walls of HATSHEPSUT's temple to legitimize her usurpation of the throne in 1473 B.C., and they depict 'Ahmose as giving birth to Hatshepsut, the divine child of the god. 'Ahmose died comparatively young and was buried at THEBES.

Queen 'Ahmose of the 18th Dynasty, as depicted in Hatshepsut's Deir el-Bahri relief commemorating the latter's divine birth.

'Ahmose Hent-Tenemu a princess of the 18th Dynasty, the daughter of 'AHMOSE I (1550–1525 B.C.) and Princes INHAPI. A stela to her memory was erected in Thebes.

'Ahmose Meryt-Amon a queen of the 18th Dynasty, the daughter of 'AHMOSE I and wife of AMENHOTEP I (1525–1504 B.C.). Her mummified remains were discovered at DEIR EL-BAHRI, having been rewrapped and reburied by the priests of the 20th Dynasty, who discovered her tomb violated by robbers. She appears to have died in her early thirties, with arthritis and scoliosis evident.

'Ahmose-Nefertiry a queen of the 18th Dynasty, wife of 'AHMOSE I (1550–1525 B.C.), and the daughter of Sekenenre'-TA'O II and Queen AHHOTEP. It is possible that she was married to 'Ahmose's predecessor, KAMOSE, the last king of the 17th Dynasty, who died while campaigning against the HYKSOS. There is also some speculation that she may have been only a half-sister to 'Ahmose.

'Ahmose-Nefertiry is mentioned on an inscription depicting the honors being given to Queen TETISHERI, her grandmother, and her name was listed in the Sinai and on the island of Sai in inscriptions. A stela found at KARNAK shows her with the king, bringing offerings to AMON. She bore four daughters and two sons.

Ahmose-Nefertiry lived during the early part of the reign of her son, AMENHOTEP I, who gave her many honors. When she died she shared a mortuary temple and a tomb with him, and her mortuary cult remained popular.

'Ahmose Pen-Nekhebet a nobleman of EL-KAB who served in the military campaigns of the first kings of the 18th Dynasty (1550–1307 B.C.). His tomb inscriptions provide detailed information about this critical period of the New Kingdom. The inscriptions even mention a military campaign conducted in the reign of HATSHEPSUT.

The reliefs of 'Ahmose Pen-Nekhebet, when combined with the inscriptions of 'AHMOSE, SON OF EBANA, clarify other documents of the era and provide insight into the military efforts of these 18th Dynasty rulers. (See HYKSOS)

'Ahmose Sipar a prince of the 18th Dynasty, the son of 'AHMOSE I (1550–1525 B.C.) and Queen 'AHMOSE-NEFERTIRY. 'Ahmose Sipar may have served as regent or co-ruler with 'Ahmose because his tomb at THEBES had the markings of a king. He died before he could succeed his father, however, and AMEN-HOTEP I became king. He was buried with honors on the western shore of Thebes.

'Ahmose Sitayet   an official of the 18th Dynasty, named viceroy of Nubia by 'AHMOSE I (1550–1525 B.C.) after 'Ahmose's Nubian campaign. 'Ahmose Sitayet was not a member of the royal family. As viceroy of NUBIA, however, he assumed the title "King's Son of Kush." He ruled the territories below the First Cataract and the region of Aswan for the king, with administrative offices in Aswan and on ELEPHANTINE Island. His son, Tjuroy, succeeded him in the viceroyalty.

'Ahmose, Son of Ebana   a nobleman of El-Kab, who served in the army of Sekenenre'-TA'O II (c. 1560 B.C.) when that ruler began the military campaigns to oust the HYKSOS from Egypt. 'Ahmose's tomb at El-Kab, discovered in the cliffs, provides information about the wars of the first kings of the 18th Dynasty. As royal records of that era are rare, his biographical inscriptions, when combined with those of 'AHMOSE PEN-NEKHEBET, provide a valuable source of information about the period. These mortuary texts, personalized as they are, add dimension and immediacy to the formal annals and temple reliefs of the times. (See AHMOSE PEN-NEKHEBET and HYKSOS.)

'Ahmose Tumerisy   a princess of the 18th Dynasty, the daughter of AMENHOTEP I (1525–1504 B.C.) and Queen 'AHHOTEP II. She outlived her royal parents and witnessed the reign of King TUTHMOSIS I, who honored her with ranks and titles. 'Ahmose Tumerisy was buried in an unfinished platform in the Deir el-Bahri mortuary complex of King MENTU-HOTPE II.

Ahset   a royal consort of the 18th Dynasty, married to TUTHMOSIS III (1479–1425 B.C.). Nothing is known of her life except the fact that she was of royal blood. She did not hold the title of queen.

Aigyptos   the Greek word for Egypt, dervied from the Egyptian name for MEMPHIS, Hiku-Ptah, or "Mansion of the Soul of Ptah." The Greek version evolved over the centuries into the Western name for the nation. The Egyptians used the word *Khemet* to refer to their land. The Arabic word for Egypt is Misr or Masr.

Aker   an ancient Egyptian god in the form of a lion, popular in certain historical periods. The Aker was supposed to guard the passage of the god RE on his solar bark. A lion cult connected to Aker and to the worship of lions was started at To Remu, the modern Tell Migdam. The Greeks called the site LEONTOPOLIS in honor of the cult. Akeru, the plural form, were depicted in the tomb of Queen NEFERTARI, wife of RAMESSES II in the 19th Dynasty (1290–1224 B.C.).

Portrait of an Aker cult lion that was in the tomb of Queen Nefertari of the 19th Dynasty in the Valley of the Queens at Thebes.

Aker Papyri   surviving only in fragments, a version of the BOOK OF THE DEAD from a Saite tomb. The papyri described the journey of the god RE through Tuat or the underworld.

akh   one of three primary terms used by the Egyptians to express the quality of the individual human being after death. *BA* and *KA* were the other designations. None of these terms can be translated into

English properly, as the word "soul" does not convey an all-encompassing explanation of their meaning. The *akh* was believed destined to become part of the circumpolar stars, those that remained constant in the night sky.

Akhenaten originally Amenhotep IV (Neferkheprure' Wa'enre'), ninth king of the 18th Dynasty (1353–1335 B.C.). He is called the "heretic pharaoh" in some records because of his break with the traditional religious structure of his time. Throughout history Akhenaten has raised considerable interest and debate because of his unique religious views and the monuments they inspired. He has been called brilliant, saintly, revolutionary and even the most remarkable king to sit upon Egypt's throne.

The son of AMENHOTEP III and QUEEN TIY (1391–1353 B.C.), Akhenaten was raised in the traditional manner and observed the religous rituals of AMON, the god of the Thebes who had reached an exalted position throughout Egypt. In time, however, Akhenaten turned exclusively to another deity, ATEN, the sun god, known in Egypt in earlier reigns. (TUTHMOSIS IV had carried the god's insignia into battle, and Amenhotep III dedicated one of his royal barges to Aten.)

Soon after ascending the throne, Akhenaten repudiated his royal name and his allegiance to Amon. He took the name Akhenaten, meaning "He Who is of Service to Aten." Queen NEFERTITI, Akhenaten's wife, was remaned Nefer-Nefru-Aten, "Beautiful is the Beauty of Aten." The royal couple abandoned Thebes to begin a great city in Middle Egypt, at a site called Akhetaten, the "Horizon of Aten" (modern el-'AMARNA). The court followed and artisans joined them to begin the great artistic efflorescence that would characterize the brief period of the new capital's predominance, despite the opposition of the priests and devotees of the god Amon. At 'Amarna the couple erected extraordinary buildings. Akhenaten conducted elaborate ceremonies in the new temples and palaces.

'Amarna rose in splendor on the banks of the Nile, its artisans displaying the new modes and methods, termed naturalistic, of decorating the complex. Examples of this style surviving today depict the king and his family with strange deformities and peculiar physical traits. Aten, originally depicted by Akhenaten in the form traditionally reserved for Re'-Harakhte, became a rayed solar disk.

From his new capital Akhenaten attacked the cults of other deities in Egypt, especially Amon. Agents went about destroying their statues and desecrating

Akhenaten (Amenhotep IV) of the 18th Dynasty, from a statue typical of the 'Amarna art style.

sites and other evidence of their worship. Even the CARTOUCHE of Akhenaten's father, Amenhotep III, was destroyed because it bore Amon's name. Opposition to Akhenaten grew out of the radical changes that were the result of his new monotheism. His insistence upon the sole cult of Aten left the general populace of Egypt in a state of unrest and anger. All of the religous aspects of their lives had been abolished. The great temples of THEBES, MEMPHIS and HELIOPOLIS, and the local temples up and down the Nile, were deprived of their estates and plantations. These estates and their revenue reverted to the crown. These confiscations were carried out to such an extent that they gave rise to mismanagement and eventually corruption.

Akhenaten appears to have been militarily active to a degree, despite the claims of those coming to the throne after him. He initiated a campaign in Nubia and responded to the crises in the Levant with military action. He was still receiving tributes from other lands, and reliefs depict him, accompanied by Nefertiti and their daughters, accepting the offerings.

The Queen Mother, TIY, joined Akhenaten in 'Amarna in the 12th year of his reign, bringing Princess Baketaten (later BAKETAMON) with her. Akhenaten provided her with a residence and with a small temple. Another of his daughters, Princess MEKETATEN, died soon afterward, probably in childbirth, and reliefs depict the mourning of Akhenaten and Nefertiti. Within a short time, Nefertiti disappeared from the scene, probably having fallen out of favor. She was replaced by her daughter, MERYTATEN (also called Meryt-Amon), who took over her duties and her residences. Meryt-Aten was then replaced by Ankhesenpaaten (ANKHESENAMON). Another queen, KIYA, possibly the Mitanni princess Tadukhipa, was called Akenaten's "favorite" and bore him a daughter and two sons. Akhenaten did not live long after his assault on the other deities. He apparently died in 'Amarna in the 18th year of his reign. It is believed that his mummified remains were destroyed by those bitter enough to seek vengeance upon his corpse and upon his holy city and other traces of his reign were abolished to the point that HOREMHAB, the military leader coming after him, claimed his kingship to date from the time of Amenhotep III.

akhet   the season of inundation in the ancient Egyptian calendar. The rising of Sirius, the dogstar, called Sopdet by the Egyptians and Sothis by the Greeks, signaled the beginning of the annual flooding of the Nile. When this sign appeared in the heavens the river was set to spread over the fields and orchards along its banks, revitalizing the land with silt and effluvium from Africa's core. *Akhet* was the first season of the year, starting as it did with the rising of the Nile, a factor that all Egyptians understood as basic to the nation's vitality. *Akhet* was one of the three major seasons of the Egyptian calendar year, with a duration of four 30-day months. *Akhet* was followed by PROYET and SHOMU. (See CALENDAR and SEASONS.)

Akhetaten   See 'AMARNA, EL-.

Akhmin   called Khent Menu or Apu by the ancient Egyptians and Panopolis by the Greeks, the center of Upper Egypt's ninth NOME and a cult center for the worship of the god MIN. The goddess TAIT was also honored in Akhmin. Only the necropolis areas remain today. A temple dating to the 18th Dynasty was found there. Egypt's linen industry was important to Akhmin in later eras.

Akhmin's goddess, Tait, shown carrying mounds of linen used for wrapping the bodies of the deceased.

Amada   a site north of ABU SIMBEL, where a temple dating to the reign of TUTHMOSIS III (1479–1425 B.C.) of the 18th Dynasty was discovered. The temple contained a court, columned portico, a vestibule and sanctuaries. AMENHOTEP II refurbished the temple during his reign, and court pillars were added by

TUTHMOSIS IV. SETI I of the 19th Dynasty restored the temple and built an addition.

'Amara a fortified town almost 150 miles south of WADI HALFA on the Nile, founded by SETI I (1306–1290 B.C.) and given the name the "House of Men-ma'atre'," to honor one of the king's royal names. Wadi Halfa and the surrounding area were given new defenses during the Ramessid era.

'Amarna (el-'Amarna) Arabic name of the modern city on the site of ancient Akhetaten, the "Horizon of ATEN," built by AKHENATEN (Amenhotep IV of the 18th Dynasty, 1353–1335 B.C.) and destroyed by HOREMHAB a few decades later. Erected on a level plain between the Nile and the eastern cliffs north of ASSIUT, 'Amarna was 6 miles long and marked by boundary stelae. The districts of the city were well planned and laid out with geometric precision and artistry. All of the areas of 'Amarna were designed to focus on the royal residence and on the temple of the god Aten.

Officials and courtiers lived in the principal districts, and the homes provided for them were large and lavish. Most contained gardens, pools and summer villas, as well as reception areas, festival halls and bathrooms. The temple and the palace were located on the Royal Avenue, designed to run parallel to the Nile. This thoroughfare was spanned by an immense brick bridge, which was not only a startling architectural innovation but achieved an artistic unity that became the hallmark of the god's abode. The bridge joined two separate wings of the royal residence and contained the famed WINDOW OF APPEARANCE, which was discovered in reliefs of the area. Akhenaten and Nefertiti greeted the faithful of the city in the window and honored officials and artisans there, forming an appealing portrait of regal splendor in this setting.

The palace did not serve as a royal residence but as a site for rituals and ceremonies. The royal family occupied limited space in separate apartments. The rest of the structure was dedicated to altar areas, halls, stables, garden, pools, throne rooms and ceremonial chambers. The entire palace was adorned with delicate and distinctive reliefs and paintings in the 'Amarna style. Waterfowl and marsh scenes graced the walls, adding a natural and pastoral quality to the residence. The main throne room for official ceremonies in honor of Aten was set between pillared halls, one with 32 rows of 17 pillars each. Adjacent to the palace was the temple of the god. This site had a rectangular wall that measured 2,600 by 900 feet. The temple, as many of the other structures in

Merytaten, a daughter-consort of Akhenaten, at 'Amarna.

'Amarna, was adapted to the Nile climate and designed for outdoor services. There were few roofs evident in the architectural planning of the complexes. The homes of the 'Amarna artisans were in the southeastern section of the city, surrounded by another wall. Six blocks of such residences were laid out in this area, between five parallel streets.

Akhetaten, also called the "City of the Solar Disk", is supposedly named 'Amarna, or Tell el-'Amarna today to commemorate a tribe of Bedouins that settled on the site approximately two centuries ago. A vast cliff cemetery was established nearby connected to 'Amarna by the ROYAL WADI.

Am Duat See BOOK OF THE DEAD.

Amemait a mythical beast called "The Devourer" in ancient Egyptian mortuary lore. The creature was part lion, part crocodile and part hippopotamus.

AMEMAIT   the mythical beast that was part crocodile, part lion, with the hind quarters of a hippopotamus. Amemait was in the Judgment Halls of Osiris, waiting beside the sacred scales to devour the unworthy.

Amemait waited beside the scales in the JUDGMENT HALL OF OSIRIS, where souls were deemed fit or unfit for eternal bliss. The beast was entitled to eat any of the deceased Egyptian souls that did not measure up to the ideals required for paradise. (See ETERNITY, MA'AT and MORTUARY RITUALS.)

Amenemhab a military official in the 18th Dynasty, serving TUTHMOSIS III (1479–1425 B.C.) and his son AMENHOTEP II (1427–1401 B.C.). Amenemhab had been introduced to Tuthmosis by his wife, who was a nurse for the royal family. He entered military service and was promoted to the rank of general during the imperial period, when Egypt was on the march against city-states and rival confederacies.

Amenemhab's mortuary reliefs gave particular insight into the battles of Tuthmosis, Egypt's warrior king. On one occasion Amenemhab is said to have saved the king's life by cutting off the trunk of a charging elephant. On another occasion he claimed that he cut out the belly of a mare sent into the ranks of the stallion cavalry units by the enemy, thus avoiding a mating frenzy.

Ever at Tuthmosis' side, he served his king and then maintained his rank and position during the reign of Amenhotep II who was eager for battle in the first years after his accession to the throne. (See TUTHMOSIS III'S MILITARY CAMPAIGNS.)

Amenemhet I (Sehetepibre') the first king of the 12th Dynasty (1991–1962 B.C.), a usurper who had served under the previous dynasty as a vizier. He assumed the throne when the last king of the 11th Dynasty died, and took a fleet of ships up and down the Nile to settle claims with his rivals. (It is also possible that Amenemhet usurped the throne of the reigning king.) He later claimed to have been prophetically named by a sage called NEFERTI, who predicted that a king named Ameni would come from Upper Egypt to restore the land.

During his reign, Amenemhet campaigned against the Libyans and the Asiatics in the Sinai, where he erected the WALL OF THE PRINCE (also supposedly foretold by Neferti). The Wall of the Prince was a series of fortresses designed to guard Egypt's eastern border regions. He created another fortress at Semna and is credited with establishing the fortified trading post at Kerma as well, both outposts in Nubia. His capital was on the site of modern LISHT, on the border of Upper and Lower Egypt, and he named the city ITJ-TAWY, "Seizer of the Two Lands." Despite usurping the throne, his dynastic line started an era that would be regarded by later Egyptians as the nation's golden age.

A commoner by birth, Amenemhet was supposedly of Nubian descent on his mother's side. She

Amenemhet I, of the 12th Dynasty, from a statue that acknowledges his Theban origins by representing him in the white war helmet of Upper Egypt.

was named Nefret, and her reliefs and inscriptions carry no titles except that of "King's Mother." Amenemhet married several women. Nefrutotenen was one of his principal consorts and probably the mother of SENWOSRET I. Queen Sit-Hathor was the mother of Princess NENSEB-DJEBET, and Queen DEDYET, Amenemhet's sister, was another wife. Late in his reign, Queen NEFRU-SOBEK became a royal consort, probably replacing a retired or deceased favorite. A daughter named Nefrusheri became the wife of Senwosret I, and a Princess Nyetneb was also his daughter.

Amenemhet named his son Senwosret I co-ruler in 1971 B.C. and dictated his famous *Instructions* to warn him against rivals. The document provides a remarkable portrait of a ruler and much information about the king's personal difficulties.

Amenemhet died while Senwosret was on a military campaign. He was buried in a funerary pyramid that he had erected at Lisht in which he is called the "Horus of Repeating Births." His death is a key element of the plot of the *Tale of SINUHE THE SAILOR.* There had been one attempt on his life in the past, and this story makes use of that failed assassination to add impact to the adventures of the hero. (See AMENEMHET'S *INSTRUCTIONS* and NEFERTI.)

Amenemhet II (Nubkaure')   the third king of the 12th Dynasty (1929–1892 B.C.) and the son of SENWOSRET I and Queen Nefrusheri. He served for three years as co-ruler with his father and went on an expedition to NUBIA, which seems to have been the extent of his military career. His efforts were directed toward Egypt's internal affairs and to the rebellious nature of the various NOMARCHS, who maintained as much independence as possible and were easily provoked by royal commands.

His Queen was Mereryet, although another wife, Kemanub, is mentioned in some records, along with his daughters: Ata, Atuart, KHNUMT, Sit-Hathor, Sit-Hathor Hormeret and Sit-Hathor Meryt. His son was SENWOSRET II. Amenemhet was buried at DASHUR.

Amenemhet III (Nima'atre')   the sixth king of the 12th Dynasty (1844–1797 B.C.), the son of SENWOSRET III and Queen Sebekshedty-Neferu. He was one of the outstanding kings of the 12th Dynasty, bringing economic stability and prosperity to Egypt by completing the system of water regulation in the FAIYUM. The flood waters of the Nile were allowed to overflow into Lake Moeris there. The irrigation system that he completed in the Faiyum also accommodated the draining of marshes and the construction of an overflow canal. To celebrate the reclamation of a vast stretch of land (estimated at 153,600 acres), Amenem-

Amenemhet III, as depicted in a restored colossal statue that exemplifies the artistic sophistication of his era.

het raised two colossal statues of himself nearby. The famed LABYRINTH was built nearby, once identified as the tomb of the king but now considered a palace, temple or local administrative center.

Amenemhet also worked to ensure Egypt of natural resources from the Sinai, exploiting the copper mines there steadily. He provided the mine workers housing and fortifications in order to defend against raiding Bedouins. Within Egypt's borders he also had local mines and QUARRIES worked.

His reign was comparatively free of military campaigns, except for brief punitive expeditions, which stabilized Egypt's possessions. In NUBIA, his forces reached the Third Cataract of the Nile.

Amenemhet's consorts were A'AT and Nefruptah (probably his chief consort). His pyramid was built at DASHUR, where other members of his royal line had erected tomb complexes. Another pyramid stands at Hawara, where he constructed the famed Labyrinth. He also raised colossal statues at BIAHMU.

Amenemhet IV (Ma'akherure')   seventh king of the 12th Dynasty (1799–1787 B.C.); probable son of AMENEMHET III. Because of the length of his father's reign, he was of advanced age when he assumed the throne. It is believed that he served as co-ruler with Amenemhet III for a time. Monuments to him were found at several sites, including a small temple at Medinet Ma'adi in the FAIYUM. The temple, probably built by both kings, was dedicated to the goddess RENENET.

Amenemhet IV received tributes from Byblos, Syria and other lands during his brief reign. A pyramid at Mazghuna was thought to have been his tomb site, but that is now discounted. He died without a male heir and was succeeded by his sister or half-sister, NEFRU-SOBEK.

Amenemhet V (Sekhemkare') reportedly the fourth king of the 13th Dynasty (c. 1760 B.C.), but little is known of his reign. His name appears on monuments, and despite the presence of Asiatics in the eastern territories and the general unrest of the provinces, his rule was relatively peaceful.

Amenemhet VII (Sedjefakare') reportedly the 15th king of the 13th Dynasty (c. 1740 B.C.). His name appears on monuments in Tanis, Medamud, the ELEPHANTINE and elsewhere, but little is known of him.

Amenemhet an official of the 18th Dynasty, counselor to Queen-Pharaoh HATSHEPSUT (1473–1458 B.C.). The brother of SENENMUT, he served as a priest of AMON and as a supervisor for the bark of the god. He was buried in THEBES. (See BARKS OF THE GODS.)

Amenemhet's *Instructions* a document attributed to AMENEMHET I of the 12th Dynasty (1991–1962 B.C.) and dedicated to his son and heir, SENWOSRET I, also called the *Testament of Amenemhet*. It was probably written after his death as a commemorative.

The king solemnly declares that intimacy on the part of any ruler will bring about his destruction. He gives an account of a failed attempt on his life as an example of the perils awaiting any lax king. The work contains some 88 verse lines and purports to be the counsel of a deceased king, now a ghost, to his son.

The *Instructions* also embody the world's first statement about the duty of a king. The document clearly defines royal obligations based upon the needs of the people. Amenemhet made a point of stating that a ruler must be willing to endure personal sacrifices and loneliness. The text was included in the Milligan Papyrus and the Papyrus Sallier II.

Amen-em-Opet Clan a NOMARCH family involved in the New Kingdom dynasties, known also as Amu-nemope or as Amen-em-Ope. This family, like many other aristocratic NOME clans, served the kings of Egypt in various capacities and proved unstinting in their loyalty and dedication. Such men brought remarkable abilities to the various offices of the nation. A sage named Amenemope served as the viceroy of NUBIA for SETI I of the 19th Dynasty (1306–1290 B.C.). Bakenkhonsu and other members of the clan held similar positions throughout that era of Egyptian history.

Amenhemet a NOMARCH of BENI HASAN, listed in some records as Ameni. Amenhemet flourished in the reign of SENWOSRET I (1971–1926 B.C.) of the 12th Dynasty. He was a military commander of the court, supervising the affairs of the territories below the First Cataract and leading expeditions for the benefit of the royal treasury. A campaign in Nubia allowed Amenhemet to distinguish himself, and he was given charge of a gold mining venture near COPTOS.

Amenhirkhepshef a prince of the 20th Dynasty, the son of RAMESSES III (1290–1224 B.C.). Amenhirkhepshef served in Ramesses' military campaigns and perhaps died in battle. He had been the heir apparent until his death. He was buried in an elaborate tomb in the Valley of the Queens at Thebes.

Amenhotep I (Djeserkare') the second king of the 18th Dynasty (c. 1525–1504 B.C.). He was the son of 'AHMOSE I and Queen AHMOSE NEFRETIRI. An older brother, 'AHMOSE SIPAR, appears to have been 'Ahmose's original heir and probably served as co-ruler for a time. He died before he could assume the throne, however, and Amenhotep became king.

Amenhotep faced a Libyan uprising in his first year as sole ruler of Egypt, an event that occurred chronically when new young kings acceded to the throne. He led an army to the western border and overcame the Libyans and their allies on two separate occasions, thus preventing an invasion in the Delta territories. The Nubians were the next to rebel, and Amenhotep sailed south with another army and defeated the southern enemy, bringing back many captives to THEBES. During this campaign he visited the cataract defenses and refurbished many of the strongholds in the Egyptian chain of fortifications there. Such fortresses were vital to the interests of the nation because they were strategically placed to halt massive units of Nubians and to alert the viceroy at Elephantine Island at Aswan to the north.

Interested in art and in architecture, Amenhotep initiated elaborate building projects at the KARNAK temple complex in Thebes. Innovative and enthu-

Amenhotep I, as depicted in a Theban relief. He is wearing a royal headdress of the New Kingdom.

siastic, he had many types of stone brought to the site, including alabaster from Hatnub. Amenhotep also designed a station for the Bark of Amon for use on processional feast days. Because of his military valor and his interest in restoring and repairing the ancient shrines of the Nile, Amenhotep was considered a good king by his contemporaries. The Theban kings, 'Ahmose and KAMOSE had stopped clan rebellions stemming from the HYKSOS domination and the Egyptians were comfortable with the Theban dynasty and its achievements. Amenhotep was declared a titular god by the Amonite priests soon after his death, an honor not given to many kings.

Amenhotep's queen was his sister, AHHOTEP II, but he also wed Princess 'AHMOSE MERYT-AMON, who died young. A son was born to Amenhotep and Queen Ahhotep, Amunemhet, but he died in infancy.

This king was the first pharaoh of Egypt to devise a plan to separate his actual tomb from his prominent mortuary temple. Such temples had been part of the funerary complexes of royalty since the Archaic Period, designed with chambers and courts for offerings and rituals. He was probably aware of the looting taking place in such mortuary complexes, and he chose an inconspicuous site overlooking the western shore of Thebes.

Amenhotep died before reaching the age of 50, leaving the throne to a military commander who in time would become the great TUTHMOSIS I. Statues of Amenhotep depict him as a vigorous man who stood just under 6 feet, with a prominent nose and the dynastic overbite. Amenhotep was entombed in a coverlet of yellow, red and blue flowers, all well preserved and containing their original perfumes. A wasp had settled onto one of the flowers when Amenhotep's body was placed in its original sarcophagus. That insect remained with him throughout the centuries, unearthed only when his royal host was discovered in the Valley of the Kings. When his mummy was discovered it was so beautifully prepared that no one wanted to open it for forensic studies. The mortuary rituals had evolved during his reign, and the embalmers had taken great pains to honor his royal remains and to prepare them for eternity, indicating their affection and the reputation of the king.

Amenhotep II (Akheprure')   the seventh king of the 18th Dynasty (1427–1401 B.C.). The son of TUTHMOSIS III and Queen MERYT-RE HATSHEPSUT, Amenhotep II was taller than most of his contemporaries and muscular in build. His queen consort was MERIT-AMON, the daughter of Tuthmosis III, although another queen, Teo, bore him a son and heir, TUTHMOSIS IV.

He took pride in his ability as a horseman and as a horse breeder. He excelled in battle and in archery, having received expert training in both. His entire life had been spent in preparation for his eventual rule. One of his first assignments was the command of the main Egyptian naval base at PER-NEFER, near MEMPHIS. Amenhotep developed a preference for this region and maintained estates there all of his life. He served as co-ruler while performing his princely obligations.

When Amenhotep II came to the throne, Egypt had an extensive empire; millions of subjects paid tribute and honor to Egypt and to its royal line. When Tuthmosis III died, the Asiatic city-states and their allies attempted to throw off the Egyptian yoke. They put the young new king's military prowess to the test but did not find him wanting.

He delighted in hand-to-hand combat and led his troops into battle with howls of royal rage. His ferocity was reported to have dismayed enemy troops in many skirmishes.

He spent the second year of his reign in Syria and Phoenicia, following in Tuthmosis III's footsteps. He

Amenhotep II, from a Karnak relief.

put down various rebellions there and then marched to the Euphrates River, where his father and grandfather had erected stelae to commemorate their victories. Amenhotep raised his own pillar there to record his accomplishments and his military successes. Returning to Egypt in triumph, the young king displayed unusual barbarism. Hanging upside down on the prow of his ship were captive Asiatic chiefs, whom he personally beheaded in religious ceremonies. Amenhotep died at the age of 45. His remains show evidence of rheumatism and a type of systemic disease. They also show clear signs of severe dental decay, probably the source of the infection that resulted in his death.

Amenhotep III (Nebma'atre')   ninth king of the 18th Dynasty (1391–1353 B.C.). Amenhotep III ruled over a peaceful, prosperous and indulgent Egypt. The son of TUTHMOSIS IV and Queen MUTEMWIYA, he married a commoner named TIY, the daughter of YUIA, the Hurrian master of horse at THEBES (who was from a northern territory famed for horsemen) and led a life of splendor. His empire extended from the area of northern Sudan to the shores of the Euphrates River. Slaves, raw materials and tribute flowed into Thebes, his capital, and he retained a small army of trained adminstrators whose families had a long tradition of service to the throne.

Peace and prosperity enabled the king to dedicate himself to artistic renewal and to pleasure. Commemorative scarabs were used to convey to the people his skill as a hunter, wisdom as a ruler and staunch defense of traditions. Amenhotep consolidated his

international position by marrying the daughters of foreign kings, including one or two Mitanni princesses and one from Babylon.

He probably fought or directed his military commanders, in one campaign in NUBIA, and he had inscriptions made to commemorate that punitive expedition. His great accomplishment was his patronage of the arts. Temple sites were refurbished and enlarged, monuments were raised to honor the king's patron deities, and he surpassed even his own artistic ambitions in erecting MALKATA, his pleasure palaces on the western shore of the Nile. The vast complex was called "The House of Nebma'atre' as Aten's Splendor." The resort boasted a lake over a mile long, which appears to have been created in only 15 days by advanced hydraulic sluicing techniques. The complex contained residences for Queen Tiy and for AKHENATEN (Amenhotep IV), the king's son and heir. Amenhotep even had a pleasure bark dedicated to the god Aten, built for outings on the lake.

While Amenhotep busied himself with his own affairs, Queen Tiy worked tirelessly with officials and scribes overseeing the administrative aspects of the empire. She was devoid of personal ambition and served Egypt well during her tenure. Tiy also arranged for Princess SITAMUN, her daughter by Amenhotep, to marry her father. This custom was practiced by some royal lines that wished to secure several royal heirs to the throne. Theories concerning the actual origins of SMENKHKARE' and TUT'ANKHAMUN (who appear to have been brothers) stem from that union, but no definitive evidence can link the siblings to Sitamun.

Amenhotep spent years improving the complex of KARNAK as well, erecting a hypostyle hall with pylons and rows of ram-headed sphinxes, and linking that shrine with the temple of AMON at LUXOR. A shrine built to honor the goddess MUT was erected in a southern religious complex and was provided with a similar avenue of sphinxes. In time Amenhotep dismantled the monuments of some of his predecessors in order to provide his workmen with materials. The foundation of his Karnak pylon, for example, was originally from a chapel of SENWOSRET I of the 12th Dynasty (1971–1926 B.C.).

This king celebrated the SED festival on three separate occasions. His health was deteriorating when he celebrated the last one, however, caused by severe dental problems. He appealed to Istar of Nineveh, the goddess known for healing powers, and survived. Retiring to Malkata with his vast harem, Amenhotep occupied himself with his own diversions; Tiy remained at her post with her able administrators. Amenhotep died at the age of 54 or 55. His

Amenhotep III, wearing the khepresh, "helmet of victory," from a basalt statue.

mummified remains, once seriously disputed, indicate that Amenhotep was 5 feet tall; his narrow, handsome face had almond-shaped eyes with heavy lids. His heir was Akhenaten, and he had many children by his harem companions. His royal daughters, born by Queen Tiy, included the princesses Ast, Hentmerheb, Sitamun, Hentaneb and BAKETAMON.

Amenhotep's Colossi   See COLOSSI OF MEMNON.

Amenhotep, Son of Hapu   an official of the 18th Dynasty and one of Egypt's two official saints or demigods. Amenhotep was a high-ranking priest in a temple at ATHRIBIS and an architect of considerable merit. He supervised many building projects for the royal family but retired to pursue his religious activities, refusing further honors or appointments. Reaching the age of 80, and having seen many changes on the Nile, he exerted considerable influence in his own era. Young men came to the temple at Athribis to hear Amenhotep's counsels. In the process he gained a reputation for piety. In honor of his piety, his mortuary cult was established throughout Egypt

in later years by royal decree. As a result, Amenhotep shared divinity with IMHOTEP, the builder of the famed STEP PYRAMID at Saqqara for DJOSER. A clinic or sanitarium was operated in honor of Amenhotep at DEIR EL-BAHRI, on the western shore of Thebes in later eras.

Amenken   an official of the 18th Dynasty, serving AMENHOTEP II (c. 1427–1401 B.C.). Amenken was a high official of the treasury, concerned with the tabulation and the distribution of gifts to court favorites and NOME officials. The kings of Egypt presented outstanding servants with golden collars and other costly insignias of honor on feast days.

Amenmose   a prince of the 18th Dynasty, the son of TUTHMOSIS I and Queen 'AHMOSE (1504–1492 B.C.). He was an older brother of Queen-Pharaoh HATSHEPSUT. Records indicate that he became a general of his father's armies before he died. He was obviously set aside for TUTHMOSIS II upon the death of their father. Amenmose may have died at a young age. He was buried in the royal necropolis on the western shore of Thebes.

Amenti   the mythological domain of the dead on the western shore of the Nile, considered to be the residence of the god OSIRIS.

ames   the ancient Egyptian name for the scepter in the form of a club or mace that was used as a royal insignia in most eras. The *ames* dates back to the early period of Egypt, when the warriors of the south invaded the Delta, subduing the Bee King's armies and unifying the nation. The kings maintained the insignias of ancient times and incorporated them into the newer rituals of office.

amethyst   a semiprecious stone, a variety of quartz, usually lavender or purple in color. These stones were discovered in the southern desert regions of ancient Egypt and were highly prized.

Amherst Papyrus   a document from THEBES that contains an account of the Ramessid-era TOMB ROBBERY TRIALS. With the ABBOTT PAPYRUS, which includes an account of the same event, this text provides detailed information and insight into the 20th Dynasty, a period of declining royal authority and law and order in the Nile Valley.

Amon   a god of ancient Egypt known in early eras but attaining dominance during the New Kingdom at THEBES. Amon, whose name means "hidden,"

The god Amon, the principal deity of Egypt's New Kingdom, from a Theban temple relief.

figured in the Hermopolitan myths associated with the dynamic force of life. The deity, and a female counterpart, Amonet, were mentioned in the PYRAMID TEXTS in the 5th and 6th Dynasties. The first evidence locating the god in Thebes is an inscription by a NOMARCH, Rehuy, also of the 6th Dynasty, who claimed to have performed services for Amon.

When the Thebans began to exert influence over Egypt's political scene, Amon's cult began its ascendency. During the New Kingdom the god was elevated in status and conferred many attributes of other divine beings. Amon was declared to have given birth to himself, and it was stressed that no other god had such power. All other deities in Egypt's pantheon traced their being and their powers to his self-creation. Amon was included in the OGDOAD of HERMOPOLIS, then at the primeval mound of MEMPHIS, at which time he was supposed to have formed all the other gods. He then left the earth to abide as RE in the heavens, taking the form of a divine child revealed in the LOTUS.

In statues Amon was normally depicted as a handsome, virile young man or as a ram with curled horns. The kings of the New Kingdom carried his banners everywhere in their establishment of the empire, and the temple in Thebes received tributes from many lands. Amon was the "Greatest of Heaven, Eldest of Earth," and the priests of his temple wrote tender hymns in his honor.

The generosity of 'AHMOSE I (1550–1525 B.C.), who made donations to the temple of Amon in thanksgiving for his victories, set a pattern in the New Kingdom, and the god was showered with costly gifts by 'Ahmose's successors. Both the temples at KARNAK and LUXOR benefited from royal patronage. In time Amon was revered throughout Egypt, as the Amonite priests assumed more and more political control. There was a shrine in the SIWA Oasis, which was later called Jupiter Ammon by the Romans, and pilgrimages were undertaken in every era to worship the god there.

At Thebes, Amon was provided with a consort, the goddess MUT, and with a son, KHONS, or Khonsu. The ram, the symbol of the god's true spiritual power, was kept at Thebes for religious ceremonies, embodying the energies of the deity and his beauty. During the AMARNA Period, the temples of Amon were attacked and closed by order of AKHENATEN. When TUT'ANKHAMUN came to the throne in 1333 B.C., he returned the court to Thebes and restored the god's primacy over Egypt. This move was calculated to appease the priests of the temple and to settle the unrest caused by the abandonment of the deity by Akhenaten.

Many FESTIVALS were celebrated in honor of Amon. One of these, the Beautiful Feast of the Valley, was especially popular. The god's statue was taken across the Nile to the western shore of Thebes, where people waited to greet the retinue of priests and devotees. Ritual meals and mortuary offerings were set before the tombs of the dead, while people held picnics in the various mortuary chambers and courts. Amon's priests visited each tomb or grave site, and special Bouquets of the God were placed at the tombs as mementoes. Singers and dancers, accompanied by lively bands, followed the priests and conducted rituals. The festivals of Amon were popular throughout Egypt in the New Kingdom.

Amon's Bark a vessel called *Userhetamon*, or the "Mighty of Brow Is Amon," a floating temple for the god Amon at THEBES. The bark was supposedly a gift of 'AHMOSE I (1550–1525 B.C.) in thanksgiving for his successful military campaigns. The vessel was a divine ark, and special "stations" were erected throughout Thebes to greet it on its holiday rounds. The bark was deemed a potent symbol of Amon's power and was refurbished or rebuilt in almost every region of the empire period. On the Feast of Opet the Bark of Amon was moved with great ceremony from KARNAK to LUXOR and back. On other feasts the floating temple sailed on the Nile or on the sacred lake of the shrine. It was covered in gold from the waterline up and was filled with cabins, obelisks, niches and elaborate adornments. (See BARKS OF THE GODS.)

Amon's Wives a title assumed by high-ranking royal women who took part in religious ceremonies of the god at KARNAK and LUXOR during the New Kingdom. Queens AHHOTEP and 'AHMOSE-NEFRETIRI, in the reign of 'AHMOSE I (1550–1525 B.C.) were the first such women to assume the role, serving as patronesses for festivals and cultic rites.

When the priests of Amon usurped the throne in the 21st Dynasty (1070 B.C.) the role of the Wife of Amon was altered. A princess of the royal house was consecrated as the god's spouse, served by virgins in the Harem of Amon.

Amratian See Naqada I in EGYPT, PREDYNASTIC.

Amtes a queen of the 6th Dynasty, a consort of PEPI I (2289–2255 B.C.). Some records indicate that she was involved in a harem plot to overthrow Pepi. The conspiracy was unsuccessful, and an official named Weni was called upon to investigate the charges against Amtes and her fellow conspirators. No record is available to give an account of the verdict given at the trial. (See HAREM.)

Am Tuat (also Am Duat) See BOOK OF THE DEAD.

Amu (also A'am) the Egyptian name for the Asiatics who entered the Nile Valley in the periods of dynastic weakness, eras called Intermediate Periods by historians because no royal line was able to maintain control of the land. Manetho, the Ptolemaic historian, referred to such Asiatics as the HYKSOS, a term derived from Hikau-Khasut, "Shepherd Kings," a phrase used by one of the usurping rulers. (See HYKSOS, MANETHO'S KING LIST.)

AMU Hyksos nomads, as depicted on the wall of Khnumhotep's tomb in Beni Hasan, dating to the 12th Dynasty.

amulet a decoratively carved object that was worn by the ancient Egyptians in keeping with their religious traditions. Called *wedjau*, the amulets were made out of metal, wood, faience, terracotta or stone and believed to contain magical powers, providing the wearer with supernatural benefits and charms. The potential power of the amulet was determined by the material, color, shape or spell of origin. Living Egyptians wore amulets as pendants, and the deceased had amulets placed in their linen wrappings in their coffins. Various styles of amulets were employed at different times and for different purposes. Some were carved as sacred symbols in order to attract the attention of a particular deity, thus ensuring the god's intercession and intervention on behalf of the wearer.

The *DJED* for example, was the symbol of stability that was associated with the god Osiris, and was normally worn on the chest, on a cord or necklace. The amulet was placed on the neck of the deceased,

The Amulet of the Eye, the sacred symbol associated with Re' and Horus and considered a powerful magical talisman.

in order to protect that part of the anatomy in the afterlife. The *djed* was normally fashioned out of glazed stone, faience, gold, gilded wood, lapis lazuli or from some other semiprecious material. The *djed* as a national symbol was used at festivals and celebrations.

The ANKH, the eye, the Amulet of the Heart, the PAPYRUS SCEPTER and images of the vulture were all popular. The favored amulet, however, appears to have been the SCARAB, the sacred beetle symbol that represented all of the mystical connotations and links between earth and resurrection. The scarabs were normally fashioned out of stone, wood, metal, schist, steatite and bronze (discovered in a 20th Dynasty site), and they could be tiny in size or large.

The BOOK OF THE DEAD, the mortuary text used throughout Egypt's later eras, contained a list of amulets required for the proper preparation of a corpse. One amulet found on almost every mummy was the *djed*. The scarab and other amulets were placed according to tradition and had to be fashioned out of specific materials, colored red or green normally, and incanted with spells supposedly provided by the god THOTH in HERMOPOLIS in the Old Kingdom.

Amunnakhte's Instructions   a text of a didactic nature which was written by a scribe of the PIR ANKH or House of Life (a medical and educational institution) at THEBES. Discovered in the Chester Beatty Papyrus IV, the instructions were addressed to an assistant, urging the young man to take up the noble profession of scribe, an important position in Egyptian society. The Egyptians revered such didactic literature, seeking wisdom and purpose in such texts. (See LITERATURE and SCRIBE.)

Amunemhet   a prince of the 18th Dynasty, the infant son of AMENHOTEP I (1525–1504 B.C.) and Queen

AHHOTEP II. His body was discovered in the cliffs of DEIR EL-BAHRI, having been rewrapped and reburied by the priests of the 20th Dynasty, who discovered his original tomb plundered. The child died in the first or second year of his life.

Amunemhet   an official of the 18th Dynasty, serving in the reign of AMENHOTEP II (1427–1401 B.C.). Amunemhet was a high priest of the god AMON but served the court in other capacities as well, as did most of the Amonite priests of that period. He was an accomplished architect and supervised royal building projects. He was buried in Thebes.

Amunet   a queen of the 11th Dynasty, a consort of MENTUHOTPE II (2061–2010 B.C.), called Amuniet in some records. Amunet was buried in the royal mortuary complex at DEIR EL-BAHRI on the western shore of Thebes, where Mentuhotpe and his other female companions were entombed.

Amunmesse (Menmire')   the sixth king of the 19th Dynasty, involved in the reign of SETI II (1214–1204 B.C.), possibly as a usurper. Considerable differences of opinion abound as to the chronological succession of the throne at this time. At some point, however, Amunmesse did assume the throne, holding it temporarily. No dates are ascribed to his reign, which was obviously brief. The only monument that honors him is a tomb in the VALLEY OF THE KINGS. Records indicate that he was related to RAMESSES II through his mother, Takhaet. His consorts were Baktwerel and possibly TIA, who has been suggested by some as the mother of SIPTAH, his successor.

Ana   a queen of the 13th Dynasty, a wife of SEBEK-HOTPE I (c.1750 B.C.). She is listed in some records as the mother of the princesses Ankhetitat and Fent-Ankhet.

Anastasi Papyri   a collection of Egyptian documents collected from various sources by the Swedish consul to Egypt during the period when extensive exploration was beginning on the Nile. Some of the papyri date to the Ramessid era and contain hymns to the god AMON and accounts from that period of Egyptian history.

Andjeti   See OSIRIS and BUSIRIS.

Anen   an official of the 18th Dynasty, serving in the reign of AMENHOTEP III (1391–1353 B.C.). Anen was the high priest of HELIOPOLIS' temple complex and the brother of Queen TIY. A statue of him in his priestly attire is in the Turin Museum.

Anhai Papyrus   one of the most elaborately illustrated papyri of the BOOK OF THE DEAD, the ancient Egyptian mortuary rituals texts that evolved over the centuries. This document, discovered in Thebes, depicts the rites of burial and the judgments of the dead. The Anhai Papyrus measures 14 feet, 6 inches and is now in the British Museum.

Anhur   a god of ancient Egypt, called Onouris by the Greeks. His name meant the "Sky-Bearer," and he was worshipped in conjunction with the god Shu, as another solar deity. Anhur was believed to be the warrior aspect of Re', but he also represented the creative powers of humans. He was depicted as a muscular human with an embroidered robe and a headdress of four plumes. He was especially popular in the New Kingdom era, when he was addressed as the "Savior" because of his martial powers and his solar connection. Mock battles were conducted at his festival, and he was a patron against enemies and pests. Anhur remained popular in later eras, after the fall of the New Kingdom, especially in Abydos.

Ani Papyrus   a document that is one of the surviving BOOKS OF THE DEAD, written for a man named Ani. It measures 178 feet, 3 inches and contains mortuary texts from the New Kingdom (1550–1070 B.C.). The Ani Papyrus is noted for its illustrations and its tales and legends, some of which are not included in other available papyri of that nature. The Litany of Osiris and a treatise on the origins of the gods and the union of Re' and Osiris distinguish the papyrus as well. A feature of the Ani Papyrus is a section that contains the opinions of the various priestly colleges in existence in the New Kingdom.

'Aniba   the site of a New Kingdom fortress, south of modern Cairo. The fort was originally surrounded by three walls and contained the remains of a temple and storage facilities. The structure dates to the 18th Dynasty (1550–1307 B.C.). A necropolis near Aniba was used for New Kingdom tombs and pyramids. Rock chapels were discovered on the western shore of the Nile, opposite the site, as well as an ancient cemetery plot.

animals, sacred   See GODS AND GODDESSES.

ankh   the symbol of eternal life in ancient Egypt, as well as the word for physical life. The *ankh* resembles a cross with a loop at the top and represented eternity when positioned in the hands of deities. The symbol dates to the establishment of the cults of the deities ISIS and OSIRIS in the Early Dynastic Period. The original meaning of the symbol was lost in later

ANKH   the cruciform insignia representing life, shown here in the hands of the goddess Ma'at; taken from a mortuary illustration.

periods, but it remained a constant hieroglyphic insignia for life. The *ankh* was used in rituals, especially in those involving the royal cults, and it had special significance when used in various temple ceremonies. (See AMULET.)

Ankhkhaf   a prince of the 4th Dynasty, a son of SNOFRU (2575–2551 B.C.) who served as vizier during one period of KHUFU's region. His MASTABA was discovered in a necropolis area at GIZA. His statue, a bust of exquisite artistry, is in the Museum of Fine Arts in Boston.

Ankhesenamon   originally called Ankhesenpa'aten, a queen of the 18th Dynasty, the daughter of AKHENATEN and Queen NEFERTITI (1353–1335 B.C.). Born to the royal family in residence at the city of 'Amarna, she was married to TUT'ANKHAMUN and became the queen when he succeeded SMENKHKARE' in 1333 B.C. The royal couple ruled only ten years. Tut'ankhamun was eight years old when he became king, and Ankhesenamon was thirteen.

Perhaps fearful of the priests and the growing power of HOREMHAB, a general of the armies who had stirred up opposition to 'Amarna and the worship of the god Aten, Ankhesenamon took a drastic step when Tut'ankhamun died. She wrote to King

Ankhesenamon and Tut'ankhamun from a Theban relief, which accentuates their extreme youth.

Shuppiluliumash of the Hittites, an emerging power on the northern Mediterranean, offering herself and the throne of Egypt to one of his royal sons. A prince ZANNANZA set out for Egypt and the wedding but was murdered at the border of Egypt, probably by Horemhab's military agents.

AYA, a master of horse in Thebes, was chosen to succeed Tut'ankhamun. As the royal widow, Ankhesenamon was given to him as his bride. Some question has been raised as to the possibility that Aya was the father of Queen Nefertiti, which would have made him Ankhesenamon's grandfather. The couple assumed the throne before the burial of Tut'ankhamun, thus performing the required ritual that each successor had to provide a deceased king in the tomb. Aya died in 1319 B.C., but Ankhesenamon disappeared from the royal scene before that, giving way to Aya's wife, TEY.

Ankhnesmery-Re' I   a queen of the 6th Dynasty, the wife of PEPI I (2289–2255 B.C.). The daughter of an official named Khui and the sister of Djau and Ankhnesmery-Re' II, she became the mother of NEM-TYEMZAF. Ankhnesmery-Re' I is reported to have died giving birth to Pepi's heir (Nemtyemzaf) or soon afterward.

Ankhnesmery-Re' II   a queen of the 6th Dynasty, the wife of PEPI I (2289–2255 B.C.). The daughter of an official named Khui and the sister of Djau and ANKHNESMERY-RE' I, she became the mother of PEPI II. When the young Pepi II succeeded his brother, NEMTYEMZAF, Ankhnesmery-Re' II served as regent for her child. She was aided by her brother, Djau, who was vizier. They raised the young heir and kept Egypt stable until he reached his majority. The story of the two sisters, Ankhnesmery-Re', was discovered on a tablet at ABYDOS.

Ankhnes-Pepi   a queen of the 6th Dynasty, wife of PEPI II (2246–2152 B.C.). Ankhnes-Pepi lived to see her son or grandson become the founder of the 8th Dynasty. She was buried in a storage chamber, entombed in a sarcophagus borrowed for the occasion from a family friend who had prepared it for his own funeral.

Ankh-tawy   the ancient name for the city of MEM-PHIS or part of its environs, meaning "Life of the Two Lands." The city's name was changed to Memphis in the 6th Dynasty by PEPI I.

Annals of Tuthmosis III   See TUTHMOSIS III'S MIL-ITARY CAMPAIGNS.

ANKHNESMERY-RE' II   shown here in a statue with her son, Pepi II of the 6th Dynasty.

Anubis   the Greek rendering of the Egyptian Anpu or Anup, opener of the roads for the dead, the guide of the afterlife. From earliest times this deity presided over the embalming rituals and received many pleas in the mortuary prayers recited on behalf of deceased Egyptians.

Anubis, the god of the rituals of the tomb, from a temple relief.

He was normally depicted as a black jackal with a bushy tail or as a man with the head of a jackal or a dog. In the PYRAMID TEXTS Anubis was described as a son of RE' and given a daughter, a goddess of freshness. In time he lost both of those attributes and became part of the Osirian cultic tradition, the son

The goddess Anukis, from a temple relief.

of NEPHTHYS, abandoned by his mother who had borne him to OSIRIS. ISIS raised him, and when he was grown he accompanied Osiris, aiding Isis when SETH slew Osiris and dismembered his corpse. Anubis invented the mortuary rites at this time, taking on the title of "Lord of the Mummy Wrappings." Anubis henceforth ushered in the deceased to Osiris' JUDGMENT HALLS. Anubis remained popular in all periods of Egyptian history and even in the time of foreign domination.

Anukis a goddess of the First Cataract of the Nile and the wife of the god KHNUM. Anukis was depicted as a woman carrying a staff and wearing a feather crown. She was popular in most periods of Egypt's history, especially when the nation held vast territories below the Cataracts.

Aoh a queen of the 11th Dynasty, the consort of INYOTEF III (2069–2061 B.C.) and the mother of MENTUHOTPE II. She was depicted in the company of her royal son on a stela.

Apet See TAUERET.

Apis the sacred bull, a theophany of the Ptah-Sokar-Osiris cult at MEMPHIS. The PALERMO STONE and other records give an account of the festival honoring this animal. The ceremonies date to the 1st Dynasty (c. 2900 B.C.) and were normally called "The Running of Apis." The animal was also addressed as Hapi. The name Apis is Greek for the Egyptian Hep or Hapi. The sacred bull of Apis was required to have a white crescent on one side of its body or a white triangle on its forehead, signifying its unique character and its acceptance by the gods. A flying vulture patch on the back of the animal was also considered a sign that it was eligible for ceremonies. A black lump under its tongue was enough to qualify a bull if all other signs were absent.

When a bull of Apis died, an immediate search began for another animal with at least one of the markings required. Such animals were dressed in elaborate golden robes and paraded in the ceremonies of PTAH. It is believed that the bull was always born of a virgin cow, impregnated by Ptah for a life of service in the temple.

The bulls were used as ORACLES on FESTIVAL days. In a special chamber in Memphis the animal was turned loose to decide which gate it would enter to seek its food. The gates held symbols as to the positive or negative response to questions put to the animal by believers. Each bull was cared for by the priests for a period of 25 years and then drowned. Various parts of the animal were then eaten in a sacramental meal in the temple, and the remains were embalmed and placed in the SERAPEUM or in another bull necropolis structure. (See BUCHIS, A'ANEFER, MNEVIS; see also GODS AND GODDESSES, ANIMALS.)

Apophis (Apep in some lists) a giant serpent with mystical powers who was the enemy of the god RE'. Apophis lived in the waters of NUN (the cosmological area of chaos) or in the celestial waters of the Nile (the spiritual entity envisioned in Egyptian religious texts) and attempted each day to stop Re'

Apis bull, from an ornate gilded Old Kingdom statue.

Apophis, the serpent of the Tuat or Underworld. This stela relief shows a dead Egyptian man paying homage.

from his appointed passage across the sky. In some traditions Apophis was a previous form of Re' that had been discarded, a myth that accounted for the strength of the creature. Apophis was viewed as a genuine threat to Re' by the Egyptians. On sunless days, especially on stormy days, the people took the lack of sunlight as a sign that Apophis was becoming victorious over Re'. When there was an eclipse, the Egyptians believed that Apophis had swallowed Re and his solar bark (See SOLAR BOAT.).

Apophis never gained a lasting victory, however, because of the prayers of the priests and the pious. The ritual document, "Book of Overthrowing Apophis," discovered at KARNAK, contained a list of the serpent's secret names and a selection of hymns to be sung to celebrate Re' 's victories. A series of dreadful assaults were committed on Apophis each time the serpent was defeated, but he rose in strength again on the following morning, an image of evil always prepared to attack the righteous. (See OVER-THROWING APOPHIS.)

Apophis ('Awoserre') a king of the 15th (HYKSOS) Dynasty ruling from AVARIS while the 17th Dynasty (c. 1585–1542 B.C.) ruled Upper Egypt from Thebes. He was mentioned in the Sallier Papyrus and on the Karnak Stelae. His contemporaries were Sekenenre' TA'O II and Wadj-Kheperre' KAMOSE in Thebes. These Theban kings began to reclaim land during his reign, forcing the Hyksos to retreat northward.

Apophis sent word to Sekenenre' Ta'o II that the snoring hippopotami in the sacred temple pool at Thebes kept him awake at night by their unseemly noises. This was perhaps a sheer literary device used by the Thebans, to justify their cause, but Sekenenre' Ta'o, receiving the message, decreed that it was an insult, because Apophis' bed chamber was more than 400 miles away. He promptly declared official war on Avaris and began to campaign to push the Hyksos out of Egypt. He was slain in battle or in an ambush, and KAMOSE, his eldest son, took up the crusade with renewed vengeance. The Hyksos gave way up and down the Nile, and Apophis died in Avaris, possibly from old age or from the stress of seeing the Thebans' victorious advance on his kingdom.

"appearing" an ancient Egyptian term for the dawning of a god or the coronation and or anniversary of a king. As a manifestation of a deity, the term was considered appropriate in the names of barks and buildings. (See WINDOW OF APPEARANCE.)

Apuwat See WEPWAWET.

Arabian Desert the eastern desert of ancient Egypt, mountainous and rutted by deep wadis or dry riverbeds. This hostile area protected Egypt from invaders crossing the Red Sea. The sandy terrain is marked by a chain of hills, from north to south, which rise in some places to a height of 7,000 feet above sea level. The hills provided Egypt with vast quarries and mining areas that yielded granite, diorite and other stones.

Armant See ERMENT.

Arsaphes See HARSHAPHES.

Art and Architecture the important and often stunning expressions of Egyptian life and religious beliefs that have made that nation the focus of study and examination for centuries. Art and architecture gave testimony to the religious creeds of the various eras as well as to the presence of individuals of note, illuminating the national concern with the gods and eternity.

Late Pre-dynastic Period (4000–3000 B.C.)

Art

The people of the Nile Valley began producing art as early as the 7th millenium B.C. Decorative patterns consisted of geometric designs of varying shapes and sizes and very obscure symbols. Direct representational drawings, mainly of animals, hunters and traps, came at a slightly later date. Evidence of artistic advancement among the Neolithic cultures in Upper Egypt and Nubia is provided by the drawings of boats and domesticated animals, most notably at HIERAKONPOLIS, where some elements of the Mesopotamian and Saharan styles are evident.

Pottery of the Predynastic Period, as well as figures fashioned out of bone and ivory, initiated the artistic motifs that would be influential for many centuries. Vessels and palettes accompanied fine black-topped pottery, leading to red polished ware decorated with cream-colored paint. The light on dark painting technique made the pottery of this period distinctive. While geometric designs were developed first, artisans began to experiment with human, plant and animal forms. An excellent example is the bottom of a bowl with entwining hippopotami. Such bowls can be dated to the NAQADA I Period, also called Amratian (from el-'Amra). The ultimate achievement of this period was the mastering of Egypt's most famous artistic medium: stone.

In the NAQADA II Period (also called the Gerzean—

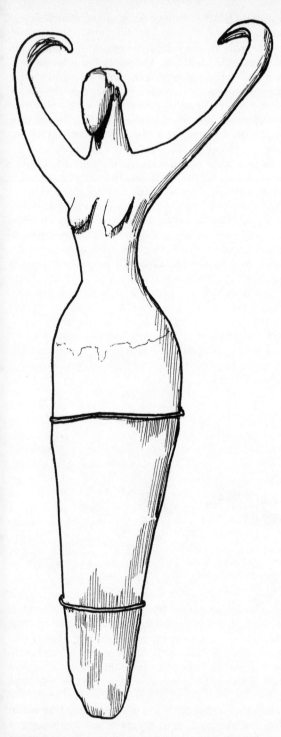

from Girza), stone pieces were being fashioned, some of the most notable discovered in a cemetery in the Girza district, the Thinite NOME of Upper Egypt. Ivory and stone figures were carved in cylindrical form, crude in detail but remarkable for their size. Reliefs in stone and statuary were used by the cult of the god MIN. Technical advances are evident in the pieces recovered in Hierakonpolis (both in stone and in faience), in ABYDOS and HELWAN.

Stone palettes and mace heads appeared at the end of the Predynastic Period but with a clarified sense of composition. The Oxford palette from Hierakonpolis is probably the earliest of this form, along with the Louvre fragment and the mace head of the SCORPION KING. Of primary importance in the development of composition, of course, was the NA'RMER PALETTE, a green slate slab from Hierakonpolis originally intended to serve as a tablet on which cosmetics for the eyes were blended. The palette, utilitarian in purpose, was crucial nevertheless from an artistic standpoint.

The style of later Egyptian art is visible in the depiction on the palette of the military campaigns in the Delta. Vitality, power and a certain sense of

PREDYNASTIC ART   the famed Amratian (Nagada I) female figure, probably a goddess, made of painted clay. The figure is in the Brooklyn Museum.

The Na'rmer Palette, from the Old Kingdom, commemorating the unification of the Two Kingdoms.

drama are incorporated into the carvings. The palette thus was a model for later generations of artists. Increased regulation of human representation came later with the canon of Egyptian art (see box).

Architecture

Architecture in the Predynastic Period evolved at the same pace as relief, painting and sculpture. Writing and the construction of tombs and temples were both tied to the rise of political centralization in the late Naqada II or Gerzean Period. The few remains of this era point to the use of mud brick, seen in the painted chamber ("Decorated Tomb 100") at Hierakonpolis. Cities were being built with walls, projecting towers, and gates, the designs of which were preserved on the palettes of the era and thus survived to influence later periods.

Of particular interest architecturally are the dwellings of the period. The earliest homes were probably versions of tents or roofless areas protected from the wind and rain by walls or thickets. Eventually mud was utilized to make walls, allowing for the first actual residences. The mud, daubed at first on thatched walls, was later turned into bricks, sun dried and considerably more durable. Buildings were circular or oval in design, but innovations in wall construction, battering, the process of sloping walls to provide sturdier bases, provided artistic flair and balance. Windows and doors were employed. The windows were set into walls at high levels, and both portals were trimmed with wood, a material that became scarce in later periods.

In Upper Egypt there were definite advances, but generally speaking, one of three basic plans was followed in construction. The first was a rectangular structure with paneled sides and a hooped roof. The second was a rectangular pavilion with a vaulted roof surmounting a cornice. The third was the SEREKH design. This was a large system of elaborately paneled facings and niches. Flax chalk lines (lines drawn in chalk after being measured with taut ropes) were used early for construction measurements.

Early Dynastic Period and the Old Kingdom

Art

Although the Early Dynastic Period and especially the Old Kingdom are noted for the rapid and impressive development of architecture—in tombs, TEMPLES, chapels and the evolving MASTABA, alongside the PYRAMID—the decorative arts flourished as well. Craftsmen produced exceptional pieces, and statuary, painting, furniture, jewelry and household implements all benefited from experimentation and innovations.

Sculpture in the round (freestanding statues) fulfilled a ceremonial need for display in religious matters and provided symbolic representation of the royal lines. Most statues were made of limestone, sandstone or granite. Sometimes wood, clay and even bronze were used, but such materials were rare. Sculpture followed the same conventions as painting and relief, and displays a stylistic similarity.

Statues were compact and solid, notable for the air of serenity and idealized features they imparted to their subjects. Such idealization was a key element in the art of the time, formalized into powerful conventions. Portraiture was not practised on the elite, but realism emerged in the statues of commoners or lesser-known individuals. The eyes of statues were sometimes brought to life by the insertion of crystals into the eye sockets.

Paintings and reliefs displayed a religious orientation. As part of the decoration of mortuary complexes they depicted architectural and hunting scenes, paradise and everyday life, with references to the Nile and its marshlands. One remarkable tomb painting of geese at MEIDUM depicts the fowl with engaging naturalism.

MEIDUM GEESE   detail of the magnificent paintings from the tomb of Princess Itet.

At the close of the 4th Dynasty (c. 2465 B.C.) the style of depicting figures and scenes in sunken relief began. The outline of the form was cut sharply into the surface of the walls, leaving enough space to emphasize the figure. Shadows thus emerged, accentuating line and movement while protecting the forms from wear.

In this era the solar temples (designed to honor Re', the sun god, and to catch the sun's rays at dawn) were being erected along the Nile, and artists began to depict the natural loveliness of the landscape and the changing seasons, all under the stars of the heavens. The progress of painting developed.

THE CANON OF THE HUMAN FORM

The canon followed by the ancient Egyptians for representing the human figure in reliefs and paintings evolved within the perimeters of religion. The predynastic Egyptians, already deeply concerned with spiritual concepts, had a need to communicate ideas and ideals through the representation of divine beings, human personages and events. From the beginning the Egyptians understood the propagandistic aspects of art and formulated ways in which artistic representation could serve a didactic purpose. Art was meant to convey information. The canon of the human form resulted, and it was a convention by which representation could convey metaphysical concepts while at the same time bringing a vision of the material world to the viewer.

The canon dealt mainly with paintings and reliefs as they were used in mortuary structures and religious shrines, and governed the representation of three-dimensional elements on a two-dimensional surface, which demanded anatomical knowledge, perspective and idealized composition.

Early examples demonstrate an increasing sophistication in such compositions, culminating in the Na'rmer Palette of the predynastic age. The Na'rmer Palette integrated all of the earlier artistic elements while displaying a unique energy and vitality. With the start of the Old Kingdom (2575 B.C.), artistic conventions were being codified to provide generations of artists with formal guidelines on the proper positioning of human figures within a scene or pictorial narrative, or a framework of hieroglyphs and religious symbols.

According to the canon, the human figure was to be composed in a prescribed manner. To facilitate execution in reliefs and paintings, a surface was divided into 18 rows of squares (the 19th reserved for the hair). In later historical periods more rows were added.

The human figure, when sketched or traced onto a surface, was depicted from a dual perspective. The head was always rendered in profile, but the human eye and eyebrow were depicted in full view. The shoulders and upper torso were also shown in full view, so that the arms, hands and fingers were visible. The abdomen from the armpit to the waist was shown in profile and the navel was normally placed on the side of the figure, directly on the edge. The legs and feet were also in profile, balancing the head, and until around the mid-18th Dynasty the inside of the feet was preferred over the outside in human representations.

The canon was strictly observed when artists portrayed the ruling class of Egypt. The formality allowed by the canon and its idealized conception lent grace and authority, critical to royal portraits. While one might expect rigidity and staleness to result from this type of regimentation, the canon provided a framework for continual elaboration, and the teams of artists who worked together to adorn the private and public shrines found a common ground for individual expression.

Artistic quality was maintained, and the needs of each generation were provided for among the standards regulating fine art.

Wall surfaces were marked by red and black lines, allowing the artists to set scope and perspective. Once the carvings were completed, the walls were given a light coat of stucco, and some were then touched with paints of various hues. The figures were outlined one last time so that they would come to life against the neutral backgrounds.

Furniture from this period shows the same remarkable craftsmanship and fine detail, as evidenced by the funerary objects of Queen HETEPHERES I, the mother of KHUFU (2551–2528 B.C.). Wooden furniture inlayed with semiprecious stones graced the palaces of the era and Hetepheres was buried with chairs, beds, a canopy, and gold covered boxes. She had silver bracelets and other jewelry of turquoise, lapis lazuli and carnelian. Crowns and necklaces, all of great beauty, adorned the royal mother while she lived and were placed in her tomb to adorn her through eternity.

Architecture

By the time the Early Dynastic Period was established in MEMPHIS, experimentation and the demands of the mortuary rituals challenged the architects of Egypt to provide suitable structures for the dead. The mastaba, the rectangular building erected with battered walls and subterranean chambers and shafts, became more and more elaborate.

Small temples were fashioned out of stone, and one such place of worship, constructed at the end of the 2nd Dynasty (c. 2649 B.C.) was composed of granite. STELAE began to appear (the round topped stone slabs designed to hold inscriptions commemorating great events and personages, religious and secular). SAQQARA became an elaborate necropolis for Memphis, and other mortuary complexes were erected at Abydos.

The turning point in such complexes came in the reign of Djoser (2630–2611 B.C.) when IMHOTEP, his chancellor or vizier, fashioned the STEP PYRAMID, the earliest structure in stone of its size and Egypt's first pyramid, on the Saqqara plain. This structure, composed of mastabas placed one on top of another, became the link between the original tomb designs and the true pyramids of the next dynasty. The pyramid complexes that emerged in the 5th Dynasty consisted of valley temples, causeways, mortuary temples and accompanying subsidiary buildings, and they became the symbol of Egypt.

These pyramids reflected not only mathematical and construction skills but other aspects of Egyptian civilization. Rising from the plain of Giza and in other locations, the structures were no longer simple tombs but stages for elaborate ceremonies where priests offered continual prayers and gifts, as part of an ongoing mortuary cult. Later kings were forced to reduce the size of their pyramids, eventually abandoning the form entirely because of a lack of resources, but the Giza monuments remained vivid examples of Egypt's architectural glories.

The Middle Kingdom

Art

At the close of the Old Kingdom, the authority of Egypt's rulers had eroded and the country suffered from civil unrest. One of the consequences was a decline in both art and architecture. The 11th Dynasty reunited Upper and Lower Egypt in 2040 B.C. and resumed patronage of the arts and the building of monuments. The art of this new age, called the Middle Kingdom, was marked by realism and a new degree of classicism revived from the Old Kingdom. An elegant and elaborate style was popular and detail became paramount, as evidenced in the head of SENWOSRET III (1878–1841? B.C.) of the 12th Dynasty in which age and weariness are frankly depicted.

The jewelry of this period is famous in modern times because of a cache of necklaces bracelets and pectorals discovered in DASHUR, the mortuary region of the 12th Dynasty. Beautifully crafted of enamel gold, and semiprecious stones, it attests to the artistic skill of the period. Another treasure, found at LAHOUN yielded golden wire diadems with jeweled flowers, as well as a dazzling variety of bracelets, collars and pectorals of semiprecious stones set in gold.

Architecture

Under the nomarchs, the rulers of the nomes or provinces in outlying districts who were able to maintain their authority amid general civil unrest, architecture survived the fall of the Old Kingdom. Their patronage continued into the Middle Kingdom, resulting in such remarkable sites as BENI HASAN (c. 1900 B.C.), with its rock carved tombs and large chapels complete with columned porticos and painted walls. The 11th Dynasty, however, resumed royal sponsorship of architectural projects, symbolized by the great mortuary complex of Mentuhotpe II (2061–2010 B.C.), at DEIR EL-BAHRI on the western shore at THEBES. The temple there very much influenced New Kingdom architects and was the first complex set on terraces of varying height with a columned portico at the back of the terrace. This formed the facade of the tomb. The actual tomb area was recessed into the cliff.

During the Middle Kingdom most of the temples

SENWOSRET III   a Middle Kingdom statue.

Little is known of the palaces or royal residences of this period because they too were fashioned out of brick and wood. It is clear that the palaces (PERO or per-a'a) always contained two gateways, two main halls and two administrative sections to reflect the upper and lower regions of the nation. Flagstaffs were used at the gates, as they were placed before temples. The remains of the 17th Dynasty (1640–1550 B.C.) palace at DEIR EL-BALLAS, on the western shore north of Thebes, indicate somewhat luxurious surroundings and innovative decoration, following the "double" scheme. In some instances the walls and floors were designed to imitate ponds of fish and vast tracts of flowering shrubs.

The Second Intermediate Period and the domination of northern Egypt by the Hyksos curtailed artistic endeavors along the Nile, although the arts did not vanish. A renaissance took place, however, with the arrival of the New Kingdom after the Hyksos were driven from the land.

New Kingdom

The New Kingdom is recognized as a period of great artistic efflouresence, with art and architecture evolving in three separate and quite distinct eras: the Tuthmossid period, from the start of the New Kingdom (1550 B.C.) to the end of the reign of AMENHOTEP III (1353 B.C.), the 'AMARNA period (1350–1335 B.C.) and the Ramessid era (1307–1070 B.C.).

Art

Tuthmossid Period
With the expulsion of the Hyksos and the reunification of Upper and Lower Egypt, the kings of the 18th Dynasty (the Tuthmossids) began elaborate rebuilding programs in order to reflect the spirit of the new age. Sculpture in the round and painting bore traces of the Middle Kingdom standards while exhibiting innovations such as polychromatics and the application of a simplified cubic form.

Osiride figures (depictions of Osiris or of royal personages assuming the deity's trappings) of the period found at Deir el-Bahri are of painted limestone, with blue eyebrows and beards and red or yellow skin tones. Startling in appearance, color was applied even on black granite statues. Cubic forms popular in the period are evidenced by the statues of Chief Steward SENENMUT and Princess NEFERU-RE, his charge, of HATSHEPSUT's era (1473–1458 B.C.). The figures, encased in granite cubes, are nonetheless touching portraits, enhanced by hieroglyphs that interpret their rank, relationship and affection for one another. Other statues, such as one in granite of

of Egypt were built with columned courts, halls and chambers for rituals. The sanctuaries of these shrines were elaborate, and most had small sacred lakes within the precincts. KARNAK was begun in this era, and in time the temple would become the largest religious complex in the history of the world. The famed temple of LUXOR would be linked to Karnak by an avenue of ram-headed sphinxes.

Residences of the upper classes and some of the common abodes began to assume architectural distinction as well. Made of sun-baked brick and wood, most villas or mansions had two or three floors eventually, connected by staircases. Storehouses, a separate kitchen area, high ceilings and vast gardens were a part of residential designs. Some had air vents for circulation, and all of the houses, whether owned by aristocrats or commoners, had gently sloping roofs on which the Egyptian families slept in warm weather. Made of vulnerable materials, no examples of domestic architecture survive.

TUTHMOSIS III (1479–1425 B.C.) demonstrated both the cubist and polychromatic styles.

Sculpture was but one aspect of New Kingdom art where innovations were forged. In painting artists adhered to the canon set in predynastic eras but incorporated changes in their work. Egypt's military successes, which resulted in an empire and made vassals of many Mediterranean nations, were commemorated in pictorial narratives of battles or processions of tribute-bearers from other lands. A grace and quiet elegance permeated the works, a sureness born out of prosperity. The surviving tomb paintings of the period display banquets and other trappings of prosperity. The figures are softer, almost lyrical. The reign of Amenhotep III (1391–1353 B.C.) brought this new artistic mastery to its greatest heights.

'Amarna

The city of 'Amarna, erected by AKHENATEN (1353–1335 B.C.) in honor of the god ATEN, set off an artistic revolution that upset many of the old conventions. The rigid grandeur of the earlier periods was abandoned in favor of a more naturalistic style. Royal personages were no longer made to appear remote or god-like, and in many scenes Akhenaten and his queen, NEFERTITI, are depicted as a loving couple surrounded by their offspring. Physical deformities are frankly protrayed, and the royal household is painted with protruding bellies, enlarged heads and peculiar limbs.

The famed painted busts of Nefertiti, however, demonstrate a mastery that was also reflected in the magnificent pastoral scenes adorning the palaces. Only fragments remain, but they boast a wondrous range of animals, plants and water scenes that stand

The 'Amarna art style, as evidenced in a painting from Akhenaten's city depicting two of his daughters.

unrivaled for anatomical sureness, color and vitality. The palaces and temples of 'Amarna were destroyed in later reigns, with men like HOREMHAB (1319–1307 B.C.), who razed the site in order to use the materials for personal projects.

Ramessid Period

From the reign of RAMESSES I until the end of the New Kingdom, art once again followed the canon, but influences from the Tuthmossid and 'Amarna periods were evident. The terminal years of the 20th Dynasty brought about a degeneration in artistic achievement, but until that time the Ramessid accomplishments were masterful. Ramesses II embarked on a building program unrivalled by any previous Egyptian ruler.

RAMESSES II and his contemporaries were involved in martial exploits, and the campaign narratives (so popular in the reign of Tuthmosis III) became the dominant subject of temple reliefs once more. Dramatic battle scenes were carved into temple walls, and paintings in the royal tombs, especially that of Queen NEFERTARI, the wife of Ramesses II (1290–1224 B.C.), offer stunning glimpses of life on the Nile. RAMESSES III's battle scenes at MEDINET HABU (1194–1163 B.C.) are of equal merit and are significant because they are among the major artistic achievements of the Ramessid period.

Architecture

Tuthmossid Period

Architecture at the start of the New Kingdom reflected the renewed vitality of a united land. Its focus shifted from the tomb to the temple, especially those honoring Amon and those designed as mortuary shrines. The mortuary temple of Hatshepsut (1473–1458 B.C.) at Deir el-Bahri allowed the architects of her age the opportunity to erect a masterpiece: three ascending colonnades and terraces set into the cliffs on the western shore and reached by two unusual ramps. The temples of other kings of the period are less grand but equally elegant. The great palace complex of Amenhotep III (1391–1353 B.C.), which included chapels, shrines and residences set into a man-made lake, was a masterpiece of architectural design.

Karnak and Luxor both massive in scale, reflect the enthusiasm for building of the Tuthmossids. Although several stages of construction took place at the sites, the architects were able to integrate them into graceful and powerful monuments of faith.

'Amarna

The entire city of 'Amarna was laid out with precision and care, leading to the great temple of the

COLUMNS IN EGYPTIAN ARCHITECTURE

One of the most appealing and awe-inspiring aspects of Egyptian temple architecture are the spectacular rows of columns, resembling groves of soaring stone trees. These columns, especially at KARNAK and LUXOR, dwarf human beings and bear inscriptions, carved reliefs and a weighty majesty unequaled anywhere else in the world.

Columns held special significance for the Egyptians, representing as they did the expanse of nature. Columns alluded to the time when vast forests dotted the land, forests which disappeared as the climate changed and civilization took its toll upon the Egyptian environment. They also symbolized the Nile reed marshes.

The columns were introduced into temples in order to simulate nature, and to identify mankind again with the earth. The first tentative columns are still visible in the STEP PYRAMID of SAQQARA, but they are engaged columns, attached to walls for support and unable to stand on their own. IMHOTEP designed rows of such pillars at the entrances to various buildings and incorporated them into corridors for DJOSER's shrine (c. 2600 B.C.).

In the 4th Dynasty (2575–2465 B.C.) masons experimented with columns as a separate architectural entity. In one royal tomb at GIZA built in the reign of Khufu (2551–2528 B.C.) limestone columns were used effectively. In the tomb of Sahure' of the 5th Dynasty (2458–2446 B.C.) the columns are made of granite, evincing a more assured style and level of skill.

Wooden columns graced a site in the reign of Kakai (2446–2426 B.C.) in that same dynasty, and another king of the royal line, Izi (2416–2392 B.C.), had limestone columns installed in his ABUSIR necropolis complex.

At BENI HASAN in the 11th Dynasty (c. 2134–2040 B.C.) the local nomarchs, or clan chiefs, built their own tombs with wooden columns. The same types of columns were installed in tombs in the 12th Dynasty (c. 1991–1773 B.C.), but they were made of wood set into stone bases.

With the coming of the New Kingdom (c. 1550–1070 B.C.) the columns became part of the architectural splendor that marked the capital of THEBES and the later capital of PER-RAMESSES (in the eastern Delta). Extensive colonnades stood on terraces, or in the recesses of temples, opening onto courts and shrines.

The accompanying illustrations are examples of the various types of columns used by the Egyptians.

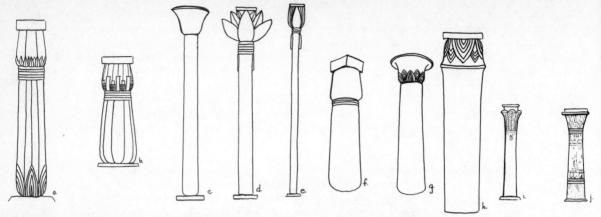

COLUMNS: a) papyrus bundle design from 5th Dynasty; b) papyrus bundle variation; c) papyrus stem from Old Kingdom; d) lotus stem design from Middle Kingdom; e) lotus stem variation; f) bud column from New Kingdom; g) bud column variation; h) inverted bud column design; i) palmiform from 5th Dynasty; j) campaniform design from Karnak.

god Aten. The distinctive aspect of these buildings was the absence of a roof. The rays of the divine sun, a manifestation of Aten, was allowed to reach into every corner, providing light and inspiration.

Ramessid Period

The period of Ramessid architecture, which can be said to include Horemhab's tomb at Saqqara, was marked by lavish construction on a gigantic scale. Three of the greatest builders in Egyptian history, SETI I (1306–1290 B.C.) and Ramesses II (1290–1224 B.C.) of the 19th Dynasty and Ramesses III of the 20th Dynasty (1194–1163 B.C.), reigned during this period.

Seti began work on the second and third PYLONS of Karnak, and instituted the Great Hall, completed by his son, Ramesses II. Ramesses II also built the RAMESSEUM in Thebes. He left an architectural legacy as well at PER-RAMESSES, the new capital in the eastern Delta. MEDINET HABU, Ramesses III's mortuary temple complex, which included a brick palace, displays the same architectural grandeur. This was the last great work of the Ramessid era of the New Kingdom.

The most famous of the Ramessid monuments, other than the great mortuary temples at Abydos, was ABU SIMBEL, completed at the 30th anniversary of Ramesses' reign. The rock-art temple was hewn out of pink limestone. With the fall of the Ramessids, Egypt entered into a period of decline. Later dynasties would arise, and foreign peoples would rule the land, but the magnificent artistic endeavors of ancient Egypt continue to intrigue visitors to Egypt today. (For details on the various works mentioned or the sites, see the individual entries. See also TEMPLES.)

Asar See OSIRIS.

Asasif a depression on the western shore of the Nile near DEIR EL-BAHRI, across from the city of THEBES. Tombs of the Saite dynasty era (see SAIS) were discovered in the area, as well as mortuary complexes from the 11th Dynasty (2134–1991 B.C.). RAMESSES IV (1163–1156 B.C.) also started a temple on the site.

Aser the ancient Egyptian name for the tamarisk tree.

Asiatics See HYKSOS.

Ashait a royal wife of the 11th Dynasty, married to MENTUHOTPE II (2061–2010 B.C.). She was buried with him in his elaborate mortuary complex at DEIR EL-BAHRI, on the western shore of the Nile at Thebes. Her tomb reliefs supposedly identify her as an Ethiopian or Negress. Ashait's coffin contained an enchanting hymn about the four winds, delineating the sort of weather and abundance that came from the four cardinal points of the earth, all brought to Egypt by mythical maidens.

Assiut called Lykopolis or Lyconpolis in some lists, the center of the 13th NOME of Upper Egypt, located south of HERMOPOLIS on the eastern side of the Nile. Assiut was dedicated to the god WEPWAWET, the wolf deity. The city was important because it was the terminus of the caravan route from the KHARGAH OASIS and the lands below the First Cataract. The

NOMARCHS of Assiut were famous in many eras of Egyptian history for their military prowess and were enlisted to aid some rulers during periods of unrest.

Inscriptions carved into the tombs which were hewn out of the cliffs overlooking Assiut indicate the power and independent stance of the locals. Most of these tombs date from the period of the 9th and 10th Dynasties (2134–2040 B.C.), when the Herakleopolitan kings looked to the Assiut warriors to defend their lands against the encroaching Thebans. One interesting relief among those discovered in the tombs is that of a female nomarch named SITRE', who served as regent and kept the clan's hereditary lands intact until her son reached his majority. (See DEIR DU-RUNKA.)

astrology the practice attributed to the ancient Egyptians, highly dramatized in the modern world. The Egyptians practiced a form of astrology, but it had little in common with that of later eras. The Egyptians practiced "Astral-Theology," a form of divination that responded to the astronomical observances of their day but held no independent value.

The Egyptians were always anxious to equate human endeavors with cosmic events as observed in the night sky, and much of their writings and teachings about the spirit of MA'AT were concerned with a need to mirror the divine order demonstrated by the heavenly bodies. Horoscopes in the modern sense of the word were not known by the Egyptians before the fall of the New Kingdom. They did not have the traditional signs of the zodiac or the concept of planetary houses. When the Egyptians did learn about horoscopes and the attendant lore, it was from Mesopotamian and Hellenistic sources late in the Ptolematic period.

The Egyptians had other methods of divination and fortune telling, such as the mythological calendars that dealt with lucky and unlucky days, especially as they pertained to births. When other cultures dominated Egypt, or when later dynasties arose along the Nile, the priests would become world famous for their skills.

Astronomical Room See RAMESSEUM.

astronomy the ancient Egyptian science of the stars, prompted in the early eras by the demands of agriculture. Because the harvest seasons and the fertilization of the fields and orchards depended upon the annual inundation of the Nile, the priests of the formative years of Egypt's history began to chart the heavenly bodies and to incorporate them into a religious tradition that would provide information about the Nile and its patterns of inundation.

There was a fascination with celestial activities as evidenced by tomb inscriptions of the Old Kingdom (2575–2134 B.C.) and the First Intermediate Period (2134–2040 B.C.), which continued into later eras and were elaborated in the Ptolemaic time. These inscriptions contained lists of the divisions of the sky, called *dekans* by the Greeks. The *dekans* were the so-called 12 hours of the night, represented by pictures. Each *dekan* was personified and given a divine attribute. Nut, an important sky goddess of Egypt, was associated with the inscriptions and their depictions. As the goddess of the heavens, the celestial bodies were incorporated into her body.

Certain priests, designated as the "Keepers of Time," watched the nightly movement of the stars. They were required to memorize the order of the fixed stars, the movements of the moon and the planets, the rising of the moon and the sun, as well as their setting times, and the orbits of the various celestial bodies. Such learned individuals were then ready to recite this information in counsel and to provide details about the changes taking place in the sky in any given season.

One set of stars known to the temple astronomers was called the Ikhemu-Seku, the "Stars That Never Fail." These were the polar stars that remained fixed in the night sky and were much venerated as special souls having attained true bliss. The second set of stars, actually planets, were the Ikhemu-Weredu, the "Never Resting Stars," which followed distinct orbits in the night sky. There is no information as to whether or not the Egyptians made a true distinction between the planets or the stars. Both sets of "stars" were believed to accompany the solar bark on its nightly voyage.

The stars noted were: Sirius the Dogstar, called Sopdu or Sopdet, considered the true symbol of the coming inundation of the Nile, signalling the rising of the river; Orion, called Sah, the "Fleet-Footed, Long-Strider"; Ursa Major (Great Bear or Big Dipper), called Meskhetiu. Also noted were Cygnus, Cassiopeia, the Dragon, Scorpio and the Ram. There is no evidence that the Egyptians charted the Pleiades until the Ptolemaic period.

The planets noted were: Hor-tash-tawy (Jupiter), called "Horus Who Binds the Two Lands"; Hor-ka-Pet (Saturn), called "Horus the Bull of Heaven"; *Horus-Desher* (Mars), the "Red Horus"; *Sebeg* (Mercury), meaning unknown; *Seba-Djai* (Venus), the "Star that Crosses." The sun was preeminent in Egyptian religion from predynastic times, represented as the scarab beetle, Khepri, rising in the morning, Re' at noon (overhead), and Atum at night. The sun only became important to Egyptian astronomy in the 26th Dynasty. The Egyptians had no special interest in the stars and planets in themselves. It was enough for them to recognize the astral bodies as part of the cosmic harmony that had to be maintained by mankind so that the world could prosper and survive.

In the tomb of SENENMUT, an official of the 18th Dynasty during the reign of HATSHEPSUT (1473–1458 B.C.), a chart painted on the ceiling points to the astronomical knowledge of the period. It is the first known star chart.

Aswan named Sunnu by the Egyptians and Syene by the Greeks, a city located at the First Cataract of the Nile. The area was famous for its red granite, called Syenite in later eras. Aswan also served as provincial administrative headquarters for the territories below the cataract, and the viceroys of NUBIA were stationed on the ELEPHANTINE Island there. Settlement on the Elephantine at Aswan predates the dynastic period. In time the region became a center for the trade conducted with Nubia and the African interior. The district honored the ram god Khnum and his two consorts, Satet and Anuket. The Nile god, Hapi, was also believed to live in a cave in the region, and another Aswan site was believed to have been the grave of Osiris.

On the west bank of the Nile at Aswan there are graves of the Egyptian officials who conducted the trade expeditions and administered the affairs of the region. Some of the graves date from the Old Kingdom (2575–2134 B.C.). The tomb belonging to HARKHAF, an official of the 6th Dynasty, contains a long historical text concerning PEPI II (2246–2152 B.C.).

Atbara a Nile tributary that enters the river at the Fifth Cataract, bringing vast quantities of alluvium and red mud to the Nile Valley. The Greeks called this tributary the Astaboras.

Aten the deity also known as "Aten of the Day," the solar disk that shone on the river, considered by some to be a form of Re'-Harakhte. AKHENATEN (Amenhotep IV–1353–1335 B.C.), upon ascending the throne in Thebes, proclaimed a great religious reformation and decreed worship of Aten as the only true religion of the land. Aten was not an invention of Akhenaten, having been known in the reigns of his predecessors TUTHMOSIS IV and Amenhotep III.

He established a new capital in honor of the god, Akhetaten, the "Horizon of Aten," now known as el-'AMARNA north of Thebes. Vast temple complexes arose on the shore of the Nile, but there were no statues of the god; the deity was represented by a great red disk from which long rays, complete with hands, extended to the faithful. Akhenaten and his queen, NEFERTITI, accompanied by their daughters, conducted religious ceremonies. Until the close of the reign, Akhenaten was the only priest of the new religion.

Ceremonies to Aten consisted mainly of offerings of cakes and fruits and the recitaion of lovely hymns composed in his honor. Aten was lauded as the creator of man and the nurturing spirit of the world. A distinct strain of brotherhood and equality of all races and peoples was expressed in the hymns. Aten's worship was a modified form of monotheism, and as long as Akhenaten was alive the deity was the official god of Egypt. Stern measures were taken against the temple of AMON in particular and against the veneration of other deities as well. Even the CARTOUCHE of Akhenaten's father, AMENHOTEP III, was damaged because the name Amon was part of it. When Akhenaten died in 1335 B.C., 'Amarna fell victim to the many enemies of the new god, and Aten was banished.

Athribis an ancient town in the southern, central Delta region, at Benha, called Hut-hery-ib by the Egyptians, capital of the 10th NOME of Lower Egypt and associated with the worship of the black bull and the god HORUS KHENTIKHETY. A temple honoring the latter was erected in Athribis, and one of the priests of that shrine, AMENHOTEP, SON OF HAPU, achieved lasting fame in the nation.

Atum the oldest earth god in ancient Egypt, part of the Heliopolitan COSMOGONY. Atum was thought to have emerged from NUN, the watery chaos, or to have created himself. His name meant "Completed One," indicating that he rose alone and unaided on the site of the temple at HELIOPOLIS. In the Old Kingdom (2575–2134 B.C.), Atum had been identified with the god RE', becoming Atum-Re'. He was considered a form of the setting sun but could also appear in the guise of a MONGOOSE. In some eras Atum was depicted as a man wearing the double crown of Egypt, with the royal scepter and the ANKH. In time he was associated with PTAH and then with OSIRIS.

aut the ancient Egyptian name for funerary offerings to the deceased, when such offerings could be afforded by the family or contracted for before death.

The priesthood maintained special groups of trained officials who offered goods to the deceased as part of MORTUARY RITUALS.

auta the ancient Egyptian name for the cobra in striking position represented on the crowns of the kings. (See URAEUS and WADJET.)

Auibre a prince of the 4th Dynasty, the son of Prince Hardedef (c.2530 B.C.). The *Instructions of Hardedef* were addressed to him. (See LITERATURE.)

Avaris (Greek for the Egyptian Hut-waret) a city located in the eastern Delta, northeast of BUBASTIS, in the region of Khatana and Qantir, the site of PER-RAMESSES, the residence of the 19th Dynasty rulers. Avaris dates to ancient times and was considered a shrine city of the god Osiris; a piece of the god's body was supposed to be preserved there as a holy relic. Avaris became the capital of the HYKSOS, the Asiatics who dominated the northern territories in the Second Intermediate Period (1640–1532 B.C.).

Avaris was constructed or adapted by the Hyksos, who provided the city with walls, causeways and various devices to protect the inhabitants against sieges and missile attacks. KAMOSE of the 17th Dynasty (1555–1550 B.C.) tried to reach Avaris with his southern army in order to expel the Hyksos, but the task fell to his brother, 'AHMOSE I of the 18th Dynasty (1550–1525 B.C.). He used both land and sea forces to assault the capital. Avaris endured the siege, and the withdrawal of the Hyksos appears to have been the result of negotiations, although the Egyptian army pursued them even beyond the border. The surrender of Avaris in 1532 ended the Hyksos domination and the division of Egypt.

In the Ramessid era the site would become a spectacular metropolis again. Avaris appears to have been the home of the first Ramesses, and his successors transformed the city into a vast complex of temples, palaces, shrines and military encampments.

awet the ancient Egyptian name for the crook, the royal symbol of the kings adopted from the god OSIRIS and the ancient shepherd deity Andjeti. The crook denoted pharaoh's role as the guardian of the people of the Nile. The crook and the flail were used in all royal ceremonies and were part of the mortuary regalia of the kings.

Ax of Ahhotep a New Kingdom military emblem that was discovered in the tomb of Queen AHHOTEP, the mother of 'AHMOSE I (1550–1525 B.C.). Made of

Aya, as depicted presiding over the burial rites of Tut'ankhamun.

gold, the ax signified the emblem of honor in military events. A common form of the ax was used in all parades. (See MILITARY.)

Aya (Mereneferre') the 27th ruler of the 13th Dynasty (1704–1690 B.C.). This king is believed to have been a native of AVARIS and a vassal of the HYKSOS, the Asiatics who dominated the northern territories at the time. A diorite capstone from his pyramid was found in the eastern Delta.

Aya (Kheperkheprure') the 13th king of the 18th Dynasty (1323–1319 B.C.), he ascended the throne upon the death of TUT'ANKHAMUN and apparently married ANKHESENAMON, the boy-king's widow. She does not appear after the initial accession of Aya however. The queen who is shown with him on all surviving texts is TEY. She had served as a nurse of NEFERTITI originally, having married Aya years earlier.

Aya had been the Master of Horse for AKHENATEN at 'AMARNA, but he followed the process of reorganizing the government and the aggrandizement of the god AMON during his brief reign. He built a mortuary temple at MEDINET HABU in western Thebes but did not provide a tomb for himself there. In the VALLEY OF THE KINGS a tomb was decorated for him and for Tey, but his remains have never been found. When Aya died without an heir, HOREMHAB assumed the throne of Egypt.

ba the human-headed bird representing the soul or the vital principle of human beings. The *ba* appears at the moment of union between the *ka* and the body, leaving the mortal remains at death with the *ka*. The *ba* can survive in the afterlife only if it remains in close proximity to the *ka*, whose servant it appears to be at that time.

The translation of the actual name *ba* is uncertain. In many eras it was listed as the soul of the *ka*. For human affairs the *ba* played the role of a moral sense or a conscience. Great care was taken that the *ba* was not led astray after death by evil influences, as it appears to have had mobility, and rituals were designed to lead the *ba* safely to the *ka* and the mortal remains of the deceased after wandering. (See ETERNITY, KA and MORTUARY RITUALS.)

ba **house** a small house-type container, fashioned out of pottery in most eras and placed in the tombs of commoners who could not afford the elaborate offertory chapels of the larger PYRAMIDS or MASTABAS. The *ba* house was fashioned as part of the mortuary ritual and was designed to offer the KA a resting place

Ba, the human-headed, winged form depicted in mortuary reliefs.

and a proper receptacle for funerary offerings. Some houses contained clay images of foods and gifts to imitate the costly offerings given in the tombs and chapels of the royal family and the aristocrats. This custom was started in the Middle Kingdom, when the priests wanted to provide ordinary Egyptians with as many mortuary rituals and magical implements as possible to ensure their eternal bliss. (See ETERNITY.)

Bab el-Hosan the name given to the tomb under the pyramidal complex of MENTUHOTPE II (c. 2061–2010 B.C.) of the 11th Dynasty at DEIR EL-BAHRI.

Baboon originally called Hedjwerew, or the "Great White One," a theophany of the god Thoth. Baboon sat in the JUDGMENT HALLS OF OSIRIS, erect upon the scales used to weigh souls. The animal informed the gods when the balance was achieved upon the scale between the symbol of righteousness, and the soul. Some temples kept baboons as mascots.

Badarian See EGYPT, PREDYNASTIC.

Ba'eb Djet the ancient Egyptian name for the sacred ram of MENDES. Depicted with elaborate horns surmounted by the URAEUS, the animal was carefully sought and tested for signs of its fitness to serve as a manifestation of RE', OSIRIS and PTAH. In some eras the ram was believed to house Osiris' soul. The name Ba'eb Djet was altered to Banaded in time, which the Greeks translated as Mendes. A living ram was kept in the temple at Mendes to ward against misfortunes taking place. Thoth, the god of wisdom, is supposed to have recommended this practice in ancient times. The ram was a popular subject for statues and reliefs. In later eras the animal stood as a symbol of the great god AMON. In this form the ram had great curved horns and an elaborate crown.

Baboon, a theophany of Thoth, honored in all Egyptian rituals. Holding the Amulet of the Eye, this was a New Kingdom statue.

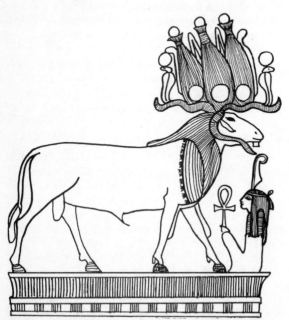

Ba'eb Djet depicted as a statue with the goddess Ma'at in attendance. The ram served the Mendes deity and was incorporated into the worship of Amon in the New Kingdom as well.

Baharia Oasis located in the Libyan Desert, southwest of HERACLEOPOLIS, it was considered one of the more important of the ancient Egyptian OASES. KAMOSE of the 17th Dynasty (c. 1553 B.C.) rested at this oasis with his troops while campaigning against the Asiatics in the northern territories. The Baharia Oasis, hidden in an expanse of sand and wilderness, served as a sanctuary for Egyptians in this era. The oasis was also the starting point for desert caravans to the Nile. The wines of the region were popular in ancient times and were considered important tribute from the area.

Bahr Libeini a waterway through Memphis dating to the Early Dynastic Period. Legend stated that AHA altered the course of the Nile in order to reclaim the region of MEMPHIS as the site of Egypt's first capital.

Bahr Yusef a natural canal connecting the Nile to the FAIYUM between Hermopolis & Meir. This stream was allowed to enter the Faiyum region but was trapped there, forming a lake and a rich agricultural area. The name, translated as "Joseph's River," is not of biblical origin but honors a local hero of Islam. The canal is supposed to have been regulated by AMENEMHET III (c. 1844–1797 B.C.) of the 12th Dynasty during the reclamation and irrigation projects conducted at that time.

Bakenkhonsu an official of the 19th Dynasty serving RAMESSES II (1290–1224 B.C.). Bakenkhonsu was appointed as the High Priest of AMON by Ramesses. He was a member of the Amenemope clan of that era. He supervised the building of one of Ramesses' temples and erected sacred barques for the gods of Thebes. Bakenkhonsu also served in the Egyptian court system. He was mentioned in the Berlin Papyrus and on some statues now in the possession of the Cairo Museum. His name is associated with Queen NEFERTARI also, as some lists place her as a member of his family.

Baketamon a princess of the 18th Dynasty, the last daughter of King Amenhotep III (c. 1391–1353 B.C.) and Queen TIY. Baketamon was a sister of AKHENATEN (Amenhotep IV) and witnessed the 'AMARNA episode, living there with her mother for a time. She bore the name Baketaten in 'AMARNA.

Barks of the Gods sacred boats, either in miniature form or full-size, used as part of ancient Egyptian religious ceremonies. These vessels were important because they accentuated the nurturing role of the

Nile in Egyptian life through the centuries. The religious significance of the barks can be traced to the belief in the sacred Nile, which carried the dead to the various levels of eternal paradise and bliss.

RE' sailed across the heavens on solar barks, using the Mandet to ascend the sky each morning and the Meseket to descend at twilight. He also employed a bark on his nightly voyage through Tuat, or the Underworld.

The Bark of OSIRIS was mentioned in the PYRAMID TEXTS. An elaborate vessel, this bark had a cabin for the shrine and was decorated with gold and other precious metals and stones. In the New Kingdom the Bark of Osiris was called the Neshmet or the Kha'emhet, and it was refurbished or replaced by each king.

AMON's Bark, called the Userhetamon, or Weseghatamon, ''Mighty of Brow Is Amon,'' was Egypt's most famous ritual boat. The vessel was replaced or redecorated almost every year and was used for special Amonite ceremonies in and around Thebes. A special lake was built for certain rites, and the temple was designed to house the bark when it was not in use.

Most barks followed a similar design. They were fashioned as floating temples, fronted by miniature obelisks, with flagstaffs and highly adorned cabins, which served as the sanctuary of the god.

Other Egyptian deities sailed in their own barks on feast days, with priests rowing the vessels on sacred lakes or on the Nile. KHONS' Bark was called ''Brilliant of Brow'' in some eras. The god MIN's boat was named ''Great of Love.'' The Hennu Bark of SOKAR was kept at MEDINET HABU and was paraded around the walls of the capital on holy days. This bark was highly ornamented and esteemed as a cultic object.

The barks could be actual sailing vessels or carried on poles in festivals. The gods normally had both kinds of barks, for different rituals.

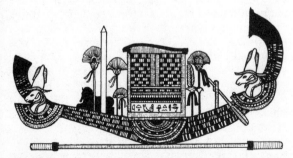

Bark of Amon, from a temple relief in Thebes. Such vessels sailed on the Nile and on temple lakes or were carried in gala processions.

Barramiyeh a site on the eastern desert near Edfu. This was a rich gold mining area for the ancient Egyptians. SETI I (c. 1306–1290 B.C.) of the 19th Dynasty recorded his efforts to dig wells for the benefit of the local miners there. Such projects were royal obligations throughout Egypt's history. A temple at WADI MIA celebrated his concerns and care. (See METALS.)

Bastet a goddess of ancient Egypt, whose theophany was the cat. Bastet's cult center was at BUBASTIS. She was the protector of pregnant women and the pleasure-loving goddess who served as the patroness of music and dance. Bastet was also believed to protect men from diseases and from demons. The goddess was considered the personification of the warming rays of the sun on the Nile. She was normally depicted as a woman with a cat's head, holding a SISTRUM and the sign of life, the ANKH.

The goddess remained popular to Roman times. Her festivals at Bubastis were some of the most well attended in Egypt. People set out on festooned barges, and music accompanied all who made the pilgrimage to her shrine. The festival was a time of pranks as well as another designated period of intoxication. A gigantic parade culminated the celebration, and on that day few Egyptians were sober. (See BUBASTIS.)

Bata in some records listed as Bet, a god of archaic eras, whose theophanies were both the ram and the bull. Bata was immortalized in the Egyptian ''TALE OF THE TWO BROTHERS.''

Batn el-Hagar called the ''Belly of Stones'' by the local inhabitants, a site near the Second Cataract. The ''Belly of Stones'' is a desolate region extending for more than 100 miles, filled with white water rapids and surrounded by harsh wastelands. Such stark landscapes were part of the natural defenses of ancient Egypt throughout its history. The kings normally fortified areas such as Batn el-Hagar, using them to deter invasions. (See DAL ISLAND, FORTRESS and NUBIA.)

Bauerdat called Bauerded in some records, an official of the 5th Dynasty serving Izezi (c. 2388–2356 B.C.) as a leader of expeditions to the regions below the cataracts of the Nile. Bauerdat and his companions journeyed as far south as Sudan in the service of the king. He is supposed to have returned to court with a DWARF, probably of the Deneg variety. Dwarfs were highly prized in the Egyptian royal households in every era. Bauerdat recorded his honors and service on a mortuary stela.

Baufre' a prince of the 4th Dynasty, the son of KHUFU (2551–2528 B.C.) who is listed in older studies on Egypt as the successor of KHEPHREN. Baufre' was the brother of HARDEDEF, a renowned sage. His role in dynastic affairs, however, remains obscure, and there is no evidence that he assumed the throne at any time. Baufre' was mentioned in the Westcar Papyrus

Bay also known as Irsu, an official of the 19th Dynasty, serving both SIPTAH and Queen-Pharaoh TWOSRE (c. 1204–1196 B.C.). Bay was supposedly of Syrian descent, a fact that irritated many Egyptian aristocrats of his era. He was a confidant of Twosre and began his usurpation of power while she was regent for the young Siptah.

When Twosre ruled in her own right, Bay served as her chancellor. He was listed in Siptah's mortuary texts. The official was not praised by his contemporaries, however, and has generally been recorded as a usurper and an interloper during the days of failing pharaonic power.

bay an instrument used by the ancient Egyptians for surveying Nile sites and for architectural planning. The *bay* gave the builders an accurate sighting of the horizon and the terrain, an important element in the construction of temples and shrines.

beards sacred symbols in the early eras of Egypt. The first conquerors, men such as NA'RMER and the SCORPION KING, were depicted as having beards. Reliefs of the Early Dynastic Period kings display beards as well. References to the kings and gods even in later periods noted that these divine beings wore "beards like lapis lazuli."

Beatty Papyrus IV, Chester a document that dates to the Ramessid period, 19th and 20th Dynasties (c. 1307–1070 B.C.). The papyrus contains medical diagnoses and prescriptions for the treatment of diseases of the anus. The breast, heart and bladder are also discussed, indicating an advanced knowledge about the human anatomy and about organ functions. Such papyri have offered modern scholars an insight into the sophisticated medical knowledge and practices of the ancient Egyptians, a science that was not attributed to them in the past. (See MEDICINE.)

Bebi an official of the 11th Dynasty, serving MENTUHOTPE II (c. 2061–2010 B.C.). Bebi was the chancellor for Mentuhotpe, but was also a nomarch, an hereditary nobleman of Dendera.

Bedwi (*or Bedway*) an ancient Egyptian term for the Bedouin or Asiatic, nomad tribes of the southern SINAI, on Egypt's eastern border. The Bedwi tried to hold their ground against the many expeditions sent by the Egyptians in the early eras of the nation. Such expeditions were designed to locate quarries, mines and other natural resources. In time full-scale mining operations were conducted in Bedwi territories, resulting in military campaigns and the eventual displacement of the tribes. (See METALS.)

beer called *heneket*, a popular drink in ancient Egypt. The brew was made from barley. Pieces of bread were soaked in water, and the beer was drained off after a proper period of fermentation. Beer was kept in vats in cellars and storehouses and was consumed by rich and poor alike. Modern excavations of Egyptian brewery sites indicate that the brew was potent. A brewery at HIERAKONPOLIS was recently discovered.

Behdet See EDFU.

Beit el-Wali a temple site south of Aswan, erected by RAMESSES II (c. 1290–1224 B.C.) of the 19th Dynasty. A detailed account of the king's military campaigns was inscribed on the walls of this temple. A narrow court, adorned with reliefs and scenes, led to the interior chambers.

Beit Khallaf a site near the old town of Thinis, where a mastaba made of brick was discovered. This mortuary structure had both ground-level and subterranean chambers. The seals of KHUFU (2551–2528 B.C.) were discovered in the lower rooms. The site also contained a mortuary structure of DJOSER (2630–2611 B.C.).

Bekhtan's Princess See BENTRESH STELA.

benben the ancient Egyptian insignia kept in the shrine of the god RE' at HELIOPOLIS and incorporating the pyramidal symbol with the rays of the sun. This sign evoked the concept of RESURRECTION. Re' was associated with the *benben* in his cultic rites, and the symbol was an influence on the builders of the massive pyramids of the Old Kingdom. As such, the PYRAMIDS, gigantic *benbens*, served as a stage for rituals and commemorative ceremonies that served the Egyptians in all eras.

Beni Hasan a site located north of HERMOPOLIS, which was a NOME stronghold in the First Intermediate Period (2134–2040 B.C.) and in the 12th Dynasty

(1991–1783 B.C.). Beni Hasan was known as Menat-Khufu in some eras. Tombs of the nomarchs of the 11th and 12th Dynasties were discovered in the upper range of the necropolis area there, all having elaborate chambers, columns and offering chapels, with elegant vestibules. Almost 900 smaller burials from the late 6th Dynasty (2323–2150 B.C.) to the First Intermediate Period are in the lower cemetery, now stripped of their decorations. HATSHEPSUT (1473–1458 B.C.) of the 18th Dynasty, started the unique rock shrine located just to the south of Beni Hasan. The Greeks named it the Speos Artimidos. The temple on the site was completed by SETI I of the 19th Dynasty (1306–1290 B.C.).

Benimeryt   an official of the 18th Dynasty, serving TUTHMOSIS III (1479–1425 B.C.). Benimeryt was the royal architect and a director of public works. He also served as an overseer of the royal treasury. Much honored for his skills, this official was given the title of Tutor of Princess MERIT-AMON, an honorary post held by officials in the capital.

Bennu   the phoenix-like bird of ancient Egyptian legends and religious mythology, sheltered in the PERSEA TREE at HELIOPOLIS. The solar and Osirian cults used the bird in rituals as a symbol of RESURRECTION. Eggs of the Bennu bird, actually created by the priests out of precious spices, were entombed at Heliopolis as part of the rites there.

Bent Pyramid   See PYRAMIDS.

Bentresh Stela   a stela dating to 300 B.C. relating a story concerning the reign of RAMESSES II (1290–1224 B.C.) at Thebes. The story details the arrival of the Princess of Bekhtan (identified as the land of the Hittites). She was given to Ramesses as a wife and her name is listed in the stela as Bentresh, although she was probably MA'AT HORNEFRURE. When Bentresh arrives in Egypt she is found to be possessed by a demon, but she is so lovely that the king makes an effort to free her of the evil spell. Finally, when all else fails, an image of the god KHONS is brought into her presence, and the demon flees. The story appears to have been a commemorative fancy concerning the marriage of Ramesses II to a Hittite princess during his reign. It was obviously fostered by the priests of Khons in an attempt to bolster the reputation of their god, by linking him to the reputation of Ramesses. (See HITTITE ALLIANCE.)

Berkat al Kurun   See QURUN.

Berenib   a queen of the 1st Dynasty, supposedly the wife of AHA (2920 B.C.) and probably the ranking Memphite royal woman of the time. Her marriage to Aha would have provided legitimacy to his claims and stabilized the reign.

Berlin Papyri   a series of documents from various eras of Egypt, now in the Egyptian Museum, West Berlin. Some date to the Middle Kingdom (2040–1640 B.C.) and others to the Ramessid period (1307–1070 B.C.) One of the papyri, discovered at Saqqara, contains 204 separate paragraphs and discusses medical conditions and treatments. The papyrus repeats much of the Ebers and Hearst texts but is supposed to have dated to the Old Kingdom's dynasties (2575–2134 B.C.). Diagnoses and treatises on rheumatism, ear problems, fertility and the conditions of the heart are treated in this document. Another papyrus contains literary and popular mythological works. Also included in the texts are the TALE OF SINUHE THE SAILOR, the story of KHUFU AND THE MAGICIANS, the ELOQUENT PEASANT, all valued for their insight into Egyptian LITERATURE.

Bersha   a site north of 'Amarna, where Amenhotep III (1391–1353 B.C.) reopened a quarry. Bersha was

Bennu bird, from a temple relief.

located near the famous Turra quarry, valued for its high-quality limestone. Tombs of local nomarchs were discovered at Bersha, rock-cut in the cliffs of a valley. Some of the tombs date to the 12th Dynasty (1991–1783 B.C.) or earlier. The most noted of the tombs was constructed for DJEHUTIHOTPE, called the "Great Overlord of the Hare Nome." The chapel was designed as a portico with two columns and a niched inner chamber. The west wall of the interior room contained the famous scene depicting the transporting of a colossal statue from the HATNUB quarries. (See QUARRIES.)

Bes   an ancient Egyptian god who was the patron of women in childbirth. He probably appeared in Babylonia first. Bes was also the patron of war and the protector of hunters. His cultic home was supposedly PUNT. The god was depicted in reliefs and statues as a dwarf, with a leonine head and a protruding tongue. His legs were bowed, and his ears were large. He was clad in animals skins, bore a tail and wore a feathered diadem. Appealing mostly to commoners, the god was popular in the later eras of Egypt. In the Ptolemaic period his portrait adorned the walls of the "birthing palaces" erected at the time. His consort was Beset.

Biahmu   a site northeast of HAWARA in the FAIYUM region of ancient Egypt. The remains of two colossal statues of AMENEMHET III of the 12th Dynasty (c. 1844–1797 B.C.) were discovered there. The statues are the remains of a temple complex believed to have been erected at Hawara or Biahmu.

Biban el Harim   also called Biban el Sultanat in some records, the modern name for the VALLEY OF THE QUEENS on the western shore of Thebes.

Biban el Moluk   called Biban el Muluk in some records, the modern name for the VALLEY OF THE KINGS on the western shore of Thebes.

Bint-Anath   probably the Batau'anth of early records, a queen of the 19th Dynasty, the daughter of King RAMESSES II (c. 1290–1224 B.C.) and Queen IST-NOFRET. Bint Anath became Ramesses' Consort when Queens NEFERTARI and Istnofret died or retired.

bird symbols   the representations of divine aspects used by the ancient Egyptians in religious reliefs and in ceremonies. Bird theophanies were honored throughout Egypt's history. In some eras the birds were mummified and revered. The ability of birds to fly gave them special significance for the

Horus falcon, from statues and reliefs. Bird symbols figured in all religious texts and frequently appeared on temple walls.

Egyptians, because in that activity they reflected the spiritual aspirations of the people and engendered many funerary beliefs. The BA, the soul, was always depicted as a winged being.

The hawk was the insignia of HORUS and RE', the falcon identified RE'-HARAKHTE, Horus, MONT and KHONS. The ibis represented the god THOTH, and the goose symbolized GEB, known as the Great Cackler. The swallow honored ISIS and the owl was a hieroglyphic character. The sparrow was an omen of bad tidings in some periods of Egyptian history, and the sight of a dead bird, called a *zent*, was considered particularly ominous by various groups. (See *Birds* under GODS AND GODDESSES.)

Bitter Lakes   a region stretching from the Nile to the WADI TUMILAT in the Egyptian Delta. The lakes became popular in early eras, when a route was developed as a canal of passage to the Red Sea.

Biya   Egyptian word for the ancient Bee King of the Delta region and Lower Egypt. The Bee King was called the "Honey Man" in some eras.

board games   a recreation popular in all historical periods of ancient Egypt. The people delighted in all forms of amusements, and a variety of table games was played in palaces and in humbler abodes. Mortuary reliefs in the tombs of royalty and nobles depict personages engaged in such games.

Faience and ivory inlaid boxes of the game of *senet* were discovered in tombs. These boxes were designed with 30 squares and had spaces for position games, much like modern parchisi. *Senet*, and the game called Tjau were possibly of Asiatic origin. Robbers, another game, was played with two sets of five or more pieces. The moves were determined by the toss of knucklebones or by wooden or ivory wands. The game boxes had drawers held in place by ivory bolts and contained ivory pieces, which were shaped like cones or spools. Another popular game, Serpent, was played on a circular board with small balls inscribed with the names of early Egyptian kings. Jackals and Hounds, one of the most popular of the board amusements, used wands to determine moves.

Book of the Dead   a loose collection of magical spells and incantations that were normally written on papyrus, sometimes illustrated, and popular in Egypt from the New Kingdom (1550–1070 B.C.). The purpose of the Book of the Dead, which later called the *Reu nu pert em hru* (Chapters of the Coming Forth By Day), *Am Duat* or *Am Tuat*, was to instruct the deceased on how to overcome the dangers of the afterlife, by enabling them to assume the form of several mythical creatures, and to give them the passwords necessary for admittance to certain stages of Tuat or the Underworld. The spells also allowed the deceased to proclaim themselves as bearing the identity of many gods. It is estimated that there were

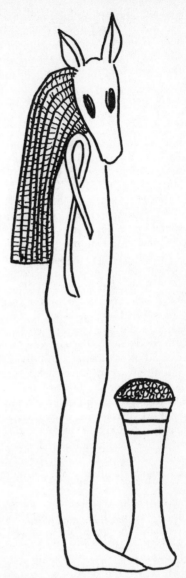

ASS OF THE TUAT   a mythical creature shown in depictions of the Book of the Dead.

approximately 190 independent "chapters" or sections of the Book of the Dead, although there is no single extant papyrus containing all of them.

The spells and passwords were placed in the tombs of the ancient Egyptians from about 1600 B.C. onward, although there are indications that they were included in the sections called "chapters" as early as the 12th Dynasty (1800 B.C.). These spells and passwords were not part of a ritual but were fashioned for the deceased, to be recited in the afterlife. Egyptians believed in the efficacy of magic and in the cultic powers of the gods. At the same time, they

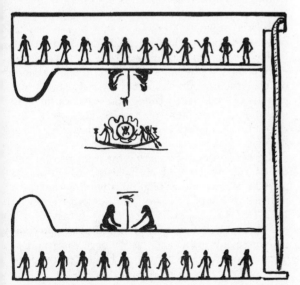

BOOK OF THE DEAD   an illustration of the First Hour of the Night in the Book of the Gates or Pylons, depicting the soul's journey through Tuat or the Underworld.

had considerable faith in life after death, a belief that included specific paradises and activities. The abundance of their material world was something cherished by the Egyptians, who translated paradise in similar terms, with the same fertile fields, light and sacred waters.

In the early periods the funerary texts were inscribed on walls, or in coffins, normally in the tombs reserved for the reigning families and other aristocrats. In time, however, these texts became more and more available to the commoners. The Book of the Dead became normal items of manufacturing, and the individual could decide the number of chapters to be included, the types of illustrations and the quality of the papyrus used. The individual was limited only by his or her financial resources.

During the New Kingdom, the papyri were lengthy, involved collections of spells and passwords, some magnificently illustrated in color. The good versions of the Theban Recension Book of the Dead, a form adopted at the time, averaged between 15 and 90 feet in length and about 13 inches in width. Some papyri were made to order for special clients, but great stocks of the Book of the Dead were available for those who could afford them, and individual names were put into them when purchased.

The extant papyri of the Book of the Dead were written in hieroglyphic script, called the *hieratic*. They contain vignettes, protests of innocence, and spells and magic words to provide comfort and security in Tuat. Three of the most famous versions of the Book of the Dead, discovered in the tombs of Egyptians, called Ani, Anhai and Hunefer, are now in the British Museum.

Other religious documents provided for the deceased during various historical periods have also been discovered. The Book of the Gates contains formulas for making the sun rise and traces the road of the gods and the deceased, showing various openings through which the boat of RE' would have to pass in order to be released from perils. The JUDGMENT HALLS OF OSIRIS and the various paradises awaiting the deceased are explained. The text also includes designs for solar barks, with arrows and magical disks. Such boats were fashioned by the faithful and then burned in cultic rituals to rejuvenate the sun in a mystical fashion each day, as part of OVERTHROWING APOPHIS.

The Book of the Opening of the Mouth, once part of the Litany of Offerings, a text developed in the 18th Dynasty with new ceremonies attached to the traditional ones, remained popular. Priests used the Ur-Heka instrument according to the rituals of this book, and magically opened the mouth of the corpse, while libations were poured out in honor of the gods. The purpose of the book and its rituals was to provide the deceased with a new body in the other world and to make him or her part of the divine cosmos there. The rites were also designed to establish contact between the living and the dead, an important aspect of Egyptian beliefs. In later eras the corpse was no longer used for the rituals. A statue was designed to take the place of the deceased during the ceremonies.

The Book of the Pylons, called the Shat en Sebau, was another version of the Book of the Dead. This work was written to provide the dead with detailed descriptions of the Underworld.

Another funerary text, called alternately the Deliverance of Mankind or the Destruction of Mankind, was discovered in the tomb of SETI I (c. 1306–1290 B.C.) of the 19th Dynasty. The document makes reference to a flood and concerns a popular myth about the nature of man.

The various religious or funerary texts called the Book of the Dead evolved over the centuries as MORTUARY RITUALS became more sophisticated and broad in their appeal. New versions appear in the New Kingdom, and another one after the fall of the pharaonic dynasties. These were recensions, formulated in Heliopolis, Thebes and Sais.

Book of Overthrowing Apophis See OVERTHROWING APOPHIS.

Books of Thoth See THOTH'S BOOK.

Bubastis a site north of Cairo that was the capital of the 18th nome of the Lower Kingdom and the cult center for the goddess Bastet. A vast temple was erected there in the Ramessid era, and some statues of this structure survive. A 6th Dynasty shrine was also discovered, with architectural seals belonging to KHUFU and KHEPHREN, of the 4th Dynasty (2575–2551). A seal of Pepi I of the 6th Dynasty (c. 2289–2255 B.C.) was also found on the site.

A great catacomb containing the remains of mummified cats was found at Bubastis, which was a popular destination for pilgrims attending the lavish festivals in honor of Bastet, and AMENHOTEP III (c. 1391–1353 B.C.) spent an anniversary of his coronation there. He left an inscription at Bubastis to commemorate the event and his military campaign in Nubia. Bubastis is recorded as having suffered an earthquake c. 2770. (See FESTIVALS and SED.)

Buchis the ancient Egyptian sacred bull residing at Erment (Hermonthis). Buchis was considered a theophany or earthly form of the god MONT in early times and then was designated as a manifestation of the Theban god AMON. Any bull selected for the temple ceremonies had to have a white body and a black head from birth. In some records the sacred bull was called Bukhe. A cemetery provided for the mummified remains of these animals was called the Bucheum and contained coffins with lids weighing up to 15 tons for the corpses. Other tombs were carved out of the walls to receive the animals' bodies. (See A'A-NEFER, APIS, MNEVIS.)

Buhen   a site between the Second and First Cataract of the Nile near the WADI HALFA settled as an outpost as early as the 2nd Dynasty. This area was marked by fortifications and served as the boundary of Egypt and NUBIA in certain eras. The New Kingdom pharaohs built extensively at Buhen. A Middle Kingdom fortress was also discovered on the site, with outer walls for defense, bastions and two interior temples, following the normal pattern of such military structures in Egypt. HATSHEPSUT, the Queen-Pharaoh of the 18th Dynasty (c. 1473–1458 B.C.), constructed a temple in the southern part of Buhen, with a five-chambered sanctuary, surrounded by a colonnade. TUTHMOSIS III (c. 1479–1425 B.C.) her successor, renovated the temple, enclosing the complex and adding porticos.

The actual fortress of Buhen was an elaborate structure, built partly out of rock with brick additions. The fort was set back from the river, giving way to a rocky slope. Thick walls supported external buttresses, which were designed to turn south and then east to the Nile. A ditch was added for defense, carved out of rock and with deep sides that sloped considerably and were smoothed to deter scaling attempts. A gateway in the south wall opened onto the interior military compound, which also contained the original temples. AMENHOTEP II is credited with one shrine erected there during his reign (c. 1427–1401 B.C.). (See FORTRESSES and MILITARY.)

Building Text   a document provided for every temple in ancient Egypt. These texts were engraved in a prominent place and provided the name of the temple, the nature of its cultic rituals and the special significances of its sanctuaries. Building Texts linked the temple to the original time of creation, following the established traditions of the Primeval Mounds. The temple thus became more than a material demonstration of spiritual truths. Because of the documentation added, the shrine was part of the original "APPEARANCE" of the god in Egypt. (See "FIRST OCCASION," PAY LANDS and TEMPLES.)

Bulls   See A'A-NEFER, APIS, BUCHIS, MNEIVIS.

Burullus   one of the four great salt lakes in the Delta of Egypt. (See LAKES.)

Busiris   a central Delta town originally called Djedu, the Per-Usire, House of OSIRIS. Busiris was dedicated originally to the local vegetation god, Andjeti. The Osirian cult, however, became popular, and Osiris assumed the titles and ceremonies of Andjeti. The god SOBEK was also honored in the town. Busiris was originally inhabited by predynastic shepherd tribes. The town never became politically powerful but remained an important shrine center for Osiris.

Buto (the goddess)   See WADJET.

Buto   a site south of Tanis in the Delta, the capital of the Lower Kingdom in predynastic times, called Pe, or Per-Wadjet, the House of Wadjet. Predynastic tombs and a temple dating to the 1st Dynasty (2920–2770 B.C.) were discovered in Buto, which remained popular as the seat of power for the legendary kings of Egypt's prehistoric periods. In all major festivals these kings were portrayed as the SOULS OF PE in Lower Egypt, as the SOULS OF NEKHEN (HIERAKONPOLIS) of Upper Egypt. These legendary kings greeted each new claimant to the throne during the CORONATION RITUALS and were called upon to serve as the guardians of the land in each generation.

byssus   the name given to the fine linen products developed in certain regions in Egypt. (See AGRICULTURE and AKHMIN.)

C

Cairo Calendar   a text discovered in a papyrus that dates to the reign of RAMESSES II (1290–1224 B.C.) of the 19th Dynasty. This was a calendar of lucky and unlucky days of the year. The good or bad fortune of a single day was determined by past events connected to that particular date, concerning the gods, omens, battles or prophecies recorded for that specific time period.

The start of a journey, the planning of a marriage or business transaction, and especially days of birth were studied in relationship to the calendar and its lucky or unlucky connotations. People born on unlucky days were doomed to a bad end according to Egyptian traditions. In the case of royal princes, children on whom the fate of Egypt depended, birth dates were critical. If such a royal heir was born on a bad day, the Seven Hathors arrived on the scene and changed the child, substituting one born on a propitious day. In that way calamities were avoided, not only for the royal family but for the nation. In time the Seven Hathors were thought to provide that service for all children, even commoners. The calendar was used by the literate or upper class Egyptians in much the same way as horoscopes are used in modern times.

calcite   the opaque white stone commonly called alabaster, used throughout Egyptian history. It was quarried at a remote site called HATNUB, east of 'Amarna and had solar connections in a mythical sense. Calcite vessels and larger sarcophagi were made out of calcite, but it was never used as a common building material. (See QUARRIES.)

calendar   a system of annual designation in use in Egypt as far back as predynastic times. Lunar in origin, the calendar was designed to meet the agricultural demands of the nation and evolved over the centuries.

The calendar that developed in the early dynastic period had 12 months of 30 days. The inaccuracy of such a calendar was self-evident almost immediately. The lunar calculations made by the priests and the actual rotation of the earth around the sun did not coincide, and very rapidly the Egyptians found themselves celebrating festivals out of season. The calendar was then revised by adding five days at the end of each year, called EPAGOMENAL DAYS, which provided some stability to the calendar calculations.

The calendar contained three SEASONS of four months each. *Akhet* was the season of the inundation, the first third of the year, starting at the end of modern August and followed by *peret* and *shemu*. *Peret* was the time in which the land emerged from the floodwaters, and *shemu* was the time of harvest.

As the calendar veered away from the true year, the Egyptians invented a corrected calendar and used it side by side with the one dating to predynastic times. They would not just set aside something so venerable, preferring to adjust their enterprises to the new calendar while maintaining the old.

The rising of a star called Sopdu or Sopdet by the Egyptians, and known in modern times as Sirius the Dog Star, started each new year on the revised calendar. The arrival of Sopdet at a given time was due to the fact the star appears just above the horizon at dawn about the same time of year that *akhet* began.

Canal of Sehel   a passage that dates to the 6th Dynasty (c. 2300 B.C.), dug alongside the First Cataract of the Nile at the island of Sehel in order to allow the Egyptians easy access to the territories below. In the 12th Dynasty, SENWOSRET II (1897–1878 B.C.) cleared the canal and mounted an inscription on the rocks of the island to commemorate the event. He claimed that he was in the process of making a new entranceway into Nubia and returned several years later to repair it. (See SEHEL ISLAND.)

Canon of the Human Figure See ART AND AR-
CHITECTURE.

canopic jars containers used in the funerary rituals to preserve the viscera of the deceased after
embalming. The jugs varied in style over the centuries but were used throughout Egypt's history, considered a vital part of the elaborate mortuary ritual.
The name given to the vessels is Greek, not Egyptian,
because the shape resembled the tributes made to
the Greek hero Canopus in their era. The vessels
were normally made of wood, pottery, faience, cartonnage or stone.

In the Middle Kingdom, the canopic jars were
squat in design, with plain stoppers and seals. In the
New Kingdom the stoppers had been designed to
represent the particular patron of the dead involved
in the protection of a specific human organ. The jar
containing the liver was under the protection of the

Canopic jar with head of the god Duamutef, from the New
Kingdom era.

god Imsety, and the stopper was carved into the
shape of a human head with a beard.

The jar protecting the lungs used Hapi as a patron,
and the stopper on those vessels was shaped to
resemble the head of a baboon. The canopic jar
containing the stomach was protected by Duamutef,
and his form was the jackal. The intestines, protected
by Qebehsennuf, had a stopper in the form of a
hawk's head. The canopic jars were enclosed within
elaborately designed cabinets and kept separate from
the mummified corpse. Various protector deities were
used to guard the cabinet. (See MORTUARY RITUALS.)

carnelian a semiprecious stone found in Nubia
and highly prized by the artisans of every era in
Egypt. Carnelian was used in AMULETS, jewelry, and
in insignias.

cartonnage a combination of plaster, linen, papyrus and other pliable materials used for the manu-
facture of sarcophagi and mummy masks. Linen sheets
were glued together with gums or resins and covered
with plaster in order to shape the masks to the
contours of the heads and shoulders of the mummies. The masks were then gilded and painted to
attempt an idealized portrait of the deceased. By the
end of the Middle Kingdom (c. 1640 B.C.), however,
the cartonnage was extended to cover the entire
mummified form. (See COFFINS and MORTUARY RIT-
UALS.)

cartouche the modern term designating the original Egyptian symbol called the SHENU "that which
encircles." A cartouche is an ellipse found in reliefs,
paintings, sculpture and papyri encircling certain royal
names of Egyptian kings since the 4th Dynasty. (See
ROYAL NAMES.)

cat an animal associated in ancient Egypt with the
goddess BASTET and considered a manifestation of
the god RE' as well. In funerary legends the cat took
up residence in the PERSEA TREE at HELIOPOLIS. The
word for cat in Egyptian is *miu*, the feminine being
mut (translated by some as "kitty"). There is some
evidence of the domestication of cats in predynastic
times, and cats were used in hunting birds, much as
dogs are used today. Cats were not represented in
tomb paintings until the Middle Kingdom (c. 2040
B.C.) and were very popular in New Kingdom (1550
B.C.) tombs. They were depicted under the chair or
on the lap of the deceased. Cats were also featured
in dream books, and the SATIRICAL PAPYRUS uses
them for ironic effects. Cats were also used as part

of medicinal practices. Mortuary texts warn against cat-shaped demons in Tuat or the Underworld.

cataracts the white water regions or rapids of the Nile River. Six in number, these dangerous regions of the Nile extended from Aswan to just above Khartoum. The First Cataract, at Aswan, served as the natural barrier along the southern border of Egypt. The kings of the various dynasties began exploring the territories to the south and the region between the First and Second Cataract was always important as a trading area. The settlement at Buhen in the 4th and 5th Dynasties indicates that the Egyptians had started a process of incorporation. The unsettled period following the 6th Dynasty (c. 2150 B.C.) caused the Egyptians to withdraw from the region to some extent, but in the 11th Dynasty (c. 2040 B.C.) control was established once again. The 18th Dynasty kings and their successors of the New Kingdom (1550–1070 B.C.) pushed as far south as Kurga. During the periods in which the territories below the First Cataract were held by the Egyptians, the administration of the region was conducted at the ELEPHANTINE at Aswan by a special viceroy. (See NUBIA and CANAL OF SEHEL; see also FORTRESS.)

Cartonnage coffin normally gilded and painted to provide an idealized portrait of the corpse, from the New Kingdom.

Cat statue, one of the strikingly unique forms of Egyptian art, from New Kingdom.

cenotaphs the mortuary complexes or simple tombs built to provide a probable religiously motivated burial site that remained empty. The cenotaphs contained no bodies but were ceremonial in nature. Much debate is now in progress concerning the cenotaph sites and purposes.

chariots used in military and processional events in ancient Egypt, the chariot was not an Egyptian invention but was introduced into the Nile Valley by the Asiatics during the Second Intermediate Period (1640–1532 B.C.).

Egyptian innovations made the Asiatic model lighter, faster and easier to maneuver. Egyptian chariots were fashioned out of wood, with the frames built well forward of the axle for increased stability. The sides of the chariots were normally made of stretched canvas, reinforced by stucco. The floors were made of leather thongs, interlaced to provide an elastic but firm foundation for the riders.

A single pole, positioned at the center and shaped while still damp, ran from the axle to a yoke that was attached to the saddles of the horses. A girth strap and a breast harness kept the pole secure while the vehicle was in motion.

Originally, the two wheels of the chariot had four spokes; later, six were introduced. These were made of separate pieces of wood glued together and then bound with leather straps.

Kamose (c. 1550 B.C.) was the first Egyptian ruler to use the chariot and cavalry units successfully. The HYKSOS, dominating the northern territories at the time, were startled when the first units of cavalry appeared against them on the field at NEFRUSY, led by Kamose. The horses of the period, also introduced into Egypt by the Asiatics, were probably not sturdy enough to support the weight of a man over long distances, a situation remedied by the Egyptians within a short time. The horses did pull chariots, however, and they were well trained by the Egyptian units.

Chemmis the sacred floating island in the western Delta near Buto that figures in the lovely legend concerning the goddess ISIS and her infant son, HORUS. Isis, impregnated by the corpse of the god OSIRIS, whom she buried, retired to the sacred isle to give birth to the child who would avenge Osiris' assassination. SETH, the murderous brother of Osiris, also a god, sought Isis and Horus, but at Chemmis mother and child remained in hiding. The goddess WADJET was in attendance, arranging reeds and foliage to keep Isis and Horus out of sight. This legend, recounted each year in Egypt, was one of the loveliest examples of the great maternal and wifely instincts of Isis, who embodies the ever-faithful wife and the mother ready to sacrifice herself for her offspring. Isis was beloved in Egypt because of this and other tales of her suffering and endurance.

Cheops See KHUFU

Cippus of Horus a form of STELA popular in the late and Ptolemaic periods, featuring Harpokrates (Horus as a child) standing on a crocodile and holding scorpions and other dangerous creatures. Magical texts accompanying the image provided protection against the beings displayed. Water was poured over the Cippus, and by drinking the water a person was thought to be rendered invulnerable.

circumcision the surgical removal of all or part of the male prepuce, practiced by the Egyptians as part of their traditional methods of hygiene. Male circumcision was not performed at birth but during adolescence.

clock a primitive instrument in the form of an alabaster vase filled with water for measuring time that was owned by Amenhotep III (1391–1353 B.C.) of the 18th Dynasty. The vase kept time by emptying itself, drop by drop.

coffins wooden boxes that appeared in the Old Kingdom (2575–2134 B.C.), designed to protect the remains of the deceased. Such boxes were placed inside of MASTABAS, which were large enough to provide chapels and chambers for offerings. The coffins were carved or painted on their sides to make

Chariot design with pharaoh in a military pose, from New Kingdom temple reliefs.

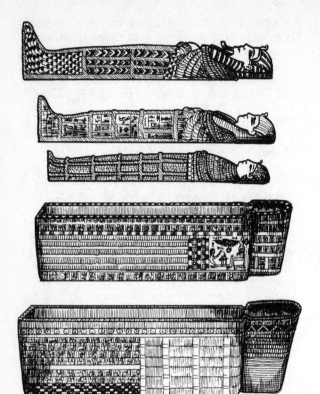

Coffins (anthropoid)—nested variety with a human mummified body encased in gilded boxes that fit one into the other.

them resemble the walls of the royal palaces. Doors, windows and even the patterns of hanging reed mats were fashioned to resemble coffins.

Maps of Tuat or the Underworld were often painted inside the coffin for the benefit of the deceased, and other maps, mortuary texts and symbols were placed on the outside, with magic spells included for protection.

Cartonnage masks were developed in the First Intermediate Period (2134–2040 B.C.) but were extended in later dynasties to cover the entire mummified remains. Both the inner and outer coffins were fashioned in cartonnage, with idealized masks of the deceased along with the usual mortuary incantations. These anthropoidal coffins were elaborately painted, dressed in the robes of HORUS or in the feathers of the goddess NEKHEBET. The *rishi* or feather design was popular in the 17th and early 18th Dynasties (1640–1400 B.C.). (See MORTUARY RITUALS.)

Coffin Texts inscriptions inside coffins of spells and incantations intended to help the deceased on their journey to the hereafter. Developed in HERAKLEOPOLIS in the First Intermediate Period (2134–2040 B.C.), they evolved from the 12th Dynasty (1991–1783

B.C.). The Coffin Texts were developments of the PYRAMID TEXTS, which had been placed only in royal tombs in the 5th and 6th Dynasties (2465–2150 B.C.). The Coffin Texts were used by all Egyptians.

colors often symbolic in nature, the various hues used in ancient Egypt were derived from mineral and vegetable sources. Colors lent a realistic, natural value in reliefs and other forms of art. Artisans began to observe the natural occurrence of colors in their surroundings and pulverized various oxides and other materials to develop the hues they desired. Some colors, their symbolism and sources are listed on page 55.

Colossi of Memnon statues that are still standing on the western shore of the Nile at Thebes. They were once part of the mortuary complex of AMENHOTEP III (1391–1353 B.C.) of the 18th Dynasty. The statues stand 65 feet high, including their bases, and depict the ruler in a seated position, allowing his figure to dominate the landscape. The Greeks, coming upon them in later eras, decided that the statues honored their hero, Memnon, who fought at Troy, and named them accordingly. In the past the northernmost statue was said to have made musical sounds at dawn, amazing visitors and bringing it world fame.

columns See ART AND ARCHITECTURE.

Coptos a site located south of Dendera, the capital of the fourth NOME of Upper Egypt and the cult center of the god MIN. Throughout its history, Coptos was linked to the important caravan route through the WADI HAMMAMAT to the Red Sea port of KUSER. Soldiers kept watch over this passage through the wastelands, aiding travelers and guarding against attacks by roving bands of nomads. Temples discovered in Coptos date to the 6th Dynasty (2323–2150 B.C.); one was erected in honor of Min by TUTHMOSIS III (1479–1425 B.C.).

Coptos Decrees, edicts dating from the 8th Dynasty (c. 2150 B.C.), exempted the estates of the god Min from all taxation and from civil duties, such as military or labor requirements. Another decree dates from the reign of INYOTEF V (c. 1640 B.C.) concerning a nobleman named Teti accused of taking sacred temple objects. Teti lost his hereditary titles, his estates and privileges, a punishment extended to his heirs.

Corners of the Earth the four cardinal points recognized by the ancient Egyptians and honored in the construction of PYRAMIDS and other monuments.

COLORS

COLOR	SYMBOLISM	SOURCE
White (hedj)	Used to represent limestone, sandstone, silver, milk, fat, honey, vegetables, teeth, bones, moonlight, some crowns. Symbolized baboon (associated with Thoth), the crown of Upper Egypt, joy, luxury and white bread (in offerings to the dead).	Made from powdered limestone.
Black (kem)	Used to represent ebony, emmer wheat, cattle, hair, eyes, Nubians. In tombs used to represent mascara. Symbolized the underworld, the dead, Osiris, fertility (from the Nile mud), the heart, Anubis and the ibis.	Made from carbonized materials, such as lampblack, burnt wood, and at times from manganese oxide found in the Sinai.
Red (desher) Blood-red (yenes) Blue-red (tjemes)	Used to represent male skin color, natron, fruits, myrrh, woods, animals, blood, fire, the red crown of Lower Egypt, hair, baboons, foreigners, some clothing and sometimes the dead. Anything bad in the calendars or bad days were written in red at times. Symbolized anger, rage, disorder or brutality, or, on the contrary, positive aspects.	Made from anhydritic iron oxide
Blue (khesbedj)	Skin color of the solar gods, wigs and beards of the gods. Popular in faience.	Made from powdered azurite, lapis or copper carbonate.
Green (wadj)	Associated with Wadjet, the cobra goddess. Name (wadj) means healthy, flourishing, etc. Green represented the fertile fields, the resurrected Osiris. Heart scarabs were made out of green nephrite. Green was popular color for amulets. Faience could be either blue or green and was favored in amulets. The "Eye" amulet was called the wadjet, "that which is healthy."	Made from malachite.
Yellow (ketj)	Represented vegetal matter, some foods and the skin color of females. Gold represented sunlight, the disc, the rays of the sun and metal.	Made from hydrated iron oxide.

The gods of the Four Corners were SOPDU, HORUS, SETH and THOTH.

coronation rituals an ancient Egyptian ceremony that evolved from the Archaic Period and was used upon the accession of a new king to the throne.

The king was shown to the people in opening rites as the heir to Upper and Lower Egypt. In some dynasties this ceremony took place while the old king was still on the throne, elevating his successor to the position of co-ruler to ensure orderly succession. Another aspect of succession not involved in the actual ceremonies of coronation but vital to the elevation of a new king was the mortuary rite. Each new king had to be present at the burial of his predecessor.

Wearing the white crown of Upper Egypt, the heir to the throne was led out to the people. He then put on the red wicker basket crown of Lower Egypt. When the crowns were united upon his head a great celebration took place.

At this point the king entered the hall of the nome gods of Upper Egypt, wearing only the white crown. When these divinities welcomed him he repeated the same ceremony in the hall of the nome gods of Lower Egypt, wearing the red crown. A stake was then put into the ground, entwined with the LOTUS and PAPYRUS symbols of both kingdoms. The monogram or CARTOUCHE of the new ruler was worked in gold and precious stones alongside the stake.

The crook and the flail, the symbols of Egyptian royalty traditionally handed down from the agricultural beginnings of the nation, were placed in the hands of the new king, who was then led in procession around the walls of the capital.

A ceremony called the "placing of the diadem in the hall" started in the Early Dynastic Period eras. By the time the New Kingdom pharaohs were elevated to the throne, the rituals had become more sophisticated and elaborate. The inscriptions detailing the coronation of Queen-Pharaoh Hatshepsut (1473–1458 B.C.) describe purifying rites and a journey from Thebes to Heliopolis, where the god Atum offered her the crown. AMENHOTEP III (c. 1391–1353

B.C.) made the same trip down the Nile on the occasion of his accession.

A proclamation of kingship was then announced at Thebes, supposedly from the god Amon, and the new king was led before the courtiers and the people. Purified once again and robed, the heir received the crown and was honored by statues of the gods, serving as attendants. The concluding ceremonies and festivals lasted for several days and were occasions of immense joy for the nation. It was also believed that the gods and goddesses took part in the celebration as the king's name was inscribed mystically on the sacred PERSEA TREE upon his coronation.

corvée the king, as the living god of the land, had the right to ask his people to assume staggering burdens of labor. This prerogative of the Egyptian kings has been viewed both as a form of slavery and as a unique method of civic responsibility. The corvée was not slavery, although that particular institution was introduced into Egypt in the Middle Kingdom. The massive construction evident along the Nile was possible only because of the seasonal enlistment of the Egyptian people. Vast armies of workers left their fields and orchards and took up their construction tasks with enthusiasm because of the spiritual rewards of their labors. Each man called to the scene of royal projects worked his alloted hours, went home filled with beer and bread. Work was seasonal and carried out in shifts, depending on the Nile's inundations and the readiness of the land for sowing or harvesting. Elaborate camps were erected on the site of building projects, and entertainment and medical care were provided for the workers during rest periods.

The corvée was possible only in times of dynastic strength and stable government. When a dynasty failed, as in the First and Second Intermediate Periods, enforced labor was not only impractical but impossible.

cosmetics the women of Egypt followed certain styles and trends in their toilette. From earliest times Egyptian women employed materials to brighten or color their faces. They were particularly concerned with mascara, which was used to recreate the sacred Eye of Re' symbol on their own eyes—at once a religious and a fashion statement.

This mascara was made of malachite, or copper ore, in the Early Dynastic Period (2920–2575 B.C.) and probably was used for the same purpose in the predynastic age. During the Old and Middle Kingdoms (2575–2134 B.C. and 2040–1640 B.C.) galena was used as mascara, and then a form of kohl (like the modern cosmetic) was popular. Mascara was either imported or obtained from a source near COPTOS.

Various red pigments were used to adorn the face, mostly ochres and natural dyes. Scents from cedar and sandal wood, barks, flowers and plants were fashionable, and perfumes were composed of sanfed fats and alcohol, or oils.

Most royal or noble women took care not to allow

COSMETIC SPOON receptacle for unquents, from the 12th Dynasty.

the sun to darken their complexions, and in funerary paintings they were depicted as fair-skinned. The cosmetics of the women were kept in beautifully carved boxes, or in chests made out of ivory or other precious materials. Spoons, palettes for grinding powders, brushes for mascara, and small tubes for ointments to adorn the lips have been found, as well as combs, mirrors and various trinkets for wigs and hair.

cosmogony the so-called creation myths of ancient Egypt, legends that assumed political and religious significance in each new era of the nation. The number and variety of these myths provide insight into the development of Egyptian spiritual values and clearly delineate the evolution of certain divine cults.

To begin with, the ancient people of the Nile did not concern themselves with doctrinal or theological purity and precision. They did not adhere to logical progression in matters of religious significance. Spiritual consciousness and a harmonious unity, both in the individual and in the nation, were the elements that kept Egyptians secure and stable.

Their religious aspirations were cultic in nature, dependent upon ritual and celebration, upon manifestations of ideals and values. Dogmas or doctrines did not concern them specifically. In fact, the Egyptians were uncomfortable with spiritual concepts that demanded logical and reasonable development. It was enough for them to see the god, to hear his or her concerns for the land, and to mirror the cosmic harmony that their astronomical abilities had gleaned for them in the sky.

There were basic systems of creation in all eras of Egypt's development. They were found at HELIOPOLIS, HERMOPOLIS, MEMPHIS and THEBES. Other local temples provided their own cosmogonic information, but the four major ones provided the framework for spiritual evolution in Egypt.

The cosmogonic tenets of the city of Heliopolis are available in the PYRAMID TEXTS of the Old Kingdom but are scant and appear to make references to what was considered common knowledge of the time. In this creation story the god ATUM emerges from the watery chaos called NUN. Atum made his first appearance on the hill that became the great temple at Heliopolis.

In time the god Atum was identified with RE', becoming Re'-Atum, symbolized by the phoenix on the BENBEN or by a SCARAB. Re'-Atum began making the other divine beings of Egypt through masturbation. SHU, his son, was then spit out of his mouth, and Re'-Atum vomited out TEFNUT.

Shu was the god of the air, and Tefnut was his consort and was also considered to represent order in the material world. Both of these gods were associated with the legends concerning the Eye of Re'-Atum. This Eye was responsible for the birth of human beings and was also the symbol of the sun.

Shu and Tefnut gave birth to GEB, the earth, and to NUT, the sky. They, in turn, gave birth to ISIS and OSIRIS, NEPHTHYS and SETH. All of these divine beings, with Re'-Atum, formed the ENNEAD (the nine) of Heliopolis. In some eras the ennead also included HORUS.

In the city of Hermopolis the cosmogonic decrees held that the original gods were formed as an OGDOAD (octet). These were Nun and his consort Naunet (the male being depicted as a frog-headed man and the woman as having a serpent's head), Huh (called Heh in later eras) and Hauhet, Kuk and Kauket, and AMON and his consort Amaunet.

This ogdoad was responsible for the Golden Age before man in the Nile Valley. Nun was water, Huh represented eternity, Kuk darkness and Amon air. Amon became popular because of his role in stirring up the waters and the darkness to cause life. The original site of the appearance of the gods took on great significance in temple lore, called Primeval Mounds or the Pay Lands.

The Hermopolitan cosmogony included the appearance of a cosmic egg laid by a celestial goose or an ibis. A popular legend from this time was that of the LOTUS, which brought the god Re' to the world. The ogdoad of Hermopolis concerned themselves with the rising of the sun and the inundation of the Nile, both vital to Egyptian prosperity.

The Memphite creation story was very old and complex. PTAH was the creator of the entire world according to the Memphite priests. The ennead of Heliopolis and other divinities were only manifestations of Ptah's creative powers. Ptah was the Heart and the Tongue, the seat of the intellect and the weapon of creative power. As Atum spat out the gods in the other creation tale, he did so at Ptah's command, the result of the will of Ptah.

This cosmogonic theory was sophisticated and demanded a considerable amount of metaphysical awareness, something that defeated the cult from the beginning. Ptah was the creative principle, setting out not only the world and human beings but moral and ethical order. Ptah not only made the other gods but instituted the formulas for their worship, the offerings, the rituals and the ceremonies. Ptah made the cities and the men and women who inhabited them, and he set the standards for personal and national behavior. In time Ptah was joined to Osiris, to extend his reign even into the afterlife, as he was also united with Sokar.

The Theban cosmogony was late in arriving on the scene, coming into being in the New Kingdom (1550–1070 B.C.). The priests of Amon, understanding the need for a creation story that would provide their deity with rank and privilege above the other gods of Egypt, used the original concept of Amon as the air divinity of Hermopolis.

Thebes became the first Primeval Mound, the original Pay Land, the place of the "Appearance" of the watery chaos and the creation of all life. Amon created himself in Thebes, and all other gods were merely manifestations of him. He was Ptah, the lotus, the Ogdoad. Amon then became Tatenen, the Primeval Mound of Memphis. Thebes also assumed Osiris into its domain, claiming that the god was born in the New Kingdom capital. (See PRIMEVAL MOUND, TEMPLES.)

crocodile   an animal revered by the ancient Egyptians as a theophany of the god SOBEK. The god and his symbol were worshipped at Gebelein, Dendera and Sais. Particular honor was given to the crocodile in the FAIYUM. Crocodiles eventually were kept in

Crocodile as a theophany of the god Sobek, from a New Kingdom statue.

pools or in small lakes, where priests tended to their daily needs. Some of the animals wore crystal or golden earrings and some had bracelets on their forepaws. When they died they were embalmed with care.

Crocodiles were plentiful in the early eras. A legend stated that 'AHA of the 1st Dynasty (2920 B.C.), was befriended by one when attacked by enemies in the Faiyum. The embalmed remains of crocodiles were discovered in the tomb of AMENEMHET III (c. 1844–1797 B.C.) and elsewhere. KOM OMBO was an important center for the crocodile cult in later eras.

Crocodilopolis   the ancient Egyptian capital city in the FAIYUM, called Medinet el Faiyum and Shedet. This was the center of the cult of the god SOBEK but was also a cultic shrine for the goddess RENENET. A temple was discovered on this site, dating to the reign of AMENEMHET III (c. 1844–1797 B.C.) but probably built by one of his predecessors, SENWOSRET I. There is some speculation that the red granite obelisk at Abgig is actually a remain of this temple. A legend from the early dynastic era credited 'AHA (2920 B.C.) with the founding of this city.

crook   a royal symbol carried by the kings of ancient Egypt, representing the early shepherds. (See AWET.)

crowns   the various royal head coverings used by the kings of ancient Egypt for specific ceremonies or rituals. The white war crown of Upper Egypt, the *hedjet*, was combined with the *deshret*, the red wicker basket crown of Lower Egypt, to form the *wereret*, the double crown of Upper & Lower Egypt. The kings also wore the *seshed*, the crown covered with a filet of ribbon with a bow at the back and fluttering pennants. A cobra was used as the insignia in the front of a circlet, which had bows shaped liked the timbrels of the papyrus plant.

The ram's horn crown, called both the *atef* and the *hemhemet*, depending upon their style and use, was a ritual head covering and was worn only on solemn occasions when the king wished to be connected with Osiris and Re' in rituals. The *nemes*, the striped head cloth with panels extended in the front, was worn only by the kings. The *khepresh*, the military crown, was made of electrum and was blue in color, worn on campaigns or in triumphal processions.

cult centers   the ancient Egyptian sites where gods were honored with special rites or ceremonies, and where temples were erected to their devotion. Each

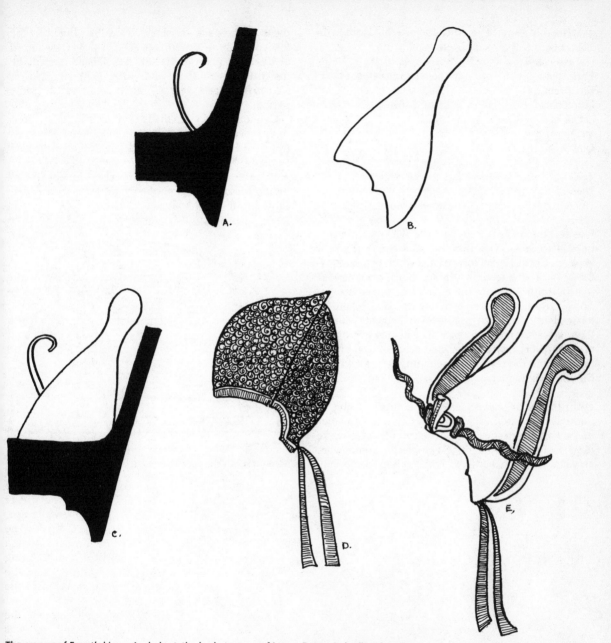

The crowns of Egypt's kings: A. *deshret,* the basket crown of Lower Egypt; B. *hedjet,* the white war helmet of Upper Egypt; C. *pschent* or *wereret,* the double crown of Upper and Lower Egypt; D. *khepresh,* the electrum war helmet; E. *atef* or *hemhemet,* ram's horn crown.

town had its own particular deity, but these were the centers of the major gods:

CENTER	GOD
Abydos	Osiris
Assiut	Wepwawet
Bubastis	Bastet

CENTER	GOD
Coptos	Min
Crocodopolis	Sobek
Dendera	Hathor
Edfu	Horus
Elephantine	Khnum
El Kab	Nekhebet

CENTER	GOD
Heliopolis	Re'
Heracleopolis	Harsaphes
Hermopolis	Thoth and the Ogdoad
Hierakonpolis	Horus
Leontopolis	Lions (Akeru)
Letopolis	Horus
Memphis	Ptah
Ombos	Set
Sais	Neith
Tanis	Set
Thebes	Amon
Thinis	Anhur (Onouris)

Cusae   the ancient Egyptian site named el-Qusiya in modern times. This was the main city of the 14th NOME of Upper Egypt, located just south of 'AMARNA. Cusae was at one time the southern boundary of HYKSOS control during the Second Intermediate Period. A fortress was erected on the site, taken by KAMOSE (c. 1550 B.C.) of the 17th Dynasty during Egypt's war for independence. The nearby necropolis of Meir (Mir) contained rock-carved tombs of the nomarchs of the region, some dating to the Old and Middle Kingdom eras.

cylinder seals   carved seals originating probably in Sumeria and entering Egypt in predynastic times or in the Early Dynastic Period. The cylinder seals were used to imprint titles on clay objects. Some were attached to metal handles, while others, especially those of the early dynasties, were hand-held in the form of a scarab. Fragments of such seals were found at Khafr Tarkhan and elsewhere. These carried the insignias of 'NARMER and 'AHA 2920 B.C. Queen NEITHOTPE's seals were also discovered from the same period.

Cylinder seals were made of black steatite, serpentine, ivory and wood. People suspended the seals from cords around their neck and then impressed symbols or CARTOUCHES into damp clay or other substances to mark items as reserved for royal use. By the Middle Kingdom the cylindrical seal was discarded in favor of SCARABS.

SCARAB SEAL   the Egyptian version of the ancient cylinder seal.

D

Dagi   listed as Dagy in some records; an official of the 11th Dynasty, serving as vizier and governor of the pyramidal city of MENTUHOTPE II at DEIR EL-BAHRI on the western shore of the Nile c. 2010 B.C. Dagi was the superintendent of the southern domains in Thebes, which was used as the home clan administrative center for the kings of the dynasties of the Middle Kingdom.

Dagi was buried at Thebes with honors, having erected a tomb on the western shore near the royal necropolis area.

daily royal rites   the ceremonies of the divine cult that were listed on the temple walls at ABYDOS and recounted in Egyptian papyri. These were rites dedicated to the god AMON and date from the New Kingdom era (1550–1070 B.C.). The god was honored by the king or by his priestly representative in the great Theban temples each day. The deity was offered unguents, wine, incense and articles of fine clothing and jewelry at the start of the services. Lavish care was taken of the statues of Amon in the temple, reserved in sanctuaries and hidden. Only the highest-ranking priests and members of the royal family could enter the sealed chambers of the god to perform the morning greetings, the washing rituals and the clothing ceremonies. Each priest knew that he was acting solely as a substitute for the king. It was only in the name of the king that such ceremonies could be performed, because they fulfilled the royal obligation designed to bring about grace of office in return.

Most New Kingdom pharaohs performed the rites personally when they were in Thebes. In other temples the same ceremonies were conducted before the other deities; again, the cult priests were aware that they were substitutes for the king. The pharaoh went to the temple to "visit his father" each day. When the king, or his high-ranking representative, arrived in the shrine, he was greeted by a priest dressed as the god. The double crown of Egypt was offered to the king as part of the ceremony, and a masked priest embraced the royal person in a fatherly manner. Dating back to ancient eras, this ritual was believed to impart to the king the SA-ANKH, the Living-Giving Waters, sometimes called the Fluids of Life. The original concept of the Sa-Ankh were part of the cult of OSIRIS and RE', although the Horus rituals at Edfu used the same tradition. On some occasions the king nursed from the breasts of a statue of HATHOR, ISIS or SEKHMET. In this manner he received divine life, a grace that he was able to extend to the people in turn. MAGIC was thus achieved and a pact was acknowledged between the deity and the king. In some eras it was believed that these ceremonies allowed the king not only to receive divine life but to transmit it back to the god in return, thus providing a daily mystical communion. Such rites were designed to give an outward and visible sign of something spiritually experienced. (See PHARAOHS.)

Dakhla   one of Egypt's major OASES in the western, or Libyan Desert. The Oasis of Dakhla was called the "Inner Oasis" from archaic times and was located directly west of the area of KHARGA.

Dal Island   a site overlooking the Second Cataract of the Nile, where it enters the gorge called BATN EL-HAGAR, or the "Belly of Stones."

Damietta   the modern name given to the branch of the Nile River on the eastern side of the Delta.

Dashur   a necropolis area on the Libyan Plateau near MEMPHIS, popular with the early dynastic families of ancient Egypt. Two pyramids of SNOFRU of the 4th Dynasty (2575–2551 B.C.) were erected there. Also located on the site were two pyramids of AMENEMHET II and AMENEMHET III of the 12th Dynasty

DASHUR PECTORAL from the 12th Dynasty, depicting Hathor with the cobras, the solar disk, the sacred eyes and with Horus and Seth. Horus is the falcon and Seth is the Typhonean animal unique to Egypt in early times.

(1991–1783 B.C.). Another, belonging to SENWOSRET III, contained a red granite burial chamber. These pyramids display a marked degree of artistic skill and are greatly prized for their artistic adornments.

Dead, Judgment of See JUDGMENT HALLS OF OSIRIS.

death See ETERNITY, MORTUARY RITUALS and RESURRECTION.

"Debate of a Man with His Soul" a didactic text written during the Middle Kingdom and contained in the Berlin Papyrus 3024. Called "The Man Who Tired of Life" in some records, this text discusses conditions of human existence. The text is similar to KHAKHEPERRESONBE'S COMPLAINTS. It takes the form of a conversation between a man and his vital principle, commenting upon events and on death as a blessed release from mortal suffering. The "soul," in turn, advises courage and a willingness to view life as a challenge.

Declarations of Innocence See NEGATIVE CONFESSIONS.

Dedi an official of the 4th Dynasty, serving KHUFU (2551–2528 B.C.). Dedi was a soothsayer who predicted the birth of the kings of the 5th Dynasty. The god RE' was supposed to have aided these kings in their rise to power. Dedi and his prophecy about the kings of the 5th Dynasty are contained in the Westcar Papyrus.

Dedu an official of the 18th Dynasty, serving in the reign of TUTHMOSIS III (1497–1425 B.C.). Dedu was a chief of the famed MEDJAY troops in the New

Daily royal rites personified in the goddess Isis, giving nourishment to the king and imparting graces and spiritual powers.

Kingdom era. These Nubian warriors distinguished themselves in Egypt's battle against the Asiatic invaders during the Second Intermediate Period and in the early stages of the New Kingdom, aiding both Kamose and 'Ahmose as they fought the HYKSOS in the Delta. When the country returned to peace, the Medjay assumed the role of the state police.

Dedu, a Nubian, served as the Superintendent of the Western Deserts and as a royal envoy to the tribes living there. He commanded police units in strategic locations and maintained the peace. Dedu was buried at Thebes on the western shore.

Dedumose II (Djedneferre')   the 37th king of the 13th Dynasty (c. 1640 B.C.). He was listed by Manetho as a vassal of the HYKSOS, who had taken control of MEMPHIS at the time. The "Great Hyksos" kings of the 15th Dynasty expanded into the region held by Dedumose's line, and he had to rule in their name. He left monuments in Thebes, Deir el-Bahri and Gebelein.

Dedun   a deity of Nubia who was honored by TUTHMOSIS III of the 18th Dynasty (1479–1425 B.C.). Tuthmosis built a temple at Semna for the worship of Dedun, obviously a tribute to pacify the local inhabitants and to establish a rapport with the region. The temple also served as a monument to the troops of the famous MEDJAY units, which had served Egypt during the struggle with the Asiatics in the Delta. Dedun was the presiding god of Nubia at the time.

Dedyet   a queen of the 12th Dynasty, the sister and wife of Amenemhet I (1991–1962 B.C.). Both the king and his sister were commoners, and of partial Nubian descent. Dedyet was not the Queen Consort, or the "Great Wife" of the king. Queen Nefru-totenen was the ranking royal woman of the reign. It would have been imperative for Amenemhet to consolidate his position by marrying into the Egyptian aristocracy.

Defufa   a site at the Third Cataract of the Nile, where twin brick fortresses were erected in the Old Kingdom period. The kings of ancient Egypt's early dynasties used the region for trade and constructed fortified outposts to protect their people and their wares.

The fortress at Defufa was in operation in the reign of Pepi II (2246–2152 B.C.), in the 6th Dynasty. Later kings refurbished and strengthened the fortress and maintained it for defensive purposes during eras of Nubian expansion. (See FORTRESS.)

Deir el-Bahri   called Djeseru-Djeseru by the ancient Egyptians, a name which meant the "Holy of

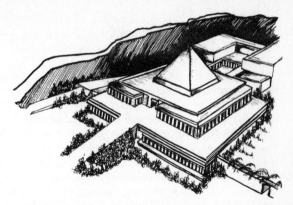
Tomb of Mentuhotpe II at Deir el-Bahri, a pioneering artistic effort of the Middle Kingdom (as reconstructed).

Holies." The present name of the site is from the Arabic, meaning "Monastery of the North," to denote an early community of Coptic Christian monks who established a religious house there. Deir el-Bahri is located on the western shore opposite the city of Thebes.

Mentuhotpe II (2061–2010 B.C.), of the 11th Dynasty, built his mortuary complex at Deir el-Bahri. He was a member of the famed Inyotef clan of Thebes and returned to his home for burial.

His temple was pyramidal in design, with terraces, walled courts, ramps, porticos and colonnaded walkways. The roof was supported by 140 separate columns. Mentuhotpe's royal female companions were buried at the rear of the complex in elaborate tombs. The entire structure was carved out of a cliff, and a vast burial chamber was fashioned under the pyramid, a chamber called Bab el-Hasan in modern times.

Queen-Pharaoh HATSHEPSUT of the 18th Dynasty (c. 1473–1458 B.C.), built a temple north of Mentuhotpe's complex. Her famous temple was designed with similar terraces and was hewn out of the cliffs also. Senenmut and other architects of that era were influenced by the splendor of Mentuhotpe's structure and incorporated the same architectural plans. A walled courtyard led to a ramp and raised terrace. A portico on this level had 22 pillars and a series of reliefs depicting an expedition to PUNT. A chapel dedicated to HATHOR and a shrine in honor of the god ANUBIS were graced with hypostyle halls. Another columned portico completed that section, while a ramp led to another court enclosed with columns and yet another portico. The sanctuary on the highest level of the complex contained a solar cult chapel and a shrine for the royal cult.

Deir el-Ballas   a site north of Thebes where the palace complex of the 17th Dynasty was discovered.

Ta'o I (c. 1600 B.C.) or perhaps one of his ancestors constructed the double palace there. It was used by TA'O II and KAMOSE, but the kings of the 18th Dynasty abandoned the site.

An enclosing wall, measuring some 900 by 400 feet, surrounded a complex of columned halls, courts, audience chambers, suites and royal apartments. Also included in the complex were silos and stables, indicating the agricultural interests of the royal family. The northern palace seems to have served as the royal residence, while the southern building was used as an administrative center. A village for staff members, workers and artisans was part of the northern enclave. The 17th Dynasty ruled in Thebes as contemporaries of the HYKSOS, or Asiatics, who dominated the Delta. Ta'o II was the Theban king who began the war to achieve Egyptian independence from the alien invaders.

Deir Durunka   a site south of ASSIUT in ancient Egypt, where tombs of nomarchs from the 19th Dynasty were discovered. The tombs were noted for their charming reliefs, which depict lush pastoral scenes, and elaborate statues, indications of the high standards of art during the Ramessid era.

Deir el-Gebrawi   the site of the Old Kingdom nomarch necropolis, located near ASSIUT in Upper Egypt. Some 100 tombs were discovered there. Several contained funerary chambers of offerings, part of the evolving mortuary rituals of the early periods. Deir el-Gebrawi was located some distance from the banks of the Nile, which makes its location typical for that era, when the southern clans used the desert fringes as necropolis regions.

Deir el-Medineh   a village of ancient Egyptian artisans attached to the New Kingdom necropolis at Thebes. These workers were formerly called the "Servants of the Place of Truth," the laborers of the tombs in the Valleys of the Kings and Queens. Such workers were valued for their skills and their imaginative artistry. In some records these artisans were called the "Servitors of the Place of Truth."

The homes of these artisans had several rooms, with the workers of higher rank enjoying vestibules and various architectural adornments. They also erected elaborate funerary sites for themselves and their families, imitations of the royal tombs upon which they labored throughout their lives. Small pyramids were fashioned out of bricks, and the interior walls were covered with splendid paintings and reliefs.

Deliverance of Mankind from Destruction   See BOOK OF THE DEAD.

Delta   See LOWER EGYPT.

Den   the fourth king of the 1st Dynasty (date of reign unknown), listed as ruling approximately half a century, probably the son of WADI. Den was considered energetic and a patron of the arts. Legends about him state that certain mortuary spells were found during his reign. He figures in the Ebers Papyrus and in the Berlin Medical Papyrus and was believed to have been medically trained. Den was active militarily in the SINAI, where the Egyptians were interested in the natural resources. He was buried at SAQQARA and built another mortuary complex at ABYDOS. His name is associated with Queen MERENITH, who possibly served as regent during his infancy.

Dendera   called Iunet or Tantere by the Egyptians, the capital of the 6th NOME of Upper Egypt, located south of Abydos. Dendera was the cultic complex for the goddess HATHOR. Crocodiles were also honored there and given sanctuary. A chapel dating to the

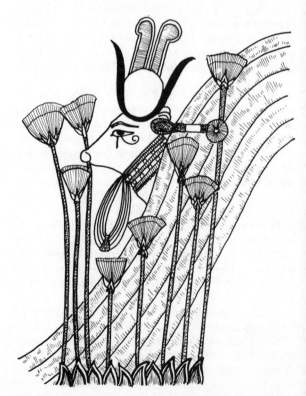

Dendera's deity, Hathor, shown as a celestial cow.

reign of KHUFU of the 4th Dynasty (2551–2528 B.C.) and a shrine from the 11th Dynasty (2134–2040 B.C.) were discovered in the western section of the city near an ancient sacred lake.

The necropolis of Dendera included tombs from the Early Dynastic Period as well as a number of mastabas belonging to the local nomarchs. On the western side of the cemetery there are brick-vaulted catacombs in which birds, cows and dogs were entombed. A small chapel from MENTUHOTPE II (2061–2010 B.C.) was also discovered in Dendera and is now in the Egyptian Museum in Cairo. The building commemorated the royal cult and had inscriptions from the reign of Merneptah (1224–1214 B.C.) of the 19th Dynasty.

The modern site of Dendera boasts a magnificent temple dedicated to the goddess Hathor, erected after the fall of the New Kingdom and extended by the Ptolemaic kings and the Roman emperors. A temple honoring the birth of Isis was decorated by Emperor Augustus, and another shrine, dedicated to Horus of Edfu, was erected in the area. Extensive building continued in Dendera throughout the ancient historical eras.

deneg See DWARF.

Derr site north of ABU SIMBEL of. a rock-carved temple dating to the reign of RAMESSES II of the 19th Dynasty (1290–1224 B.C.). This shrine was dedicated to the god Re'-Harakhte and was designed with hypostyle halls and three sanctuaries.

Deshasha an area of ancient Egypt that served as a necropolis site for the southeastern part of the FAIYUM. The tombs discovered there date to the Old Kingdom (2575–2134 B.C.) and provide documentation of that period of Egyptian history. Some 100 tombs were fashioned on the site of Deshasha.

Deshret the ancient Egyptian name meaning Red Lands, the desert wastes surrounding the narrow, fertile strip of rich black soil along the Nile. Egyptians called this fertile region Khem or Khemet, the Black Land, a name which also designated the nation as a whole. The Deshret served as a natural barrier for Egypt in the early historical periods, failing only in the late Middle Kingdom, when the eastern borders were overcome and the Asiatics entered into the Nile Valley. The Deshret is very much visible in the land today, especially at Thebes, where the red cliffs stand as spectacular guardians on the western shore of the Nile, a stark contrast to the lush green and black fields below. (See EGYPT and NILE.)

deshret See CROWNS.

District of Tekhenu-Aten a tract of land on the western shore of Thebes, once part of AMENHOTEP III's vast palace complex of the 18th Dynasty (c. 1397–1353 B.C.). The area, known in modern times as MALKATA, was called the District of Tekhenu-Aten in the Ramessid era and was listed as a royal tract in throne records.

Divine Companions a group of ancient Egyptian divinities who were considered protectors of the temples and the throne. These gods date to predynastic or Early Dynastic times. The Divine Companions were four in number, but each had 14 attendants or spiritual aides. They were magical, supernatural and powerful.

Djar an official of the 11th Dynasty serving in the reign of MENTUHOTPE II (c. 2061–2010 B.C.). Djar was overseer of the royal HAREM, an important position in his time. The pharaoh maintained a large harem and buried several of his royal female companions with him at DEIR EL-BAHRI. Djar was provided with a tomb near the vast complex on the western shore of Thebes, indicating his reputation and rank.

djeba an ancient Egyptian name for the sacred perch or reed that was associated with the creation tales. The reed, split in two at the moment of creation, rose out of the waters of chaos to serve the emerging deity. It was a popular symbol throughout Egyptian history. The *djeba* was the perch upon which the god landed. Several Egyptian deities were involved with the reed in their own cultic rites. The god HORUS, called the Falcon, was called the Lord of the *Djeba* in some rituals. (See "FIRST OCCASION," PAY LANDS and TEMPLES.)

djed the ancient Egyptian symbol of stability. The *djed* was a pillar, crossed by bars and depicted with inscriptions and reliefs to serve as an amulet in mortuary rituals. It was the sacred sign of the god OSIRIS, a powerful weapon of magic for all deceased Egyptians, considered necessary to aid in the transformation of the human flesh into the spiritual form assumed by the dead in eternity.

The *Djed* Pillar Festival, a cultic celebration of the symbol and of its powers, was held annually in Egypt and was a time of great enthusiasm and spiritual refreshment for the people. The priests raised up the *djed* pillar on the first day of *shemu*, the season of the harvest on the Nile. The people paid homage to the symbol and then conducted a mock battle between

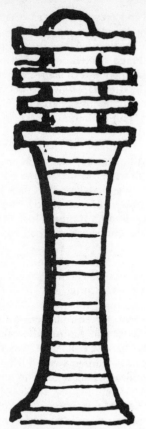

Djed pillar amulet, from the cult of Osiris, denoting stability, and the object of festivals and rites.

good and evil. Oxen were then driven around the walls of the capital, honoring the founding of the original capital of Memphis by 'Aha (2920 B.C.). Various reliefs in early tombs depict the procession, which was celebrated from early times. AMENHOTEP III (1391–1353 B.C.), of the 18th Dynasty, took part in the *Djed* Pillar Festival and had an inscription made to commemorate his royal presence. He concluded the festival by sailing in his royal bark on his sacred lake.

Djehutihotep   an official of the 12th Dynasty, serving in the reigns of AMENEMHET II (c. 1929–1892 B.C.) and SENWOSRET II (1897–1878 B.C.). Djehutihotpe was a NOMARCH with considerable prestige. He accompanied Senwosret II on a military campaign in Syria and performed other services for the royal family. He is best remembered, however, for the reliefs in his tomb at BERSHA. Reliefs depicting the transporting of a colossal statue from the quarry at HATNUB provide insight into the architectural and construction methods of his era, a time of vast building projects

on the Nile. The statue weighed more than 60 tons and was hauled on a gigantic sledge by the Egyptians as part of their CORVÉE obligations.

Djer   the second king of the 1st Dynasty of ancient Egypt at MEMPHIS. He was the son of 'AHA and a lesser wife named HENT (or Khenthap). Djer built a palace at Memphis and is reported to have ruled approximately 50 years. He probably fought a military campaign on the SINAI, and his name was also found in an inscription on the WADI HALFA below the First Cataract. Djer's mortuary complex at Abydos was supposedly named the true grave of the god Osiris after reign. His wife was Queen Herneith.

Djeseru-Djeseru   See DEIR EL-BAHRI.

Djoser (Netjerykhet)   the second king (2630–2611 B.C.) of the 3rd Dynasty. Inherting the throne as the son of KHA'SEKHEMWY and a lesser ranked queen, HAPNYMA'AT, he ruled during an age witnessing advances in civilization on the Nile such as the construction of architectural monuments, agricultural developments, trade and the rise of cities. Djoser ruled for almost two decades, and during his reign territories were consolidated and NOMES subdued.

Djoser, from a reconstructed statue discovered in the Step Pyramid at Saqqara.

He is remembered, however, for the great architectural achievement of his reign, the STEP-PYRAMID at SAQQARA. His chancellor or vizier, IMHOTEP, was the architect who directed the building of that great complex, which was Djoser's tomb.

Djoser fought the nomads on Egypt's eastern border and the Libyans on the west as the nation strove to evolve without foreign interference. He was also involved in an event that assumed legendary importance in Egyptian records, being recorded in the Famine Stela at SEHEL ISLAND. A famine lasted in Egypt for a period of seven years, and Djoser counseled with Imhotep and with his governor of the south, a man named MEDIR. Both advised him to sail to the ELEPHANTINE at Aswan, where the cult of the god KHNUM was located. Khnum was believed by the Egyptians to control the annual flow of the Nile, and Djoser had dreamed that the god appeared to him and complained about the sorry state of his shrine. He arrived at the Elephantine and erected a new temple on the site to honor Khnum, which brought about a miraculous end to the famine. Djoser's wife was Hetephernebty, thought to be a daughter of Kha'sekhemwy.

dogs   animals that were probably domesticated in Egypt in predynastic eras. The dogs served as hunters and as companions for the Egyptians, and some mentioned their hounds in their mortuary texts. Several basic types of dogs were evident from early times, mostly hounds (still seen in modern breeds).

Dogs of Egypt—[normally types of hounds or daschund in shape.] Dogs were popular as pets and hunting companions from early in Egypt's history.

Douao   a god of MEDICINE, associated with treatments of eye diseases in some eras. (See also WERET.)

Dra-abu'l Naga   the oldest section of the Theban necropolis on the western shore of the Nile opposite the New Kingdom (1550–1070 B.C.) capital. Tombs dating to the 11th Dynasty (2134–2040 B.C.) were discovered there, as well as New Kingdom funerary complexes.

dress   As the warm climate of Egypt dictated the agricultural seasons, so it influenced the style of dress. There were cool seasons, and on some evenings the temperature was cold because of the surrounding deserts, but normally the climate remained consistently warm and dry. In accordance with the temperature, the Egyptians devised simple styles and comfortable materials in which to dress from early on. Cotton was a major crop put to good use, and linen and the special material called BYSSUS became the basis for clothing for upper classes.

In the predynastic periods both men and women wore kilts, skirts that hung in simple folds or were adorned with narrow belts made of rope, fibers and leathers. In time women wore an empire-type long skirt that hung just below their uncovered breasts. Men kept to the simple kilts. These could be dyed in exotic colors or designs, although white was probably the color used in religious rituals or in court events.

In the Early Dynastic Period, both men and women wore their hair short, adorned with various bands or flowers. Then the women of Memphis began to appear in long cotton gowns with sleeves. Others adopted the empire style with bands over the shoulders. Men added simple cotton tops to their kilts when the weather cooled. That style remained consistent throughout the Old Kingdom and Middle Kingdom, although an extra panel, sometimes gauffered, sometimes stiffened, was attached to the kilts for special occasions. Furs were used in cold weather, and the Egyptians probably had capes and shawls.

Wigs were used and various types of head coverings were worn to protect the hair or bare scalp from dust and the heat of the sun. During the Old and Middle Kingdoms wigs made of fiber or human hair were adapted for use by the upper classes. Such wigs were often long, with great masses of hair pulled together in a stiff design. In some instances beads were woven into the hair at set intervals to form an intricate pattern.

Styles expanded with the coming of the New Kingdom (1550 B.C.), as the Egyptians were exposed to foreign elements. During that period, red girdles, clearly visible under the sheer cotton fabrics, were

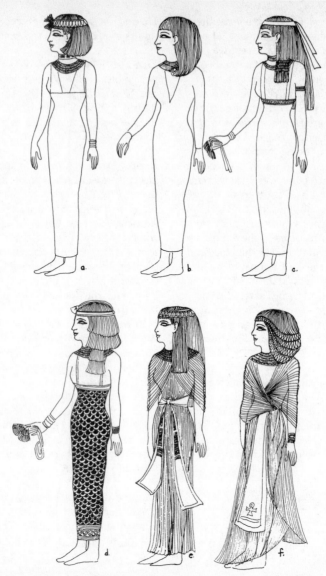

Dress styles: a) simple long skirt and short hair of Old Kingdom era; b) long cotton gown and hairstyle of Middle Kingdom; c) typical gown with shoulder straps and wig or natural hair; d) beaded gown and fringed hair of the Middle and New Kingdoms; e) capelet and embroidered sash in gauffered linen of the New Kingdom; f) elaborate wig and gauffered gown with collars of gold beads.

considered stylish. Also popular were dresses of patterned beadwork set into the material, and elaborate designs made out of bits of shell and small stones were embroidered the length of women's gowns.

The capelet, made of sheer linen, was the fashion innovation of the New Kingdom, a time in which men wore kilts and sheer blouses with elaborately pleated sleeves. Great panels of woven materials hung from the waist, and intricate folds were visible under sheer overskirts.

Viziers kept to a simple skirt of white cotton, and priests used white for all temple functions, placing animal skins or colored sashes and pectorals on their costumes to signify their rank and function. Priests wore shaved heads, and some wore the lock of youth as part of their insignia. This lock was also affected by the royal princes, who shaved their heads but maintained a single lock of hair on the side of their skull, normally entwined with beads and bits of metal.

(Men's styles) a) simple kilt of the predynastic and Old Kingdom period; b) elaborate kilt with pleated front panel; c) sheer shirt and elaborately pleated kilt, worn by nobles; d) *nemes* crown and short kilt worn by pharaohs under a sheer overskirt; e) nobleman's gauffered linen shirt and kilt, with court-style wig; f) temple dress of pharaoh, with modified war helmet, embroidered panels, capelet and slippers (made out of fibers and painted with images of enemies, so that the king could trod on them each day; g) war uniform, with golden feather design of Horus as armor, with the electrum helmet and a short, gauffered kilt; h) simple skirt of vizier, unchanging throughout Egypt's history.

Duauf's Instructions a didactic text included in the PYRAMID TEXTS that date to the era of the Old Kingdom (2575–2134 B.C.) in ancient Egypt. These *Instructions* were adages about morality and the true purpose of human life. Duauf urged his fellow Egyptians to love books and learning and to aspire to the honorable and prosperous career of a SCRIBE.

dwarf called *muu, nem* or *hua,* several dwarfs in Egypt attained high positions and honors, marrying normal-sized women and raising families. They figure in government offices and in festival rites. Records from the reign of Izi (Neuserre') of the 5th Dynasty (2416–2392 B.C.) indicate that a particular type of dwarf, called a *deneg,* was brought to the king to dance with the royal princesses in rituals. A particularly touching incident involving a dwarf (or pygmy) took place in the reign of PEPI II of the 6th Dynasty (2246–2152 B.C.). Pepi was a child when one of his officials, a man named HARKHUF, sent word

Portrait of a dwarf of ancient Egypt, taken from a tomb decoration.

from the cataracts that he was to bring a dwarf back to Memphis. The little king wrote a letter giving explicit details about the care of the dwarf on the return trip. He was exact about the sort of treatment that the dwarf should receive and even alerted the governors of the cities along the way to extend hospitality to the dwarf and his companions.

dynasties the royal houses of ancient Egypt from the beginning of the dynastic era (2920 B.C.) to the end of the New Kingdom (1070 B.C.). The kings of each royal line exemplified a particular era in Egyptian history, some serving as victims of change and political upheaval, and others leaving a profound imprint upon the life of the land. The rulers listed below are also to be found under their own entries, and the dynasties mentioned without specific rulers are in separate entries as well. Each king is listed below with his or her prenomen (first cartouche name) in parenthesis:

Early Dynastic Period   2920–2575 B.C.

1st Dynasty   2920–2770 B.C.
  'Aha
  Djer
  Wadj
  Den
  'Adjib
  Semerkhet
  Qa'a
2nd Dynasty   2770–2649 B.C.
  Hetepsekhemwy
  Re'neb
  Ninetjer
  Peribsen
  Ka'sekhemwy
3rd Dynasty   2649–2575 B.C.
  Zanakht (Nebka)   2649–2630
  Djoser (Netjerykhet)   2630–2611
  Sekhemkhet   2611–2601
  Kha'ba   2603–2599
  Huni   2599–2575

Old Kingdom   2575–2134 B.C.

4th Dynasty   2575–2465
  Snofru   2575–2551
  Khufu (Cheops)   2551–2528
  Ra'djedef   2528–2520
  Khephren (Ra'kha'ef)   2520–2494
  Menkaure' (Mycerinus)   2490–2472
  Shepseskhaf   2472–2467
5th Dynasty   2465–2323 B.C.
  Userkhaf   2465–2458
  Sahure   2458–2446
  Kakai (Neferirkare')   2446–2426
  Ini (Shepseskare')   2426–2419
  Ra'neferef   2419–2416
  Izi (Neuserre')   2416–2392
  Menkauhor   2396–2388
  Izezi (Djedkare')   2388–2356
  Wenis (Unas)   2356–2323
6th Dynasty   2323–2150 B.C.
  Teti   2323–2291
  Pepi I (Meryre')   2289–2255
  Nemtyemzaf (Merenre')   2255–2246
  Pepi II (Neferkare')   2246–2152
7th Dynasty   2150–2134 B.C.
8th Dynasty

First Intermediate Period   2134–2040 B.C.

9th Dynasty
  Khety
  Merikare'   } 2134–2040 B.C.
  Ity

10th Dynasty
11th Dynasty (Theban)   2134–2040 B.C.
  Inyotef (Sehertawy)   2134–2118
  Inyotef II (Wah'ankh)   2118–2069
  Inyotef III (Nakhtnebtepnufer)   2069–2061

Middle Kingdom   2040–1640 B.C.

11th Dynasty (All Egypt)   2040–1991 B.C.
  Mentuhotpe II (Nebhepetre')   2061–2010
  Mentuhotpe III (S'ankhkare')   2010–1998
  Mentuhotpe IV (Nebtawyre')   1998–1991
12th Dynasty   1991–1783 B.C.
  Amenemhet I (Sehetepibre')   1991–1962
  Senwosret I (Kheperkare')   1971–1926
  Amenemhet II (Nubkaure')   1929–1892
  Senwosret II (Kha'kheperre')   1897–1878
  Senwosret III (Kha'kaure')   1878–1841?
  Amenemhet III (Nima'atre')   1844–1797
  Amenemhet IV   (Ma'akherure')   1799–1787
  Nefrusobk (Sebekkare') Q.   1787–1783
13th Dynasty   1784 to after 1640 B.C.
  Wegaf (Khutawyre')   (1) 1783–1779*
  Amenemhet V (Sekhemkare')   (4)
  Harnedjheriotef (Hetepibre')   (9)
  Sebekhotpe I (Kha'ankhre')   (12)   c. 1750
  Hor (Awibre')   (14)
  Amenemhet VII (Sedjefakare')   (15)
  Sebekhotpe II (Sekhemre'-khutawy)   (16)
  Khendjer (Userkare')   (17)
  Sebekhotpe III (Sekhemre'-swadjtawy)   (21)   c. 1745
  Neferhotep I (Kha'sekhemre')   (22)   c. 1741–1730
  Sebekhotpe IV (Kha'neferre')   (24)   c. 1730–1720
  Sebekhotpe V (Kha'hotepre')   (25)   c. 1720–1715
  Aya (Merneferre')   (27)   1704–1690
  Mentuemzaf (Djed'ankhre')   (32 c.)
  Dedumose II (Djedneferre')   (37)
  Neferhotep III (Sekhemre'-s'ankhtawy)   (41a)
14th Dynasty Xois Kings, contemporary with 13th
  or 15th Dynasty
*position in dynasty listed in parenthesis

Second Intermediate Period   1640–1532 B.C.

15th Dynasty   1640–1532 B.C. (Hyksos)
  Salitis
  Sheshi
  Khian (Swoserenre')
  Apophis ('Awoserre')   c. 1585–1542
  Khamudi   c. 1542–1532
16th Dynasty Hyksos, minor and contemporary
  with 15th Dynasty

17th Dynasty (Theban)   1640–1550 B.C.
  Inyotef V (Nubkheperre')   (1)   c. 1640–1635
  Sebekemzaf (Sekhemre'-wadjkha'u)   (3)
  Nebireraw (Swadjenre')   (6)
  Sebekamzaf II (Sekhemre'-shadtawy)   (10)
  Ta'o (or Djehuti'o) (Senakhtenre')   (13)
  Ta'o II (or Dejhuti'o) (Sekenenre')   (14)
  Kamose (Wadjkheperre')   (15)   1555–1550

New Kingdom   1550–1070 B.C.

18th Dynasty   1550–1307 B.C.
  'Ahmose (Nebpehtire')   1550–1525
  Amenhotep I (Djeserkare')   1525–1504
  Tuthmosis I (Akheperkare')   1504–1492
  Tuthmosis II (Akheperenre')   1492–1479
  Tuthmosis III (Menkheperre')   1479–1425
  Hatshepsut (Ma'atkare') Q.   1473–1458
  Amenhotep II (Akheprure')   1427–1401
  Tuthmosis IV (Menkheprure')   1401–1391
  Amenhotep III (Nebma'atre')   1391–1353
  Amenhotep IV (Akhenaten)   1353–1335
  Smenkhkare' ('Ankhkeprure')   1335–1333
  Tut'ankhamun (Nebkheprure')   1333–1323
  Aya (Kheperkheprare')   1323–1319
  Horemhab (Djeserkheprure')   1319–1307
19th Dynasty   1307–1196 B.C.
  Ramesses I (Menpehtire')   1307–1306
  Seti I (Menma'atre')   1306–1290
  Ramesses II (Userma'atre'setepenre')   1290–1224
  Merneptah (Baenre'hotephirma'at)   1224–1214
  Seti II (Userkheprure'setepenre')   1214–1204
  Amunmesses (Menmire)   usurper in reign of
Seti II
  Siptah (Akhenre'setepenre')   1204–1198
  Twosre (Sitre'meritamun) Q.   1198–1196
20th Dynasty   1196–1070 B.C.
  Sethnakhte   (Userkha'ure'meryamun)   1196–1194
  Ramesses III   (Userma'atre'meryamun)   1194–1163
  Ramesses IV (Heqama'atre'setepenamun) 1163–1156
  Ramesses V (Userma'atre'sekheperenre')   1156–1151
  Ramesses VI (Nebma'atre'meryamun)   1151–1143
  Ramesses VII (Userma'atre'setepenre'meryamun)   1143–1136
  Ramesses VIII   (Userma'atre'ankhenamun)   1136–1131
  Ramesses IX (Neferkare'setenre')   1131–1112
  Ramesses X (Khenerma'atre'setepenre')   1112–1100
  Ramesses XI (Menma'atre'setepenptah)   1100–1070

E

Ebers Papyrus one of the longest papyri from ancient Egypt, dating to the reign of AMENHOTEP I of the 18th Dynasty (1525–1504 B.C.). The Ebers Papyrus is a medical text, measuring 65 feet, with 108 separate pages. The document is one of the modern world's major sources of information concerning the medical knowledge and techniques of Egypt's priest-physicians. These medical practitioners gained a considerable reputation throughout the ancient world.

Sections on digestive diseases, worm infestations, eye ailments, skin problems, burns, fractures, rheumatism and anatomy are included in the text, as well as discussions of the treatment of tumors and abcesses. More than 900 diagnoses and prescriptions are listed in this papyrus. They indicate the fact that the priest-physicians of the pharaonic periods understood pain as they recognized the pulse and the problems related to the main artery. These priests also displayed a remarkable awareness of the circulation of blood in the human body. The Ebers Papyrus is now in Berlin. (See MEDICINE.)

Edfu a city located north of Aswan in Upper Egypt, called Behdet by the ancient Egyptians. Edfu was the capital of the second NOME of Upper Egypt and the cult center of HORUS-Falcon worship from early times. The city was called the "Exaltation of Horus" in some eras. Tombs dating to the 6th Dynasty (2323–2150 B.C.), erected by the regional NOMARCHS, were discovered in the city's necropolis, as well as a step pyramid dating to the 3rd Dynasty. Mastabas and reliefs from the reign of RAMESSES III of the 20th Dynasty (c. 1194–1163 B.C.) were also discovered. In the Ptolemaic period a great temple was erected on the site.

The Nile enters the great valley at Edfu, and the city was always considered militarily strategic for the defense of the nation against Nubian forces. During the Second Intermediate Period (1640–1532 B.C.), when the Asiatics ruled the northern Delta territories, Edfu

EDFU PYLON the great entrance to the temple of the god Horus.

was fortified by the Theban kings who maintained control over Upper Egypt.

Edku an important salt lake in Egypt's Delta region. (See LAKES.)

Egypt the nation situated on the northeastern section of the African continent. The name Egypt is the modern version of AIGYPTOS, the Greek word derived from the Egyptian for the city of MEMPHIS, Hiku-Ptah, the "Mansion of the Soul [or *ka*] of PTAH." Egyptians call their land Msr today and in Pharaonic times Khem or Khemet.

Geographical Designations

Egypt has always been a narrow, fertile strip of land along the NILE River surrounded by deserts, called the Red Lands, or Deshret. The northern border was the Mediterranean Sea, called the Uat-ur or Wadj-ur, the "Great Green." The southern border was the First Cataract at ASWAN until the Middle Kingdom (2040–1640 B.C.), although the armies of

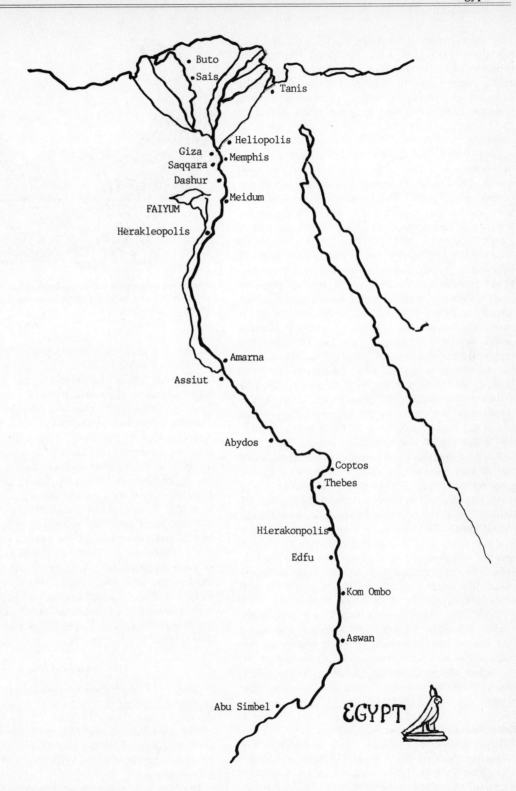

Buto
Sais
Tanis
Heliopolis
Giza
Saqqara   Memphis
Dashur
Meidum
FAIYUM
Hèrakleopolis
Amarna
Assiut
Abydos
Coptos
Thebes
Hierakonpolis
Edfu
Kom Ombo
Aswan
Abu Simbel

EGYPT

the Early Dynastic Period (2920–2575 B.C.) and Old
Kingdom (2575–2134 B.C.) conducted trading and
punitive expeditions and even fortified settlements
and centers south of Aswan. During the Middle
Kingdom the southern border was extended some
250 miles, and in the New Kingdom (1550–1070 B.C.)
the southern outpost was some 600 miles south of
ASWAN.

Egypt was composed of the Nile Valley, the DELTA,
the FAIYUM and the eastern (ARABIAN or Red Sea)
desert. The LIBYAN or western desert served as the
border on the west. Traditionally there has always
been another geographic duality in Egypt: the Upper
and Lower Kingdoms, now called Upper and Lower
Egypt.

Lower Egypt, in the north (called Ta-Meht), is
believed to have encompassed the land from the
Mediterranean Sea to Ith-tawy (LISHT) or possibly
ASSIUT. There is evidence that Lower Egypt was not
actually a kingdom when the armies of the south
came to dominate the region and to bring about a
unified nation (3000 B.C.). A depiction of a king was
seen on a major historical source from the period,
but no events or details were provided. The only
kings listed by name from the late predynastic age
are from the south. The concept of Lower Egypt
standing as a kingdom with its own geographical
and social uniqueness quite probably was a fabrica-
tion with religious and political overtones. The Egyptians had a great sense of symmetry, and the idea of
two parallel geographical units cohesing to form one
great nation would have appealed to them.

It is not certain that there was any sort of provincial
designation in the northern lands in the predynastic
period either. The NOMES, or provinces, date to the
first dynasties, and it is possible that Lower Egypt
was not one unified region at all. Whether a confederation of small groups or a people under the command of a single king, Lower Egypt called the city
of BUTO its capital (Pe in Egyptian), then SAIS.

Lower Egypt was always dominated by the Delta,
originally formed by perennial swamps and lakes
that turned into seasonally flooded basins as the
climate stabilized and inhabitants left an impact on
the region. Originally as many as seven river branches
wound through this area, and the annual inundation
of the Nile deposited layers of affluvium and silt.
There was continued moisture, gentle winds and a
vastness that encouraged agriculture.

Upper Egypt, the territory south of Ith-Tawy (or
Assiut) to the First Cataract of the Nile at Aswan,
was called Ta-resu. It is possible that the southern
border of Egypt was originally north of Aswan, as
the kings of the 1st Dynasty added territory to the

Royal symbols of Upper and Lower Egypt: the vulture, Nekhebet,
of the south, and Buto, the cobra from the north, from a New
Kingdom pectoral design.

nation. It is also possible that Upper Egypt included
some lands south of Aswan in predynastic times.

The Nile Valley dominated Upper Egypt, which
had sandstone cliffs and massive outcroppings of
granite. These cliffs marched alongside the Nile,
sometimes set back from the shore and sometimes
coming close to the river's edge. There were river
terraces, however, and areas of continued moisture,
as the remains of trees and vegetation indicate that
the region was once less arid. The original settlers of
the area started their sites on the edges of the desert
to secure themselves from the floods.

There were probably rudimentary forms of provincial government in Upper Egypt as well, specific
multi-family groups that had consolidated. Totems
of some of these groups or provincial units are evident in the unification documentation. The nomes,
as they were recognized throughout Egypt's history,
were established by the kings of the first dynasties,
but it is probable that Upper Egypt was advanced in
that regard.

Historical Periods

Because of its geographical position on the African
continent, and because of its relative isolation, Egypt
developed in a unique fashion. The natural defenses
of the cataracts of the Nile and the eastern and
western deserts kept the land comparatively free of
foreign domination in the early stages of growth and
confederation.

The Nile was the primary factor in this development, as the region offered no other rivers and little

rainfall. The annual inundation provided a bountiful agricultural economy and also prompted a remarkable sense of cooperation among the Egyptians. This spirit illuminated much of their religious and political thinking and left an imprint on their lives and on their future.

Predynastic Period

The era in which hunters and gatherers abandoned the heights and plateaus to enter the lush Valley of the Nile, discovering safety there and a certain abundance that induced them to begin settlements. These first settlements were not uniform throughout Egypt, and a list of predynastic cultural sequences has been developed to trace the development of cultural achievements in Upper and Lower Egypt.

Lower Egypt

Faiyum A (4400–3900 B.C.) a cultural sequence that emerged on the northern and northeastern shores of an ancient lake in the Faiyum district, possibly seasonal in habitation. The site was occupied by agriculturalists, but it is evident that they depended upon fishing and hunting and may have moved with the changes of the yearly migrations of large mammals. Fish were caught with harpoons and beveled points, but the people of this sequence did not use fishhooks.

Mat or reed huts were erected on the sheltered sides of mounds beside fertile grounds. There were underground granaries, removed from the houses to higher ground, no doubt to protect the stored materials from flooding. Some evidence has been gathered at these sites to indicate that the people used sheep, goats and possibly domesticated cattle. The granaries also showed remains of emmer wheat and a form of barley.

The stone tools used by the people of Faiyum A were large, with notches and denticulates. Flints were set into wooden handles, and arrowheads were in use. Baskets were woven for the granaries and for the daily needs, and a variety of rough linen was manufactured. Pottery in the Faiyum A sites was made out of coarse clay, normally in the form of flat dishes and bag-shaped vessels. Some were plain and some had red slip.

The people of this era appear to have lived in micro-bands, single extended family groups, with chieftains who provided them with leadership. The sequence indicates the beginning of communities in the north.

Merimda (4300–3700 B.C.) a site on the western edge of the Delta, covering a very vast territory with layers of cultural debris that give indications of up to 600 years of habitation. The people of this cultural sequence lived in pole-framed huts, with windbreaks, and some used semi-subterranean residences, building the walls high enough to stand above ground. Small, the habitations were laid out in rows, possibly part of a circular pattern. Granaries were composed of clay jars or baskets, buried up to the neck in the ground. The dead of the Merimda sequence were probably buried on the sites, but little evidence of grave goods has been recovered.

El-Omari (3700–3400 B.C.) a site near the Wadi Hof, between modern Cairo and Helwan. The pottery from this sequence was red or black, unadorned, with some vases and some lipped vessels discovered. Flake and blade tools were made, as well as millstones. Oval shelters were constructed, with poles and woven mats, and the people of the El-Omari sites probably had granaries.

Ma'adi (3400–3000 B.C.) a site located to the northwest of the El-Omari sequence location. A large area was once occupied by the people of this sequence. They constructed oval huts and windbreaks, with wooden posts placed in the ground to support red or wattle walls, sometimes covered with mud. Storage jars and grindstones were discovered beside the houses. There were also two rectangular buildings there, with subterranean chambers, stairs, hearths and roof poles.

Three cemeteries were in use during this sequence, as at Wadi Digla, although the remains of some unborn children were found in the settlement. Animals were also buried there. The Ma'adi sequence people were more sedentary in their life-style, probably involved in agriculture and in some herding activities. A copper ax head and the remains of copper ore (the oldest dated find of this nature in Egypt) were also discovered. There is some evidence of Naqada II influences from Upper Egypt and some imported objects from the Palestinian culture on the Mediterranean, probably the result of trade.

Upper Egypt

Badarian (4500–4000 B.C.) one of the cultural groups living in the Nile region in the regions of El-Hammamiya, El-Matmar, El-Mostagedda, and at the foot of the cliffs at El-Badari. Some Badarian artifacts were also discovered at Erment, Hierankopolis and in the Wadi Hammamat. A semisedentary people, the Badarians lived in tents, made of skins, or in huts of reeds hung on poles. They cultivated wheat and barley and collected fruits and herbs, using the castor bean for oil. The people of this sequence wove cloth and used animal skins as furs and as leather. The bones of cattle, sheep and goats were found on the sites, and domesticated and wild animals were buried in the necropolis areas.

Weapons and tools included flint arrowheads, throwing sticks, push planes and sickle stones. These were found in the grave sites, discovered on the eastern side of the Nile between El-Matmar and El-Etmantieh, located on the edge of the desert. The graves were oval or rectangular and roofed. Food offerings were placed in the graves and the corpses were covered with hides or reed matting. Rectangular stone palettes were part of the grave offerings, along with ivory and stone objects. The manufactured pottery of the Badarians demonstrates sophistication and artistry, with semicircular bowls dominating the styles. Vessels used for daily life were smooth or rough brown. The quality pottery was thinner than any other forms manufactured in predynastic times, combed and burnished before firing. Polished red or black, the most unique type was a pottery painted red with a black interior and a lip formed while the vessel was cooling.

Naqada I (Amratian) (4000–3500 B.C.) located from Deir Tasa to Nubia, including Hierakonpolis and Naqada, with a large concentration of sites evident between Naqada and Abydos. The people of this sequence erected oval huts (a type used in Naqada II as well), containing hearths and wattled and daubed. There were no windows evident, but these could have been placed in the upper levels. Windbreaks and cooking pots were also found.

The tools of the people were bifacial flint knives with cutting edges and rhombodial knives. Basalt vases were found, along with mace-heads, slate palettes and ivory carvings. Ritual figures, depicting animals and humans, were carved out of ivory or molded in clay. A black-topped pottery gave way to red wares in this sequence, some with white cross designs or scenes. Metal was very rare.

Naqada II (Gerzean) (3500–3000 B.C.) a cultural sequence that left sites from the Delta to the Nubian border, with most of the habitation centers located south of Abydos. This sequence is marked by the changes brought about in contacts with other peoples and other lands. The period also indicates growing institutions and traditions.

Accelerated trade brought advances in the artistic skills of the people of this era, and Palestinian influences are evident in the pottery, which began to include tilted spouts and handles. A light-colored pottery emerged in Naqada II, composed of clay and calcium carbonate. Originally the vessels had red patterns, changing to scenes of animals, boats, trees, and herds later on. It is probable that such pottery was mass-produced at certain settlements for trading

Flint knife from the predynastic era demonstrating early skills, with golden handle carved with the totems of the hunter clans.

purposes. Copper was evident in weapons and in jewelry, and the people of this sequence used gold foil and silver. Flint blades were sophisticated, and beads and amulets were made out of metals and lapis lazuli.

Funerary pottery indicates advanced mortuary cults, and brick houses formed settlements. These small single-chambered residences had their own enclosed courtyards. A temple was erected at Hierakonpolis with battered walls. Graves erected in this period were also lined with wooden planks and contained small niches for offerings. Some were built with plastered walls, which were painted.

The cultural sequences discussed above were particular aspects of a growing civilization along the Nile, prompted to cohese by that great waterway. The Nile, the most vital factor in the lives of the Egyptians, was not always bountiful; it could be a raging source of destruction if allowed to surge uncontrolled. Irrigation projects and diverting projects were necessary to tame the river and provide water throughout the agricultural seasons. The river, its bounty, and the rich soil it deposited gave birth to a nation.

Sometime in the late part of the predynastic era, attempts were made by leaders from Upper Egypt to conquer the northern territories. Upper Egypt probably was united by that time, but Lower Egypt's political condition is not known for certain. Men like SCORPION (Zekhen) and NA'RMER have been documented, but their individual efforts and their successes have not been determined. There was, however, a burgeoning of the arts, a force which would come to flower in the Early Dynastic Period (also called the Archaic Period).

The Early Dynastic Period (Archaic) 2920–2575 B.C.

The founding of the Egyptian state and the start of its ruling dynasties. The 1st Dynasty, begun at MEMPHIS by 'AHA (Menes), was marked by significant cultural achievements. He cemented his claims to the throne by marrying a Memphite heiress and by instituting, or reinforcing, the previous modes of governmental and religious traditions that would become unique aspects of Egypt's heritage. PAPYRUS, writing and a CALENDAR were in use, and linear measurements, mathematics and ASTRONOMY were practiced. A census, tax assessments, the reestablishment of boundaries after the yearly Nile inundations, and the development of new astronomical instruments moved the nation to new heights. The kings of the Early Dynastic Period raided LIBYA and the SINAI and began the exploitation of natural resources so vital to Egypt. Some punitive expeditions were conducted in NUBIA as well as the annexation of land around Aswan.

It cannot be verified that the first kings of this period accomplished the unification of Egypt. They ruled portions of the land and tried to gain control of the other nomes or provinces that were independent. Regions such as the northeastern Delta remained outside of their domination for a long period, as did other territories. It is assumed that the reign

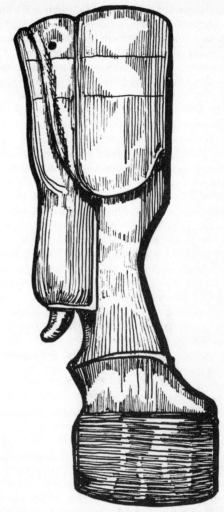

A carved chair leg made of ivory, from the Early Dynastic Period, demonstrates the swiftly evolving artistic skills in the Nile Valley.

of KHA'SEKHEMWY, the last king of the 2nd Dynasty (c. 2649 B.C.) witnessed the cohesion of the southern and northern regions, and the confederation of Upper and Lower Egypt was completed. Kha'sekhemwy also started a settlement at BUHEN in NUBIA.

Religious texts permeated Egyptian society during this period, and elaborate funerary complexes were constructed by the kings, as well as secondary tombs, called CENOTAPHS. Egypt was governed firmly by these rulers, with the aid of nome officials and dedicated administrators.

ART AND ARCHITECTURE, especially those forms associated with MORTUARY RITUALS, showed an increased degree of innovation and competence. The first evidence of the use of stone in large monuments dates to this period, and the conventions of Egyptian art developed at the same time. Cities flourished, and temples were raised to the local cults and to the emerging national deities. The achievements of the Early Dynastic Period culminated in the splendid mortuary complex erected for DJOSER (2630–2611 B.C.) by IMHOTEP, the chancellor or VIZIER of the king.

The Egyptians believed in material comforts and enjoyed amusements and pleasures, tempered by the ideal of moderation, quietude and a respect for the wisdom of elders. While they were obedient to superiors, the Egyptians firmly acknowledged an unprecedented awareness of human free will. This aspect of free will they translated into personal responsibility for one's actions, summarized in time by the concept of MA'AT. Sages such as PTAH-HOTEP, who is reported as having lived in this era, wrote didactic literature, extolling the virtues to the nation.

All of these virtues were linked to an emerging sense of the "other" in the world, to the concept of eternity and spiritual values. Egyptians were taught that they were truly one with the divine and with the cosmos. Such communion made resurrection inevitable. The Egyptians looked forward to eternal bliss in the afterlife or to celestial transmigration.

The Old Kingdom (2595–2134 B.C.)

The age of the great pyramid builders of the 4th Dynasty (2575–2465 B.C.), whose monuments rise from the sands of Giza as eternal testaments to the vigor and dynamism of this age. The kings of the Old Kingdom sent exploratory and punitive expeditions into Libya, Syria, and Nubia. A navy came into use in this era and land-based forces were frequently engaged. Quarries and mines were opened, and new expeditions ventured as far south as northern Sudan. Mining operations and other activities to extract foreign natural resources demanded a military presence and a commitment of men and material. By the close of the Old Kingdom the defensive posture of the Egyptian military was altered by General WENI (c. 2402 B.C.), who began aggressive campaigns, using veteran troops and mercenaries.

The last two dynasties of this historical period were unable to resist the growing independence of the provinces. The 7th Dynasty was short-lived (having no real power), and the 8th Dynasty could not maintain its grip on the various nomes and territories that were rebelling against this last line of kings in an effort to establish political autonomy.

The First Intermediate Period (2134–2040 B.C.)

An age of turmoil and chaos that began with the collapse of the Old Kingdom and ended with the military campaigns of MENTUHOTPE II of the 11th Dynasty (2061–2010 B.C.). Following the 7th and 8th Dynasties, ruling out of Memphis, the capital shifted to the south to HERAKLEOPOLIS, in the Faiyum. This was the home of the kings of the 9th and 10th Dynasties, (called KHETY by some and Achthoe by others), and 18 kings of this line are listed in part or in whole in the TURIN CANON.

The first of the royal line was so ferocious in attempting to gain control of the nomes surrounding his capital that he earned a reputation for cruelty. This was also the period in which the *Instructions for Merikare* and the ELOQUENT PEASANT were written.

The INYOTEF line (contemporaries who ruled the southern nomes) in THEBES began an assault on Herakleopolis. The last king of the 10th Dynasty lost his capital to Mentuhotpe II in 2040 B.C..

The Middle Kingdom Period (2040–1640 B.C.)

The era that began with the fall of Herakleopolis to Mentuhotpe II, an era of great artistic gains and stability in Egypt. A strong government fostered a climate in which a great deal of creative activity took place. The greatest monument of this period was at THEBES, on the western bank of the Nile, at a site called DEIR EL-BAHRI. There Mentuhotpe II erected his vast mortuary complex, a structure that would influence the architects of the 18th Dynasty.

The Mentuhotpe royal line encouraged all forms of art and relied upon military prowess to establish new boundaries and new mining operations. The Mentuhotpes, as the Inyotefs before them, were fierce competitors on the battlefield. They campaigned in Nubia, Libya, the Sinai, Palestine and perhaps even visited Syria on a punitive campaign.

The Mentuhotpes were followed by a royal line started by a usurper named AMENEMHET. Having served as a vizier and military commander for Egypt, Amenemhet took the throne and then sailed a fleet of 40 galleys up and down the Nile to put down rebellious nomes. He built his new capital at Ith-tawy (LISHT), south of Giza and Saqqara. He also established a WALL OF THE PRINCE, a series of fortresses on Egypt's eastern and western borders. Both Amenemhet and the Wall of the Prince were supposedly foretold by a sage named NEFERTI, who was reported to have lived in the 4th Dynasty and promised that a savior would appear to help Egypt in a time of need.

The 12th Dynasty kings raided Syria and Palestine and marched to the Third Cataract of the Nile to establish fortified posts. They sent expeditions to the Red Sea, using the overland route to the coast and the way through the WADI TUMILAT and the BITTER

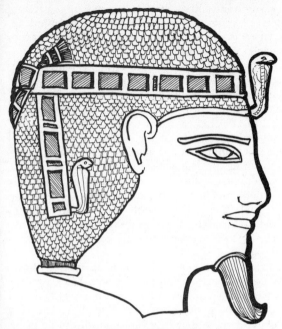

Mentuhotpe II, the founder of the Middle Kingdom.

LAKES. To stimulate the national economy, these kings also began vast irrigation and hydraulic projects in the Faiyum to reclaim the lush fields there. The agricultural lands made available by these systems revitalized Egyptian life.

The kings built vast pyramids at Ith-tawy and at DASHUR, including the multichamber LABYRINTH, which was an administrative center. It was an age of cultural and literary achievement on the Nile, prompted by the leadership of the royal family. By 1799 B.C., however, the line had waned. Amenemhet IV ruled for a decade, followed by Nefrusobek, the first woman to appropriate all the royal names of a pharaoh. Her reign lasted only four years, and the 13th Dynasty came to power in a futile effort to retain a grip on the nation. This royal line was listed in the Turin Canon, which credited between 50 and 60 kings to a period of 140 or more years. They continued to conduct building projects and governmental administration, but they were more and more harassed by the growing number of Asiatics in the northeastern Delta, and in time they collapsed or served as vassals to the new foreign regime.

In XOIS, in the western Delta, another dynasty, the 14th, contemporaries of the 13th or the 15th dynasties, maintained independence of a sort and promulgated a long line of kings (76 according to MANETHO). Scarcely any evidence remains of this royal line, but its kings are mentioned in the Turin Canon.

The Second Intermediate Period (1640–1532 B.C.)

An era of struggle and confusion, marked by the presence of the HYKSOS, the Asiatics who conquered the northeastern territories of Egypt. MANETHO, the 3rd century B.C. historian, stated that the Asiatics, whom he called the Hyksos, arrived in a whirlwind of devastation to conquer the land. The Hyksos did come to the Nile and did assume kingly roles, but their introduction into the land was gradual and dependent upon many factors.

Slavery had been introduced as an institution into Egypt during the Middle Kingdom, whose last kings were ushered into office in several fashions in Memphis or Thebes. While Egypt's military powers declined, the clamor for slaves increased, especially for the feudal and priestly estates of the Delta and the Faiyum.

The Asiatics, called the *Amu, Seteyu, Hikau Khoswet* (Manetho's Hyksos), came willingly into Egypt as prisoners or as indentured servants because Egypt offered them opportunities. As their numbers increased they began to insinuate themselves into various positions of power. IPUWER's complaints about the presence of the "Desert" in Egypt provides a cunning image of the changes taking place. The "Desert," the coarse nomads, consolidated their gains and opened Egypt to more and more migrations from the Mediterranean region.

The 15th Dynasty, ruling from AVARIS in the eastern Delta, was the royal line of the Hyksos. These kings ruled from 1640–1532 B.C. A second group of Hyksos kings ruled contemporaneously as the 16th Dynasty, but exercised less political control and held limited territory. Both Asiatic royal lines ruled at the same time as the 17th Dynasty, the kings of Thebes, who maintained a tight grip on Upper Egypt. The 17th Dynasty is dated from c. 1660–1550 B.C. and was entirely Egyptian.

In the beginning, when the Hyksos and their allies were entrenched in the eastern Delta and constructing their capital at Avaris, the Thebans maintained cordial relations with them. The Hyksos sailed past Thebes on their way to the lands below the cataracts in order to trade there, and the Theban cattle barons grazed their herds in the Delta marshlands without incident. The cordiality vanished after a time, however, and the Hyksos had to abandon all hopes of penetrating deep into Theban territories. They withdrew their forces to CUSAE, unable to maintain their dominance of more southerly lands.

Then APOPHIS III of Avaris sent an insulting message to TA'O II of Thebes, words recorded on two Karnak stelae. The Thebans declared war on the

Hyksos c. 1570 B.C., and Ta'o II mobilized his armies and struck at the Asiatic outposts. He died in battle or as a result of an ambush, but his son, KAMOSE, took up the war with equal vigor.

Kamose, the last king of the 17th Dynasty, used the famed MEDJAY troops and other military strategies and was approaching the defenses of Avaris when he died. His brother, 'AHMOSE I, the founder of the 18th Dynasty and the New Kingdom, laid siege to the city and ran the Asiatics out of Egypt, pursuing them to Sharuhen and then into Syria.

The arts and architecture of Egypt waned a bit during the Second Intermediate Period, although the tombs of the nomarchs in the outlying provinces were adorned with vivacious scenes that reflected the continuity of life in areas untouched by Egypt's warring dynasties. The Second Intermediate Period did have one lasting effect, however. Egypt was brought to the realization of the military and political realities of the age. The Thebans, watching the domination of the Asiatics in the northeast section of the nation, resolved to oust them from the Nile and to seal the borders once again.

The New Kingdom (1550–1070 B.C.)

The era following the departure of the Asiatics, a time of empire, prestige and military prowess. The New Kingdom was actually a combination of three separate historical periods: the beginning of the empire, the 'Amarna era and the Age of the Ramessids.

'Ahmose I destroyed Avaris and put down rebellions within Egypt and Nubia, and then set about conducting the affairs of state with a keen and energetic mind. He reduced the status of the hereditary princes and counts of the various nomes, thus putting an end to the petty rivalries that had plagued the nation in the past.

He established the Viceroyalty of Nubia and conducted all other government affairs through a series of judges and governors, who were sworn to serve him and the cause of his dynasty. This early part of the New Kingdom was particularly graced by talented Egyptians who brought loyalty and dedication to their tasks. AMON, the god of Thebes, honored by the Mentuhotpes of the 11th Dynasty, became the supreme deity of Egypt and the occupied territories. Costly offerings and gifts were presented to the god at KARNAK and at the LUXOR temple, which were expanded during this era.

AMENHOTEP I, the second king of the New Kingdom period, followed in his father's footsteps, but it was his successor, TUTHMOSIS I, who began the empire in earnest. He fought against enemies in far-flung lands and conquered territories all the way to the Euphrates River, where he put up a stela of victory to commemorate his success. His grandson, TUTHMOSIS III, would be one of the greatest warrior kings in Egypt's history.

Tuthmosis III was named heir by his father, Tuthmosis II, a frail man, but he was unable to assume the throne because Queen Hatshepsut usurped the titles and the role of pharaoh. She ruled Egypt from 1473 to 1458 B.C., and her reign was a time of comparative peace and stability. It was also a period of intense building in the northern and southern regions of Egypt. Hatshepsut remained powerful with the support of the priests of Amon and her able courtiers until Senenmut and Neferu-Re', her daughter, died. Then the forces of Tuthmosis III began to press for her abdication. She disappeared while Tuthmosis was on his major military campaign at MEGIDDO, possibly slain.

Tuthmosis III not only conquered vast territories but set in place an imperial system. He placed his own officials in the palaces of vassal rulers and brought back the young nobles of other lands to be educated as Egyptians so that they could return to rule in his name. Treaties, tributes, a standing army, a vast naval force and garrisons installed throughout the Mediterranean consolidated his military conquests. Tuthmosis's son AMENHOTEP II maintained the same firm hold on the territories and loved hand-to-hand combat and sports. His son, TUTHMOSIS IV, did not undertake many military campaigns, because the lands won by his ancestors remained firmly in Egyptian hands. He is remembered for his restoration of the SPHINX at GIZA.

AMENHOTEP III came to the throne in 1391 B.C., when Egypt's empire was at its height. He was not particularly martial or attentive to his duties, but his commoner wife, Queen TIY, worked with talented officials to keep the government stable. Amenhotep III also cemented ties with other lands by marrying

Asiatic tribute bearers depicted in a relief from the tomb of Tuthmosis IV.

their royal princesses, including one from Babylonia.

His son Amenhotep IV, called AKHENATEN, abandoned Thebes and Amon and initiated the 'AMARNA period, a time of great artistic innovation and political disaster. He remained isolated in his new capital, where he worshipped the god ATEN, and the empire almost collapsed around him. When he died in 1353 B.C., Egypt had lost some of its territories, and its allies had suffered severe military setbacks.

After the brief reigns of Kings SMENKHKARE', TUT'ANKHAMUN and AYA, General HOREMHAB came to the throne. He worked to restore lost lands and to bring cohesion and order to the government of the nation. His laws were stern and effective, and he managed to lift Egypt to greatness again. Horemhab died childless and left the throne to a military companion in arms, RAMESSES I.

The Ramessid Period began in 1307 B.C., and lasted until 1070 B.C., with the 19th and 20th Dynasties. Ramesses I did not rule more than a year, but his son, SETI I, was a trained military commander who was anxious to see the empire fully restored. He and his son RAMESSES II (c. 1290–1224 B.C.), called the Great, took the field against Near Eastern powers, gaining territories and securing Egypt's prominence. Ramesses II also endowed Egypt with a multitude of monuments honoring his reign. The kings following Ramesses II were not as vigorous or talented, although MERNEPTAH stopped an invasion of the SEA PEOPLES in the Delta.

The 19th Dynasty came to a close with the reign of the widow of SETI II, TWOSRE. She had served as regent for the young king SIPTAH and had usurped the throne with the aid of BAY, her counselor.

The 20th Dynasty began with SETHNAKHTE, who started his royal line in 1196 B.C. RAMESSES III, another military giant, managed to maintain the trappings of empire and restored Egypt's artistic and cultural traditions. He was followed, however, by eight additional Ramesses with little military or administrative competence. The 20th Dynasty, and the New Kingdom, was destroyed when the powerful priests of Amon divided the nation and usurped the throne.

The New Kingdom was a time of flowering, both militarily and artistically. Egypt received tribute from lands from the Sudan to the Euphrates, and vassal kings waited upon the pharaoh in his palace. The original capital of the New Kingdom was Thebes, but the Ramessids had come from Avaris, the former Asiatic capital in the Delta, and returned there to build a splendid new city called PER-RAMESSES.

Thebes was a wondrous site, and the Greeks, coming upon it centuries later, sang the praises of the ancient capital. Homer, in fact, spoke of its hundred gates and of its eternal charms. Other magnificent sites, such as ABU SIMBEL, MEDINET HABU, ABYDOS, DEIR EL-BAHRI, and countless shrines and temples up and down the Nile, stand as reminders of the glories of this age.

Third Intermediate Period

After the Fall of the New Kingdom, Egypt entered a period of decline and foreign domination. This period was marked by the rise of the Amonite priests, who usurped the title of king even before the death of RAMESSES XI. These priests acknowledged the 21st Dynasty kings of Tanis in Lower Egypt and married into that royal family but ruled Upper Egypt from Thebes. The Libyans had also intervened in Egyptian affairs and had come to hold certain territories. Military campaigns were conducted, especially by Shoshenq I in Palestine and trade was revived, bringing new prosperity. By the end of the 8th century B.C., however, there were many kings in Egypt, each ruling over a small area. A 25th Dynasty king, Piye (750–712 B.C.), set out to subjugate other rulers in Egypt but fell short of his ambition.

Late Period

Starting in 712 B.C. with the reign of Shabaka, this era was one fraught with civil wars. The Nubians inhabited the Nile Valley, eventually taking Memphis and making it their capital. The Nubians did not actually dispossess local rulers, who maintained a firm hold on their own domains. Throughout their tenure, however, the Nubians built massive structures and brought about a certain renaissance of the arts. Another priest of Amon, Montemhet, rose up in Thebes and controlled much of Upper Egypt. In 671 B.C. the Assyrians took Memphis and forced all of Egypt to pay tribute. Egypt, no longer isolated, was thus engaged in the struggles of the Mediterranean.

Greek mercenaries, used by the Egyptian rulers in their unification struggles, had set up their own communities on the Nile and by the 4th century B.C., and influenced much of the nation through their skill in trade and warfare. Reunification was eventually accomplished by a new royal line, and Egypt prospered under a central authority. The era of prosperity was not long lived, however, and in 567 B.C. the Babylonians attempted an invasion. The Egyptians defeated the Babylonians, only to face a growing Persian menace. The Persians attacked during the reign of Psammetichus III (526–525 B.C.), successfully defeating the armies of Egypt. A line of Persians ruled Egypt until 404, when Amyrtaios of Sais freed the Delta of the foreigners. Amyrtaios was listed as the sole ruler of the 28th Dynasty. The 29th and 30th Dynasties presided over troubled times until 343 B.C., when the Persians once again gained control of the land. This decade-long period of occupation is listed in histories as the 31st Dynasty.

Greco-Roman Period

In 332 B.C., Alexander the Great took control of Egypt, founding the city of Alexandria, and at his death the nation became the property of Ptolemy, one of his generals. For the next 250 years the Greeks successfully ruled Egypt, imbuing the land with Hellenic traditions. Their rule began as a time of economic and artistic prosperity, but by the 2nd century B.C. there was a marked decline. Family feuds and external forces took their toll, even though the Ptolemaic line remained in power. This royal house died with Cleopatra. Octavius (the future Augustus) took control and began the period of Roman occupation, c. 31 B.C.

Egypt and the East   from the Early Dynastic Period, (2920–2575 B.C.) Egypt guarded its borders, especially those which opened eastward, as Egyptians had ventured into the Sinai and opened copper and turquoise mines in that area, repulsing the Asiatics and staking their claims. The Egyptians maintained camps and fortresses in the area, to protect this valuable fount of natural resources.

In the Old Kingdom (2575–2134 B.C.), the Egyptians led punitive raids against their rebellious eastern vassals, and defended their borders furiously. In the 6th Dynasty (2323–2150 B.C.), the leadership of General WENI ushered in a new period of Egyptian military expansion, and the people of southern Palestine began to look toward the Nile uneasily. Weni and his Nubian mercenaries and conscripts raided the lands and the natural resources of much of southern Palestine.

During the First Intermediate Period, the Asiatics, Egypt's eastern neighbors, came into the Delta, establishing communities there. The Middle Kingdom pharaohs secured Egypt's borders again and established a firm rule, which lasted until the Second Intermediate Period, at which time vast hordes of Asiatics entered the Nile region with ease. In this era it appears as if no border existed on the eastern side of the nation, and many peoples in southern Palestine viewed themselves as Egyptians and lived under the rule of the HYKSOS kings of the eastern Delta.

The 18th Dynasty changed that condition. 'Ahmose I (1550–1525 B.C.) chased the Asiatics from Egypt and sealed its borders, reestablishing the series of fortresses called the WALL OF THE PRINCE during the Middle Kingdom period.

Amenhotep I maintained this firm rule, but it was his successor, Tuthmosis I (c. 1526–1508 B.C.), who defeated the Mitannis, once Egypt's principal Asiatic enemies, and marched to the Euphrates River with a large army. The Mitannis remained firm allies of Egypt from that time onward, and many treaties and pacts maintained the partitioning of vast territories between them. Mitanni princesses also entered Egypt as wives of the pharaohs. The Mitanni people flowered as an empire, having started their invasion of neighboring lands during Tuthmosis I's era. In time they controlled city-states and kingdoms from the Zagros Mountains to Lake Van and even to Assur, proving to be loyal allies of Egypt. They suffered during the 'Amarna Period, when AKHENATEN failed to meet the challenge of the emerging Hittites and their cohorts and the roving bands of barbarians who were migrating throughout the Mediterranean region. (The Ramessids, coming to power later, could not protect the Mitannis, either. They had already been subjugated by the warrior Hittites.) When Tuthmosis III came to the throne in 1479 B.C., the Mitannis were still in power and the Hittites were consumed by their own internal problems and by wars with their immediate neighbors.

He began campaigns in southern Palestine and the city-states on the Mediterranean Coast, eventually reaching the Euphrates. Palestine and the Sinai had been under Egypt's control since Tuthmosis I. A confederation of states threatened by Egypt or in the process of seeking total independence, banded under the leadership of the King of Kadesh. Tuthmosis III met them at MEGIDDO, near Mount Carmel, and laid siege. He then attacked Lebanon and fortified the coastal cities there, placing them all under Egyptian control. Egypt, as a result, received gifts and tribute from Babylon, Assyria, Cyprus, Crete and all of the small city-states of the Mediterranean region. Even the Hittites were anxious to send offerings and diplomats to the Egyptian court at Thebes.

Tuthmosis' son, AMENHOTEP II, conducted ruthless campaigns in Syria and governed the provinces with a firm hand. His heir, Tuthmosis IV (1401–1391 B.C.) did not have to exert himself, because the tributary nations were not anxious to provoke another Egyptian invasion. Amenhotep III came to power in an era of Egyptian supremacy, and he too did not have difficulty maintaining the wealth or status of the nation. His son, Akhenaten, however, lost control of many territories, ignoring many of the pleas of his vassal kings and allies when they were threatened by hostile forces instigated by the Hittites.

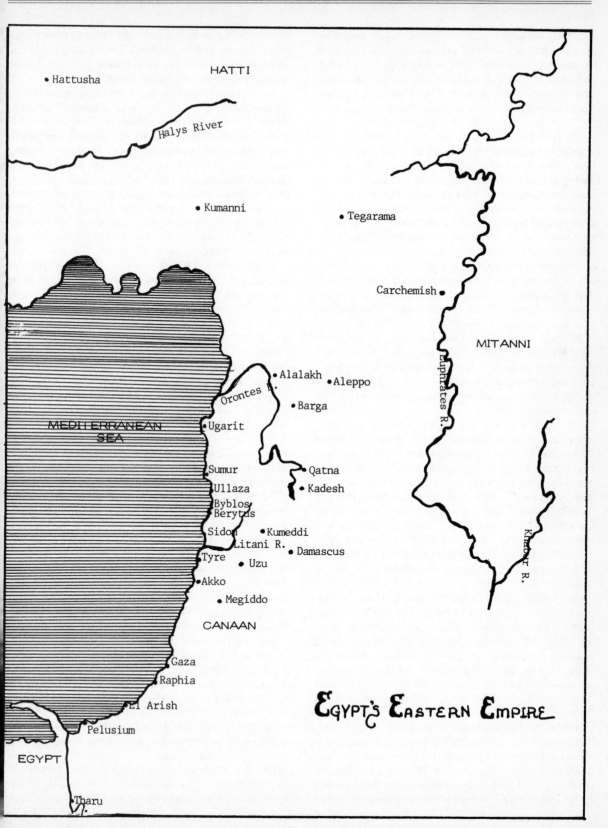

HATTI

• Hattusha

Halys River

• Kumanni

• Tegarama

Carchemish •

MITANNI

MEDITERRANEAN
SEA

Orontes R.

• Alalakh

• Aleppo

• Barga

• Ugarit

• Sumur

• Qatna

Ullaza

• Kadesh

Byblos
Berytus

Sidon

• Kumeddi

Litani R.

• Damascus

Tyre

• Uzu

• Akko

• Megiddo

CANAAN

Gaza

Raphia

El Arish

Pelusium

EGYPT

Tharu

Euphrates R.

Khabur R.

Egypt's Eastern Empire

The Hittites were a people never really identified as to homeland or tribal relationship. They arrived at the city of Hattus sometime in the 17th century B.C. and renamed it Hattusa. This capital became a sophisticated metropolis in time, with vast fortified walls complete with stone lions and a sphinx gate. In time they conquered vast regions of Asia Minor and Syria. The Hittites worshipped a storm god and conducted administrative, legislative and legal affairs ably. They worked silver, gold and ELECTRUM skillfully, maintained three separate languages within their main territories, kept vast records and protected the individual rights of their own citizens. Their legal code, like the Hammurabic code before it, was harsh but just. The Hittites were warriors, but they were also capable of statecraft and diplomacy.

The son of Hittite King Suppiluliumas was offered the Egyptian throne by Tut'ankhamun's young widow. Prince Zannanza, however, was slain as he approached Egypt's border. HOREMHAB, who became the last pharaoh of the 18th Dynasty (c. 1319–1307 B.C.), was probably the one who ordered the death of the Hittite prince, but when he came to power he was able to arrange a truce between the two nations. He needed to maintain such a pact in order to restore Egypt's internal affairs, greatly deteriorated by Akhenaten's reign.

The first Ramessid kings, all military veterans, were anxious to restore the empire again, and began to assault Egypt's former provinces. They watched the Hittites begin their own assaults on new territories with growing annoyance. The Hittites had conducted a great Syrian campaign, defeating the Mitanni king and attacking that empire's vassal states as a result. The city-state of Amurru also rose to prominence as the Amurrian king and his heir conducted diplomatic maneuvers and statecraft skillfully as agents of Hatti. Many loyal Egyptian states fell to them.

The Hittites next assaulted the Hurrian region, taking the city of Carchemish. The Hurrians had come into this territory from an unknown land, bringing skills in war, horses and chariot attacks. In time the Egyptians were the beneficiaries of the Hurrian skills, as many of them entered the Nile Valley to conduct training sessions and programs. Some even became the "Father of the God," a title given to the Master of Horse at the royal court in Thebes.

When the Hittites began to invade Egyptian territories, SETI I (c. 1306–1290 B.C.) started a counteroffensive. He easily overcame Palestine and Lebanon with his vast and skilled army. He then advanced on Kadesh, a Hittite ally, and consolidated his victories by reaching an agreement with the Hittites over the division of lands and spoils. The Hatti and the Egyptians thus shared most of the Near East with Egypt maintaining the whole of Palestine and the Syrian coastal regions to the Litani River.

Seti's son RAMESSES II faced a reinvigorated Hittite nation, however, one that was not eager to allow Egypt to keep its fabled domain. The battles displayed on Ramesses' war memorials and on temple walls, especially the celebrated "Poem" of Pentaur, depict the clash between the Hittites and the Egyptians. Ramesses and his army were caught in a cleverly devised ambush, but he led his troops out of the trap and managed an effective delaying effort until reinforcements arrived. This, the Battle of KADESH, resulting in heavy losses on both sides, lead to the HITTITE ALLIANCE.

From that point on, the Hittites and the Egyptians maintained cordial relations. Both were suffering from the changing arenas of power in the world, and both were experiencing internal problems. It is significant that the successors of Ramesses fought against invasions of Egypt as the Hittites faced attacks from enemies of their own. The SEA PEOPLES, the SHERDEN PIRATES and others were challenging the might and will of these great empires. Men like WENAMON, traveling in the last stages of Egyptian decline, faced hostility and contempt in the very regions once firmly within the Egyptian camp.

electrum   a metal popular in the New Kingdom era, although used in earlier times. Electrum was a naturally occurring combination of gold and silver. It was fashioned into the war helmets of the kings. It was called *tjam*, or white gold, by the Egyptians; the Greeks called it electrum. The metal was highly prized, particularly because silver was scarce in Egypt.

Elephantine   an island at the northern end of the First Cataract of the Nile near ASWAN, called Abu or Yebu by the ancient Egyptians. The island and the region of Aswan was the capital of the first NOME of Upper Egypt and the cult center of the god KHNUM. One mile long and one-third of a mile wide, Elephantine contained inscriptions dating to the Old Kingdom. DJOSER of the 3rd Dynasty (c. 2620 B.C.), visited the shrine of Khnum to put an end to a seven-year famine in Egypt. His visit was commemorated in a Ptolemaic era stela, the Famine Stela at Sehel.

A NILEOMETER was placed on the Elephantine, as others were established in the southern regions and in the Delta. Ruins from a 12th-Dynasty structure and others from the 18th Dynasty were discovered on the island. When 'AHMOSE I of the 18th Dynasty (c. 1550–1525 B.C.) established the Viceroyalty of NU-

ELEPHANTINE TRIAD the deities of the Elephantine and the First Cataract of the Nile—Khnum, Satet and Atet.

BIA, the administrative offices of the agency were located on the Elephantine. Similar officials, given other names in other eras, had served in the same capacity in the region. The Elephantine was always considered militarily strategic.

A small pyramid dating to the Old Kingdom was also discovered on the island, and the Elephantine was supposedly noted for two nearby mountains, called Tor Hapi and Mut Hapi, or Krophi and Mophi. These were venerated in ancient times as the "Cavern of Hopi and the Water of Hopi." The region was considered the "Storehouse of the Nile" and had great religious significance, especially in connection with the god Khnum and with celestial rituals.

A calendar was discovered in fragments on the Elephantine, dating to the reign of TUTHMOSIS III of the 18th Dynasty (1479–1425 B.C.). The calendar was inscribed on a block of stone. This unique document was called the Elephantine Calendar. Another inscription was discovered on a stela at the Elephantine. This commemorated the repairs made on a fortress from the 12th Dynasty and honors SENWOSRET III (1878–1841 B.C.). The fortress dominated the island in that era, giving it a commanding sweep of the Nile at that location. The stela is now in the British Museum.

The Elephantine Papyrus, found on the island, is a document dating to the 13th Dynasty. The papyrus gives an account of the era.

el-Kab See KAB.

el-Kula See KULA.

Eloquent Peasant of Herakleopolis a commoner named Khunianupu who supposedly lived in the 10th Dynasty, probably in the reign of Khety II. The Eloquent Peasant endured harsh treatment at the hands of officials and petitioned the king for justice with style and wit. Stating that "righteousness is for eternity," the Peasant eventually made his way into the royal court, where he was applauded and honored. The king supposedly invited Khunianupu to address his officials and to recite on state occasions. The popular account of Khunianupu's adventures and sayings is included in four New Kingdom papyri, now in Berlin and London. Such tales delighted the Egyptians, who appreciated didactic texts and especially admired the independence and courage of the commoners, whether or not they were real people or fictitious characters.

Embalming See MORTUARY RITUALS.

Ennead a system of nine deities established at HELIOPOLIS in the Early Dynastic Period as part of the cosmogonic or creation myths. The Ennead varies according to ancient records, but the usual gods involved were RE'-ATUM, SHU, TEFNUT, GEB, NUT, ISIS, SETH, NEPHTHYS and OSIRIS. In some lists THOTH or HORUS are included. PTAH also was given an Ennead at Memphis. (See COSMOGONY.)

Epagomenal Days the five days at the end of the ancient Egyptian calendar that were used to commemorate the birthdays of the gods with gala festivals and ceremonies. The Epagomenal Days were added to the calendar by IMHOTEP, the vizier of DJOSER of the 3rd Dynasty (2630–2611 B.C.). He used the additional time to correct the calendar, which had been in existence since the Early Dynastic Period. The original, lunar, calendar did not correspond to the actual rotation of the earth around the sun, thus veering steadily away from real time. The Epagomenal Days were added to make the necessary adjustments, although the traditional calendar was never accurate. The birthdays celebrated on these additional periods of time were: first day, OSIRIS; second, HORUS; third, SETH; fourth, ISIS; and the fifth NEPHTHYS. The days were actually called "The Gods' Birthdays." (See CALENDAR.)

Erment (Armant in some lists) called Iun-Mut in Egyptian and Hermonthis in Greek, a site south of THEBES. Erment was once the chief town of the fourth NOME of Upper Egypt but was replaced by Thebes as early as the Middle Kingdom. The god MONT had a cult center at Erment, associated with BUCHIS. Remains of an 11th-Dynasty palace was discovered on the site. A temple from the 18th Dynasty, built by Queen-Pharaoh HATSHEPSUT (c. 1473–1458 B.C.) and restored by TUTHMOSIS III was also found in Erment.

erpati hati'o (or Iri Pat) the ancient Egyptian term for the nobility of the NOMES or provinces of the nation. In some eras WOMEN inherited rights and rank.

Esna a site north of ASWAN in the Upper Kingdom. Tombs from the Middle Kingdom, Second Intermediate Period and the New Kingdom were discovered there. Esna is noted, however, for a Ptolemaic era temple. It was called Enit by the ancient Egyptians in some eras, and served as a cult center for the god KHNUM and the goddess Nebtu'u.

eternity the ancient Egyptian concept that gave impetus to the mortuary rituals and to the religious philosophy of every era on the Nile. Early on the people of the Nile Valley determined that the earth reflected the cosmos, a vision glimpsed nightly by the astronomer-priests and incorporated into spiritual ideals.

The Egyptians feared eternal darkness and unconsciousness in the afterlife because both conditions belied the orderly transmission of light and movement evident in the universe. They understood that death was the gateway to eternity. The Egyptians thus esteemed the act of dying and venerated the structures and the rituals involved in such a human adventure.

Heh, called Huh in some eras, was one of the original gods of the OGDOAD at HERMOPOLIS and represented eternity—the goal and destiny of all human life in Egyptian religious beliefs, a stage of existence in which mortals could attain everlasting bliss.

Eternity was an endless period of existence that was not to be feared by any Egyptian. One ancient name for it was *nuheh*, but it was also called the *shenu*, which meant round, hence everlasting or unending, and became the form of the royal cartouches.

The term "Going to One's *ka* [astral being]" was used in each age to express dying. The hieroglyph for a corpse was translated as "participating in eternal life." The tomb was the "Mansion of Eternity" and the dead was an *akh*, a transformed spirit. The PYR-

Heh, the god of eternity, shown seated on a sacred *djeba*, or perch, carrying rods of life, and the *ankh*, the symbol of life. He wears a solar disk, surmounted by cobras, the protectors of Lower Egypt and the kings of Egypt.

AMID TEXTS from the Old Kingdom Period proclaim that the *akh* went to the sky as the mortal remains went into the earth.

The PYRAMID TEXTS were provided to each deceased Egyptian king to offer him spells, incantations and wisdom for survival on the journey into Tuat or the Underworld. The COFFIN TEXTS came into being in order to instruct the non-royal deceased Egyptians about the JUDGMENT HALLS OF OSIRIS, where the soul of each mortal was weighed. These texts were used during the First Intermediate Period by nobles and nomarchs for their private tombs.

While the concept of eternity provided the impetus for the rituals and ceremonies of the mortuary rites, the arts and architecture benefited from the same vision of the afterlife. The monuments of Egypt were all related to the mortuary rites, insignias of the Egyptian contemplation of eternity. The pyramids rising up on the sands of GIZA were symbols of everlasting power and transformation. The elaborate tombs and temples were introductions into the supernatural ways of the realm beyond the grave.

Eternity itself was not some vague concept. The Egyptians, pragmatic and determined to have all things explained in concrete terms, believed that they would dwell in paradise, in areas graced by lakes and gardens. There they would eat the "cakes of Osiris" and float on the LAKE OF FLOWERS. The eternal kingdoms varied according to era and cultic belief, but all were located beside flowing water and blessed with breezes, an attribute deemed necessary for comfort. The Garden of A'ARU was one such oasis of eternal bliss. Another was Ma'ati, an eternal land where the deceased buried a flame of fire and a scepter of crystal—rituals whose meanings are lost. The goddess MA'AT, the personification of cosmic order, justice, goodness and faith, was the protector of the deceased in this enchanted realm, called Hehtt in some eras. Only the pure of heart, the *uabt*, could see Ma'at. For those deceased who feared judgment, the embalmers provided a collar amulet, as the symbol of eternity.

This concept was also the foundation of the role of the kings of Egypt. Each pharaoh was the god RE' while he lived upon the earth. At his death, however, he became Osiris, the First of the Westerners, the Lord of the Dead. Thus the kings were divine and destined for everlasting happiness. WENIS of the 5th Dynasty (c. 2323 B.C.) declared in his tomb at SAQQARA that the stars would tremble when he dawned as a soul. Eternity was the common destination of each man, woman and child in Egypt. Such a belief infused the vision of the people, challenged their artists to produce soaring masterpieces, and gave them a certain exuberance for life unmatched anywhere in the ancient world. (See MORTUARY RITUALS.)

exemption decrees documents issued in various eras of ancient Egypt to exempt certain temple complexes from taxes, enforced labor and other civic responsibilities. The most famous of these decrees were issued at Coptos. (See COPTOS and CORV'EE.)

extradition a clause placed in the HITTITE ALLIANCE between RAMESSES II of the 19th Dynasty (c. 1290–1224 B.C.) and the Hittites. The clause provided that persons of rank or importance would be returned to their own rulers if they tried to flee from one territory to the other in order to escape punishment for crimes. This clause, sophisticated and remarkably advanced for this period, exemplified the complex judicial aspects of Egyptian law in that era.

F

faience glassy manufactured substances of the ancient Egyptians. The process developed by the artisans of the Nile Valley may have been prompted by a desire to imitate highly prized turquoise, although there was a great diversity of color in faience. The usual Egyptian faience was composed of a quartz or crystal base, covered with a vitreous, alkaline compound with calcium silicates to provide the colors and the glassy finish. The Egyptians called faience *tjehenet*.

Faiyum the region of ancient Egypt called Ta-she, meaning the Land of the Lakes. In some eras it was called Pa-yuum, or Pa-yom. The Faiyum is a natural depression extending along the western side of the NILE, approximately 65 miles south of modern Cairo. It was settled in Paleolithic times, when hunters and gatherers came down from the arid plateaus, attracted by the abundant game and grasses.

The region was fed by the BAHR YUSEF, an Arabic name meaning "Joseph's River" (not a Biblical reference but one honoring an Islamic hero of later times). The Bahr Yusef was a diverted stream of the Nile, leaving the main waterway at ASSIUT. This stream was allowed to enter the Faiyum but was not provided with a natural route of exit, thus inundating the region and transforming it into a lush garden and marsh site.

The capital of the area was Shedet, or CROCODILOPOLIS, near Lake Moeris, now called Karun or Qarun. The lake is now considerably smaller than its original size. The Faiyum trapped the water of the Nile and became an area of lush vegetation and home to a variety of aquatic life. In time the region was clogged and reduced to stagnant marshes. The kings of the 12th Dynasty (1991–1783 B.C.), seeing the condition and realizing the need for increased fields, began a series of hydraulic systems to reclaim the entire Faiyum. Amenemhet III (1844–1797 B.C.) is recorded as having put up dikes and retaining walls,

with sluices and canals that partially reduced Lake Moeris and regulated the flow of the Bahr Yusef. In the process he provided Egypt with vast tracts of arable land, all of which served to strengthen the economic base of the nation. The adaptation of the Faiyum also provided Egypt with an emergency holding area in times of great floods.

One of the most beautiful regions of Egypt, the

Faiyum priestly crown, as worn by a Middle Kingdom pharaoh, from a temple relief.

Faiyum was reclaimed again and again to serve as an economic and agricultural base for the nation. Papyrus plants, palms and other harvests were available to the people of each era. The Greeks, coming upon Faiyum after the fall of the New Kingdom, remarked that the olives grown in the region were the tastiest of all. At various times the Faiyum extended over 4,000 square miles.

Famine Stela See SEHEL and DJOSER.

Faras a site near ABU SIMBEL, below ASWAN, which contained temples and a rock chapel from the New Kingdom era. Also on the site a temple of TUT'ANKHAMUN was discovered (c. 1333–1323 B.C.) from the 18th Dynasty. This temple had a stylish portico and a HYPOSTYLE HALL. The shrine measured 81 by 182 feet originally.

Fara'un Mastaba the modern name given to the ancient tomb of Shepseskhaf of the 4th Dynasty (c. 2467 B.C.) meaning "Seat of the Pharaoh." This MASTABA was erected in the southern part of the necropolis area of SAQQARA, near the Old Kingdom capital of MEMPHIS.

fate called *shoy* or *shai* by the ancient Egyptians, who put great stock in the destiny of each individual. *Shoy* was the good or ill laid down for each Egyptian at the moment of his or her birth by the SEVEN HATHORS. If the fate was good, it was called Renenet, or Renenutet, after the goddess of generation. In the case of royal princes, the heirs to the throne, the Seven Hathors guaranteed a favorable fate. They arrived at the crib of any prince born on an unlucky day and changed him, putting a lucky child in his

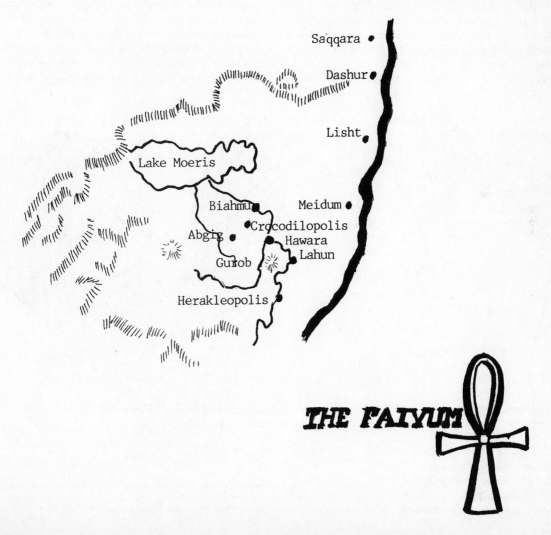

THE FAIYUM

place to avoid disaster for the nation. (See CAIRO CALENDAR and SHAI.)

festivals the celebrations of ancient Egypt, normally religious in nature and held in conjunction with the lunar CALENDAR in temples. Some festivals, mortuary or funerary in nature, were held in the royal and private tombs. The Egyptians liked visible manifestations of their beliefs and used festivals to make spiritual concepts meaningful. Most of the cultic celebrations were part of the calendar and based on local temple traditions. In some eras of Egypt there were as many as 75 such celebrations observed throughout the nation.

Starting in the Old Kingdom (2575–2134 B.C.), the first, sixth and fifteenth of every month were festivals associated with the lunar calendar. The seventh and twenty-third days had similar significance each month. The festival of the first day was a celebration of the new moon. The festival and the first day were both called *pese djentiu*. The most common name for a festival was *heb*, taken from the hieroglyph for an alabaster bowl.

Festivals were designed to commemorate certain specific events in the daily lives of the people. The Festival of the DJED PILLAR, for example, depicted growth and the movement of the sap in the trees, as part of rebirth. In two separate times of the year the festival of Wepet or Wepet-renpet, the New Year, were celebrated. Other festivals honored the Nile, and on these occasions elaborate shrines were floated onto the river, with flowers and hymns saluting the nurturer of all life in the land. In the fall the death of OSIRIS was staged at ABYDOS, and the Festival of Sowing and Planting followed.

The purpose of most of the festivals was to allow the people to behold the gods with their own eyes. Particular images of the gods, sometimes carried in portable shrines, were taken out of the temple sanctuaries and carried through the streets or sailed on the Nile. STATIONS OF THE GODS were erected throughout the various cities in order to provide stages for the processions. ORACLES were conducted on these festivals, as the images of the deities moved in certain directions to indicate negative or positive responses to the questions posed by the faithful.

One of the major Osirian festivals was epitomized by a golden ox clad in a coat of fine black linen. The

CELEBRATIONS from a tomb relief of the New Kingdom that depicts the festivities of the Egyptians on their holy days.

sacred animal was exhibited to the people during the season of the falling Nile, a time in which the Egyptians symbolically mourned the coming death of Osiris, a sign that the growing season was ending. When the river rose again, rituals were conducted on the banks of the Nile to greet Osiris' return. The priests used precious spices and incense to honor the god in his rejuvenated form.

The Beautiful Feast of the Valley, in honor of the god AMON, held in THEBES, was celebrated with procession of the barks of the gods, with music and flowers. The feast of HATHOR, celebrated at DENDERA, was a time of pleasure and intoxication, in keeping with the myths of the goddess' cult. The feast of the goddess ISIS at BUSIRIS and the celebration honoring BASTET at BUBASTIS were also times of revelry and intoxication.

The festivals honoring Isis were also distinguished by elaborate decorations, including a temporary shrine built out of tamarisk and reeds, with floral bouquets and charms fashioned out of lilies. The Harris Papyrus also attests to the fact that the tens of thousands of Egyptians attending the Isis celebrations were given beer, wine, oil, fruits, meat, fowls, geese and waterbirds, as well as rations of salt and vegetables.

These ceremonies served as manifestations of the divine in human existence, and as such wove a pattern of life for the Egyptian people. The festivals associated with the river itself date back to primitive times and remained popular throughout the nation's history. At the First Cataract there were many shrines constructed to show devotion to the great waterway. The people decorated such shrines with linens, fruits, flowers and golden insignias. (See NILE FESTIVALS, RELIGION, TEMPLES and PRIESTS.)

Festival Song of the Two Weepers See LAMENTATIONS OF ISIS AND NEPHTHYS.

First Occasion

an ancient term which meant the primeval times, called *pat, paut* or *paut-taui*. The First Occasion denoted the appearance of a god on earth, commemorating the emergence of the deity in the Primeval Mound before the god created other forms of life. (See COSMOGONY, PAY LANDS and TEMPLES.)

First of the Westerners See OSIRIS.

First Under the King

a title used by court officials in ancient Egypt, denoting a particular rank and the right to rule a certain region in the king's name. In Upper Egypt the senior officials were also called "Magnates of the Southern Ten." This affirmed their hereditary or acquired rights as an elite group of governors and judges.

Most areas of Egypt had a court of law, a treasury, a land office (for settling boundary disputes after the inundations), conservation bureaus for irrigation and dike control, scribes, a militia and storage facilities for harvests. Tax assessors were normally attached to the storage offices, which were temple-operated in many provinces. The governors of the NOMES and the judges of these area courts bore the titles of privilege and rank and reported directly to the VIZIER and to the royal treasurer in the capital. In some periods there were viziers for both the Upper and Lower Kingdoms. (see GOVERNMENT and LEGAL SYSTEM.)

flagstaffs

called *senut* by the ancient Egyptians, the symbolic poles used in the front of the pylons (entrance gates) at all major temples and shrines. Originally the cult centers had two insignias of the god visible in the court of the shrine. These were adorned with religious symbols and perhaps even with clan and NOME totems. When the kings began their massive building programs along the Nile, they copied the original cultic design and erected tall poles to fly the particular pennant of the temple or the god. These poles were made of pine or cedar and tipped by ELECTRUM caps.

flail

one of the most important insignias, used with the crook to represent the majesty of the kings of ancient Egypt. The flail, carried by the god OSIRIS, is normally shown in the hands of dead kings. It was once described as a whip but is now believed to represent the *ladanisterion*, the instrument used by early goatherds in the Near East. Such a symbol, dating back to the ancient eras, would have had magical connotations. Agricultural workers used the flail to gather labdanum, an aromatic shrub that yielded gum or resin.

The crook and the flail, both identified with the god Osiris and his patronage of vegetation and eternal life, were used in representations of the Kings of Egypt. It associated them with the past traditions, with Osiris and with the nurturing or shepherding aspects of their roles. (See PHARAOH.)

Fluid of Life See DAILY ROYAL RITES.

Followers of Horus

three distinct groups in ancient Egypt, each with its own unique role in the life of the nation. The first group, the supernatural, hence magical, company bearing this name, were creatures who supposedly accompanied the god HORUS, the

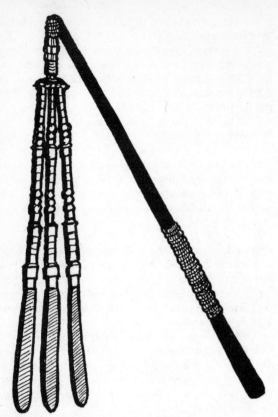

The flail, an important symbol from the early eras.

son of OSIRIS. Such companions, called Shemsu-Heru, were honored in all Horus' shrines and temples.

In the mortuary texts the Followers assume even more dramatic roles. They purify the deceased on their journey and are described in some documents as predynastic rulers who welcome the dead into their domains of eternal bliss. The second group of Followers are associated with the SOULS OF PE and the SOULS OF NEKHEN, the legendary godlike kings before the predynastic period. At the various Osirian and Horus festivals, a group called the Followers of Horus, the third group, conducted mock battles with the Followers of Seth. The Horus Companions always won these "wars."

The Followers of Horus, deemed both mythical companions and predynastic rulers of legend, may have been historically no more than the original confederation of nome warriors who followed NA'RMER north on his quest to overcome the Delta and unify Egypt. These Followers of Horus may also have been the king's retinue, accompanying him when he conducted his biennial tours of inspection along the Nile.

Followers of Seth a group of ancient Egyptians who participated in staged mock battles in the cere-

monies honoring OSIRIS and HORUS. The Followers of SETH were always overcome by the Followers of Horus in such struggles. They were called *mesu-betesht*, or *desheru*, the red ones.

fortresses military installations known in Egyptian as *mennu*. Traces of fortifications dating to the Old Kingdom (2575–2134) were found at ABYDOS and HIERAKONPOLIS, but the actual fortresses employed by the Egyptians were positioned on rocky elevations overlooking the Nile below the First Cataract and were probably constructed in the 12th Dynasty (1991–1783 B.C.). These fortified positions guarded the Nile between the Elephantine and the Second Cataract, and a cluster of them were built at the Second Cataract, which marked Egypt's southern border for a time.

Among them was the famed fortress of BUHEN, originally an Old Kingdom settlement, located on the western shore of the Nile opposite Wadi Halfa. This defense worked in conjunction with the Gebel Turob, a hill where Egyptians kept watch on all native movements. During the 12th Dynasty Nubians were not allowed to move northward without permission, and the sentries on Gebel Turob were stationed in a strategic position to enforce this royal policy. Watchers ran down the hill to the fortress the instant they saw large groups of Nubians in the vicinity. The watchers were provided shelters, and several men remained on duty there at all times. They were required to send detailed reports of each day's watch to their Buhen commander and to the commander of the fort at SEMNA. A similar sentry operation was undertaken at Gebel Sheikh Suleiman, also beside Buhen.

Buhen fortress itself was fashioned out of the rocky point on which it sat and was surrounded by temples and administrative offices—a pattern used for most fortresses in Nubia. It was constructed of large sun-dried bricks, laced with granite gravel for support. A wall with external buttresses followed the contours of the ledge and then swept downward to the river. This main wall was protected by two other walls and by a ditch carved out of rock and sloped with smooth sides to protect against enemy footholds. The fortress also held a garrison and storage areas.

Such fortresses were built southward into Nubia as the Egyptians expanded their territories and their interest in the region's natural resources. The fortresses on the Nile have been studied over the past decades. The garrisoned outposts as erected by the ancient Egyptians included walls and towers and were positioned in strategic locations so that southern forts could signal the ones to the north in times of emergency. It is estimated that these fortresses

Buhen fortress on the Nile, typical of the structural defenses employed by the Egyptians at the cataracts.

each contained from 2,500 to 3,000 men. Most of these troops were composed of veteran units and conscripts.

Another important Middle Kingdom fortress was built at Semna, designated as the Middle Kingdom southern border. Senwosret I started the garrison (1971–1926 B.C.), and it was completed in the reign of Senwosret III (1878–1841? B.C.). A fortress at Kumma was constructed in the normal rectangular pattern. Just below that another fortress was built at Uronati, triangular in shape. At Shalfak, on the western bank opposite the town of Sarras, another garrison was erected, and at Mirgissa a fort built in the style of Buhen was put up to command a strategic position.

At Dabnarti a fortress dominated an island, complete with towers and ramparts. Another garrison was located at the Second Cataract, opposite the island of Mayanarti. Buhen was at Wadi Halfa, and two more fortresses were erected between that site and 'Aniba, where a vast garrison was manned year-round. At Kubban, Ikkur and Bigga there were fortresses that guarded the last approach to the interior of Egypt. (See MILITARY.)

Forty-Two Judges the mythical divine beings in the JUDGMENT HALL OF OSIRIS, where deceased Egyptians were called upon to give an account of their lives on earth. Each of the judges sat in council with the god OSIRIS to determine the worthiness of the mortals in their presence. The Forty-Two Judges were awesome creatures, some bearing titles indicating their ferocity and purpose such as Long of Stride, Eater of Shades, Stinking Face, Crusher of Bones, Eater of Entrails and Double Lion. Some of the judges assumed other roles in the mortuary mythologies, as Hraf-haf, "HE-WHO-LOOKS-BEHIND-HIM." This creature was the ancient, cranky ferryman who had to be placated by the deceased in order for him to row them to the sites of eternal bliss.

Fraser Tombs the modern designation given to tombs found at ACHORIS in the central valley of the Nile. These tombs date to the 5th Dynasty (2465–2323 B.C.).

Friends of the King a rank popular in the Old Kingdom and conferred throughout all historical periods. An honorary rank, the title distinguished officials who had access to the king as a counselor or attendant. Courtiers could also be styled Well-Beloved Friends or Nearest to the King, as in the reign of Pepi II of the 6th Dynasty (2246–2152 B.C.). These titles, which gave the bearer prestige in the court, were inscribed on mortuary stelae in the tomb complexes.

frog a symbol of generation, rebirth and fertility in ancient Egyptian lore. The frog goddess was HEKET, shaped as a frog or frog-headed. The four male gods of the OGDOAD of HERMOPOLIS were also frog-headed, a symbol of their role in the rejuvenation and fertilization of Egypt at the creation. Frog AMULETS were used to ensure rebirth for the deceased. (See COSMOGONY.)

funerals See MORTUARY RITUALS.

G

Garf Husein a site below the First Cataract near the WADI ALAKI, where a temple of RAMESSES II of the 19th Dynasty (c. 1290–1224 B.C.) was discovered. The shrine was dedicated to the Memphite god PTAH and was built into a rocky cliff. A PYLON led to a court where three porticos were stylishly decorated. The subterranean level contained a pillared hall and five sanctuaries designed in the form of crosses.

Geb one of ancient Egypt's oldest gods. He was the brother-husband of NUT, the goddess of the sky. SHU separated Geb and Nut by command of the god RE'. Geb, inconsolable over his loss, wept until his tears formed the oceans and seas of the world.

Geb was a member of the ENNEAD, the pantheon at HELIOPOLIS. He was also known as the Great Cackler and was normally depicted as a man. On some occasions he was shown in a prone position, weeping for Nut. In this stance Geb represented the mountains and valleys of the earth. He was also shown in some reliefs as having a goose on his head, a reference to his having laid the cosmic egg that contained the sun.

Geb was honored as the father of OSIRIS and the other gods. In mythological episodes he fared badly on the throne, proving too curious. Geb opened a box containing the sacred URAEUS of the god RE'. The serpent promptly slayed his companions and burned Geb, who ruled wisely after that incident and gave the throne to OSIRIS in time. Henceforth the throne of Egypt was always considered Geb's, and each king claimed to be a descendant of this god.

gebel arabic for "hill."

Gebel Abu Rowash See ABU ROWASH.

Gebel Adda site of a rock-cut temple of HOREMHAB of the 18th Dynasty (1319–1307 B.C.). The shrine was dedicated to the gods AMON and THOTH. The temple was graced with a staircase, columned halls and with three shrines for offerings and devotional ceremonies.

Gebel el-Ahmar a site, located northeast of modern Cairo, for quartzite. The stone discovered there, reddish in color, was one of the most beautiful and hardest materials available to Egyptian artisans over the centuries. Limestone was also quarried there.

Gebel Barkal a site near the Fourth Cataract of the Nile where a temple of AMON was constructed in the 18th Dynasty and then restored by SETI I of the 19th Dynasty (1306–1290 B.C.). This was one of the southernmost frontiers of Egypt during the time of the empire. It was probably abandoned when the New Kingdom collapsed.

Gebelein the modern name for a site on the western shore of the Nile, south of ERMENT (Hermonthis). It was called Pi-Hathor by the Egyptians and Pathyris by the Greeks. Gebelein was a center for the goddess HATHOR from ancient times. Temples were discovered there dating to the 11th and 12th Dynasties, all dedicated to this popular deity. The necropolis area of the city contained tombs from the First Intermediate Period. Fragments from the Gebelein temple include inscriptions from the reign of MENTUHOTPE II (2061–2010 B.C.). They commemorate the king's victories. The inscriptions do not specify whether the enemies were Egyptians or foreign, and they possibly refer to Mentuhotpe's victory over the city of HERAKLEOPOLIS in 2040 B.C. The kings of the 9th and 10th Dynasties ruled from that city during the First Intermediate Period. Its collapse brought an end to the turmoil besetting a divided nation and marked the beginning of the Middle Kingdom era. The kings of the 11th Dynasty, who ruled from Thebes fought to defeat the KHETYS at Herakleopolis. The first Theban

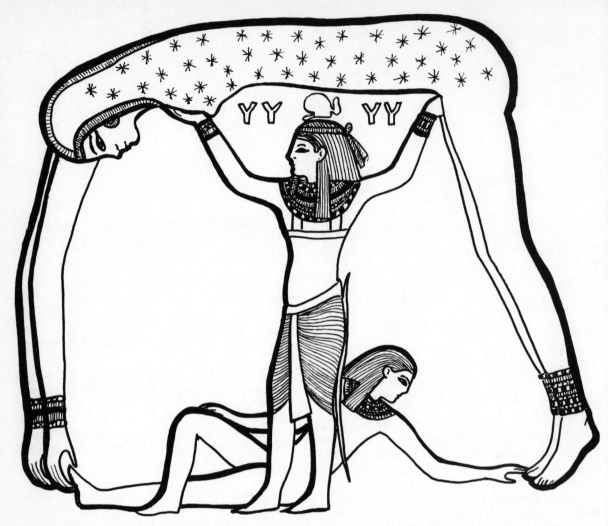

Geb and Nut separated from one another by Shu, in the cosmogonic tale depicted in temple reliefs of every era of ancient Egypt.

kings of this royal line served contemporaneously with the Herakleopolitans.

Gebel Mokattem site near modern Cairo of a limestone quarry that provided stone used for royal building projects from the Early Dynastic Period of Egypt until the fall of the New Kingdom. The quarry provided the fine materials used at GIZA and at other royal necropolises in the region. The limestone, which was of a high quality, was used for the STEP PYRAMID complex at Saqqara. (See TURA.)

Gebel Sedment the necropolis region of the city of HERAKLEOPOLIS, south of MEMPHIS. Herakleopolis was the capital of the 9th and 10th Dynasty Kings,

who controlled only a small part of Egypt. The site also contains Old and New Kingdom tombs.

Gebel el-Silsila the modern name for a site on the western shore of the Nile north of ASWAN. This was a quarry for standstone, much used by the kings of the late eras of ancient Egypt. Stelae and rock-cut shrines were discovered in the area, as well as a temple of HOREMHAB of the 18th Dynasty (c. 1319–1307 B.C.), commemorating his victory over the Nubians. The temple has pillared halls, a rectangular vestibule and a sanctuary, all containing reliefs depicting Horemhab's military campaigns. Ceremonies in honor of the god KHNUM, associated with the ebb and flow of the Nile, were also offered here.

ROCK TOMBS   the carved grave sites at Gebel Silsila.

Gebel Zebara   a gold mining area in the eastern desert near EDFU. SETI I of the 19th Dynasty (c. 1306–1290 B.C.) dug wells there and improved the living conditions of the Egyptian miners there. This site was near the WADI MIA. (See METALS.)

genitals   the reproductive organs surgically removed from some royal corpses in certain eras of ancient Egypt, notably that of the Ramessid kings. The genital organs were prepared separately and placed in a wooden box shaped in the form of the god OSIRIS. Obviously this was done to commemorate the loss of Osiris' genitals when he was slain by Seth. What prompted such commemoration is not known. RAMESSES III of the 20th Dynasty (1163 B.C.) was definitely embalmed in this fashion. The Ramessids were from AVARIS, an area dedicated to the god Seth, as the names of some of the kings indicate, and it may have been in tribute to Seth that the genitals were embalmed separately.

Gerzean Period (Naqada II)   See EGYPT PREDYNASTIC.

Gerze   a site in the FAIYUM called the Lower Valley. A large necropolis was discovered there, containing tombs from predynastic times. Oval-shaped graves were found, with linings made of wood or brick. (See EGYPT, PREDYNASTIC.)

Girdle of Isis   an ancient Egyptian magical sign, an ANKH-shaped form with its lateral arms drooping on either side. This AMULET, called the *tit*, was made of red materials, often jasper or carnelian. The amulet honored the blood of ISIS. It was believed that the symbol would confer strength upon the living and the dead. Girdle of Isis amulets were sometimes fashioned out of gold. When used in MORTUARY RITUALS, the amulet was dipped into a bowl of water filled with flowers and then placed on the corpse to protect it from various forms of putrefaction.

Girga   See THINIS.

GIRDLE OF ISIS   the amulet personified in an inscription.

Giza   a plateau area southwest of modern Cairo that served as the necropolis site for the Old Kingdom royal families and court officials. The PYRAMIDS of KHUFU (2528 B.C.), KHEPHREN (2494 B.C.) and MENKAURE (2472 B.C.) dominate the region. Private tomb complexes of nobles and officials of these kings are located to the east and west. Giza's non-royal tombs were laid out with precision and artistry, but later officials of less prestigious rank intruded on the site and disrupted the original pattern by introducing their own grave complexes.

gods and goddesses   the mythological divine beings who comprised the great patheon of ancient Egypt.

Some were defined by their cosmogonic role, while others were associated with a particular geographic location. The former were "universal" gods, those not limited to a particular place.

The numerous gods of Egypt were the focal points of the nation's cultic rites and personal religious practices. They also played a part in the great MORTUARY RITUALS and in the Egyptian belief in posthumous eternal bliss. There are several theories relating to the gods and goddesses of Egypt, including the assumption that they evolved from the practice of animism and fetish rites.

Animism was probably part of the predynastic religion of the Nile Valley before 3000 B.C., mirroring the basic urges displayed by primitive peoples all over the world. Through animism humankind sought to explain natural forces and the place of human beings in the pattern of life on earth. Animism involved the worship or the placating of human souls and other immaterial entities, particularly those inhabiting the realms of the dead.

The Egyptians believed firmly that death was just a doorway to another form of existence, so they acknowledged the possibility that those who had died were more powerful in their resurrected state. Thus politically, spiritually or magically powerful members of each community took on special significance in death, or in the realm beyond the grave. Special care was taken to provide such souls with all due honors, offerings and reverence. Dead persons were thought to be able to involve themselves in the affairs of the living, for good or ill, and thus had to be placated with daily sacrifices. Even recently, the people of some districts of Egypt still write letters to the dead and deliver them to the tombs so that the deceased will know about a problem and intercede on their behalf.

Animism in Egypt was concerned with the spirits of all natural things as well. The Egyptians lived with forces that they did not understand. Storms, earthquakes, floods and dry periods all seemed inexplicable, yet the people realized acutely that natural forces had an impact on human affairs. The spirits of nature were thus deemed powerful, in view of the damage they could inflict on humans. It was also believed that the spirits of nature could inhabit human bodies.

Two other forms of worship coexisted with animism in predynastic times: fetishism and totemism. Fetishism recognized a spirit in an object (as in animism) but treated the object as if it had a conscious awareness of life around it and could bring to bear certain magical influences. Fetishes had two significant aspects: one as the object in which a spirit was

LOTUS MOTIF   popular in various artistic forms in Egypt, used in temples and in private residences, depicting the emergence of the god Re' into the material world.

present and, secondly, as an object used by the spirits for a specific purpose (such as AMULETS or talismans.) Totems evolved out of NOME emblems, a particular animal or sign that signified the province's spirit. Such totems appeared on the nome staffs used in battle, and each nome army unit marched behind its own leader and its own insignia in the early historical periods.

Several ancient gods and goddesses of Egypt were associated with totems. NEITH, HATHOR, MONT and MIN, for example, were early symbols of fertility, hunting, pleasure and war. Fetishes appeared early in amulet form. The DJED pillar, which was associated with the cult of the god OSIRIS, became the nation's symbol for stability. The GIRDLE OF ISIS represented the virtues of that goddess as a wife and divine mother. As the predynastic period drew to a close, certain fetishes and totems were given human traits and characteristics, a process called anthropomorphism. The Egyptian gods evolved during this period, particularly Osiris, who represented not only the death of the earth at the end of the growing season but the regeneration of plant life as well. At that time, animals became objects of cultic devotion because of their particular abilities, natures or roles on earth. Some were made divine because of the dangers they posed to humans, in an effort to constitute what is called sympathetic magic. In time, others were used as theophanies, manifestations of the gods, because of their familiar traits or characteristics.

Although the Egyptians were polytheists, they displayed a remarkable henotheism—the practice of worshipping one god while not denying the existence of others. This is particularly evident in the hymns, didactic literature and the tales of the Egyptians where sages address one god as the self-created supreme being. The Egyptians had no problem with a multitude of gods, and they seldom shelved old deities in favor of new ones. Characteristics and roles of various gods, were syncretized to reconcile differing religious beliefs, customs or ideals. For political and religious reasons, for example, the Theban god AMON, who was considered the most powerful deity in the New Kingdom, was united with RE', a sun god whose cult dated to the beginnings of Egypt.

Worship of the gods of Egypt evolved over time as large cults developed on a local and then on a national scale. The following is a summation of the gods of Egypt in their various roles:

Major Gods and Goddesses

Amon
The state god of Egypt in the New Kingdom, (1550–1070 B.C.), with major temples at KARNAK and LUXOR in THEBES and in other large cities, such as MEMPHIS. The god also was worshipped in the OASES of the desert in time, and his popularity remained strong to Roman times. Amon was depicted as a handsome young man, sometimes ithyphallic, wearing two plumes. He is also portrayed as a ram.

Anubis
A god of the dead, dating to the Old Kingdom as part of Osirian myths. Anubis was the patron of embalmers and had a vital role in the travels of the deceased in TUAT or the Underworld. He was shown as a jackal or as a man with a jackal head.

Anukis
A goddesss of the cataract region, part of the triad formed with the god KHNUM and the goddess SATIS at the ELEPHANTINE. Her temple was also on SEHEL Island, and she was depicted as a woman wearing a tall feathered headdress. Anukis was associated with the inundation of the Nile and in the creation of mankind.

Atum
One of the creator gods in the HELIOPOLITAN cosmogony, whose characteristics were later assumed by other gods in a new cosmic order. Atum was normally portrayed as a man.

Bastet
A goddess with an ancient cult center at BUBASTIS in the DELTA, depicted as a cat-headed woman or as a lioness. She was at times a war goddess and at other times the protector of pregnant women.

Geb
An ancient earth god, involved in cosmogonic legends, always represented as a man in connection with the NUT and SHU myths. Geb was known as the Great Cackler in some eras and was shown as a man with a goose on his head to signify that he laid the first cosmic egg of creation.

Hapi
The personification of the Nile, honoring the river's inundations and fertile deposits on the fields of Egypt. Hapi was normally depicted as a fat man, holding the symbols of abundance. In some reliefs he was depicted as two men, in a mirror image.

Hathor
Called the "Golden One," a favorite in Egypt for centuries, the goddess of the sacred sycamore and an important sky goddess. She was honored at DENDERA, Thebes, Memphis, Abu Simbel and in other important sites. Known also as a patroness of pleasure and music, Hathor was represented as a woman wearing the sun disk and cow horns or as a cow, holding the SISTRUM.

Horus
The falcon god, sky deity and the living ruler, who was eventually involved in the Isis-Osiris myths. Worshipped originally in Upper and Lower Egypt, he became the first state god of Egypt, associated with the royal cult.

Isis
The wife of Osiris and the mother of Horus, one of the longest-lived deities of Egypt, surviving into Roman times. One of the great mother goddesses, she was shown as a woman with a throne headdress. A protector of the living and the dead, she was especially revered for her magical powers.

Khnum
A creator god especially worshipped at the Elephantine, and associated with Anukis and Satis. He was depicted as a man with a ram's head, often shown seated at his potter's wheel, where he brought

forth the forms of mankind. A legend concerning his shrine at the ELEPHANTINE dates to the reign of DJOSER in the 3rd Dynasty (2630–2611 B.C.) and stresses this deity's role in the annual inundation of the Nile.

Khons

A moon god, depicted often as a mummified youth with a lock of hair on his head, sometimes with the crescent of the moon. Khons was associated with Amon and Mut at Thebes. He could be depicted with a falcon's head as well.

Ma'at

The goddess of truth, who presided over the judgments of the deceased in Osiris' domain. She was depicted as a woman with a feather on her head, and in time her name was used to signify the spirit of calm and cooperation that was viewed as the ideal for human society.

Min

An early god of COPTOS, a patron of the desert who was later associated with Amon and the temple of Luxor. Min was involved in the fertility rites and was sometimes shown as an ithyphallic figure, carrying the flail and wearing plumes.

Montu

A war god associated with the BUCHIS bull at ERMENT and then with Thebes. He was normally shown as a falcon, protecting the kings in battle, or as a man wearing a falcon's head, with the sun disk and two plumes.

Mut

A war goddess, given as a wife of Amon at Thebes. She was depicted as a woman with a vulture headdress or with crowns. She could be portrayed as a lion-headed woman as well. Her great temple at Thebes demonstrated her position of honor in Egypt.

Neith

The goddess of SAIS, the patroness of war and hunting. Neith was closely connected to the god SOBEK and protected the dead and the CANOPIC JARS. She was shown as a woman wearing the red crown of Lower Egypt and carrying a shield and crossed arrows. She was especially honored in Memphis, and the Faiyum, as well as in Esna, in the southern domains.

Nekhebet

The patroness of Upper Egypt, a vulture goddess. She was involved in the coronation rituals and was depicted as a vulture or as a woman wearing the white crown of Upper Egypt.

Nepthys

Part of the Osirian legend, sister of Seth, Osiris and Isis, and Seth's wife. She was depicted in the Egyptian reliefs as a patroness of the dead, taking part with Isis in the Osirian traditions.

Nun

Part of the early cosmogonic legends, depicted as the watery chaos before creation.

Nut

A sky goddess, involved in the cosmogonic legends as the wife of Geb, the earth. Nut was normally depicted as a woman stretched above the earth, with the celestial bodies embedded in her flesh.

Osiris

The god of the dead in Egypt, dating to ancient times and maintaining popularity throughout the nation's history. He was the lord of Tuat, the Underworld, and a form of the dead kings and other deceased. He began as a fertility god but became the judge of the dead in later eras. He was normally depicted as a man in mummy wrappings, wearing a plumed crown.

Ptah

The creator god of Memphis and a patron of craftsmen. Ptah was depicted as a man in the form of a MUMMY, holding the *djed*. In time he was merged with SOKAR and Osiris to form Ptah-Sokar-Osiris, connected with the bull of APIS.

Re'

The sun god of HELIOPOLIS, from the earliest eras, and believed to be the father of the kings of Egypt while they lived. He headed the ENNEAD of Heliopolis and was then assumed by Amon of Thebes, who bore the incorporated title of Amon-Re'. Re' was represented as a man with a falcon's head or with a ram's head. He was involved in the mortuary rituals and in the daily crossing of the sun in the heavens.

Sekhmet

A lion headed goddess who was part of the Memphite triad as the wife of Ptah and the mother of NEFERTEM. Sekhmet, who represented the powers of the sun's rays, fought against the enemies of Re' and once nearly destroyed all of mankind.

Seth

The brother of Osiris, Isis and Nepthys, who slew Osiris. He was associated with the northeastern Delta and the deserts and was represented by the mythical Typhonean animal.

Sobek

The crocodile god of Egypt, particularly worshipped at the Faiyum. Sobek was involved in legends concerning Egypt's first king, 'AHA (2920 B.C.). He was normally represented by the crocodile or depicted as a man wearing a crocodile's head.

Taweret

The hippopotamus goddess who was the protector of women in childbirth. She was depicted as a composite woman and hippopotamus, with the paws of a lion and the tail of a crocodile.

Thoth

The god of wisdom, dating to HERMOPOLIS and associated with the ibis. Thoth was represented by the moon, and was also the patron of writing and counting. He was depicted as a man with an ibis head or by a BABOON.

Wadjet

The cobra goddess, patroness of Lower Egypt, and involved in the coronation of the kings. Wadjet was part of the Osirian myths and was always viewed as a protectress of Egypt, depicted as a woman with a cobra head or as a cobra about to strike at the nation's enemies.

Wepwawet

The jackal-headed god of ASSIUT, known as the opener of the Ways. Wepwawet was a mortuary god, associated with the legends of Osiris. He was depicted as a man wearing a jackal's head. (For details see these and lesser gods under individual entries.)

Animals

(Thought by the Egyptians to represent certain aspects, characteristics, roles or strengths of the various gods.)

Sacred bulls were manifestations of power in Egypt in every era. The gods were called "bulls" of their reign, and even the king called himself the "bull" of his mother in proclaiming his rank and claims to the throne. The bull image was used widely in predynastic times and can be seen on maces and palettes from that period. The bulls A'A NEFER, APIS, Buchis and MNEVIS were worshipped in shrines on the Nile.

Rams were also considered a symbol of power and fertility. The ram of MENDES was an ancient divine being, and Amon of Thebes was depicted as a ram in his temples in the New Kingdom. In some instances they were also theophanies of other deities, such as Khnum.

The lion was viewed as a theophany, as was the cat, and the deities Shu, Bastet, Sekhmet and the SPHINX were represented by one of these forms.

The hare was a divine creature called Wenu, or Wen-nefer. The hare was an insignia of Re's rising as the sun and also of the resurrective powers of Osiris.

The jackal was Anubis, the prowler of the graves who became the patron of the dead. As Wepwawet, the jackal was associated with the mortuary rituals at Assiut or Lykonpolis and in some regions identified with Anubis. Wepwawet was sometimes depicted as a wolf as well.

The pig, Shai, was considered a form of the god Seth, and appeared in some versions of the BOOK OF THE DEAD, where it was slain by the deceased.

The ass or the donkey, A'a, was also vilified in the mortuary texts.

The mongoose or Ichneumon, was called Khaturi, and was considered a theophany of Re as the setting sun.

The mouse, Penu, was considered an incarnation of Horus.

The leopard had no cultic shrines or rites, but its skin was used by priests of certain rank.

The baboon, Yan, was a theophany of Thoth, who greeted Re each dawn, howling at the morning sun in the deserts.

The elephant, Abu, was certainly known in Egypt but is not often shown in Egyptian art or inscriptions. Ivory was prized and came from Nubia.

The hippopotamus, a manifestation of the god Seth was vilified. As Taweret, however, she also had characteristics of crocodile and a lion.

The bat was a sign of fertility, but no cultic evidence remains to signify that it was honored.

The oryx, Mahedj, was considered a theophany of the god Seth.

Birds

The BENNU bird, a type of heron, was considered an incarnation of the sun and was believed to dwell in the sacred PERSEA tree in Heliopolis, called the soul of the gods. The phoenix, similar to the bennu, was a symbol of resurrection and honored in shrines of the Delta.

The falcon (or hawk) was associated with Horus, who had important cults at Edfu and at Hierakonpolis.

The vulture was Nekhebet, the guardian of Upper Egypt.

The goose was sacred to the gods Geb and Amon and called Khenken-wer.

The ibis was sacred to the god Thoth at many shrines.

The ostrich was considered sacred and its unbroken eggs were preserved in temples.

The owl was a hieroglyphic character. (See BIRD SYMBOLS.)

Reptiles

The turtle, Shetiu, was considered a manifestation of the harmful deities and was represented throughout Egyptian history as the enemy of the god Re'.

The crocodile was sacred to the god Sobek, worshipped in temples in the Faiyum and at Kom Ombo in Upper Egypt.

The cobra, Wadjet, was considered an emblem of royalty and throne power. The cobra was also the guardian of Lower Egypt, with a special shrine at Buto.

Snakes were symbols of new life and resurrection because they shed their skins. One giant snake, Methen, guarded the sacred boat of Re' each night, as the god journeyed endlessly through the Underworld. Apophis, another magical serpent, attacked Re' each night.

Frogs were symbols of fertility and resurrection and were members of the Ogdoad at Heliopolis.

The scorpion was considered a helper of the goddess Isis, and was deified as Serqet.

Fish

The oxyrrhynchus was reviled because it ate the phallus of the god Osiris after his brother, Seth, dismembered his body.

Insects

The bee was a symbol of Lower Egypt. The royal titulary "King of Upper and Lower Egypt" included the hieroglyph for the bee.

The SCARAB beetle in its form of KHEPRI, was considered a theophany of the god Re'. The image of a beetle pushing a ball of dung reminded the Egyptians of the rising sun, thus the hieroglyph of a beetle came to mean "to come into being." The scarab beetle was one of the most popular artistic images used in Egypt.

Sacred Trees

The tamarisk, called the Asher, was the home of sacred creatures, and the coffin of the god Osiris was supposedly made of its wood. The Persea, at the site Shub, was a sacred mythological tree where Re rose each morning at Heliopolis and the tree upon which the king's name was written at his coronation. This tree was guarded by the cat, and in some legends was the home of the Bennu bird. The Ished was a sacred tree of life upon which the names and deeds of the kings were written by the god Thoth and the goddess Sashat.

The sycamore, Nehet, was the abode of the goddess Hathor and mentioned in the love songs of the New Kingdom. According to legends, the lotus, Seshen, was the site of the first creation when the god Re' rose from its heart. The god Nefertum was associated with the lotus as well. The flower of the lotus became the symbol of beginnings.

Mythical Animals

The Saget was a mythical creature of uncertain composition, with the front part of a lion and a hawk's head. Its tail ended in a lotus flower. A painting of the creature was found in Beni Hasan, dating to the Middle Kingdom.

Amemait, the animal that waited to pounce upon condemned humans in the JUDGMENT HALLS OF OSIRIS, had the head of a crocodile, the front paws of a lion and the rear end of a hippopotamus. Other legendary animals were displayed in Egyptian tombs, representing the peculiar nightmares of local regions. One such animal gained national prominence. This was the Typhonean animal associated with the god Seth, depicted throughout all eras of Egypt.

Golden Horus Name   See ROYAL NAMES.

goose   the symbol of the god GEB, who was called the Great Cackler, the legendary layer of the cosmic egg that contained the sun. The priests of AMON adopted the goose as a theophany of Amon in the New Kingdom. The bird was sometimes called *Kehnken-wer*, the Great Cackler. (See SMENT.)

SAGET   a mythical creature found on a tomb wall in Beni Hasan and dating to the 12th Dynasty.

"go to one's *ka*" an ancient Egyptian expression for the act of dying. In some periods the deceased were referred to as having "gone to their *kas* in the sky." (See ETERNITY and MORTUARY RITUALS.)

government Egypt was a theocracy governed according to religious tenets and autocratic traditions. The PHARAOH, a manifestation of the god RE' while he lived and a form of OSIRIS beyond the grave, was the absolute monarch of Egypt in stable eras. He relied upon officials, however, to oversee the vast bureaucracy, as he relied upon the priests to conduct ceremonies in the temples as his representative.

Under the rule of the pharaohs the various regions of Egypt were grouped into NOMES or provinces, called *sepat*. These nomes had been designated in the Early Dynastic Period and each one had its own capital, its own god, totems and list of venerated ancestors. There were 20 nomes in Lower Egypt and 22 nomes in Upper Egypt (this number being institutionalized in the Greco-Roman period). Each was ruled by a *heri-tep a'a*, called the "great overlord." The power of such local rulers was modified in times of strong pharaohs, but generally they served the central government, accepting the traditional role of being FIRST UNDER THE KING. This rank denoted an official's right to administer a particular nome or province on behalf of the pharaoh. Such officials were in charge of the region's courts, treasury, land offices, conservation programs, militia, archives and storehouses. They reported to the vizier and to the royal treasury on affairs within their jurisdiction.

In general, the administrative offices of the central government were exact duplicates of the traditional provincial agencies, with one significant difference. In most periods the offices were doubled, one for Upper Egypt and one for Lower Egypt. This duality was carried out in architecture as well, providing palaces with two entrances, two throne rooms, etc. The nation viewed itself as a whole, but there were certain traditions dating back to the legendary northern and southern ancestors, the semidivine kings of the predynastic period, and to the concept of symmetry.

A prime minister, called a VIZIER, *tjaty*, ruled in the king's name in most eras. Beginning in the New Kingdom (1550 B.C.) or earlier, there were two such officials, one each for Upper and Lower Egypt, but in some dynasties the office was held by only one man. Viziers in the Old Kingdom (2575–2134 B.C.) were normally related to the royal house. One exception was Imhotep, the commoner who became high priest of the temple of PTAH and vizier of DJOSER (c. 2630 B.C.) in the 3rd Dynasty. These viziers heard all

A rare wooden statue of a vizier from the Middle Kingdom, wearing the robe worn by such governmental officials in all historical eras.

territorial disputes within Egypt's borders, maintained a cattle census, controlled the various reservoirs and food supplies, collected taxes, supervised industries and conservation projects and repaired all dikes. The viziers were also required to keep accurate records of rainfall (as minimal as it was) and to maintain current information about the expected levels of the Nile's inundations.

All documents had to have the vizier's seal in order to be considered authentic. Each vizier was normally assisted by members of the royal family or by aristocrats. This office was considered an excellent training ground for the young princes of each dynasty. Tax records, storehouse receipts, crop assessments and a census of the human inhabitants of the Nile Valley were constantly updated in the vizier's office by a small army of scribes. These scribes aided the vizier in his secondary role in some eras, that of the Mayor of THEBES. In the New Kingdom the mayor of Thebes' western shore served as an aide, maintaining the necropolis areas on that side of the Nile. The viziers of both Upper and Lower Egypt saw the king every day or communicated with him on a daily basis. Both served as the chief justices of the Egyptian courts, giving all decisions in keeping with the traditional judgments and penalties.

The royal treasurer, normally called the treasurer of the god, had two assistants, one each for Upper and Lower Egypt. In most eras this official was also the keeper of the seal, although that position was sometimes given to the chancellor. The treasurer presided over the religious and temporal economic affairs of the nation. He was also responsible for quarries and national shrines. He paid workers on all royal estates and served as the paymaster for both the Egyptian army and navy. The chancellor of Egypt, sometimes the Keeper of the Seal, assisted the other officials and maintained administrative staffs for the operation of the capital and royal projects.

In the 18th Dynasty, 'AHMOSE I (1550–1525 B.C.) established the viceroyalty of Nubia, an office bearing the title of "King's son of Kush." Many officials in previous dynasties had served in the same capacity at the ELEPHANTINE Island at ASWAN, but 'Ahmose made it a high-level rank. This officer controlled the affairs of the land below the cataracts, which extended in some eras hundreds of miles to the south. Certain Governors of the Northlands were also appointed during the New Kingdom period in order to maintain control of Asiatic lands under Egypt's control and western and eastern borders. Some officials served as well as resident governors of occupied territories, losing their lives when caught in rebellions.

The government of ancient Egypt was totally dependent upon the competence and goodwill of thousands of officials. The kings of each age appear to have been able to inspire capable decent men to come to the aid of the land and to serve in various capacities with dedication and a keen sense of responsibility. During certain eras, particularly in the waning years of the Rasmessid era of the 20th Dynasty, officials turned self-serving and corrupt. Such behavior had serious consequences for the nation.

Governors of the Northlands   officials of the New Kingdom era (1550–1070 B.C.) who governed three provinces of the eastern territories beyond the nation's borders and quite possibly some western border regions as well.

granite   a stone called *mat* by the Egyptians, much prized from the earliest eras and quarried in every historical period. Hard granite was *mat-rudjet*. Black granite was *mat-kemet*, and the red granite quarried at ASWAN was called *mat-en-Abu*. Other important quarries were established periodically and granite was commonly used in sculptures and in reliefs. It served as a basic building material for Egypt's mortuary temples and shrines. Made into gravel, the stone was even used as mortar in FORTRESSES, designed to strengthen the sun-dried bricks used in the construction process. (See QUARRIES.)

Great Cackler   See GEB and GOOSE.

Greatest of Seers   a title used for some of the prelates of the temples of KARNAK, MEMPHIS and HELIOPOLIS. (See PRIESTS and RELIGION.)

Great Primeval Mound   See PRIMEVAL MOUND and PAY LANDS.

Gurob Shrine Papyrus   a document containing details of a special shrine erected by TUTHMOSIS III (1479–1425 B.C.) in the 18th Dynasty. The shrine was a casket made of gilded wood. The papyrus commemorating the event, in a single roll, is now in London.

Ha an ancient Egyptian god of fertility and the desert regions. In various eras he was regarded as a defender of Egypt's borders and the protector of the throne. In the later periods he was honored in the seventh NOME of Lower Egypt.

hat the human heart when described anatomically or in physical terms. The literary designation was AB.

Hammamat a quarry site near COPTUS where several inscriptions from the 11th Dynasty (2134–1991 B.C.) were discovered. Men were pressed into service in order to conduct an expedition to this region, and the inscriptions state that 3,000 were used to transport a stone lid for a royal SARCOPHAGUS. In later eras, when the Egyptians moved into the area to operate the desert way stations for trade caravans, the region was well traveled and watched by patrols. The caravan route was from Coptos to the Red Sea.

Hapi 1. one of the four divine sons of HORUS and ISIS, the guardian of the lungs of the deceased. Hapi was portrayed by the head of a baboon in the stopper of the CANOPIC JARS used as part of the embalming processes in Egypt.

2. the ancient Egyptian manifestation of the NILE River's inundation. Hymns to Hapi speak of the river in cosmic terms, associated with the celestial stream in TUAT or the Underworld, but there are refrains of individual gratitude for the abundance of the yearly inundations as well. As the god Hapi, the Nile was normally depicted as a man with full breasts, symbolizing the nurturing aspects of the river, with its abundant affluvium and mud, which served to fertilize the fields of Egypt. Several rituals were held in Egypt to symbolize the return of Hapi in each year's inundation, and Nile FESTIVALS honored this manifestation of the river.

Hapnyma'at listed as Nyma'athap in some records, a queen of the 2nd and 3rd Dynasties, the

Hapi, the god of the Nile, as depicted in temple reliefs.

mother of DJOSER (2630–2611 B.C.) and the wife of KHA'SEKHEMWY, the last king of the 2nd Dynasty. She is mentioned in the biographical work of METJEN and in various seals and documents.

Hapuseneb   an official of the 18th Dynasty, serving in the reigns of TUTHMOSIS II (1492–1479 B.C.) and Queen-Pharaoh HATSHEPSUT (1473–1458 B.C.). He was the high priest AMON at THEBES and supervised many of the royal building projects of the era. He was also one of Hatshepsut's main supports during her reign.

Hardadef   called Djedefhor in some lists, a prince of the 4th Dynasty, the son of KHUFU (2551–2528 B.C.) and probably Queen MERITITES. Hardadef has long been considered one of the heirs to the throne along with his brother, BAUFRE, but did not succeed his father. He was buried in a large MASTABA beside the Great PYRAMID of Khufu, and his name appears in a royal CARTOUCHE in the WADI HAMMAMAT inscriptions. A famous literary text of that period had been attributed to Hardadef, a series of instructions, addressed to his son, Prince AUIBRE. Didactic in tone, these urge the prince to marry, to raise up "stout sons" and to remember that the "house of death is for life," an admonition concerning the resurrection of the dead. Hardadef may have authored other texts, and sages throughout Egypt's history quoted him.

harem   the harem, or household of lesser wives of the kings, called the *per-khenret* in ancient Egypt, was a highly organized bureaucracy that functioned primarily to supply male heirs to the throne, particularly when a male heir was not born to a ranking queen. The earliest evidence for a harem dates to the Early Dynastic Period and the tombs of several women found beside that of DJER (c. 2900 B.C.) at ABYDOS. These women were obviously lesser-ranked wives who lived in a harem. By the 6th Dynasty (2323–2150 B.C.), the institution was presided over by a queen and included educational facilities for the royal children and those of important officials.

In the reign of AMENHOTEP III (1391–1353 B.C.) in the 18th Dynasty, the harem was located at MALKATA, his pleasure domain on the western bank at THEBES. AKHENATEN had a harem at 'AMARNA (1353–1335 B.C.), and the administration of it has been well documented. Harems of this period had overseers and agricultural lands, cattle and weaving centers, which served as training facilities and as sources of materials, attached to them. Harems employed scribes, inspectors and craftsmen, as well as dancers and musicians to provide entertainment for royal visits.

Foreign princesses given in marriage to the Egyptian kings as part of military or trade agreements also resided in the harem. In some periods, harem complexes were built in pastoral areas, and older queens, or those out of favor, retired there. In RAMESSES II's reign, such an institution was near the FAIYUM.

The harem could be a source of conspiracy. The first recorded one dates to the Old Kingdom and the reign of PEPI I (2289–2255 B.C.). An official named WENI was called upon to conduct an investigation of a queen, probably AMTES. Because the matter was so confidential, Weni left no details as to the circumstances surrounding the investigation. A second harem intrigue occurred in the reign of AMENEMHET I (1991–1962 B.C.) of the 12th Dynasty. Amenemhet had usurped the throne, and an attempt was made on his life, as he recorded himself in his *Instructions* (also called *The Testament of Amenemhet*). The king fought hand to hand with his attackers, later stating that the plot to kill him stemmed from the harem before he named SENWOSRET I (the son to whom he addressed his advice) his co-ruler. Amenemhet died while Senwosret was away from the capital, giving rise to speculation that he was finally assassinated by another group of plotters. There is no evidence proving that he was murdered, but the *Tale of Sinuhe the Sailor*, dating to that period, makes the death a key story element.

The third harem plot, and the best documented, took place in the reign of RAMESSES III (1194–1163 B.C.) in the 20th Dynasty. The conspiracy was recorded in the Judicial Papyrus of Turin and in other papyri of the same period. Tiye, a minor wife of Ramesses III plotted, with 28 high-ranking court and military officials and an unknown number of lesser wives of the king, to put her son on the throne. A revolt of the military and the police was planned for the moment of Ramesses' assassination. With so many people involved, however, it was inevitable that the plot should be exposed.

The coup was not successful. Ramesses III is believed to have died of natural causes in the 32nd year of his reign. He commissioned a trial but took no part in the subsequent proceedings. The court was composed of 12 administrators and military officials. Five of the judges made the error of holding parties with the accused harem women and with one of the indicted men during the proceedings and found themselves facing charges for their indiscretions. Three of these judges lost their ears and noses as a result. One was forced to commit suicide and the last judge got off with a stern reprimand. The fate of Tiye is not given in the papyri. Twenty-eight of the important administrative and military officials and an unknown number of harem women were found guilty. Many of them were forced to commit suicide, including Tiye's son. The rest were presumably executed, although their fate is not clearly stated in the papyri.

Harkhaf an official of the 6th Dynasty serving PEPI II (2246–2152 B.C.). Harkhaf was a leader of expeditions below the cataract and was eventually named the governor of the region. On one such journey he captured a dancing dwarf and sent word to the king, who was a child at the time, that he was bringing home the little one as a gift. Pepi responded with a letter detailing the care and comfort to be extended to the dwarf. He stated that the official would be handsomely rewarded if the dwarf arrived "alive, prosperous and healthy." The governors of the various regions on the Nile were also notified by Pepi to offer hospitality and every assistance to Harkhaf and his cherished traveling companion.

Harmachis See SPHINX.

Harnedjheriotef the ninth king of the 13th Dynasty (c. 1760 B.C.), who is called the "Asiatic" in some lists. A statue and a scarab bearing his name were found in the DELTA and a stela commemorating his reign was discovered in Jericho.

Haroeris the Greek form of Hor Wer, meaning Horus the Great or Horus the Elder. This Horus was mentioned in the PYRAMID TEXTS and represented the sky. His eyes were the sun and the moon, epitomizing the eternal struggle between darkness and light, good and evil. In some records this form of Horus was called the Hor Nubti, the Vanquisher of SETH.

Harpokrates the greek form of Horpakhered, the ancient name for Horus the Child.

Harris Papyrus a document discovered in a tomb near DEIR EL-MEDINEH and dating to the reign of RAMESSES IV of the 20th Dynasty (1163–1156 B.C.). This is the most elaborate of the extant papyri, measuring 133 feet with 117 columns. The Harris Papyrus is famous for its detailed account of the donations made to temples by RAMESSES III, as well as a history of his reign. The document was obviously commissioned by his son and heir as part of his mortuary regalia and covers the three decades of his rule. It is now in the British Museum.

Harsaiset called Harsiesis by the Greeks, one of the most popular forms of the god HORUS. The name meant Horus, the son of ISIS.

Harsaphes the Greek form of Harshaf an ancient Egyptian ram-headed god. His cult center was at HERAKLEOPOLIS from the earliest times. A shrine was built for him there in the 1st Dynasty. His name was He Who Is on His Lake in some eras.

Hat Aten the ancient name for a villa of the god ATEN in the city of Aketaten, called 'AMARNA in modern times. Queen NEFERTITI moved out of the royal place of AKHENATEN (Amenhotep IV) (1353–1335 B.C.) and resided in this mansion soon after the death of one of her daughters. She remained in 'Amarna but was no longer part of the rituals of the new god.

Hathor an ancient Egyptian goddess revered throughout that nation's history. In the Early Dynastic Period and perhaps in the predynastic times, Hathor was the female consort of the "Bull of Amenti," the first deity of the necropolis. In later eras she became a sky goddess and was associated with other cults, called the daughter of RE' and the wife of HORUS. Actually, her name meant the "Temple of Horus", which denoted the great myth that Horus entered her mouth each night to rest there, emerging as the sun again in the morning. It was in this role that she assumed the designated role of the celestial cow. Hathor was pictured as a woman with cow's ears or as a cow in reliefs.

The SISTRUM, or *seses*, was her favorite instrument, and the goddess played it to drive evil from the land. The protectoress of women, Hathor was also the patron of love and joy. She was the mistress of song and dance and a source of royal strength. In the DAILY ROYAL RITES, as shown on temple reliefs, Hathor nursed the king or his priestly representative from her breasts, thus giving him the grace of office and the supernatural powers to protect Egypt. She was also the Queen of the West, a mortuary title that made her the protectress of the necropolis regions of the Nile. Many New Kingdom shrines were erected for her cult, and her most important temple was at DENDERA. The inscriptions give lavish accounts of this goddess, dating to the late periods.

Hathor was associated with several minor goddesses, who were also represented as cows. She was called the mother of Re' in some rites because she carried the sun between her horns. She was called the daughter of Re' because she was assimilated with the stars, which were Re''s children. Hathor is sometimes seen in tomb paintings as a cow with stars in her belly. Two of her other titles were the "Lady of the turquoise" and the "Lady of the sycamore." In every way Hathor was the benefactress of the nation,

Hathor, shown with the solar disk and horns, from a temple relief.

but the people recounted one event that marked her in a different manner. Re' supposedly became angry with mankind and sent Hathor to slay them. She performed her task with a vengeance, and Re' experienced a change of heart. He spread blood-colored beer on the ground to distract her, and drinking it, Hathor proceeded to become intoxicated, thus ending her rampage. A yearly festival held in her honor commemorated this myth.

Hatnub   called the "House of Gold," an alabaster quarry near 'Amarna. The quality of the stone and the yield of this site made it a favorite quarry of the Egyptians. An inscription dates the use of Hatnub to the reign of SNOFRU (2575–2551 B.C.) of the 4th Dynasty. An expedition sent to the site in that period obtained alabaster for the royal buildings.

Hatshepsut (Ma'atkare')   the fifth ruler of the 18th Dynasty (1473–1458 B.C.), the daughter of TUTHMOSIS I and Queen 'AHMOSE. As was common in royal families, Hatshepsut married her half-brother, TUTHMOSIS II. They had a daughter, NEFERU-RE'. By a minor wife, Isis, Tuthmosis II had a son, TUTHMOSIS III.

Tuthmosis II was suffering from a systemic illness and died in 1479 B.C., managing to appoint his harembred son his heir before dying. Hatshepsut stood as regent, because Tuthmosis III was quite young. They ruled jointly from all appearances until 1473, when Hatshepsut had herself declared pharaoh, assuming all of the office's masculine titles and masculine attire. She had considerable backing in the court, being able to count on the high priest of AMON, HAPUSENEB and other officials. It is possible that her daughter, Neferu-Re', married Tuthmosis III. This princess lived until the 11th year of Hatshepsut's reign.

Administering the affairs of the nation, Hatshepsut also began work on her temple at DEIR EL-BAHRI, on the western shore of the Nile at Thebes. Reliefs on the walls of that shrine portray her fictional divine birth as the daughter of Amon and her right to rule Egypt. She also laid claim to a previous coronation, an equally fictitious event that supposedly happened in the reign of her father, Tuthmosis I. The reliefs portrayed Tuthmosis I making her his co-ruler. At her side in this period was her chief steward, SENENMUT, who had entered the service of the royal family during the reign of Tuthmosis II. Other high-ranking officers of the court also aided her until Neferu's death and the downfall or death of Senenmut, in or before the 19th year of her reign. A few years later the Asiatic rebelled in the principalities of the east. During her reign, Egypt remained secure, and Hat-

Queen-Pharaoh Hatshepsut in a festival crown, exhibiting the radiant beauty for which she was famed in her own era.

shepsut initiated many building projects. Although she professed hatred for the Asiatics in her reliefs, Hatshepsut apparently did not sponsor punitive campaigns against them. When Kadesh and its allies started a revolt in c. 1458 B.C., Tuthmosis III led the army out of Egypt, and Hatshepsut disappeared. Her statues, reliefs and shrines were mutilated by the Tuthmosis camp in time, and her body was never found. There is some speculation concerning a female corpse discovered in the tomb of AMENHOTEP II. It is known that Hatshepsut's corpse was hidden from Tuthmosis' allies. The body discovered in Amenho-

tep's tomb had been embalmed in the royal manner, and the corpse was positioned so that its hands could hold the crook and the flail in the traditional mode. The head of this mummy, covered by long curls of brown hair, bears a striking resemblance to the Tuthmossid line.

Hauhet a member of the sacred pantheon called the OGDOAD in HELIOPOLIS. A female, this goddess was depicted with the head of a serpent.

Hauwareh the ancient Egyptian name for the channel called Bahr Yusef, leading from the Nile to the FAIYUM region.

Hawara a site in the FAIYUM, northwest of LA-HOUN, where the LABYRINTH of AMENEMHET III (1844–1797 B.C.) was discovered. The pyramid contained shafts, corridors, stone plugs and a burial chamber cut from a single piece of quartzite, estimated to weigh 110 tons. A funerary chapel was once located on the site but is now gone. (See BIAHMU.)

Hawawish the necropolis area of the ancient city of AKHMIN.

headrests the ancient Egyptian wooden or stone forms used instead of pillows on beds. The earliest

Alabaster headrest from Giza dating to the Old Kingdom. Egyptians used such headrests, made of wood and other materials, in all eras.

example is from the 3rd Dynasty (2649–2575 B.C.), although headrests were probably used earlier. Occasionally they were padded for comfort.

Hearst Papyrus   a medical document discovered at DEIR EL-BALLAS, several miles north of THEBES (a 17th Dynasty complex). The text, which dates to the 17th or 18th Dynasties, repeats much of what was found in the similar Ebers Papyrus, but adds other diseases and medical conditions. A section on the treatment of injured bones is especially interesting. Bites, ailments of the fingers and other medical matters are discussed in the documents. The Hearst Papyrus is now in the possession of the University of California at Berkeley.

heb   the ancient Egyptian word for festival. Its hieroglyph depicted a primitive reed hut on a bowl. The hut represented vegetation or reed growth and the dish was the insignia for purity. All festivals were celebrations of renewal in Egypt, a time in which the divine aspects of existence were manifested in ordinary life. (See SED.)

Hebenu   a site in Upper Egypt, perhaps occupied by the modern village of Zawiet el-Meitin, one of the cult centers of the falcon. Hebenu was among the oldest settlements in Egypt. A pyramid of undetermined date was discovered in the necropolis of Hebenu.

Heb Sed   See SED.

Hedjhekenu   a queen of the 4th Dynasty, a lesser ranked wife of KHEPHREN (2520–2494 B.C.) and the mother of Prince Sekhenkare'. She was buried in the pyramidal complex of Khephren.

Heh   See ETERNITY.

heka   See MAGIC.

Hekaib   an official of the 6th Dynasty serving PEPI II (2246–2152 B.C.) as a commander of troops and a leader of expeditions to the Red Sea coast, where ships were built for a voyage to PUNT. He was murdered at KUSER on the Red Sea, and his body was recovered by his son and brought to ASWAN for burial. (See TRADE.)

Heket   a goddess of fertility and regeneration in ancient Egypt, represented by a frog because such animals appeared when the Nile was inundating the land, hence served as heralds of the coming season of abundance. Heket was a protector of women in childbirth.

Heliopolis   called Iunu or Iunet Mehet, the "Pillar" or the "Northern Pillar" by the ancient Egyptians, and the On of the Bible. This city was spiritually and politically powerful in the Old Kingdom. It is situated in a suburb of modern Cairo today.

Heliopolis served as the early cult center for the god RE', in his form as Atum. The temple there was called Atum the Complete One, which denoted Re''s self-creation. The priests serving Re' had the reputation of being learned and politically important. There were also shrines for the PHOENIX and Re'-Harakhte, Atum, of the MNEVIS bull in the city. The ENNEAD, the pantheon which evolved out of the religious traditions of Heliopolis, was known and revered throughout Egypt. Heliopolis, in its association with Atum, was known as the PRIMEVAL MOUND. The cosmogonic teachings of the city remained influential for many centuries, and the kings began to assume their royal titles from Re' and from his powers.

Only a single OBELISK, taken from the temple of SENWOSRET I (1971–1926 B.C.) at Heliopolis, now marks the site of the once famed center of religion and learning. A STELA discovered at Heliopolis commemorated the offerings made by TUTHMOSIS III (1479–1425 B.C.). He provided gifts for the temple of Re' and renovated the city complex. Another stela gave an account of RAMESSES II of the 19th Dynasty (1290–1224 B.C), who also honored the city. Temple inscriptions dating to the 12th Dynasty (1991–1783 B.C.), or a copy of a text from that period, were also discovered on leather. The inscriptions are in the form of a poem and praise SENWOSRET I for the restoration of the temple there.

Helwan   a region opposite SAQQARA that supported predynastic settlements and cemeteries from the Early Dynastic Period. The walls of the burial chambers were made of brick and hard stone, believed to be the earliest use of stone for monumental architecture in ancient Egypt. Storerooms and stairs were incorporated into the design, and the ceilings had wooden beams and stone slab supports. The Helwan culture is classified by scholars as part of the Neolithic Age of Egypt.

Hemamiyeh   a predynastic site of ancient Egypt in the central Nile Valley. Settlements in the area are evidenced by the remains of circular houses there. The site dates to the Badarian cultural sequence (4500–4000 B.C.). (See EGYPT, PREDYNASTIC.)

HELIOPOLITAN TRIAD the gods sacred to Heliopolis: Ptah, Sekhmet and Nefertem.

hemet the ancient Egyptian word for wife, royal or commoner. (See QUEENS.)

Hemetch a serpent demon of ancient Egyptian mythology, depicted in the pyramid of WENIS of the 5th Dynasty (2356–2323 B.C.). This creature was one of many waiting to attack the unwary deceased in TUAT or the Underworld. The various mortuary texts provided the dead with incantations in order to placate Hemetch and its serpent companions. (See MORTUARY RITUALS.)

Hemiunu a prince of the 4th Dynasty, the son of Prince NEFERMA'AT and Princess Atet, and a nephew of KHUFU (2551–2528 B.C.). He served the latter as vizier and royal seal bearer. He also appears to have built Khufu's pyramid at GIZA, placing his own tomb at the base of the famed structure. So great was the esteem in which he was held that he was the only private person in Khufu's reign allowed to have a statue in his tomb. A statue now in Hildesheim, West Germany, depicts him as a robust, heavy-set man, a sign of his prosperity. He was involved in the reburial of the famous mortuary regalia of Queen HETEPHERES, Khufu's mother, when it was discovered that her original grave had been robbed.

Heneb an ancient Egyptian god of grain and agriculture, dating to the early eras. Heneb disappeared when OSIRIS assumed popularity and became one of Egypt's major patrons of harvests and grains in the later periods.

Henenu an official of the 11th Dynasty, serving MENTUHOTPE II (2061–2010 B.C.) as a steward and an overseer of herds. This was a position of importance in that period. He also collected taxes and represented the king in various regions. Henenu was honored with a tomb at DEIR EL-BAHRI, in the mortuary complex of Mentuhotpe II.

Henhenit a queen of the 11th Dynasty, wife of MENTUHOTPE II (2061–2010 B.C.), who was buried in the vast mortuary complex of the king at DEIR EL-BAHRI on the western shore of Thebes. She was not the mother of the heir.

hennu boat See BARKS OF THE GODS and SOKAR.

Hent a queen of the 12th Dynasty, the wife of SENWOSRET II (1897–1878 B.C.). She was buried near the king at LAHOUN. She was not the mother of the heir.

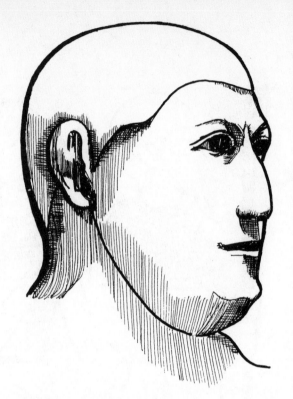

Head of Hemiunu, vizier of Khufu (Cheops), from a remarkable Old Kingdom statue.

Henutsen a queen of the 4th Dynasty, a wife of KHUFU (2551–2528 B.C.), and the mother of Prince KHUFU-KHAF and possibly of KHEPHREN, the fourth king of the dynasty. Her small pyramid was constructed beside Khufu's GREAT PYRAMID at Giza. She was listed in the INVENTORY STELA and in some modern accounts is said to be a daughter of Khufu.

Heptet an ancient Egyptian goddess believed to have been one of the cow nurses of OSIRIS during the mystical ceremonies of his resurrection. She was sometimes pictured as a woman with the head of a bearded snake.

Hepzefa an official of the 12th Dynasty serving SENWOSRET I (1971–1926 B.C.) and a NOMARCH of ASSIUT. He is noted for the contract that he had inscribed on his tomb walls concerning the mortuary offerings and rituals to be conducted on behalf at his death. Such wills or contracts were part of the funerary rites of ancient Egypt, and these inscriptions provide detailed information about the pact made between the deceased and the priests involved in such ceremonies. His wife, Princess SENNUWY, was

PRINCESS SENNUWY from a statue found at Kerma.

immortalized by a beautiful statue discovered at KERMA and now in the Museum of Fine Arts in Boston.

Herakleopolis called Ninsu, or Nen-nesut, by the ancient Egyptians, a city on the sites of modern Innasya-el-Medina, just south of the entrance to the FAIYUM. Herakleopolis was the capital of the 20th NOME of Upper Egypt and the cult center for the god HARSAPHES. It was also the home of the KHETY clan, the kings of the 9th and 10th Dynasties. During the reign of the Khetys, a canal linked Herakleopolis and MEMPHIS, but the city was lost by the clan when MENTUHOTPE II of the contemporary 11th Dynasty attacked it in 2040 B.C.

An Old Kingdom shrine and a temple of Harsaphes, from the 1st and 12th Dynasties, were discovered there. The necropolis of Herakleopolis was at GEBEL SEDMENT, where Old Kingdom tombs were discovered. Nothing remains of the city itself, which stood even into the Christian era.

Herihor and official of the 20th Dynasty who usurped the throne of ancient Egypt. Herihor served as high priest of AMON in the reign of RAMESSES XI (1100–1070 B.C.). He had come to THEBES as part of a contingent designed to put down a rebellion led by a former High Priest of Amon. PANHESY, in charge

of putting down the rebellion, placed Herihor in command of the city, and he promptly had himself named high priest and then became the VIZIER of both Upper and Lower Egypt. The king, feeble and easily manipulated, did nothing to halt Herihor's ambitions. When Ramesses XI died, thus ending the 20th Dynasty and the New Kingdom, Herihor and a confederate, SMENDES, divided up the land between them.

Heri-hor-Amon a city once located on the western bank of the Nile opposite the New Kingdom capital of THEBES. The name was translated as My Face Is Upon Amon. For a time Heri-hor-Amon served as the northern boundary of the Theban NOME. It disappeared over the centuries.

Herit a princess of the 15th Dynasty, the daughter of the HYKSOS APOPHIS (1585–1542 B.C.). Fragments of a vase bearing her name and rank were discovered in a Theban tomb, perhaps taken by the Egyptians when the Asiatic capital of AVARIS, the home of the Hyksos kings, surrendered to the army of 'AHMOSE I.

Hermonthis See ERMENT.

Hermopolis called Khemenu, the "Eight-towns," or *Per-Djehuty*, the House of Thoth, now el-Ashmunein. Hermopolis was the capital of the 15th NOME of Upper Egypt and a cult center for the god THOTH. The cosmogonic texts of the city, including the OGDOAD, had impact on the development of Egyptian religion. Ruins of an Old Kingdom shrine were discovered at Hermopolis, as well as an 18th Dynasty shrine restored by Queen-Pharaoh HATSHEPSUT (1473–1458 B.C.). Three monuments from the 12th and 19th Dynasties were also found. SETI I (1306–1290 B.C.) and RAMESSES II (c. 1290–1224 B.C.) of the 19th Dynasty built a temple there, with a PYLON, HYPOSTYLE HALL and four rows of columns. The temple was constructed out of materials taken from the destroyed city of Akhenaten at 'AMARNA, and contained many important reliefs of that temporary New Kingdom capital.

el-Hesseb Island a site at the First Cataract of the Nile at Aswan. Called Hesseh in some records, the island contained a stela from the 6th Dynasty.

Hetepheres I a queen of the 4th Dynasty, the wife of SNOFRU (2575–2551 B.C.) and the mother of KHUFU. Hetepheres' funerary regalia, including her furnishings, which were gold inlaid and covered with semiprecious stones, was moved to a new site by Khufu's vizier, HEMIUNU. Her mummy was not in its original sarcophagus, which was also reburied, having been stolen by grave robbers. Hetepheres was honored by Khufu and his court. Her furnishings and toilet articles, which include razors made of layers of gold, are famous and have provided scholars with details about the royal luxuries and the comforts of her era. The contents of her burial chamber are divided now between the Egyptian Museum in Cairo and the Museum of Fine Arts in Boston.

Hetepheres II a queen of the 4th Dynasty, the wife of Prince KEWAB, who was the rightful heir of KHUFU (2551–2523 B.C.). RA'DJEDEF took the throne after murdering Kewab, and he then married Hetepheres. Her daughter, Queen MERESANKH III, was honored by Hetepheres with an elaborate tomb in GIZA.

Hetephernebty a queen of the 3rd Dynasty, the consort of DJOSER (2630–2611 B.C.). She is believed to have been the daughter of KHA'SEKHEMWY, the last ruler of the 2nd Dynasty. She was much honored with her sister, Intakaes, in Djoser's court.

Hetepsekhemwy the first king of the 2nd Dynasty (2770–? B.C.). His name meant "The Two Mighty Ones Are at Rest", in reference to the gods HORUS and SETH. He is believed to have ruled for more than 35 years and was on Egypt's throne when an earthquake struck in the vicinity of BUBASTIS in the DELTA. It is possible that he was overthrown by his successor, RE'NEB.

He-Who-Looks-Behind-Himself a divine being, named Hraf-hef, who served as the ferryman on the celestial lake of TUAT, or the Underworld, in the

HE-WHO-LOOKS-BEHIND-HIMSELF the ferryman of Tuat or the Underworld.

mortuary myths. He also served as one of the FORTY-TWO JUDGES in the JUDGMENT HALLS OF OSIRIS, where the deceased had to prove their worthiness of eternal bliss. He-Who-Looks-Behind-Himself, called the "Great Fowler" in some texts, had to be convinced of the dead person's virtue. Litanies were provided by the priests to allow the deceased Egyptians to persuade this creature of their virtue, and magical ointments were also placed in the tombs to provide some protection from this irritable ferryman. The NET SPELLS included in the mortuary documents were to be used against He-Who-Looks-Behind-Himself.

Hibis an ancient capital of the Kharga OASIS. Its Egyptian name was Hebet, dating to the period of Persian occupation.

Hierakonpolis the site of the city called KEKHEN, named Hierakonpolis by the Greeks, to signify its long standing role as a cult center for HORUS. Some very important archaeological finds were made at Hierakonpolis, including the NA'RMER PALETTE. The predynastic tombs situated to the southeast contain wall paintings, with scenes depicting hunting, ships, animals and humans. A fort was found at Hierakonpolis, as well as a temple dating to the Early Dynastic or Old Kingdom historical periods. The SCORPION mace-head and the copper statues of PEPI I and his son (2289–2255 B.C.) were found, and a remarkable golden hawk's head.

Hieratic See LANGUAGE.

Hieroglyphs See LANGUAGE.

High Gates of Medinet Habu remarkable crenelated towers, designed with indented parapets or battlements, which graced the eastern and western sides of the complex built by RAMESSES III of the 20th Dynasty (c. 1194–1163 B.C.) on the western shore of THEBES. The gates of this mortuary complex, which was used as a villa by Ramesses while he lived, contained upper chambers that were extensively decorated and kept ready for the use of the king and his royal HAREM. (See MEDINET HABU.)

Hiku-Ptah See AIGYPTOS.

hippopotamus an animal considered good and evil by successive generations of ancient Egyptians. When in the form of Herpest, the hippopotamus was the symbol of HORUS' spiritual victory, an emblem displayed in the temple of EDFU, a center of the falcon cult. When in the form of Tuaret, the animal was

Blue faience hippopotamus. Lilies denote the creature's abode in the river.

considered benevolent, the protector of women in childbirth. Seth took the form of the hippopotamus in some legends.

Hippopotami were involved in the argument, which developed between Sekenenre'-TA'O II and the HYKSOS APOPHIS III in c. 1560 B.C. This confrontation led to the war between the Theban kings and the Asiatic invaders who had control of the eastern Delta.

Hittite Alliance an Egyptian text translated from cuneiform, describing the pact between Egypt and the Hittites, and recorded on the walls of the temple of KARNAK and at the RAMESSEUM. The alliance was formed between RAMESSES II (c. 1290–1224 B.C.) and the ruler of the Hittite empire. It was the result of a military confrontation in which both armies suffered near-defeat. The collision between the two states forged a reasonable approach to the division of territories and vassal nations. An unusual extradition clause was part of the alliance. A silver tablet was sent to Egypt by the Hittites requesting a truce, and Ramesses played host to a delegation from that land for the occasion. Two versions of the treaty are still in existence. (See EXTRADITION CLAUSE, MA'AT HORNEFRURE', BENTRESH STELA.)

Hittites See EGYPT and EGYPT AND THE EAST.

honey a symbol of resurrection in ancient Egypt, also considered a poison to ghosts, the dead, or evil spirits in a New Kingdom lullaby.

Hor (Awibre') the 14th king of the 13th Dynasty (c. 1760 B.C.), who left inscriptions on monuments from TANIS to the ELEPHANTINE. Details of his reign are obscure, but it is probably his likeness on the remarkable wooden statue that was discovered in a pyramid. This statue, bearing the outstretched arms

A rare wooden statue of Hor, depicting him as a ka.

of the KA sign on his head, is unusual because it depicts the ruler completely naked.

Horemhab (Dejserkheprure') the 14th and last king of the 18th Dynasty (1319–1307 B.C.), whose name means "Horus is in festival." Horemhab claimed NOME aristocracy. He was appointed chief of the army by TUT'ANKHAMUN, having risen through the ranks, and served as an escort for the boy king on one campaign. When Tut'ankhamun died, Horemhab remained in favor with AYA, his successor. Aya died without an heir, and Horemhab assumed the throne, marrying Queen MUTNODJMET, who had some connection to the royal family.

He marked his reign with extensive programs to restore order and to rebuild Egypt's decimated shrines. Tributes flowed into the land during his reign, and lesser city-states and nations sent delegations to keep cordial relations with him; he was called stern by contemporaries.

Horemhab moved his capital to MEMPHIS, deciding to rule from the northern site once again. Having put external affairs in order, he set about restoring Egypt's internal condition. He returned all of the properties of the temples to the rightful priests, lands which AKHENATEN had confiscated during the 'AMARNA period. He also dated his reign to the death of AMENHOTEP III in 1353 B.C., thus erasing the 'Amarna period and its aftermath. His reign was also marked by building programs, including restorations and the start of additions to KARNAK, Nubian shrines, a temple to PTAH and tombs at Memphis and Thebes. Horemhab restored the tombs of two of his predecessors, TUTHMOSIS IV and Tut'ankhamun, which had been invaded by robbers.

His most ambitious and beneficial act was the reestablishment of law and order in the Nile Valley. His famous edict concerning firm government was found on a fragmented stela in Karnak. The edict concerned itself with legal abuses taking place because of the laxity of Akhenaten's rule. Horemhab declared that officials of the state and provinces would be held accountable for cheating the poor, for pocketing funds, and for misappropriating the use of

Horemhab receiving gold collars from Tut'ankhamun, from the former's Saqqara tomb.

slaves, ships and other properties. The king singled out higher-ranked officials especially, promising swift judgments and the death penalty for offenses. The edict also announces the appointments of responsible men as VIZIERS and gives information about the division of the standing army into two main units, one in Upper Egypt and one in Lower Egypt. Horemhab not only published his edict throughout the land but took inspection tours to make sure that all of the provisions were being carried out in the remote areas as well as in the cities.

When he died without an heir, Horemhab appointed a military companion to succeed him, RAMESSES I. He built two tombs, one in SAQQARA and one in the Theban necropolis, the VALLEY OF THE KINGS. He was buried in Thebes.

Horus the Greek name for the Egyptian Hor, one of the oldest gods of the nation. The original form of Horus was that of a falcon (or hawk). He was a solar deity, considered a manifestation of the living king, as OSIRIS was the manifestation of the king in the afterlife. Early inscriptions depict Horus with his wings outstretched as a protector of the nation's kings.

In the Early Dynastic Period and in the Old Kingdom, the kings used the god's name as part of their royal titles. The SEREKH, the earliest of the king's symbols, depicted a falcon (or hawk) on a perch. As a result, devotion to Horus spread throughout Egypt, but in various locales the forms, traditions and rituals honoring the god varied greatly. In each NOME cult center Horus was known by a different epithet.

In the form of Horus the Elder, the Egyptian Horwer, Horus' eyes were the sun and the moon, and his battle with the god SETH epitomized the eternal struggle between darkness and light, good and evil. In this form, Horus was addressed as Haroeris by the Greeks. As Horus of Gold, Hor Nubti, the god was the destroyer of Seth. The Egyptian name Harakhtes meant "Horus of the Horizon," who merged with RE' at HELIOPOLIS, gradually losing identity and becoming Re'-Harakhte.

Horus the Behdetite, was a celestial falcon god with a great shrine at EDFU. When his father was attacked by Seth and his demons, this Horus soared up into the sky to scout the terrain for demons. Turning into a winged sun disk, he attacked Seth's forces and battled them, both on the earth and in TUAT, or the Underworld. The war was almost endless, but Horus proved victorious. As a result, the emblem of the sun disk became a popular symbol of Egypt. This Horus was also depicted in reliefs as the protector of each of Egypt's new dynasties. One of

Horus as a falcon, from a New Kingdom pectoral design. Inlaid stones and gold.

the most famous of the Horus images can be found in the statue of KHEPHREN, (520–494 B.C.) in the Egyptian Museum in Cairo. The falcon protects the head and shoulders of the seated king.

Hor-sa-iset, or the Greek Harsiesis, was one of the most popular forms of Horus in Egypt. This was the Horus, Son of ISIS. As a child the god was called Harpocrates by the Greeks and Horpakhered by the Egyptians, a much-loved deity. The Horus, Son of Isis had been sired by the dead Osiris and hidden on the island of CHEMMIS by his goddess mother. The goddess WADJET, the protector of Lower Egypt,

stayed on the island as a serpent to keep watch over the child and his mother. While Seth's henchmen sought out the divine pair, Wadjet kept them covered with reeds and papyrus. This Horus suffered many assaults while still a child but survived to attack Seth in vengeance for the death of Osiris. Victorious at last, having suffered the loss of his eye in combat with Seth, Horus became Horu-Sema-Tawy, the Horus, Uniter of the Two Lands. He established the authority of Osiris over the eternal realms and began the solar cycles of life on the Nile.

In the New Kingdom era, both Horus and Seth

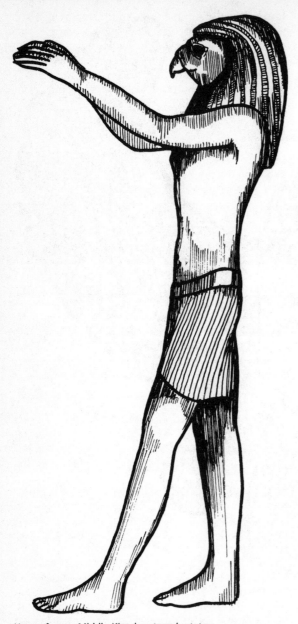

Horus, from a Middle Kingdom temple statue.

were depicted as the gods who brought the double crowns of Upper and Lower Egypt to the king. The Seth-Osiris-Horus legends continued throughout Egyptian history, varying with each new generation.

Horus Eye the symbol of the eye lost by the god Horus in his battle to avenge the death of his father, OSIRIS. Seth caused the loss of this eye, and the symbol was considered one of the most powerful in Egypt. The eye was restored by ISIS and was called the *wadjet* or "healthy eye." The eye was normally fashioned out of blue or green faience or from semiprecious stones and was popular.

Horus' Four Sons See CANOPIC JARS.

"Horus-in-the-Nest" a term used to designate the heirs to the throne of ancient Egypt when they were proclaimed in a public ritual. The title alludes to the relationship between the kings and the god. (See PHARAOHS.)

Hotepiriaket a priest of the 5th Dynasty serving in the sun temple of KAKAI (2446–2426 B.C.) at ABUSIR. The tomb of this priest contained a remarkable inscription in which he offers to commend anyone who leaves him a mortuary gift. Hotepiriaket, practical to the end, promises to intercede for anyone who leaves bread, beer, clothing, ointments, grains, etc., "in great quantity."

House of the Adorers called the House of the Adoratress in some records, a religious institution involved in land during the Ramessid era. Part of the priestly complex, this institution dedicated to AMON was mentioned in texts of the period.

House of Life See PER-ANKH.

Hua a mountain or high hill in the region below the cataract at Aswan, mentioned in several documents from the New Kingdom era. The kings, in recording their campaigns in NUBIA, stated that they went south to the height of Hua. The mountain was a navigational point for Egyptian ships.

Hudet a winged form of the ancient Egyptian god RE', called the "Splendor." The Hudet was incorporated into the cultic rituals at EDFU, commemorating the traditional myths about Horus. That falcon deity soared into the heavens to scout for the enemies of the king in these tales, becoming a winged disk in order to strike at the demons of evil. (See HORUS, RE', and SOLAR CULT.)

Hunefer Papyrus an important copy of the BOOK OF THE DEAD, dating to the reign of SETI I of the 19th Dynasty (1306–1290 B.C.). The text was composed in this era or copied from an earlier version. This papyrus is beautifully illustrated and is in the British Museum.

Huni the fifth king of the 3rd Dynasty (2599–2575 B.C.). He built a fort at the ELEPHANTINE and started

HORUS-IN-THE-NEST a princely heir, with feather of power and the *sere*, or lock of youth.

a pyramid at MEIDUM. His queen, MERESANKH I, was the mother of SNOFRU. KAGEMNI, the famous sage, was a VIZIER of Egypt during Huni's reign as the last king of his dynasty.

Hurbeit a site in the Delta, northeast of BUBASTIS, where the remains of a Ramessid-era temple were discovered. Building blocks with the seals of RAMESSES II (1290–1224 B.C.) were also found on the scene, dating the structure. Called Pharbaites by the Greeks, the site was also used as a necropolis for the remains of sacred bulls from the cultic observances.

Hurrians See EGYPT and EGYPT AND THE EAST.

Hyksos the name applied by MANETHO to the various Asiatic groups who entered into Egypt in the later part of the Middle Kingdom and in the Second Intermediate Period (1640–1532 B.C.). These Asiatics, called Hikau-Khoswet, Amu, A'am or Setetyu by generations of people on the Nile, were recorded by Manetho as having suddenly appeared in Egypt. He wrote that they raced on horse-drawn chariots to establish a tyranny in the land. They did enter Egypt, but they did not appear there suddenly, with what Manetho termed "a blast of God." The Hyksos entered the Nile region gradually over a series of decades until the Egyptians realized the danger they posed in their midst. Most of the Asiatics came across Egypt's borders for centuries without causing much of a stir. Some had distinguished themselves as leaders of the vast trading caravans that kept Egypt's economy secure. Others were supposedly veterans of the various units of Egypt's border police, started in the Middle Kingdom when AMENEMHET I (1991–1962 B.C.) constructed the WALL OF THE PRINCE, the series of fortresses that guarded the entrances into the land. If there was a single factor that increased the Asiatic population in Egypt, it was slavery, introduced as an institution in the Middle Kingdom. Asiatics came into Egypt either as captives or as immigrants eager for employment. As workers they were assimilated into Egyptian society. During the Second Intermediate Period, when several rival dynasties competed in the land, the Asiatics gained control of the eastern DELTA. Moving steadily southward and making treaties with some NOMES or subduing them with the aid of Egyptian allies, the Asiatics established themselves firmly. Only THEBES stood resolute against their expansion, and the Hyksos were denied most of Upper Egypt. Their hold on the western Delta is also poorly documented. For a time the nome clan of XOIS stood independent. The Xois Dynasty, the 14th, was contemporaneous with the 13th or the 15th Dynasties. While these rulers remained independent, the Asiatics moved around them and built their domain, with AVARIS, a site in the eastern Delta, as their capital.

In the beginning it appears as though Thebes and

HYKSOS depiction of a captive Asiatic found on the tomb walls of King Seti I of the 19th Dynasty.

Avaris managed to conduct their affairs with a certain tolerance. The Hyksos sailed to the cataracts to conduct trade without being hindered, and the Theban cattle barons grazed their herds in the Delta without incident. There were two separate royal lines of Hyksos in operation in the Delta, the 15th, called the "Great Hyksos," and a contemporaneous 16th Dynasty, ruling over minor holdings. The 15th Dynasty lasted from 1640–1532 B.C.

The Thebans were soon contesting the Asiatic's control, and the kings of the Theban 17th Dynasty (1640–1550 B.C.) began to harass their caravans and ships. APOPHIS, the Hyksos ruler who came to the throne in 1585, then sent an insult to Sekenenre'-TAO' II of Thebes and found himself in the middle of a full-scale war as a result. KAMOSE took up the battle when Sekenenre'-Ta'o died, using the desert OASES as hiding places for his army. This young Egyptian king was in striking distance of Avaris when he died or was slain. Apophis died a short time before him. 'AHMOSE I, the founder of the 18th Dynasty and the New Kingdom, took up the battle of his father and brother and laid siege to Avaris. The city fell to him in 1532 B.C., and the Asiatics fled to Sharuhen in Palestine, with the Egyptians in hot pursuit. When Sharuhen fell to the same Egyptian armies, the Hyksos ran to Syria. Thus Hyksos domination of Egypt was ended.

The Asiatics had come to the Nile to to absorb the material benefits of Egyptian civilization. In turn, the Hyksos introduced the horse and chariot, the *shaduf* (the agricultural implement that revolutionized the

HYPOSTYLE HALL OF THE RAMESSEUM a forest of stone pillars.

Egyptian farming techniques) and military weapons that transformed the armies of the Nile into formidable forces.

The Hyksos episode also brought an awareness to the Egyptians that they could not remain in isolation. That served as an impetus for later expansion. The Tuthmossid kings would march in conquest to the Euphrates River lands as declared instruments of vengeance for the Asiatic dominance of Egypt for more than a century.

Hymn of Rising   a ceremony conducted each morning in the palaces of ancient Egypt, in which courtiers and priests wakened the king and the gods with songs and hymns of praise. The lyrics of the songs were dedicated to NEKHEBET and WADJET, the protectors of the Upper and Lower Egypt. (See PHARAOH.)

hypostyle hall   a Greek term for a room or a chamber that has many columns. This architectural innovation developed gradually in Egypt, starting with the first outlined pillars placed by IMHOTEP in the courtyard of the STEP PYRAMID at SAQQARA (c. 2611 B.C.). These halls became a feature of Egyptian architecture, a reference to the reeds of the primordial marsh.

I

iban the Egyptian word for the highly prized ebony wood.

Ibhet a site near the Second Cataract of the Nile, south of ASWAN, where vast quantities of black granite were discovered by the ancient Egyptians. As far back as the 6th Dynasty the quarry there was known to the people of the Nile. By the Middle Kingdom era the Egyptians were active on the site. AMENEMHET III (1844–1797 B.C.) fought against the local Nubian inhabitants of Ibhet in the fifth year of his reign. Egypt valued the granite quarried at Ibhet and maintained a fortified operation there.

Ibi an official of the 6th Dynasty, a cousin of PEPI II (2246–2152 B.C.) and the son of the vizier DJAU. Ibi served as the Governor of the South, the Old Kingdom term for the later office of Viceroy of NUBIA. His clan was from Thinis, and the two queens ANKHNES-MERY-RE were his aunts. In his tomb, Ibi promised to "pounce" on anyone who entered his burial chamber with evil intentions. He announced as well his skill in all kinds of magical spells and curses and prominence at the court of TUAT, or the Underworld. Ibi's tomb at Deir el-Bebrawi near ASSIUT, served as the artistic inspiration for another Ibi, who lived in the 26th Dynasty and was buried at Thebes.

ibis the bird that the ancient Egyptians associated with the god THOTH, the scribe of the gods and the moon deity, the patron of writing, mathematics and language.

Ichneumon See MONGOOSE.

Idu called Idut in some records, an official of the 6th Dynasty, serving in the reign of PEPI I (2289–2255 B.C.). Idu was a supervisor of mortuary priests, concerned with the ceremonies and maintenance of the pyramidal complexes of KHUFU, and KHEPHREN. This position gives evidence of the lasting importance of the pyramidal tombs and of the rituals conducted there in honor of the deceased kings. Some temples and pyramidal complexes evolved into small cities, in which everyone was engaged in the funerary rites conducted within them.

ikh called *akh* in some texts, the mental and spiritual attributes of all human beings, which the ancient Egyptians believed were transformed at death into a transparent, luminous essence. (See MORTUARY RITUALS.)

Ikernofert called Ikhernofret in some records, an official of the 12th Dynasty, serving in the reign of SENWOSRET III (1878–1841? B.C.). Ikernofert was a supervisor of mining operations and the chief of artisans for royal projects. An aristocrat, he served as a treasurer for his NOME and prepared a portable shrine for the god OSIRIS, as well as other monuments and temples. Ikernofert's main work was the restoration of the ABYDOS temple complexes. His mortuary stela recounts his long period of service and his accomplishments.

Ikudidy an official of the 12th Dynasty, serving in the reign of SENWOSRET I (1971–1926 B.C.). Ikudidy led a caravan and military units into the oases regions of the western, or Libyan Desert, something never attempted in previous eras. The Egyptians had explored much of the Arabian or eastern desert, taking many natural resources from that region, but Ikudidy led the first military campaign in the west. He was buried at ABYDOS after long and faithful service to the crown.

Imhotep (Imouthes in Greek) an official of the 3rd Dynasty who served four kings of Egypt but is best known for his role as vizier and high priest of PTAH during the reign of DJOSER I (2630–2611 B.C.).

Statue of Imhotep.

A commoner by birth, Imhotep rose through the ranks of officials in the temple and in the court through his natural talents and dedication to the ideals of the nation. Imhotep was called the "Son of Ptah" as the high priest of the temple of the god, but he did not limit his interests or abilities to religious matters alone. He was a gifted poet, architect and priest-physician, equated with the god Asclepios by the Greeks. The greatest achievement of Imhotep, the one which stands as a living monument to his genius and his faith in eternity, was the STEP PYRAMID at SAQQARA. He built the complex as a mortuary shrine for Djoser, but it became a stage and an architectural model for the spiritual ideals of the Egyptian people.

The Step Pyramid was not just a single pyramidal tomb but a collection of temples, chapels, pavilions, corridors, storerooms and halls. Fluted columns engaged in or attached to the limestone walls emerged from stone according to his plan. Yet he made the walls of the complex conform to those of the palace of the king, according to ancient styles of architecture, thus preserving a link with the past.

Imhotep's didactic texts were well known in later eras, as were his medical writings. The Greeks honored him, and during the Roman period the emperors Tiberius and Claudius inscribed their praises of the vizier on the walls of their Egyptian temples.

Imi called Yem in some records, a queen of the 11th Dynasty, the mother of MENTUHOTPE IV (1998–1991 B.C.). She was listed as the royal mother in an inscription discovered at the WADI HAMMAMAT. Nothing else is known of her life.

Imsety a son of Horus who assisted with the mummification of OSIRIS and was therefore designated as a protector and guardian deity of the CANOPIC JARS.

incense in Egyptian, *senetjer*, an important material for religious and royal rites in every era. Several types of incense were used in rituals in temples and in royal cult celebrations. Myrrh, a red form of incense imported from PUNT, was considered the most sacred and was reserved for the most solemn of rituals. Frankincense, or *olibanum*, was also favored. Incense was a purifying element in all Egyptian observances, as well as the material used to bestow honor upon the gods and the dead or living kings.

Ineni an official of the 18th Dynasty serving in the reigns of TUTHMOSIS I (1504–1492 B.C.) and Queen-Pharaoh HATSHEPSUT (1473–1458 B.C.). Ineni probably began his career in the reign of AMENHOTEP I, the predecessor of TUTHMOSIS I. He was one of the most famous architects of his age, supervising the various projects at KARNAK. Under his direction a protective wall was erected around Amon's Theban shrine. Pylons were added, as well as doors made of copper and gold. Ineni provided flagstaffs for Karnak, fashioned out of cedar and ELECTRUM. An aristocrat of his NOME, Ineni served in many capacities over the years, loyal to both the crown and the god Amon. He was buried at Thebes.

Inhapi a princess of the 18th Dynasty, and a lesser wife of 'AHMOSE I (1550–1525 B.C.). Inhapi was the mother of Princess Ahmose Hent Tenemu.

Ini (Shepseskare') the fourth king of the 5th Dynasty (2426–2419 B.C.). He is mentioned in the TURIN CANON and in the SAQQARA list, but nothing is known about his reign.

ink See SCRIBES.

Instructions for Merikare' See KHETY.

Intef See INYOTEF.

Intef an official of the 12th Dynasty, serving in the reign of AMENEMHET I (1991–1962 B.C.). Intef was a leader of expeditions for the king, as well as an aristocrat and a prophet of the temple of the god MIN. During his term of office he set out with expeditions into the area of the WADI HAMMAMAT and into other desert regions on the eastern side of the Nile. This era was one in which Egyptians began to take strict account of their natural resources with the purpose of exploiting all available sites.

Intef an official of the 18th Dynasty, serving in the reign of TUTHMOSIS III (1479–1425 B.C.). From the Thinite nome of Upper Egypt, Intef accompanied Tuthmosis in his military campaigns as a personal attendant. He became the royal herald as a result of his dedication and loyalty and also administered the various Libyan OASES on the western desert. His mortuary stela is in the Louvre.

Intiu the ancient Egyptian name for the predynastic inhabitants of the Nile Valley. The name Intiu is translated as "Pillar People."

Inventory Stela See SPHINX.

Inyotef I (Sehertawy) called the "Elder," the founder of the Theban 11th Dynasty (r. 2134–2118 B.C.) He is listed as the son of Mentuhotpe I. Inyotef I faced a divided Egypt and began to unite the southern nomes so that Upper Egypt could remain independent of the Herakleopolitans who ruled from that city over a limited domain as the kings of the 9th and 10th Dynasties. Inyotef was buried in THEBES, where his mortuary complex was accorded much honor by his royal successors. (See KHETY.)

Inyotef II (Wah'ankh) the second king (2118–2069 B.C.) of the Theban 11th Dynasty. It is believed that he was a younger brother of INYOTEF I. He led an army against the Heraklopolitan allies of ASSIUT, who had ravaged the city of Thinis, desecrating tombs there. Inyotef captured the Thinite nome, but he did

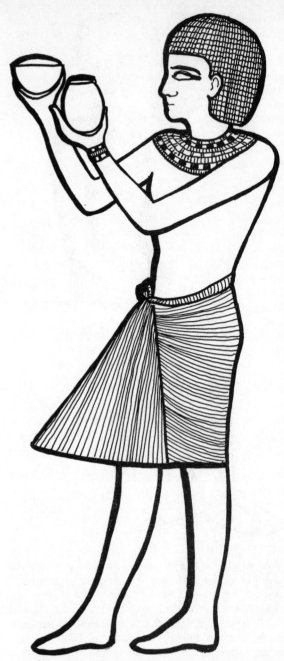

Inyotef II, as depicted in a Theban funerary relief from Upper Egypt.

not push his campaigns northward, being content to trade with the Herakleopolitans and to maintain the integrity of Upper Egypt without further conflicts. His queen was Neferukayet. Inyotef II is mentioned in the Westcar Papyrus. He was also depicted on a mortuary stela with two of his dogs. (See KHETY.)

Inyotef III (Nakhtnebtepnufer) the third king (2069–2061 B.C.) of the Theban 11th Dynasty, who was probably old when he came to the throne of Upper Egypt. He held on to the regions gained by his Theban predecessors, who had to defend their lands, especially the city of Abydos, in the face of repeated Herakleopolitan assaults. His name was inscribed on the walls at Gebel Silsileh. His queen was Aoh (called Yah in some lists), the mother of MENTUHOTPE II. His daughter, Neferu, married the heir. A second queen in his reign was Henite. (See KHETY.)

Inyotef V (Nubkheperre') the first king of the second group of the 17th Dynasty at Thebes (1640–1635 B.C.). A warrior, Inyotef V left campaign inscriptions on the temple walls at COPTOS, ABYDOS, THEBES and at other sites. He is noted for his Coptos Decree, an edict issued during his reign to punish a nobleman named Teti, who was guilty of the theft of temple materials. This Inyotef was also involved with the *LAY OF THE HARPER*, a famous mortuary text. The anthropoid coffin of Inyotef V is in the British Museum, and his diadem is in Leiden. His queen, SOBEKEMSAF, was much revered in the 18th Dynasty.

Cartonnage mask from the tomb of Inyotef V, from Thebes.

Inyotefoker an official of the 12th Dynasty, serving in the reign of SENWOSRET I (1971–1926 B.C.). He was the governor of the pyramidal complex of AMENEMHET I. In some records he is also listed as a vizier of Amenemhet. He and his wife were buried in Thebes.

Ipuki an official of the 18th Dynasty, serving in the reign of AMENHOTEP II (1427–1401 B.C.). Ipuki was a sculptor involved in the royal building projects of the New Kingdom. He was buried at Thebes near Deir el-Bahri on the western shore of the Nile, in a tomb shared by a fellow artist named NEBAMUN.

Iput a queen of the 6th Dynasty, the wife of PEPI II (2246–2152 B.C.), the daughter of PEPI I or NEMTYEMZAF. She was buried near Pepi II at Saqqara, and her tomb contained a version of the PYRAMID TEXTS.

Ipuwer See ADMONITIONS OF IPUWER.

Ipwet a queen of the 6th Dynasty, the wife of TETI (2323–2291 B.C.), and the mother of PEPI I. She is believed to have been the daughter of Wenis, the last ruler of the 5th Dynasty. She was buried at SAQQARA.

iri-pat the ancient Egyptian term for a noble, used in reference to predynastic eras normally.

Isetnofret a queen of the 19th Dynasty, the daughter of RAMESSES II (1290–1224 B.C.) and the wife of his successor, MERNEPTAH. Isetnofret was the mother of SETI II. She was buried at Thebes.

Ished Tree a sacred tree of life in ancient Egypt, thought to be the *Balanites aegyptiaca*. The goddess SESHAT and the god THOTH wrote the names of the new kings of Egypt at their accession to the throne on the leaves of this tree. (See PERSEA TREE.)

Isis the most enduring and beloved goddess of ancient Egypt, whose cult was especially popular in Greek and Roman periods. Her name means simply "the seat," ESET in Egyptian, altered to the present form by the Greeks during the Ptolemaic period. She was also called Weret-Hekau, the "Great of Magic," and Mut-netjer, the Mother of the Gods. Isis' cult began in the Delta, but as the Osirian mythology developed she became his wife. Isis is supposed to have civilized Egypt with her king husband, teaching agricultural techniques and medicine to the people. She is also credited with having instituted marriage in the Nile Valley.

When OSIRIS was slain by the god SETH, Isis began

Isis, the beloved goddess, as depicted in a temple relief from the New Kingdom.

a journey to discover his remains. The coffin in which Osiris had died was engulfed by a fragrant tamarisk tree, and Isis soon found the box and the divine body in Byblos, where it had floated on the Mediterranean Sea. Many adventures accompanied this search. Returning to the swamplands of Buto, Isis hid the coffin of Osiris, but Seth discovered it and dismembered the body into 14 pieces. Isis still persisted and began to look for the parts of her husband. She found all of his remains except for his phallus, which had been devoured by a Nile fish, called oxyrhynchus by the Greeks.

Fashioning the body together, Isis became impregnated by the corpse. She then fled to CHEMMIS, where WADJET, the goddess protector of Lower Egypt, kept her and her newborn child, HORUS, safe from the agents of Seth. In time, however, Seth attacked Horus as a serpent, and Isis had to call upon the god RE' for aid. Re' sent THOTH to be her ally. He was able to exorcise the poison from the child by reciting the cosmic disasters that would result if the baby did not recover. Horus was cured and then given to the local inhabitants to be cared for and to become their leader, thus uniting the cultic myth to the real populace of the Delta.

In another adventure the goddess Isis discovered the secret name of the god Re', viewed always as the most potent of magical weapons. She thus provided herself with additional powers, all of which she dedicated to the service of mankind. Isis was the epitome of the selfless woman, the charmer, the endurer, and the loyal spouse. To the Egyptians of every generation she was the fertile plain, the arbor and the gentle pool of life-giving waters. The cult of Isis endured because she fostered honor, courage and loyalty in the people, while evoking sympathy, admiration and a recognition of injustice. The cult of Isis continued until the reign of the Emperor Justinian. The Greeks and the Romans were entranced by the mysteries of her rituals and by the exotic, charming image which she conveyed. The goddess was normally portrayed as a woman with a throne on her head, the spelling of her name in Egyptian, and a symbol connected to the Osirian ceremonies. In many eras she was depicted as wearing the sun disk, set between the horns of a cow. In this presentation she was sometimes associated with the goddess Hathor.

Isis a queen of the 18th Dynasty, a concubine of TUTHMOSIS II (1492–1479 B.C.). The mother of TUTHMOSIS III, Isis was elevated to the rank of royal mother during her son's reign. A commoner, she had been a member of Tuthmosis II's HAREM before given birth to the heir.

Israel Stela See MERNEPTAH.

Istnofret a queen of the 19th Dynasty, a second ranked wife of RAMESSES II (1290–1224 B.C.). She bore several sons and daughters: MERNEPTAH (Ramesses' heir), Prince KHAEMWESET, BINTH-ANATH and others. Istnofret replaced Queen NEFERTARI sometime after the dedication of the temples at ABU SIMBEL. Nefertari may have died or may have retired into the harem. Istnofret soon followed her, going possibly to the retired harem enclave near the FAIYUM region.

Itawy a royal estate at Lake Moeris, called the "Great Lake" by the ancient Egyptians. This estate, was watered by a branch of the NILE, the BAHR YUSEF, through a sophisticated series of dikes and sluices. (See FAIYUM.)

Itj-tawy the capital of the 12th Dynasty on the site of modern Lisht.

Ity the last king of the 10th Dynasty of Herakleopolis, probably the obscure successor of MERIKARE', whose reign was cut short by the arrival of the armies of MENTUHOTPE II (of the Theban 11th Dynasty), who took HERAKLEOPOLIS, putting an end to the dynasty and to the First Intermediate Period of Egypt in 2040 B.C.

Iuni an official of the 19th Dynasty, serving in the reigns of SETI I (1306–1290 B.C.) and RAMESSES II (1290–1224 B.C.) as the Viceroy of NUBIA. Iuni followed the famed Amenemope in this office, indicating that he might have been a member of the AMENEMOPET clan. He was originally from the FAIYUM.

Iusas called Nebhethotep in some lists, the divine wife of the god Tem, depicted at times as the single parent of the gods SHU and TEFNUT, and sometimes considered only the female aspect of Tem. Iusas was portrayed as a woman holding a scepter and an ANKH, wearing the vulture headdress and a horned disk.

Iumeri an official of the 5th Dynasty, serving in the reign of IZI (2416–2392 B.C.) as a scribe in the royal archives. He then became a steward of the royal lands and a prophet of the enduring mortuary cult of KHUFU at his GIZA pyramid.

Izezi (Djedkare') the eighth king of the 5th Dynasty (2388–2356 B.C.), credited with using the quarries and mines at the WADI HAMMAMAT and SINAI regions. His name was inscribed also at the WADI MAGHARA and WADI HALFA. A royal son, Prince Remkuy, was Izezi's heir, but he died before he could assume the throne. Izezi was buried at southern SAQQARA.

Izi (Neuserre') the sixth king of the 5th Dynasty (2416–2392 B.C.), who is famed for his solar temple at ABU GOROB and his pyramid at ABUSIR. His tomb reliefs depict his military campaigns against the Libyans on the western desert and against the Asiatics in the SINAI. He also left an inscription at the WADI MAGHARA concerning the mines in that region. His queens were Reputneb and Khentikus, buried near him at Abusir.

J

jackal called *auau* or *a'asha*, the ancient Egyptian manifestation of the gods ANUBIS and DUAMUTEF. It is believed that the jackal was portrayed in religious inscriptions in order to placate the animal, who was a destroyer of desert grave sites. This is an example of the practice of sympathetic MAGIC.

Joppa, Capture of a famous literary work of the New Kingdom, preserved in the Papyrus Harris 500, now in the British Museum. The *Capture of Joppa* concerns a man identified as General Djehuty, who served TUTHMOSIS III (1479–1425 B.C.). Djehuty meets with a Joppa official, expressing a desire to defect to

The jackal, one of the most alluring symbols of ancient Egypt.

128

the enemy. Djehuty, instead, takes his counterpart prisoner and puts his own soldiers into covered baskets, delivering them to Joppa. The people of Joppa believe that the baskets contain the spoils of war. Once inside the city, the Egyptians leap out and slay the guards at the city gates. Some scholars see a similarity in the story of the Trojan Horse and in the tale of Ali Baba. Objects from the Theban tomb of Djehuty are housed in various European collections. The best-known object, a golden bowl, is in the Louvre in Paris.

Judicial Papyrus of Turin   a document that gives an account of the harem conspiracy of the 20th Dynasty in the reign of RAMESSES III (1194–1163 B.C.). (See HAREM.)

Judgment Halls of Osiris (or Judgment Halls of the Dead)   a mythical site located in Tuat or the Underworld and the destination of all Egyptians beyond the grave. OSIRIS, as the Lord of the Underworld, sat in judgment on all souls, aided by the goddess MA'AT, the FORTY-TWO JUDGES and other mortuary deities. The site and the rituals of the halls were depicted in various mortuary papyri. In some of these papyri they are called the "Hall of the Two Ma'at Goddesses." The entrance to this area was called the *Khersek-shu*, and the entire edifice was in the shape of a coffin. Two pools were normally

SCALES OF MA'AT from the Judgment Halls of Osiris, with attendant deities seeing that each heart is weighed against the true spirit of the land.

included in the setting, both of which were mentioned in various versions of the BOOK OF THE DEAD.

Osiris, accompanied by the Forty-Two Judges, demonlike creatures, reviewed the lives of the dead Egyptians and absolved them or condemned them. The Declarations of Innocence, also known as the NEGATIVE CONFESSIONS, and the names of the individual judges were provided to the deceased by the priests so that the corpse could effectively plead its case. Other AMULETS, spells and incantations were also available.

Gigantic scales were present in the hall, and there divine beings assisted the god THOTH in keeping an account of the deceased's heart, which determined his or her worthiness to enter the realms of eternal bliss. While the weighing of the heart took place, the corpse addressed a series of prayers and commands to his heart and recited various mortuary formulas. This effort resulted in an exact balance between the heart and the Feather of Ma'at, the symbol of righteousness. If the deceased did not manage to balance with the feather, he or she was thrown to AMEMAIT, the Destroyer, who waited by the scales to claim its victims.

Additional aspects of the ritual in the Judgment Halls of Osiris included the naming of the stones and bolts of the doors, so that they would open onto the realms of eternal happiness. The deceased was then faced with bargaining rituals with the ferryman who rowed the dead to the domain of Osiris. HE-WHO-LOOKS-BEHIND-HIMSELF was the ferryman, a testy individual. All of the rites conducted in the hall and in the ceremonies indicated a recognition of human free will and personal responsibility for moral actions during one's life on earth. Such recognition, however, was immediately countered by the use of MAGIC, which the Egyptians believed would guarantee a quick passage to the eternal fields of happiness. This ritual of death and judgment remained in Egyptian religious beliefs as eternity remained the goal of the Egyptians throughout their history. The tribunal in the Judgment Halls of Osiris and its everlasting consequences were part of the framework upon which the Egyptians based their continual spiritual aspirations. (See *Ma'at-Kheru*.)

Jupiter Ammon   See SIWA OASIS.

K

ka the ancient Egyptian term for a spiritual essence, which existed alongside human form and yet maintained individuality. The *ka* was an astral being, and yet it was also considered the guiding force for all human life. The Egyptians recognized the "double" aspect of the *ka*, and in some statues the kings were depicted as having an identical image at their side. While existing with the human being during his or her mortal life, the *ka* was the superior power in the realms beyond the grave. The term for death was "Going to one's *ka*" or "Going to one's *ka* in the sky."

Kas resided in the divine beings as well, and pious Egyptians placated the *kas* of the gods in order to receive favors. They served as guardians of places at the same time. OSIRIS was always called the *ka* of the Pyramids. The *ka* entered eternity before its human host, having served its function by walking at the human's side to urge kindness, quietude, honor and compassion. Throughout the life of the human, the *ka* was the conscience, the guardian, the guide. After death, however, the *ka* became supreme. Kings thus laid claim to multiple *kas*. RAMESSES II of the 19th Dynasty announced that he had over 20 such astral beings at his side.

The *ka* was also viewed as a part of the divine essence that nurtured all existence in the universe. KHNUM, the god who molded mankind from clay in each generation, was depicted on many occasions as forming identical figures on his potter's wheel, one being the human and the other the *ka*, which was the vital element of eternal life in Egyptian beliefs. For this reason the *ba* was supposed to stay close beside it in the grave. The rituals of embalming were performed in order to prepare the corpse for the arrival of the *ka*, as well as for resurrection. The *ka* came to visit the mummy of the deceased, bringing the *ba*. For those commoners who could not afford the elaborate embalming processes, simple statues of themselves in mummified form were provided by the mortuary priests to attract the *ka* to their grave sites. (See BA, MORTUARY RITES and ETERNITY.)

Ka'a a predynastic king who preceded Na'rmer in campaigning for unity in Egypt. (See EGYPT, PREDYNASTIC.)

Ka'aper Statue a rare wooden life-size statue of an ancient Egyptian official from the 5th Dynasty who was buried in a mastaba at SAQQARA. When the statue of Ka'aper was taken out of its mastaba chambers, the modern Egyptian workmen on the site exclaimed that he was the Sheik el-Beled, the local mayor. The ancient Ka'aper was a high priest and a lector in the Memphite temple.

el-Kab the modern name for the ancient city of Nekheb, one of Egypt's earliest settlements. El-Kab is located north of EDFU in Upper Egypt. At one time it was the capital of the southern kingdom. Nekhen, called HIERAKONPOLIS, was located directly across the Nile from el-Kab. A predynastic royal residence was built on the site, and the mud-brick ramparts can still be seen there. El-Kab was the cult center for the goddess NEKHEBET, one of the two deities who served as protectors of Upper and Lower Egypt. During the New Kingdom era the city was politically and military strategic.

El-Kab's inhabitants rose against 'AHMOSE I (c. 1550–1525 B.C.) when he started the 18th Dynasty. He had to return from the siege of the HYKSOS city of AVARIS in order to put down the rebellion. The nomarchs of the region were energetic and independent. Their rock-cut tombs on the northeastern section of the city display their vivacious approach to life and to death. A temple honoring the goddess NEKHEBET was erected by TUTHMOSIS III (c. 1479–1425 B.C.) of the 18th Dynasty. RAMESSES II of the 19th Dynasty (c. 1290–1224

KA'APER STATUE   a rare wooden statue from the 5th Dynasty.

B.C.) refurbished the site. A lion statue was also discovered at el-Kab.

Kadesh, Battle of

In the fifth year of his reign, RAMESSES II (c. 1290–1224 B.C.) marched out of the Egyptian outpost on the eastern desert, with the Regiment of Amon and with three other regiments soon to follow. He commanded an army of more than 20,000 men and made his way into the valley of the Orontes River, overlooking Kadesh, the troublesome city-state, whose king had warred on Tuthmosis III of the 18th Dynasty for more than a decade.

There was no sign of the Hittite army, and Ramesses, anxious to begin a siege of the city of Kadesh, drew away from his main units and discovered himself facing the horde of the Hittite host, under command of King Muwatallis. Ramesses had taken the word of two Asiatics of the region that no Hittites were present, not knowing that Muwatallis had sent them to lure the pharaoh into a trap.

Maneuvering deftly, the Hittite king set up a series of ambushes and stood in a position to demolish the Egyptian forces. Ramesses, however, had taken two Hittite spies captive as well and had beaten word of the enemy forces out of them. He sent for the Regiment of Ptah, which was nearby and scolded his officers for their laxity in assessing the situation. While this was happening, however, the Hittites were cutting their way through the Regiment of Re', sealing the trap. Hundreds of Egyptians began to arrive at Ramesses' camp in headlong flight. The Hittite cavalry was close behind, followed by yet another enemy cavalry amounting to some 2,500 chariots.

The Regiment of Amon was swamped by the panicking soldiers who had suffered the first losses and raced northward in the same disorder.

Ramesses, undaunted, brought calm and purpose to his small units and began to slice his way through the enemy in order to reach his southern forces. With only his household troops, with a few officers and followers, and with the rabble of the defeated units standing by, he mounted his chariot and discovered the extent of the forces against him. He then charged the eastern wing of the assembled foe with such ferocity that they gave way, allowing the Egyptians to escape the net which Muwatallis had cast for them. The Hittite king watched the cream of his command fall before Ramesses, including his own brother. The Hittites and their allies were being driven into the river, where they drowned.

Within the abandoned Egyptian camp, the enemy soldiers were looting, and they were taken by surprise by a group of Ramesses' own soldiers and slain. Ramesses gathered up the victorious unit, determined to stand his ground until reinforcements arrived. The Hittite king, in turn, threw his reserves of 1,000 chariots into the fray, but he was unable to score against Ramesses and his men. Then the banners and totems of the Regiment of Ptah came into

sight and both camps knew that the Egyptian reinforcements had arrived. The Hittite cavalry was driven
into the city, with terrible losses, and Muwatallis
withdrew.

Ramesses did not capture Kadesh, but the battle
resulted in a treaty between the Hittite and the Egyptians, cemented by a marriage. (See BENTRESH STELA,
HITTITE ALLIANCE, PENTAUR, POEM OF, and EXTRADI-
TION CLAUSE.)

Kagemni   an Egyptian official, possibly two separate individuals, who lived in the reigns of HUNI
(2599–2575 B.C.), the last king of the 3rd Dynasty,
and SNOFRU (2575–2551 B.C.), the first king of the 4th
Dynasty. The literary Kagemni is remembered for his
didactic writings, which were concerned in particular
with social behavior and with right attitudes towards
rulers and one's fellow human beings. A copy of his
texts was found in the Papyrus Prisse. Another Kagemni, or perhaps the same individual, was an overseer of the tomb complex of KHABA, one of Huni's
predecessors on the throne. He is reported to have
held the office of VIZIER for Snofru as well.

Kakai (Neferirkare')   the third king of the 5th Dynasty (2446–2426 B.C.), believed to be the brother of
SAHURE'. He is mentioned in the PALERMO STONE and
was the monarch involved with a court official named
WESHPTAH, accidentally striking him while conducting a tour of a building. The official's tomb proudly
announces that accident. Another courtier of Kakai's
reign noted in his mortuary inscriptions that he was
favored enough to kiss Kakai's foot, rather than remain prostrate on the floor. Kakai was active in
military campaigns. His tomb complex was at ABUSIR.

Kalabsha   a site south of the First Cataract, where
a fortress and a temple were erected in the 18th
Dynasty, probably by TUTHMOSIS III (1479–1425 B.C.).
The site was much expanded in the Greek and Roman periods. Like Philae, the temple was moved
north when the Aswan Dam was opened, so that it
would not be flooded.

Kamose (Wadjkheperre')   the 15th and last king
of the 17th Dynasty of Thebes (1555–1550 B.C.), the
son of Sekenenre' TA'O II and Queen AHHOTEP, and
the brother of 'AHMOSE I. He was raised at DEIR EL-
BALLAS, north of Thebes, where the kings of this
dynasty had a royal residence. During his youth he
was also trained by his grandmother, Queen TETISH-
ERI.

The Thebans went to war with the HYKSOS, the
Asiatics, when APOPHIS (Hyksos king of the contem-

Cartonnage mask from the tomb of Kamose at Thebes.

porary 15th Dynasty at AVARIS) insulted Sekenenre'
Ta'o. The Thebans gathered an army and set out to
rid Egypt of the foreigners and their allies. Kamose
came to the throne when Sekenenre' Ta'o died suddenly, and took up the war with enthusiasm. It is
possible that he married his sister, 'AHMOSE-NEFER-
TIRY, who became the wife of 'AHMOSE I when Kamose died. The elders of Thebes counseled against
the war, stressing the fact that Avaris and Thebes
had been at peace for more than a century. Kamose
rebuked them, however, declaring that he did not
intend to sit between an Asiatic and a Nubian (the
Hyksos in Avaris and the Nubians below the First
Cataract). He vowed to renew the war and to rid
Egypt of all alien elements.

The Thebans made use of the horse and chariot,
introduced into the Nile Delta by the Hyksos when
they began to swarm into Egypt in the waning days
of the Middle Kingdom and in the Second Intermediate Period, c. 1640 B.C. The Thebans had lightened
the chariots for manueverability and had trained troops
in their use. At the same time, Kamose had enlisted
a famous fighting machine to his cause. When he
went into battle the MEDJAY troops were at his side.
These Nubians loved hand-to-hand combat and served
as scouts and as light infantry units, racing to the
front lines of battle and striking terror into the hearts

of their enemies. Kamose caught the Hyksos off guard at NEFRUSY, a city north of Hermopolis, with a cavalry charge. After his first victory, he moved his troops into the oasis of Baharia, on the Libyan or western desert, and struck at the Hyksos territories south of the FAIYUM.

At the same time he sailed up and down the Nile in Upper Egypt to punish those who had been traitor to the true Egyptian cause. One Teti was singled out for particularly harsh treatment, and Kamose was proud that he had left the man's wife to mourn him on the banks of the Nile. Some documents indicate that Kamose was within striking distance of Avaris when he died of natural causes or battle wounds. Apophis had died just a short time before. Stelae discovered at Karnak provide much information about this era.

The mummy of Kamose was discovered, but it was so poorly embalmed that it disintegrated when it was taken out of its coffin. This warrior king had no heirs, and he was succeeded by his brother, 'Ahmose I, who ended the war by ousting the Hyksos and started the famed 18th Dynasty and the New Kingdom.

Karnak   the modern name for ancient Nesut-Towi, the "Throne of the Two Lands," or Ipet-Iset, "The Finest of Seats," site of the temple of the god AMON at Thebes. Karnak remains the most remarkable religious complex ever built on earth. Its 250 acres of temples and chapels, obelisks, columns and statues built over 2,000 years incorporate the finest aspects of Egyptian art and architecture into "a great historical monument of stone." Karnak was originally the site of a shrine built in the Middle Kingdom, but many rulers of the New Kingdom repaired or refurbished the structure. It was designed in three sections. The first one extended from the northwest to the southwest, with the second part at right angles to the original shrine. The third section was added by later kings.

The plan of the temple to Amon, evident even in its ruined state, contained a series of well-coordinated structures and architectural innovations, all designed to maximize the strength of the stone and the monumental aspects of the complex. Karnak, as all other major temples of Egypt, was graced with a ramp and a canal leading to the Nile, and this shrine also boasted rows of ram-headed sphinxes at its entrance. At one time the sphinxes joined Karnak and another temple of the god at LUXOR, to the south.

The entrance to Karnak is a gigantic PYLON (370 ft wide), which opens onto a court and to a number of architectural features. The temple compound of RAMESSES III of the 20th Dynasty is located here, complete with STATIONS OF THE GODS, daises and small buildings to offer hospitable rest to statues or barks of the various deities visiting the premises. The pylon entrance, unfinished, dates to a period after the fall of the New Kingdom. Just inside this pylon is a three-chambered shrine erected by SETI I of the 19th Dynasty for the barks of the gods AMON, MUT and KHONS.

The shrine of Ramesses III of the 20th Dynasty is actually a miniature festival hall, complete with pillars and elaborate reliefs. The so-called "Bubastite Portal," built in the Third Intermediate Period, is next to the shrine. The court is completed by a colonnade, also from a late period, and a portico erected by HOREMHAB, the last ruler of the 18th Dynasty.

The second pylon in the structure, probably dating to the same dynastic era, refurbished by the kings of the 19th Dynasty, is graced by two colossi of RAMESSES II, and a third statue of that king and his queen-consort stands nearby. This second pylon leads to a great hypo-style hall, the work of SETI I and Ramesses II, where 134 center columns are surrounded by more than 120 papyrus bundle type pillars. Stone slabs served as the roof, with carved stone windows allowing light to penetrate the area. The Ramessid kings decorated this hall with elaborate reliefs. At one time there were many statues in the areas as well, all removed or lost now. Of particular interest are the reliefs discovered in this hall of the Poem of Pentaur, concerning military campaigns and cultic ceremonies of Egypt during its imperial period. The HITTITE ALLIANCE is part of the decorative reliefs.

The third pylon was erected by AMENHOTEP III of the 18th Dynasty. The porch in front of the pylon was decorated by Seti I and Ramesses II. At one time four obelisks stood beside this massive gateway. One remains, dating to the reigns of TUTHMOSIS I and TUTHMOSIS III of the 18th Dynasty. A small area between the third and fourth pylons leads to precincts dedicated to lesser deities. The fourth pylon, erected by Tuthmosis I, opens into a court with Osiride statues and an obelisk erected by HATSHEPSUT. Originally part of a pair, the obelisk now stands alone. The second was discovered lying on its side near the sacred lake of the temple complex. Tuthmosis I also erected the fifth pylon, followed by the sixth such gateway, built by Tuthmosis III. These open onto a courtyard, a Middle Kingdom sanctuary, the Djeseru-djeseru, the holy of holies. Statues and symbolic insignias mark this as the core of the temple. The sanctuary now visible was built in a late era, replacing the original one. A unique feature of this part of Karnak is the sandstone structure designed by Hatshepsut. She occupied these chambers on occasion and provided the walls with reliefs. Tuthmosis III added a protective outer wall which was inscribed with the "annals" of his military campaigns. This is the oldest part of Karnak, and much of it has been destroyed. The memorial chapel of Tuthmosis III is located just behind the court and contains chambers, halls, magazines and shrines. A special chapel of Amon is part of this complex, and the walls of the area are covered with elaborate reliefs that depict exotic plants and animals, duplicate in stone of the flora and fauna that Tuthmosis III came upon in his Syrian and Palestinian military campaigns and called the "Botanical Garden."

A number of lesser shrines were originally built beyond the limits of the sanctuary, dedicated to PTAH, OSIRIS, KHONS and other deities. To the south of the sixth pylon was the sacred lake, where the barks of the god floated during festivals. A seventh pylon, built by Tuthmosis III, opened onto a court, which has yielded vast amounts of statues and other relics from the New Kingdom. Three more pylons complete the structure at this stage, all on the north-south axis. Some of the pylons were built by Horemhab, who used materials from AKHENATEN's now destroyed temple. A shrine for Khons dominates this section, alongside other monuments from later eras. A lovely temple built by SENWOSRET of the 12th Dynasty was discovered hidden in Karnak and has been restored. A shrine for the goddess MUT, having its own lake, is also of interest.

Karnak represents faith on a monumental scale; that each Dynasty of Egypt made additions or repairs to the structures gives evidence of the Egyptians' fidelity to their beliefs. Karnak remains as a mysterious enticement into the world of ancient Egypt. One Karnak inscription, discovered on the site, is a large granite stela giving an account of the building plans of the kings of the 18th Dynasty. A second stela records work being done on the Ptah shrine in the enclosure of the temple of Amon. The Karnak obelisks vary in age. Some are no longer on the site, having been moved to distant capitals, but those that remain provide insight into the massive quarrying operations conducted by the Egyptians during the New Kingdom. The Karnak pylon inscriptions include details about the New Kingdom and later eras and provide scholars with information concerning the rituals and religious practices as well as the military campaigns of the warrior kings of that period.

A Karnak stela, a record of the gifts given to Karnak by 'AHMOSE I, presumably in thanksgiving for a victory in the lands beyond Egypt's eastern border, is a list of costly materials. 'Ahmose I provided Karnak and the god Amon with golden chaplets, lapis lazuli, gold and silver vases, tables, necklaces, plates of gold and silver, ebony harps, a gold and silver sacred bark, and other offerings.

The Karnak King List, discovered in the temple site, is a list erected by TUTHMOSIS III of the 18th Dynasty. The document contains the names of more than 60 of ancient Egypt's rulers, not placed in chronological order. (See ART AND ARCHITECTURE and KING LISTS.)

Kawit a royal companion of MENTUHOTPE II of the 11th Dynasty (2061–2010 B.C.). Her burial chamber, part of the king's vast mortuary complex at Deir el-Bahri, on the western shore of the Nile at Thebes, contained elaborate and stylish scenes of her toilet rituals. Her sarcophagus listed Kawit as the "Sole Favorite of the King," a distinction repeated on the other sarcophagi in the complex.

Kebawet a goddess of early eras in ancient Egypt, called the deity of "cold water libations," an element considered vital to eternal bliss in Tuat or the Underworld. She did not remain popular for a long period and did not have an extensive cult.

Kebir (Qaw el-Kebir) a site on the eastern shore of the Nile north of ASSIUT, where tombs of Middle Kingdom NOMARCHS were discovered. Three elaborate mortuary complexes contained sophisticated architecturally elements, including porticos, terraces, halls and shrines.

Keeper of the Door to the South a title for the governors of ASWAN, the administrators of NUBIA, below the First Cataract of the Nile.

Keepers of Time See ASTRONOMY.

Kemsit called Kemsiyet and Khemsait in some lists, a royal companion of MENTUHOTPE II of the 11th Dynasty (2061–2010 B.C.). She was buried in the king's vast mortuary complex on the western shore of the Nile at Thebes. Kemsit's sarcophagus lists her as the "Sole Favorite of the King," a title that she shared with the other female occupants of the complex.

Kenamon an official of the 18th Dynasty, serving in the reign of AMENHOTEP II (1427–1401 B.C.). Kenamon was a steward of the royal estates in the northern territories, having been introduced into court service by his mother, a royal nurse. He distinguished himself in this role and held other positions in the temple and in government. His tomb is a popular tourist attraction at Thebes.

kenbet   See GOVERNMENT and LEGAL SYSTEM.

Kerma   a trading post of ancient Egypt located near the Third Cataract of the Nile. The fortress dates to the reign of Amenemhet I of the 12th Dynasty (1991–1962 B.C.). Kerma was the capital of the short-lived nation of KUSH, which was defeated by the 12th Dynasty Egyptians.

Kewab   a prince of the 4th Dynasty, the son of KHUFU, (2551–2528 B.C.). Prince Kewab was married to Princess HETEPHERES II and was the father of Queen MERESANKH III. Kewab was probably the rightful heir to the throne, and either died prematurely or was murdered by RA'DJEDEF. He is depicted as a portly man in the walls of Queen Meresankh's tomb. His own grave was situated in the eastern section of the Giza necropolis, beside the Great Pyramid.

Kha   an official of the 18th Dynasty serving in the reigns of AMEN-HOTEP II (1427–1401 B.C.) and his successors, TUTHMOSIS IV and AMENHOTEP III. Kha was an architect who supervised the vast necropolis projects of these rulers. He is reported to have lived at DEIR-EL-MEDINEH.

Kha'ba   the fourth king of the 3rd Dynasty (2603–2599 B.C.). His name was found on stone bowls in NAQADA and in the tomb of SAHURE. He is believed to have built the pyramid at Zawiet el-Aryan, in the desert of GIZA.

Kha'emweset   a prince of the 19th Dynasty, the son of RAMESSES II (1290–1224 B.C.) and Queen IST-NOFRET. He took part in a campaign in NUBIA when still a lad, and later entered the temple of PTAH in MEMPHIS. There he designed a burial for the Bulls of APIS. While stationed in Memphis, Khaemwest visited SAQQARA and began a commission for a historical study of the necropolis site, thus earning himself the modern nickname of the "Egyptologist Prince." He was very popular among his contemporaries, and his mortuary cult lasted until the Roman era, when he was incorporated into several Roman legends, mentioned in the demotic literature of the period.

khaibit   the ancient Egyptian word for the shadow of a soul, deemed to be a spiritual essence that was capable of freeing itself at the moment of death. All Egyptians desired to see their *khaibit* roaming free beyond the grave. No explanation of the actual role or purpose of the shadow has been recorded. (See ETERNITY and MORTUARY RITUALS.)

Khakheperresonbe's Complaints   a literary work composed in the late 12th Dynasty or in the Second Intermediate Period. The only copy, dating to the 18th Dynasty, is now in the British Museum. Khakheperresonbe was a priest of HELIOPOLIS, who wrote on the popular theme of national distress, carrying on a debate with his own heart and receiving counsel for silent courage in the face of general apathy. There is a similarity between this text and the *DEBATE OF A MAN WITH HIS SOUL.*

Khama'at   a princess of the 4th Dynasty, the daughter of MENKAURE' (2490–2472 B.C.) and the wife of a courtier, PTAH-SHEPSES. This courtier had been raised in the company of the royal children. Both Ptah-Shepses and the princess were married at SAQQARA.

Khamerernebty I   a queen of the 4th Dynasty, the wife of KHEPHREN (2520–2494 B.C.) and probably the mother of KHAMERERNEBTY II. She was buried in a large tomb east of Khephren's pyramid at Giza.

Khamerernebty II   a queen of the 4th Dynasty, the daughter of KHEPHREN and probably Queen KHAMERERNEBTY I and the wife of MENKAURE' (2490–2472 B.C.). She was the mother of Prince Khunere. A statue of her, discovered in the king's mortuary complex, is now in the Museum of Fine Arts in Boston.

Khamet   an 18th Dynasty official serving in the reigns of TUTHMOSIS IV (1401–1391 B.C.) and AMEN-HOTEP III (1391–1353 B.C.) as a court treasurer and as the overseer of the royal building projects. He was buried at Thebes, and his tomb is decorated with inscriptions concerning the military campaigns of his era.

khamsin   an Arabic term describing a storm condition of modern Egypt, probably dating to earlier periods. Arising in February or March and lasting about two months, with southern or southwesterly winds, and diurnal in nature (rising in velocity throughout the day hours), the *khamsin* brings sand into residences and into the shrines on the Nile. The storm period was long viewed as a season of contagious diseases and illnesses. The *khamsin* ended when the "sweet breath of the north wind" brought welcome relief.

Khamudi (Swoserenre') the last king of the HYK-SOS 15th Dynasty (1542–1532 B.C.). He saw the disintegration of the Hyksos empire. His obelisk was discovered near AVARIS, and he is listed in the TURIN CANON. Khamudi obviously negotiated the exit of the Hyksos from Egypt after the successful seige of Avaris by 'AHMOSE I of the contemporaneous 17th Dynasty at Thebes.

Kharga See HIBIS and OASIS.

Kha'sekhemwy the fifth king of the 2nd Dynasty (c. 2640 B.C.), who is believed to have been the actual uniter of Upper and Lower Egypt. He is known for a large granite door jamb in the temple at HIERAKON-POLIS, sculpted with vast reliefs. He was probably known originally as Kha'sekhem, adding the last portion to his name to celebrate his victories. He was a vigorous military campaigner. A statue of him in the Egyptian Museum at Cairo demonstrates the first evidence of the use of hard stone in the Early Dynastic Period. He also built mortuary complexes at SAQQARA and ABYDOS. His queen was HAPNYMA'AT, the mother of DJOSER.

Khendjer (Userkare') the 17th king of the 13th Dynasty (date unknown) whose reign remains obscure. Khendjer's tomb was built in the southern part of SAQQARA. The tomb was cased in limestone and contained stairs and passages leading to a quartzite burial chamber. He is possibly the king mentioned in the Louvre stela.

Khenemsu an official of the 12th Dynasty, he served SENWOSRET III (1878–1841? B.C.) as a royal treasurer and as a leader of mining expeditions, an important part of that dynasty's attempts to rejuventae Egypt's economy. He was responsible for raids in the Sinai and for the mining of copper and malachite from that region.

Khensuhotep a sage of the 18th Dynasty, noted for his *Maxims*. Religious in nature, these adages urged the Egyptians of his era to remember that the gods honored silent prayer and decreed right behavior in all creatures. The *Maxims* were popular in the New Kingdom and in later periods.

Khentemsemeti an official of the 12th Dynasty, serving AMENEMHET II (1929–1892 B.C.) as a royal treasurer entrusted with important expeditions to the mine and quarry regions. This was part of the Middle Kingdom's policy of economic restoration. Khentem-semeti claimed that he distinguished himself on such a journey into the area around the ELEPHANTINE.

Khentkawes a queen of the 4th Dynasty, the daughter of MENKAURE' or possibly of RA'DJEDEF and the wife of SHEPSESKHAF (2472–2467 B.C.). It is possible that she then married USERKAF, the founder of the 5th Dynasty, as she has been called the mother of that dynasty. She is listed as the mother of KAKAI in an Abusir papyrus. Khentkawes was buried in an unfinished tomb at GIZA, a sarcophagus shaped structure faced with limestone.

Khepesh See KHOPESH.

Khephren (Ra'kha'ef) the fourth king of the 4th Dynasty, the son of KHUFU and probably Queen HENUTSEN, who ruled from 2520–2494 B.C. He is known for his pyramid at GIZA, where he also erected the Great SPHINX. Khephren was supposedly hated by his contemporaries for his autocratic nature.

A statue in the Egyptian Museum in Cairo depicts Khephren in the protective shadow of a falcon, a monument to the artistic achievements of the period. He was mentioned in the TURIN CANON. His wife was KHAMERNEBTY I. Queen MERESANKH III bore him Prince Nebemakhet; Queen Hedjhekenu bore him Prince Sekhemkare', and Queen Persenti' bore Prince Nekaure', who became famous for his will, and Menkaure', who succeeded Khephren after a brief reign by an unknown.

khert-neter the ancient Egyptian name for a cemetery or necropolis. The name is translated as "that which is beneath the god."

khet an ancient Egyptian cultic insignia used in AMULETS or as mystical signs. This emblem was associated with GEB and OSIRIS.

Khety the name of the Herakleopolitan kings, called Achthoes or Aktoy in some lists, who came to power in 2134. The 9th and 10th Dynasties, they ruled a portion of Egypt until 2040 B.C., when MENTUHOTPE II captured HERAKLEOPOLIS. There were 17 Herakleopolitan kings listed in the records, with three of them, called Khety, rather well known. They were as follows:

Knety I (Meryibre') the founder of the dynasties and a Herakleopolitan NOMARCH who marched with his army to unite the NOMES of Egypt after the collapse of the Old Kingdom. He controlled a vast region in time, although Asiatics had entered the eastern Delta, and the Theban Inyotef kings did not surrender their lands of Upper Egypt. This Khety inscribed his name at ASWAN. He was called "cruel" by his contemporaries.

Khety II (Nebkaure'?) the Herakleopolitan king believed to have given audience to the legendary ELOQUENT PEASANT. His name was inscribed at the WADI TUMILAT.

Khety III (Wah'kare') the author of the *Instructions for Merikare'*, a didactic text that offers historical documentation of the First Intermediate Period. It was designed to serve as a guide for his son, Merikare', who succeeded him. The *Instructions* mention the raid on Thinis, conducted by Khety's ASSIUT nome allies, an assault which ravaged much of the city and resulted in the desecration of graves there. That incident so aroused the Thebans that they began their military efforts to bring about the demise of the Herakleopolitan line. Khety did not live to see the Theban victory, although he was reported to have ruled approximately 50 years.

Khian the third king of the HYKSOS 15th Dynasty (date of reign unknown) one of the "Great Hyksos." Khian was a vigorous monarch, and his monuments were discovered in both Upper and Lower Egypt. Scarabs and seals bearing his name were found as far way as Crete.

Khnum the ancient Egyptian god of the ELEPHANTINE, who assumed the form of a ram and was considered a deity of creation. His name meant "Moulder," and he was accompanied by two consorts, SATIS and ANUKIS. On his potter's wheel, Khnum molded the great cosmic egg and fashioned OSIRIS and all other living creatures. The Nubians, who worshipped a similar god, DEDUN, incorporated Khnum into their religion during the New Kingdom. Khnum was associated with DJOSER of the 3rd Dynasty (2630–2611 B.C.) in a tale about a period of famine in the land. The god was normally depicted as a man with a ram's head, wearing wavy horns, plumes and the solar disk and uraeus.

Khnumhotep Clan a remarkable NOME family of BENI HASAN during the 12th Dynasty. Khnumhotep I, whose name meant "Khnum Is Content," was appointed governor of his province by AMENEMHET I (1991–1962 B.C.) and accompanied the ruler on a military campaign against border tribes. His sons Nakht and Amenemhet also became court officials. His daughter Beket married and gave birth to a son named Khnumhotep II. This grandson of the original

The god Khnum, at his potter's wheel near the Elephantine, forming mankind.

monarch or aristocrat, wed a princess from another nome, and their descendants inherited the combined territories.

Khnumt called Khnumyt and Khnumit in some records, a princess of the 12th Dynasty, the daughter of AMENEMHET II (1929–1892 B.C.). Princess Khnumt was buried at Dashur, where a cache of her royal jewels was discovered. These necklaces and crowns are remarkable for their beauty and exquisite workmanship.

Khokha a site on the Nile's western shore across from the city of THEBES, which served as a necropolis for early eras in Egypt. Tombs dating to the 6th Dynasty were discovered there, graves of the local nomarchs who maintained their own cemetery sites and their own mortuary traditions. Several of the tombs are beautifully illustrated. Tombs from the 18th and 19th Dynasty were also discovered at Khokha.

One is of particular interest for its reliefs depicting the arts and artisans of the era.

Khons the ancient Egyptian god of healing. His name originally meant "Navigator" and he was associated in many eras with the god THOTH. Khons' cult began in THEBES, and he became the son of AMON as that deity's popularity grew. Another major shrine of his cult was at Ombos. Khons designed a statue of himself to be taken to the sick or the possessed. The Egyptians flocked to his shrine for healing, and the statue is commemorated by one famous legend of the New Kingdom, the tale recorded on the BENTRESH STELA. Khons was portrayed as a young man with a hawk's head or as a lad with the traditional lock of youth, mummy wrappings and the scepter of the god PTAH. When addressed as Khons Neferhotep of Karnak he was the exorcisor and the deity of love

KHONS   the handsome young god, from a New Kingdom statue.

and fertility. When associated with the cult of the god Re', he was known as Khonsure.

khopesh (*khepesh* in some lists) the sickle-shaped sword with a sharp outer edge used by the Egyptians of the New Kingdom in MILITARY campaigns. The weapon was introduced by the HYKSOS invaders of the Second Intermediate Period or influenced by the design of their own weapons.

Khufu (Cheops) the second king of the 4th Dynasty (2551–2528 B.C.), the son of SNOFRU and Queen HETEPHERES I and the builder of the Great PYRAMID at GIZA. He ruled a unified country and had able relatives to serve as his administrators. He was married to Queen MERITITES, but she was not the mother of KHEPHREN, his eventual heir. Prince Kewab was born to her, and there is some belief that HETEPHERES II was also her child. Queen Henutsen, another wife, bore him Prince Khufuhaf and probably Khephren. There was another queen and a separate line from which RA'DJEDEF (Khufu's son who murdered the heir KEWAB) descended. HARDEDEF and BAUFRE' were also Khufu's sons, possibly by Meritites, and they served in various administrative posts.

Only a small state of Khufu remains, now in the Egyptian Museum in Cairo. He is associated with the legendary tale that was found in the WESTCAR PAPYRUS, dating to a later period, an obvious copy of an earlier document. Actually a series of ribald stories, the text depicts Khufu's father, Snofru, sailing on a pleasure boat with his harem ladies clad only in fish nets. The prophecy concerning the 5th Dynasty kings was supposedly recited in the presence of Khufu. He is quoted as telling one story himself in this text, concerning DJOSER.

Khusebek an official of the 12th Dynasty, serving SENWOSRET III (1878–1841? B.C.) as a military commander who accompanied the king on punitive campaigns in Nubia and in Syria. His mortuary stela provides information about the military activities of his era. The stela was discovered at ABYDOS.

Khuy an official of the 6th Dynasty, serving PEPI I (2289–2255 B.C.). Khuy was a nomarch whose daughters, the two ANKHNESMERY-RE's, became the wives of Pepi. His son DJAU served PEPI II as vizier. Khuy was the grandfather of both PEPI II and NEMTYEMZAF.

King Lists the various texts that list the rulers of Egypt in chronological order or have cartouches designating their titles and eras. These kings lists include the following:

A miniature statue of Khufu, builder of the Great Pyramid. The only likeness known in existence, it is displayed in the Egyptian Museum, Cairo.

Abydos List inscribed by SETI I (1306–1290 B.C.) in his temple in Abydos, containing 80 kings' names. The list is still there, and it has some intentional omissions, including the Egyptian rulers of the Second Intermediate Period, the HYKSOS rulers of the same era, HATSHEPSUT, AKHENATEN and his immediate successors down to HOREMHAB. RAMESSES II, Seti's heir had the list copied, and this is now in the British Museum.

Saqqara List a text containing 58 names, taken from the tomb of an official of Ramesses II. The names are in retrograde order, staring with Ramesses and ending with Menes. It is now in the Egyptian Museum in Cairo.

Karnak List inscribed on the festival hall of TUTH-MOSIS III (1479–1425 B.C.), east of the main temple at Karnak in Thebes. This list contains the names of 62 kings, not all in order and not all inclusive. It is now in the Louvre.

The Turin Canon considered the most trustworthy and valuable list, compiled in the reign of RAMESSES II (1290–1224 B.C.). It is extremely fragmentary, and a number of the king's names are no longer decipherable. It appears to have contained every king from Menes to Ramesses II, in the correct order, with the year totals for each reign. This canon is now in the Egyptian Museum, Turin, Italy. Other lists are in various collections around the world.

kites the name applied to the goddesses ISIS and NEPHTHYS in the Osirian cult in the late eras but also representing the ancient Egyptian women who were hired to accompany or greet the coffins of the deceased at funerals. These were professional mourners who raised a din at the sight of the body. They were inspired by the LAMENTATIONS OF ISIS AND NEPHTHYS when they mourned the body of the god OSIRIS.

Kiya a queen of the 18th Dynasty, a lesser-ranked wife of AKHENATEN (1353–1335 B.C.), listed as "The Favorite." She held considerable power even during Nefertiti's time, and many representations of her were found at 'Amarna. Kiya is possibly a foreign princess, Tadukhipa, sent originally from Mitanni as a wife of AMENHOTEP III, Akhenaten's father. She died a short time before Akhenaten, and was buried with a considerable funerary treasury. Her body and those of her children (a daughter and possibly one or two sons) have not been discovered.

knots considered magical by the Egyptians, depending upon the way they were tied and located. A row of knots on a rope was viewed as a protective talisman or AMULET. Some Egyptians wore sets of knots on ropes to keep them safe from enemies, and on mumimes the beaded knots on the chests of the corpses were designed as shields.

kohl the Arabic term for the ancient Egyptian cosmetic used to adorn the eyes. Dried remains of kohl have been discovered in tombs, accompanied by palettes, pots and tubs for application.

KITES   the women mourners who from prehistoric times accompanied the corpse to the burial site.

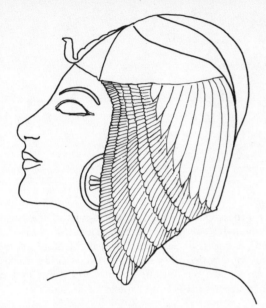

Kiya, a lesser ranked wife of Akhenaten.

Kom Ombo a site north of ASWAN, where a temple dating to the 12th Dynasty was totally renovated by the kings of the Ptolemaic period. The temple was dedicated to the cults of the gods HORUS and SOBEK. The nearby Silsileh quarries were in use in many historical eras. Sobek's cult led to the mummification of a large number of crocodiles there in later periods.

Kom Ushim the ancient site in the FAIYUM, south of Cairo, which was used extensively by the kings of the 12th Dynasty (1991–1783 B.C.) as retreats and residences.

Konosso a high water island at Philae, south of ASWAN. Konosso was used by the 18th Dynasty kings (1550–1307 B.C.) as a staging point for the Nubian expeditions of the New Kingdom. An inscription from the reign of TUTHMOSIS IV (1401–1391 B.C.) gives an account of one such Nubian adventure.

el-Kula a site on the western shore of the Nile north of HIERAKONPOLIS and el-Kab. The remains of a step pyramid were discovered there, but no temple or offertory chapel was connected to the shrine. The pyramid dates to the Old Kingdom.

Kuser a port on the Red Sea, in the region called SEWEW opposite COPTOS. Kuser was used extensively by the Egyptians, who operated shipbuilding facilities there for the expeditions to the land of PUNT.

Kush See NUBIA.

kyphi the Greek form of the Egyptian *kapet*, a popular incense or perfume of ancient Egypt, composed of many ingredients. The formulas varied considerably and were mentioned in medical texts. *Kyphi* was also used as a freshener for the air and clothes (even though some of the formulas included the excrement of animals). As a mouthwash it could be mixed with wine. *Kyphi* was sometimes used as incense in the Ptolemaic period, and formulas were discovered on the walls of Edfu and Philae temples.

L

Labyrinth the Greek name given to the temple precinct of a pyramid complex consisting of many courts and colonnades, erected at Hawara beside the FAIYUM, by AMENEMHET III of the 12th Dynasty (1844–1797 B.C.). Historically the structure has been identified as a palace, a mortuary complex, and as an administrative or cult center of the era. It is called the Labyrinth because of the complexity of its architectural design. Shafts, corridors and stone plugs were part of the original plan, all incorporated into the pyramid to protect the central burial chamber of the king. This portion of the pyramid was cut from a single block of granite and is estimated to have weighed about 110 tons. Twelve separate courts graced the Labyrinth, all facing one another in a lavish display of architectural skill.

ladder a mystic symbol and AMULET depicting the ascension of the ancient Egyptian god OSIRIS. This ladder was called a *MAQET* in some cultic centers and was used to honor the goddess NUT, one of Osiris' divine aides. Models of the ladder were placed in tombs to protect the deceased and to invoke the aid of the god of the dead. The ladder was a mythological emblem, designed by the gods to stretch mystically when Osiris was ascending. The dead received the same benefits from the *maqet* if they had faith in Osiris' resurrective powers.

Lahoun (or Lahun) a site in the FAIYUM region, named Renhone or Ro-henty by the ancient Egyptians, which translates as "Mouth of the Lake." Lahoun contained 12th Dynasty pyramid complexes, including one erected by SENWOSRET II (1897–1878 B.C.) on a rocky spur. Originally constructed out of mud, this mortuary complex was 160 feet high. The walls of the pyramid were held in place by stone and faced with high quality limestone. The facing was plundered by RAMESSES II (1290–1224 B.C.) of the 19th Dynasty for his own projects. At the northern end

of the necropolis of Lahoun the tombs of the royal family members of that dynasty were also discovered. A queen of Senwosret and eight other aristocrats were buried there. The MASTABAS of the nobles were constructed out of granite and contained a SARCOPHAGUS made out of the same stone.

Lake of Flowers one of the eternal paradises awaiting all dead Egyptians, according to the ancient mythology. The presence of fresh water, cool winds and flowers were to be essential to any paradise. (See ETERNITY and LILY LAKE.)

lakes part of the geographical composition of ancient Egypt. The scant rainfall in that nation kept the Egyptians dependent upon the bounty of the Nile, especially in the southern territories of Upper Egypt, which were particularly arid and without any major source of water other than the river. Lower Egypt, however, especially in the Delta or Faiyum regions, was blessed with seven lakes, even in ancient times. There were Qurun (or Birkat-al-Qurun), identified by the ancient Egyptians as the "Lake of Horus," situated in the FAIYUM; the Natron Lake of the Natron Valley northwest of modern Cairo; and the Delta lakes Manzilah, Edku, Abukir, Mareotis and Burullus (or Burlus).

Lamentations of Isis and Nephthys an ancient Egyptian text from the Late Period in which the two goddesses ISIS and NEPHTHYS, the divine sisters of OSIRIS, wept over his sufferings and death at the hands of the evil SETH. The two also proclaimed his resurrection from the dead and his ascension into heaven. Two priests recited the Lamentations in the annual feast of the god's ordeals in the 4th month, December 21 on the modern calendar. Another version of the Lamentations was called the Festival Songs of the Two Weepers or the Songs of Isis and Nephthy. These were probably performed in the temples with tambourines and other musical accompaniment. (See KITES.)

Lands of the Bows a legendary designation of the territory directly below the First Cataract of the Nile. The armies of the Early Dynastic Period (2920–2575 B.C.) conducted expeditions into the region, and this traditional designation, related to the NINE BOWS, remained throughout the pharaonic era. (See NUBIA.)

language the oral and written systems of communication of ancient Egypt as revealed in hieroglyphs. The earliest inscriptions date to the Early Dynastic Period (2920–2575 B.C.), although it is probable that hieroglyphs were in use before that time, and they were used throughout Egypt's history until the Christian era. The last hieroglyphs known were inscribed at Philae, dated A.D. 394.

The introduction of hieroglyphs was one of the most important developments in Egypt, as a tradition of literacy and recorded knowledge was thus begun. Not everyone in Egypt was literate, of course, but standards of education were set and maintained as a result, norms observed through the centuries by the vast armies of official scribes. In the beginning, the use of hieroglyphs was confined to a class of priests, and over the years the language in the oral form grew sophisticated and evolved, but the hieroglyphs remained comparatively traditional, protected against inroads by the priestly castes who trained the multitude of scribes. The hieroglyphs were normally used for religious texts, hence the Greek name hieroglyph ("sacred carvings"). The linguistic stages of development are as follows:

Old Egyptian the language of the Early Dynastic Period (2920–2575 B.C.) and the Old Kingdom (2575–2134 B.C.). Extant texts from this period are mostly official or religious, tomb inscriptions and a few biographical documents.

Middle Egyptian the linguistic form of the First Intermediate Period (2134–2040 B.C.) through the New Kingdom (to 1070 and probably beyond).

Late Egyptian the linguistic form used through 715 B.C.

Demotic the term applied to books and documents written in the Demotic script from the 25th Dynasty to the late Roman era.

Coptic the language in its latest form, as written from the third century A.D. to the present time, so named because of its affiliation with the Coptic Christians of Egypt.

Hieroglyphic Egyptian is basically a pictorial form, used by the early Egyptians to record an object or an event. The hieroglyph could be read as a picture, as a symbol of an image portrayed, or as a symbol for the sounds related to the image. In time the hieroglyphs were incorporated into art forms as well, inserted to specify particulars about the scene or event depicted.

Hieroglyphs were cut originally on cylindrical seals. These incised, roller-shaped stones (later replaced by hand-held scarab seals) were rolled onto fresh clay jar stoppers. They were used to indicate ownership of an object (particularly royal ownership) and designated the official responsible for its care. Such cylinders and seals were found in 1st Dynasty tombs.

Hieroglyphs accompanying the artistic renditions of the Early Dynastic Period began to conform to certain regulations. At the start of the Old Kingdom, a canon of hieroglyphs was firmly in place. From this period onward hieroglyphic writing appeared on stone monuments and bas-reliefs or high reliefs. The hieroglyphs were also painted on wood or metal. They were incorporated into temple decorations and were also used in coffins, stelae, statues, tomb walls and other monumental objects.

The obvious limitations of hieroglyphs for practical, day-to-day recordkeeping led to another, cursive form, called the hieratic. In this form the hieroglyphs were simplified and rounded, in the same way that such writing would result from the use of a reed-pen rather than a chisel on a stone surface. In the Old Kingdom the hieratic was barely distinguishable from the hieroglyphic, but in the Middle and New Kingdoms the form was developing unique qualities of its own. By the close of the New Kingdom the religious texts prepared on papyri were written normally in hieratic, and some stones depict the same script. The demotic ("popular") or enchorial form of the language made its first appearance in the Late Period, and throughout the Ptolemaic and Roman eras it was the ordinary form used, even on some stelae.

The Egyptian language in the written form (as it reflected the oral traditions) is unique in that it concerns itself with realism. There is something basically concrete about the images depicted, without speculative or philosophical nuances. Egyptians had a keen awareness of the physical world and translated their observances in images that carried distinct symbolism. Gestures or positions reflected a particular attribute or activity. The hieroglyphs were concise, strictly regulated as to word order and formal.

In the hieroglyphic writing only two classes of signs need to be distinguished: sense signs or ideograms, sound-signs or phonograms. The ideograms represent either the actual object depicted or some closely connected idea. Phonograms acquired sound values and were used for spelling. The vowels were not written in hieroglyphs, a factor which reflects the use of different vocalizations and context for words in the oral Egyptian language. The consonants remained consistent because the pronunciation of the word depended upon the context in which it appeared.

Hieroglyphic inscriptions consisted of rows of miniature pictures, arranged in vertical columns or horizontal lines. They normally read from right to left, although in some instances they were read in reverse. The signs that represented persons or animals normally faced the beginning of the inscription, a key as to the direction in which it should be read.

The alphabet is precise and includes specific characters for different sounds or objects. For each of the consonontal sounds there were one or more characters, and many single signs contained from two to four sounds. These signs, with or without phonetic value, were also used as determinatives. These were added at the ends of words to give them particular action or value.

The decipherment of hieroglyphic writing was made possible with the discovery of the ROSETTA STONE. Since that time, the study of Egypt's language has continued and evolved, enabling scholars to reassess previously known materials and to elaborate on the historical evidence concerning the people of the Nile.

Lansing Papyrus　a document in the British Museum that contains a text devoted to the praise of scribes in ancient Egypt. The papyrus also extolled the advantages of education and learning, elements much prized, although not universally shared, in almost every era of the nation.

lapis lazuli　a semiprecious stone imported from other sources that was extremely popular with the ancient Egyptians. Opaque, dark or greenish blue, often flecked with gold, lapis lazuli was used extensively in jewelry and to a lesser extent for small sculptures, scarabs and amulets. The Egyptian name for the stone was *khesbedj*, and in sculpture it represented vitality and youthfulness. The goddess HATHOR was sometimes called "The Mistress of Lapis Lazuli."

lapwing　See REKHET.

Lateran Obelisk　a monument belonging to TUTH-MOSIS III (1479–1425 B.C.) of the 18th Dynasty, now in Rome in the Vatican. Inscriptions were added by TUTHMOSIS IV (1401–1391 B.C.), who raised up the obelisk at KARNAK, where it had lain unattended for

decades. He announced that deed and his filial piety on the monument.

Layer Pyramid　the modern name given to a PYR-AMID at Zawiyet el-'Aryan, in the desert of GIZA. The pyramid dates to third Dynasty and is believed to be the complex of KHA'BA (2603–2599 B.C.) of the third Dynasty. This pyramid had a companion structure, but that was never completed.

Lay of the Harper　the name given to several texts discovered on tomb walls and on stelae from ancient Egypt. They were reflections on death, although quite distinct from the normal religious views evidenced in the various BOOKS OF THE DEAD. Most praise death, viewing it as a continuation of life. One, the Harper's Song from the tomb of INYOTEF V of the 17th Dynasty (c. 1640–1635 B.C.), is unusual because it expresses doubts about the existence of a paradise beyond the grave. Such pessimistic views were rare in Egypt. The song was not actually found on the walls of Inyotef's tomb but in the tomb of an individual buried at Thebes, citing the original.

legal system　the administrative structure developed in ancient Egypt as part of the national and provincial forms of government. The people of the Nile remained close-knit in their NOME communities, even at the height of the empire, and they preferred to have their court cases and grievances settled under local jurisdiction. Each nome or province had a capital city, dating to predynastic times. Lesser cities and towns within the nome functioned as part of a whole. In each town or village, however, there was a *seru*, a group of elders whose purpose it was to provide legal opinions and decisions on local events. The *djadjat* in the Old Kingdom (2575–2134 B.C.) and the *kenbet* thereafter made legal and binding decisions and meted out the appropriate penalties. The *kenbet* was a factor on both the nome and high-court levels. This series of local and national courts was normally a wise tradition. Only during the periods of unrest or chaos, as in the two Intermediate Periods, did such a custom prove disastrous. The popularity of the ELOQUENT PEASANT was due to the nation's genuine desire to have courts provide justice. Crimes involving capital punishment or those of treason, however, were not always within the jurisdiction of the local courts, and even the Great *Kenbet* could not always render the ultimate decision on such matters.

The Great *Kenbet* in the capitals were under the supervision of the viziers of Egypt, in several periods there being a vizier for Upper Egypt and another for Lower Egypt. This custom commemorated the unification of the nation in 3000 B.C. Petitions could be made to the lower courts or to the Great *Kenbet* by all citizens. Egyptians waited in line each day to give the judges their testimony or their petitions. The decisions concerning such matters were based on traditional legal practices, although there must have been written codes available for study. HOREMHAB (1319–1307 B.C.), at the close of the 18th Dynasty, set down an edict concerning the law in which he appears to be referring to past customs or documents.

No distinction was allowed in the hearing of cases. Commoners and women were afforded the same opportunities as aristocrats in the courts. The poor were also to be safeguarded in their rights. The Eloquent Peasant was popular because he dared to admonish the judges again and again to give heed to the demands of the poor and not to be swayed by the mighty or the well dressed. The admonitions to the viziers of Egypt, as recorded in the 18th Dynasty tomb of REKHMIRE', echo the same sort of vigilance required by all Egyptian officials.

Some of the higher-ranking judges of ancient Egypt were called "Attached to Nekhen," a title of honor that denoted the fact that their positions and roles were in the finest traditions of HIERANKOPOLIS, the original home of NA'RMER. The title alluded to these judges' long and faithful tradition of service and their role in preserving customs and legal traditions of the past. Others were called the "Magnates of the Southern Ten," and these officers of the government were esteemed for their services and for their rank in powerful Upper Egyptian nomes or capitals. When Egypt acquired an empire in the New Kingdom era, various governors were also assigned to foreign territories under Egyptian control, and these held judicial posts as part of their capacity. The viceroy of Nubia, for example, made court decisions and enforced the law in his jurisdiction.

The judicial system of ancient Egypt, collapsing when the various periods of unrest or foreign dominance, inflicted damage on the normal governmental structures, appears to have served the Egyptians well over the centuries. Under strong dynasties, the courts and the various officials were expected to set standards of moral behavior and to strictly interpret the law. (See GOVERNMENT.)

Leontopolis   called To-Remu by the ancient Egyptians, the modern Tell Yahudiyeh near Cairo. This city was a shrine and cult center for the worship of lions in early eras. A lavish palace was discovered there, dating to the reign of RAMESSES III of the 20th Dynasty (1194–1163 B.C.). The palace lies in ruins, but its remains provide an indication of the exquisite

beauty and richness of the mansion. The lion cult, and the cult of the AKER, in various forms, remained important in Egypt throughout its history. The animal was normally kept in the throne room of the king and exhibited to various dignitaries from other lands as a symbol of the strength of the pharaoh.

Letopolis   called Hem by the ancient Egyptians and now named Ausim. This site was sacred to HORUS in some eras but was never politically important.

lettuce   a vegetable considered sacred to the ancient Egyptian god MIN and endowed with magical properties. It was believed to be a magical weapon against the dead, able to prick them, as identified in a New Kingdom lullaby. Lettuce was fed to Min's sacred animals and was also part of the rituals of the god SETH.

libraries   called "houses of the papyri" and normally part of the local PER-ANKH, or "House of Life." Education was a priority in every generation in ancient Egypt, and the schools were open to the qualified of all classes, although only a small percentage of the population was literate at any given time.

The libraries were vast storehouses of accumulated knowledge and records. In the New Kingdom the pharaohs of the Middle Kingdom were much admired, indicating that the Egyptians had a profound realization of what had taken place in earlier times. Men like Prince KHA'EMWESET of the 19th Dynasty began studies of the past, surveying the necropolis sites of the first dynasties and recording their findings with meticulous care.

The priests of the Per-Ankh were required to recite or read copious documents and records of the various enterprises of the king. The levels of the Nile, the movement of the celestial bodies and the bi-annual census were some of the subjects that could be summoned up from the libraries and from the lore of the priests. In all areas the libraries were actually archives, containing ancient texts and documents. The most famed library of Egypt was erected in the Ptolemaic era and burned during Julius Caesar's campaign in Alexandria. The wealth of the recorded material lost in that conflagration is incalculable.

Libya   the land bordering the northwestern Delta of ancient Egypt. Libya is mentioned in the records of the Early Dynastic Period (2920–2575 B.C.), but the people designated in these documents are those who lived in what was called Tjehenu. They were depicted on early temple walls and shown with many of the characteristics of the Egyptians of the time. The Libyans were called Hatiu-a, "Princes," perhaps because of their splendid attire.

The separation of the Egyptians and Libyans probably happened in the predynastic periods, when the Upper Egyptians were assaulting the Delta and other northern lands, seeking to unify the nation. NA'RMER recorded victories over the people of Tjehenu.

The Old Kingdom (2575–2134 B.C.) pharaohs conducted military campaigns against the Libyans, or punitive expeditions to keep the western borders of Egypt secure. SNOFRU is listed in the PALERMO STONE as having invaded Libya (c. 2560 B.C.). SAHURE' (2458–2446 B.C.) of the 5th Dynasty depicted the goddess SESHAT recording the herds of cattle, sheep and goats that he captured in the Libyan Desert. Members of the Libyan royal family were also brought back to the Nile by this victorious king.

By the Middle Kingdom such assaults on Libya were commonplace, and Egypt's armies contained units of Libyans, dating to the last part of the Old Kingdom. SENWOSRET I (1971–1926 B.C.) of the 12th Dynasty, sent expeditions against the Libyans. It is at this time that the Libyans were designated as Tjehenu and Tjemehu.

During the Second Intermediate Period (1640–1532 B.C.), the Libyans apparently were able to penetrate the Delta region, undeterred by the HYKSOS, who ruled in AVARIS. 'AHMOSE I (1550–1525 B.C.), who united Egypt again and routed the Asiatics from their strongholds, cleared the Delta of the Libyan invaders as well. His successor, AMENHOTEP I, undertook another massive invasion to rid Egypt of Libyan encampments. He reportedly captured three hands (an expression used to record enemy dead) in this assault, which may have taken place in the Libyan Desert. There is evidence that this warfare did not continue through the 18th Dynasty.

In the 19th Dynasty, however, the Libyans were experiencing problems with the invading SEA PEOPLES, and one of their own royal line led an expedition into the Delta. He and his army took their families and their household goods with them, anticipating a permanent settlement. MERNEPTAH (1224–1214 B.C.) marched with his armies and slew 6,000 Libyans and their allies. The Libyan prince fled to his homeland but was put aside by his own people. The MESHWESH, a Libyan people, attacked Egypt in the 20th Dynasty and were routed by RAMESSES III (1194–1163 B.C.). They were defeated on two separate occasions by this Ramesses. Reliefs depicting the Libyans of this era show them wearing curls on one side of their heads and carrying uniquely designed phallus-shaped shields into battle. When the New

Kingdom collapsed c. 1070 B.C., the Libyans managed to gain control of Egypt as the 22nd Dynasty. Some vigorous kings came to the throne in that era of Libyan domination.

Libyan Desert an arid stretch of land on the western side of the Nile River, marked by low hills and sand. This desert contained widely scattered oases and was actually a part of the vast FAIYUM, which was irrigated by sophisticated hydraulic systems and reclaimed by successive Egyptian kings. The Libyan Desert was always harsher and more forbidding than the one on the eastern side of the Nile, called the Arabian or Red Sea Desert. The oases of the region, however, were famed for their wines and agricultural products, and contained shrines of the Egyptian gods that remained popular for centuries. (See OASES.)

Libyan Palette a fragment of a commemorative tablet, either predynastic or dating to the 1st Dynasty of ancient Egypt (2920 B.C.). Made from gray schist, the vessel resembles the famed NA'RMER PALETTE but depicts a variety of trees, plants and animals and an assault. The palette was discovered in ABYDOS.

Lily Lake called the Lake of Flowers in some religious texts, one of the eternal realms of bliss referred to in mortuary documents. Deceased Egyptians were to be rowed across this lake by HE-WHO-LOOKS-BEHIND-HIMSELF. (See LAKE OF FLOWERS and ETERNITY.)

"Linen of Yesterday" a poetic image employed by the ancient Egyptians to denote death and the changes that dying brings to humans. The phrase was included in the dirges sung by the KITES, the professional women mourners at funerals. The deceased is addressed by these mourners as one who dressed in fine linen but now sleeps in the "linen of yesterday." That image alluded to the fact that life upon the earth became "yesterday" to the dead. It was probably prompted by the custom of the commoners or the poor, who gave used linens to the embalmers for the ritual preparation of each mummy. The poor could not afford new linens, and so wrapped their beloved corpses in those of "yesterday."

lion an ancient Egyptian theophany, or divine manifestation, associated with the gods RE', HORUS and the AKER. Called the *ma'au*, the lion was renowned for its courage and strength. The cult center for lion worship was established at LEONTOPOLIS in the Delta in early eras. Several lion forms were honored in the temples, including MATIT, Mehit, and PAKHT, dating to the era of the 1st Dynasty. The Aker

A lion head from a 5th Dynasty statue found at Abusir.

cult was involved with the worship of Re'. The Aker guarded the sacred sites of the cult and the Gate of Dawn, the mythical abode through which Re' passed each morning.

Lions of Sebel called Sebua in some lists, a remarkable pair of stone figures erected by AMENHOTEP III of the 18th Dynasty (1391–1353 B.C.) at Sebel in southern Nubia. The lion figures were carried away by the Ethiopians when they invaded the territory and are now in the British Museum. During the 'Amarna period, when AKHENATEN (Amenhotep IV) instituted the cult of ATEN, the inscriptions on the lions were destroyed, being of a religious nature. TUT'ANKHAMUN (1333–1323 B.C.) restored the reliefs when he returned the worship of AMON at Thebes. He also added his own commemoratives.

Lisht the modern name for the 12th Dynasty capital of IT-TOWY, south of Memphis. The pyramids of AMENEMHET I (1991–1962 B.C.) and SENWOSRET I (1971–1926 B.C.) were discovered at this site, on an elevated section. Amenemhet's pyramid measured 92 yards on one side and was constructed out of various types of limestone. Designed with a shaft, the tomb was graced by a granite stela at its entrance, made of syenite, a red form of that stone from Aswan.

List of Offerings a common text from ancient Egypt that specified the gifts to be made to the deceased as part of the mortuary ceremonies. The List of Offerings was in use in ancient Egypt by the beginnings of the Old Kingdom (2575 B.C.), in private and royal tombs. Offerings of meat, drink and incense were made each day by priests of the funerary rituals, who were commissioned to perform acts of commemoration. Some entire clans of priests functioned in this capacity, especially in the royal mortuary complexes. The list evolved over the centuries into the LITURGY OF FUNERARY OFFERINGS, which continued throughout Egypt's history.

Litanies of Sokar a compilation of 100 lines, addressed to the god SOKAR, a Memphite deity of Tuat or the Underworld, associated in various eras with PTAH and OSIRIS. In the early eras he was the protector of the great necropolis at GIZA, the site of the pyramids of the 4th Dynasty. The Litanies of Sokar were discovered in the RHIND PAPYRUS, which is now in the British Museum.

Litany of Osiris a hymn or prayer to the god of the dead in ancient Egypt. This litany was included in the ANI PAPYRUS, which is now in the British Museum. (See BOOK OF THE DEAD.)

Litany of the Sun attributed to the original cult of the god RE', a religious text of ancient Egypt, discovered in the tomb of SETI I (c. 1306–1290 B.C.) of the 19th Dynasty. The text is part of the mortuary rituals of the era, Amonite in origin but embracing all traditions of Egypt's mythology.

literature a form of cultural expression and art in ancient Egypt, both religious and secular in nature and developing over the period of history from the Early Dynastic Period to the Greco-Roman Period. The literature of the Egyptians was normally didactic, but eventually it came to include tales, poems, songs, lullabies, hymns, liturgies, prayers and litanies.

The hieroglyphs that evolved into the Egyptian written language appeared in a variety of forms, as the written word became part of the decoration of monuments, tombs, stelae and instruments of daily use. Other texts, not part of monuments, were preserved by the scribes, who appear to have copied documents from earlier ages as part of their training. Some of these texts have been presented on papyri or on OSTRAKA, the boards and slates used by individual students. The literature of Egypt is so vast and covers so many centuries that it is normally accorded distinct categories. These follow.

Religious Texts

Designed to bolster the state cult of the king, the oldest religious documents are the PYRAMID TEXTS, discovered on the walls of the various chambers of the pyramids of the kings of the 5th and 6th Dynasties (2465–2150 B.C.). The texts delineate the magical spells that were designed to provide the king with a place in the world beyond the grave, where he would receive his rewards for service and be welcomed by the gods. The daily offerings to be made as part of the mortuary ritual in the pyramid were also listed.

Soon after, the nobles began to assume the same rights as the king as far as benefits beyond the grave were concerned, and they had Pyramid Texts placed in their coffins. These COFFIN TEXTS also contained spells and magical incantations to allow the dead to assume supernatural forms and to overcome whatever obstacles awaited them on their journey in the afterlife. The early forms of the BOOK OF THE DEAD date to this period (2134–2040 B.C.). The Book of the Dead underwent various changes over the centuries, remaining popular. The most complete versions date to the Ptolemaic Period, and these contain as many as 150 separate spells. The coffin variety of the Book of the Dead was placed on papyrus in the New Kingdom (1550–1070 B.C.).

Other religious texts, including the Ritual of the Divine Cult, the Book of Gates, and the Destruction of Mankind, all follow the same general pattern of magical incantations and descriptions of the various chambers or stages to be discovered in Tuat or the Underworld. The elaborately beautiful hymns to the various deities were also popular. The OVERTHROW-ING OF APEPI and other religious documents provide an insight into the religious aspects of Egyptian life. Especially graceful are the hymns to the gods AMON and ATEN, which date to the New Kingdom.

Magical papyri and mortuary stelae (placed in Abydos as part of the great Osirian cult) provide other information. The stelae announce the ranks, deeds and general goodness of the owners. Letters were also written to the deceased, on the assumption that in the afterlife the individual had powers and could remedy situations on earth. The custom of informing the dead about contemporary issues remained popular in some areas of Egypt into modern times.

Scientific Texts

While the religious mortuary texts of Egypt dealt mainly with magic and divine intercession in human affairs, the nation also focused on the practical aspects of life. As a result, various sciences were undertaken, not in a speculative way but in order to facilitate the performance of daily activities. Medical texts reflected the practical aspects of Egyptian literature. Manuscripts from the New Kingdom, the Ebers Papyrus and the Edwin Smith Papyrus, as well as others, display the anatomical knowledge and curative ability of the priests, who were regulated in their methods of diagnosis, treatment and post-treatment.

Among mathematical texts discovered are the Rhind Papyrus and one currently in Moscow. Another identifies agricultural crops, birds, animals and geographical locations. Texts on astronomy, irrigation, geography and husbandry were also found. Military texts abound, part of the record of events from the unification of Upper and Lower Egypt in 3000 B.C., with the exploits of the New Kingdom pharaohs described in detail. Travel records from that same period provide information about Egypt's relationships with other lands, and conditions in the world at the time. The REPORT OF WENAMON at the end of the 20th Dynasty is particularly enlightening. The Tale of SI-NUHE THE SAILOR, based on the death of AMENEMHET I (1991–1962 B.C.), provides insight into the court intrigues and to the cultures of other nations during the Middle Kingdom.

Legal Texts

Legal documents consist mainly of wills or accounts of court events, although legal references in the ABBOTT PAPYRUS offer a view of social changes along the Nile, dealing with tomb robberies and their prosecution at the close of the New Kingdom. Wills placed in tombs, deeds of sale, census lists and records of lawsuits have been discovered. The Edict of Horemhab has provided information about the conditions in Egypt at the close of the 18th Dynasty (1307 B.C.).

Texts concerning the government administration have been discovered as well. REKHMIRE', the vizier for TUTHMOSIS III (1479–1425 B.C.), had the instructions of the king concerning his office and the ideals of such a position inscribed on his tomb walls at Thebes. Texts from the Elephantine, concerning the work of the Viceroys of Nubia, date to many eras, as do the reports of officials on expeditions for the throne. Inscriptions of expeditions can be seen on cliffs in the various wadis and in the desert regions, announcing the mining and quarrying activities.

Fantastic Tales

The TALE OF THE SHIPWRECKED SAILOR, dating to the Middle Kingdom, remained popular in Egypt. The story elaborates on mystical creatures and magical events. The TALE OF THE DOOMED PRINCE, the TALE OF THE TWO BROTHERS and the TALE OF KHUFU AND THE MAGICIANS all relate magical happenings and even adventures rife with perils. The story concerning KHUFU (2551–2528 B.C.), the builder of the Great Pyramid has descriptions of idle hours spent on pleasure boats among harem maidens clothed only in fish nets.

Didactic Texts

The ancient Egyptians were fond of texts that admonished them, propounded idealistic views of life and encouraged them to assume a more enlightened stance. Some of these texts bemoaned conditions in the land in times of dynastic weakness, while others contained maxims and adages clearly meant to instruct. PTAHHOTEP, a sage of the 5th Dynasty (2465–2323 B.C.), and KAGEMNI, of the 3rd Dynasty (2649–2575 B.C.), were among the first to admonish royalty and commoner alike. KHETY III of the 10th Dynasty (c. 2020 B.C.) gave his son Merikare' instructions about the behavior of kings, as did AMENEMHET I of the 12th Dynasty (1991–1962 B.C.). Amenemhet's discourse details the obligations of a ruler and the needs of his subjects. Didactic literature remained a constant in Egypt, and many sages were honored by the people in all eras.

Poetic Texts

Religious and social events of the various eras were normally accompanied by music. The pleasures of music, feasting and love became part of the rhythm of life on the Nile, eventually giving rise to love songs, which often told of love-sick swains separated from their sweethearts. Sycamore trees, birds and the winds become messengers of love in the poetic texts, with the lovers pledging their hearts and vowing eternal affection. Love songs appear to have been recorded first in the Middle Kingdom; the late New Kingdom period provided many more. The songs capture the directness of the Egyptian people, as well as their sensitivity to the seasons, their easy affection and their love of metaphors and conventional imagery. The hymn to SENWOSRET III (1878–1841 B.C.) epitomizes this form of Egyptian literature.

Liturgy of the Funerary Offerings a list of the funerary gifts and rituals conducted by priests involved in the mortuary cults of the ancient Egyptians. Evolving from the LIST OF OFFERINGS, which dates to the Old Kingdom (2575–2134 B.C.), the Liturgy was devised to magically change meat, bread and wine into divine spiritual substances, which were offered to the gods and to the dead. This transmutation of offerings is documented in the tombs of the 5th Dynasty (2465–2323 B.C.) but was probably in use before that time. More than 114 ceremonies comprised the Liturgy.

The purification of the mummified remains, the incensing accompanied by magical incantations and prayers were used to perform the rituals of the burial and restoration of the deceased in the Liturgy. The priests were believed capable of revitalizing the senses and the various organs of the dead with the use of the spells provided. All was based on the resurrection of OSIRIS and on the basic creed that no life is obliterated at death but only transformed into shapes that will accommodate the environment of eternity. The Liturgy of Funerary Offerings was revised in several eras but remained popular throughout Egypt's history.

London Papyrus a palimpset or parchment upon which several texts were written, erased and then written again by ancient Egyptian scribes. This document contains medical and magical texts. It is reportedly from the 4th Dynasty originally, being a copy of a document belonging to KHUFU (2551–2528 B.C.).

Lotus the symbol of rebirth or creation in ancient Egypt. The lotus was sacred to the god NEFERTUM but was also part of the cult of the god RE'. The flower was used in temple rituals and was incorporated into bouquets and floral tributes for festivals. The lotus signified Re' 's power and birth and was celebrated in the Lotus Offering, a hymn sung in the temple on festival days, especially at the cultic center in EDFU. The hymn referred to the god Re' as the "Great Lotus," which emerged from the primeval pool at the moment of creation. (See COSMOGNY and SMA-TAWY.)

Lower Egypt See EGYPT, *Geographical Designations*.

Loyalist Instruction See SEHETEPIBRE.

Luxor the modern Arabic name for Southern Opet, the area of Thebes in Upper Egypt that was dedicated to the god AMON during the New Kingdom (1550–1070 B.C.). The modern name is derived from the Arabic *el-Askur*, the Castles, an obvious reference to the vast ruined complexes in the area.

One of the major structures in Luxor was a temple used for religious processions. (See illustration on page 86.) Erected by AMENHOTEP III of the 18th Dynasty (1391–1353 B.C.), the temple honored the Theban god Amon. The first pylon and the colonnaded court of the temple were constructed by RAMESSES II of the 19th Dynasty (1290–1224 B.C.). This section of the temple enclosed a sanctuary that was probably built by TUTHMOSIS III (1479–1425 B.C.). Tuthmosis III personally directed the construction of the sanctuary

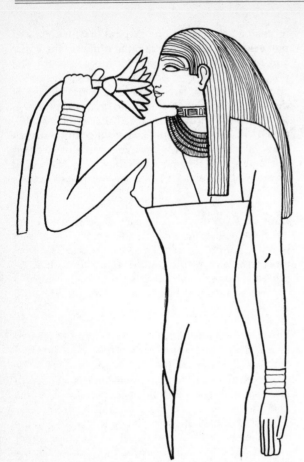

LOTUS the religious symbol of Re''s emergence from the watery chaos, from a stela in Saqqara dating to the 5th Dynasty.

during his reign in the 18th Dynasty to accommodate the famous bark of Amon. The bark was part of the elaborate festival ceremonies and was refurbished periodically and protected in a safe storage area when not in use. Amenhotep III, a successor of Tuthmosis, erected an actual temple on the site, the beginning of the complex.

Six colossal statues and two obelisks adorned the area leading to the second pylon, which was also built by Amenhotep III. There a colonnade and two rows of papyrus capital columns were bordered by papyrus-bundle pillars. A transverse hypostyle hall, with 32 more columns arranged in four rows of eight, opened onto the inner temple area. Additional hypostyle halls were surrounded by ritual chapels and led to the original sanctuary site.

Amenhotep III adorned the walls of the temple with reliefs depicting his birth and his royal parentage, an affectation used frequently by the rulers of the New Kingdom. TUT'ANKHAMUN (1333–1323 B.C.), newly converted to the worship of Amon after the fall of 'AMARNA and AKHENATEN's heretical cult of ATEN, provided the temple with more reliefs, depicting the ceremonies being conducted in the sanctuary to honor Amon. It is not certain if these reliefs were actually the original ones of Amenhotep III or added to placate the priests of Amon and the Theban people. HOREMHAB, at the close of the 18th Dynasty, attempted to use the same inscriptions to announce his own achievements and honors. Many statues and two red granite obelisks, one now in the Place de la Concorde in Paris, adorned the Luxor Temple. The barks of Mut, Khonsu and other deities rested as well in the temple area, which was linked to the massive KARNAK complex by a double row of sphinxes.

The God Amon was carried to the Luxor Temple once a year to visit his particular manifestation there. The Amon adored at Luxor was a vibrant, ithyphallic form of the god, a patron of fertility and involved with the necropolis sites on the western shore of the Nile opposite Thebes. This same form of the god was also worshipped in cultic rites at MEDINET HABU and remained popular even in the eras of occupation.

The Feast of Opet, the annual celebration of this shrine, was an elaborate festival, complete with the sacrifice of animals and gala rituals. At this time the statues and barks of the Theban deities were carried in procession on the shoulders of the priests. The procession was led by dancers, singers and musicians and cheered by the people, who came from miles around to celebrate the occasion.

The barks were placed on great barges and floated on the Nile before returning to the temple precincts. A great sacrificial feast awaited the return of the deities, with acrobats, dancers, musicians and throngs of adorers sounding the greeting.

The Greeks and Romans had a keen interest in Luxor temple, which was popular throughout all of the eras of occupation. Modern excavations, taking place as part of the restoration and preservation programs at Luxor, uncovered a trove of statues from the reign of Amenhotep III called the "Luxor Cachette." These statues, beautifully preserved works of art, are believed to have been buried by the priests of Luxor in the face of an invasion or some other political peril. (See BARKS OF THE GODS.)

Lykonpolis See ASSIUT.

Temple of Amon reconstructed at Luxor, called Opet, the southern part of Thebes in Upper Egypt.

M

Ma'adi a predynastic site just south of modern Cairo, where the remains of oval and circular-shaped houses were discovered. Posts stuck into the ground appear to have served as the simple foundation for these structures, which were composed of mud daub and wattle originally. Interior hearths, an innovation in the predynastic eras, were also discovered as part of the designs of the houses at Ma'adi. There is little indication, however, that roofs were part of the architectural planning of the residences. Windbreaks and sheltering walls served as the only form of protection for the inhabitants in the beginning. Ma'adi was near the famed TURA Quarry. (See EGYPT, PREDYNASTIC.)

Ma'ahes an ancient Egyptian god, reportedly of Nubian origin, whose cult center was at LEONTOPOLIS, called To-Remu by the Egyptians. Ma'ahes was believed to be the son of the god RE' and the goddess BAST. He was depicted normally as a man wearing the *atef* CROWN, but he was also shown as a lion in the act of devouring the enemies of Egypt. Ma'ahes was one of many lion deities, as the worship of that animal as a divine theophany remained popular over the centuries. (See AKER, LION and LEONTOPOLIS.)

Ma'at an ancient Egyptian goddess who personified the spirit of the nation from earliest times: cosmic harmony and equilibrium. The goddess Ma'at was depicted as a woman wearing an ostrich feather on her head, and sometimes with the wings of a divine being. She maintained a vital role in the mortuary rituals of Egypt, where she weighed the hearts of the deceased. This mortuary role evolved over the decades into the principle of MA'AT, the desired right attitude, which remained the ethical and moral foundation of the Egyptian people.

ma'at the spiritual ideal of the ancient Egyptians. *Ma'at* was originally personified by a goddess, whose role in the mortuary mythology was constant throughout the nation's history. In time, however, the ideals against which the goddess weighed the hearts or souls of the deceased were systematized into a single philosophical or spiritual concept that was derived, in part, from observation of the universe and the celestial "beings" in the night sky. *Ma'at* was cosmic harmony, justice, order and peace. Each new king claimed to have restored the spirit of *ma'at* upon his accession to the throne, no matter how benevolent the rule of his predecessor. *Ma'at* was the model for human behavior, in conformity with the will of the gods, the universal order evident in the heavens, cosmic balance upon the earth, the mirror of celestial beauty.

Awareness of the cosmic order was evident early in Egypt; priest-astronomers charted the heavens and noted that the earth responded to the orbits of the stars and planets. The priests taught that mankind was commanded to reflect divine harmony by assuming a spirit of quietude, reasonable behavior, cooperation and a recognition of the eternal qualities of existence, as demonstrated by the earth and the sky. All Egyptians anticipated becoming part of the cosmos when they died, thus the responsibility for acting in accordance with its laws was reasonable. Strict adherence to *ma'at* allowed the Egyptians to feel secure with the world and with the divine plan for all creation. This concept of *ma'at* was as much an outgrowth of Egyptian ideas on cosmogony as of ethical awareness. Many Egyptians made a sincere effort in almost every historical era to achieve the reflection of celestial harmony, believing that *ma'at* was the true essence of creation, evident in every new human life span and again in each hour upon the earth or in the sky.

Ma'at Hornefrure' a queen of the 19th Dynasty, married to RAMESSES II (c. 1290–1224 B.C.). Ma'at Hornefrure', probably a Hittite Princess, wed to Ramesses II as a result of the HITTITE ALLIANCE. She

Ma'at, the goddess, shown with wings of spirituality and with the feather of righteousness. From a mortuary scene.

ruled beside queens BINT ANATH and MERYTAMON in Ramesses' later years and then retired to the harem palace in the FAIYUM region. It is probable that Queen Ma'at Hornefrure' was the inspiration for the Egyptian Tale of the Princess Bekhten contained in the BENTRESH STELA. The story appeared soon after the

arrival of the Hittite delegation and the signing of the Alliance.

ma'at-kheru the ancient Egyptian expression meaning "true of voice," used to denote human beings judged as pure and worthy of eternal bliss in the realms of OSIRIS. The term appears in various editions of the BOOK OF THE DEAD. (See MORTUARY RITUALS and JUDGMENT HALL OF OSIRIS.)

Mafdet called Maftet and Mefdet in some records, a cat or lynx goddess of ancient Egypt, mentioned in the PALERMO STONE. Normally depicted as a woman wearing a cat's skin, she was a protector against snakebites and a friend of all deceased Egyptians. She aided RE' by overthrowing the serpent APOPHIS.

magic called *heka* by the Egyptians, the conduct of rituals and ceremonies in order to assume powers or to produce specific results. Magic was a traditional part of religious rites in Egypt, viewed as the enabling force by which men and gods alike succeeded in their endeavors. Magic was the binding force between the earth and other worlds, the link between mortals and the divine.

Few Egyptians could have imagined life without magic because it provided them with a role in godly affairs and an opportunity to become one with the divine. The gods used magic, and the ANKH was the symbol of power held in their hands in reliefs and statues. Magic was a gift from the god RE' to be used for the benefit of all people. Its power allowed the kings and the priests to act as intermediaries between the world and the heavens.

Three basic elements were always involved in the practice of *heka*: the spell, the ritual and the magician. Spells were traditional but also changed with the times and contained words, which were viewed as powerful weapons in the hands of the learned. Names were especially potent as magical elements. The Egyptians believed that all things came into existence by being named. The person or object vanished when his or its name was no longer evoked, hence the elaborate mortuary stelae and the custom of later generations returning to the tombs of their ancestors to recite aloud the name and deeds of each person buried there.

In many tombs acts of intentional destruction were related to magic. The damage inflicted was meant to remove the magical ability of the object, image or word. Names were struck from inscriptions to prevent their being remembered, thereby denying their existence. In the Old Kingdom tombs (2575–2134 B.C.) the hieroglyphs for animals and humans were frequently destroyed to keep them from resurrecting magically and harming the burial sites, especially by devouring the food offerings for the deceased. The Egyptians believed rituals to be a part of all religious observances and set up an elaborate system of ceremonies for common usage. Few texts survive, how-

ever, to explain these sorts of rituals. Egyptians also hoped to cast spells over enemies with words, gestures and rites. AMULETS were common defenses against *heka*, as they were believed to defend humans against the curses of foes.

magical dream interpretation an aspect of Egyptian religious and cultic observances, and a part of magic, or *heka*, as practiced in Egypt. Dreams were considered important omens or prophetic signs. Papyri available in temple archives provided traditional views of the various elements of dreams. Priests often provided interpretations.

If a man saw himself with his mouth open while dreaming, he was told that the dread in his heart would be relieved by divine intervention. If a person saw his wife in his dream the omen was good, interpreted as meaning that all evils would retreat from him. Evils could be foretold, however, by dreams experienced in a temple. If a man dreamed that he saw a dwarf, he was going to lose half of his natural life span. If he wrote on a papyrus in his dream he understood that the gods were beginning to tally up his deeds for his final judgment. If a man dreamed that he died violently, however, he could be assured of living long after his father was entombed. The interpretation of dreams was part of the ancient Egyptian's innate curiosity and concern about the future, and was practised particularly in the late periods. The people used oracles and consulted a calendar of lucky and unlucky days in order to ensure the successful outcome of their ventures. (See CAIRO CALENDAR and MAGIC.)

Magical Lullaby a charming song from ancient Egypt, crooned by mothers over their children's beds. The lullaby was intended to warn evil spirits and ghosts from tarrying or planning harm. The mother sang about the items that she possessed in order to harm the spirits of the dead. She carried lettuce, to "prick" the ghosts, garlic to "bring them harm", and honey, which was considered "poison to the dead." The lullaby is included in some modern texts on myths and literature. (See MAGIC and AMULETS.)

Magnates of the Southern Ten a title given to certain governors, normally hereditary nobles of the NOMES or provinces of Upper Egypt, who ruled their territories in the name of the king. (See GOVERNMENT and FIRST UNDER THE KING.)

Maherpa an official of the 18th Dynasty, a companion of AMENHOTEP II (1427–1401 B.C.). A Nubian, Maherpa was a boyhood friend of the pharaoh, or else a hostage companion maintained at Thebes to receive training until he assumed the throne of his own kingdom. He died at a young age and was buried in an undecorated tomb at Thebes, encased in three coffins. Part of his funerary regalia was a beautifully illustrated copy of the BOOK OF THE DEAD, in which he appears with black skin.

Mahu an official of the 18th Dynasty, serving in the reign of AKHENATEN, Amenhotep IV (1353–1335 B.C.). Mahu was the commander of the police units at 'AMARNA during the era of Akhenaten's sojourn in that capital dedicated to the god ATEN. He may have been one of the MEDJAY, the Nubians who served in the New Kingdom as members of the state police. The Medjay waged war early in the 18th Dynasty and aided KAMOSE, the last king of the 17th Dynasty, when he began the war to oust the Asiatics or HYKSOS from Egypt.

Mai an official of the 18th Dynasty, serving in the reign of AKHENATEN, Amenhotep IV (1353–1335 B.C.) at 'AMARNA. Mai was an hereditary aristocrat of his nome and commanded troops for the king in the capital of the god ATEN. He was buried in the cliffs overlooking the city dedicated by Akhenaten to the new god.

Malkata the Arabic name for the site south of Medinet Habu on the western shore of Thebes in Upper Egypt. The name means "Place Where Things Are Picked Up." Malkata was created at Dja'-rukha by AMENHOTEP III (1391–1353 B.C.) of the 18th Dynasty as his palace complex, which became a miniature city with many residences and luxurious dwellings. Several palace compounds were erected at Malkata. Each had administrative offices, houses for court officials, halls, chambers, chapels and lavish apartments. Homes for artisans were also erected on the site.

An artificial lake and harbor were constructed for the region, connected to the Nile and built within a record time. A T-shaped harbor remains visible in modern times. The king and his courtiers sailed on a barge dedicated to the god ATEN when he visited Malkata, which in time became his royal residence.

He built a palace there for his harem and constructed others for Queen TIY and for Amenhotep IV (AKHENATEN), his heir. All of the royal buildings were lavishly painted and decorated by New Kingdom artists. The entire complex, built out of sun-dried bricks, was linked to a nearby funerary temple by a causeway. The god AMON was honored in this shrine. The lavish suites of the palaces and temples were whitewashed and then painted with scenes of life along the Nile or with cultic symbols. (See DISTRICT OF TEKHENU-ATEN.)

Mandet the sacred bark upon which the god RE' rode into the sky each morning as the sun. This ancient Egyptian mythological craft allowed Re' freedom of the heavens. Re' descended each evening in a similar bark, called the MESEKET.

Manetho's King List included in the *Aegyptiaca*, the work of an historian from Sebennytus, Egypt, who lived during the Ptolemaic era, c. 280 B.C. Manetho's list divided Egypt into more than 30 separate historical dynasties. Scholars use Manetho's *Aegyptiaca* in conjunction with the TURIN CANON and other chronological records discovered in the various tombs and monuments of Egypt. Though it did not survive as a complete manuscript, it was excerpted by other ancient historians so that it could be reconstructed. (See KING LISTS.)

maqet the spiritual LADDER of ancient Egypt upon which the god OSIRIS ascended into heaven. The *maqet* was used in some mortuary rituals and then used to invoke the goddess NUT, in whose name Osiris entered the realms of heaven. The *maqet* sign was also inscribed with images of the goddess ISIS in reliefs, denoting her role in the resurrection and ascension of Osiris.

Mareotis an important lake in the Delta region of the Lower Kingdom of ancient Egypt. (See LAKES.)

marriage the union undertaken by Egyptian men and women that appears to have conferred considerable social status though a semi-legal aspect becomes clearly evident only in documents dating to the periods following the fall of the New Kingdom in 1070 B.C. There are no records of marriages taking place in temples or in government offices, but celebrations were held in conjunction with such unions. In general, ancient Egyptian marriages appear to have been based on cohabitation. Until the 26th Dynasty, prospective grooms normally sought permission for union from the intended bride's father, and in the Late Ptolemaic Period the groom offered silver and cattle as a "bride price" to put an end to a father's claims on his daughter. Late Period marriage contracts appear to have been drawn up to clarify a division of property in the case of dissolution of the union.

Royal marriages, recorded in almost every era, had several religious and administrative aspects. Most of these unions were designed to promote the royal cult and based on the need to provide royal heirs who met the blood requirements for succession. The kings of the first dynasties of Egypt married aristocratic Memphite women to augment their claims and to establish connections with the local noble families. Polygamy was an accepted part of royal life, providing heirs to the throne. Normally the son of a king (if there was one) married his sister and made her his Great Wife, the ranking queen. He then took other wives to ensure legitimate heirs. Consanguinity was not a factor considered detrimental to such unions, either on a moral or genetic basis. In many instances the heir to the throne was not born of the sister-wife but of another member of the king's retinue of lesser queens, a process by which the possible negative genetic effects of such unions were allayed. In later years, kings married foreign princesses as well, in politically expedient unions, conciliatory gestures to allies and buffer states.

There were ideals concerning marriage and the family, and many Egyptian sages, including one of KHUFU's own sons (4th Dynasty), counseled the people to marry and to raise up a patriotic and noble generation. In the case of Khufu's family, however, the presence of too many wives and offspring led to the probable murder of an heir and to division among the royal family. The various HAREMS were sources of intrigue and rivalry in some eras, as reported conspiracies and plots indicate.

Polygamy was not practiced by non-royal Egyptians, including the noble classes, but marriages were arranged for political reasons among aristocrats, as evidenced by NOME records. Family members, such as uncles, aunts and cousins, did intermarry, and the extended nome families took care to keep their holdings secure by regulating unions among their offspring.

Not all of the marriages of ancient Egypt were successful, however, and in such cases divorce was an accepted remedy. Such dissolutions of marriage required a certain open-mindedness concerning property rights and the economic survival of the ex-wife. In the eras following the fall of the New Kingdom, contracts become evident. These were possibly no more than mutually accepted guidelines for the division of property in the event of a divorce, but they could also have been legal expressions of the marriage union. A portion of these contracts were drawn up by partners who already had children. Many documents from the late periods appear to be true marriage contracts. In the case of divorce, the dowry provided by the groom at the time of marriage reverted to the wife for her support, or a single payment was given to her. In some instances the husband had to give one-third of the property acquired during the marriage, and in others the husband was obliged to provide alimony payments. The charge of adultery, if carried successfully against a wife, eliminated all legal obligations on the part of a husband.

Masara   a site on the Nile opposite ZAWIYET EL-ARYAN near Giza. Fine limestone quarried at Masara was used by the Egyptians for mortuary and other royal building projects. The limestone from this sitre was particularly popular as a facing for tombs because of its lustrous beauty. (See QUARRIES.)

mastabas   Arabic word for rectangular mud benches. The mastaba was the style of tomb used by the Egyptians when mortuary customs advanced during the last eras of the predynastic age. The simple trenches and shallow graves that had been used in earlier times no longer functioned as proper receptacles for the dead because the new traditions demanded ritual burials with funerary regalia and offerings. These religious practices, coupled with the custom of celebrating commemorative ceremonies at the tombs, demanded a certain spaciousness for the accommodation of priests, family members and ritual offerings. The walls of the graves had to be extended and reinforced in order to meet the demands of more elaborate rites, and mud and wood were used originally as foundations. When separate burial chambers and chapels were incorporated into tomb designs, unbaked bricks were employed as well. In time the tombs were covered with oblong-shaped embankments, whose interiors were faced with limestone and decorated with schemes drawn from cultic myths, spells and religious literature.

False doors were designed to serve as stelae on which the achievements, honors and aspirations of the deceased could be proclaimed to future generations. The false doors, however, were sometimes actual entrances set into the walls that led to the SERDAB, the chamber in which the statue or statues of the deceased were placed. Statues were normally deposited in the *serdab* chamber of the kings, one for each royal name or religious title. These chambers, however, were also in non-royal tombs. The *serdab* was built with a slit in the wall so that the statues could view the funerary rituals being conducted in the chapel and could observe the gifts and mortuary offerings being proffered in commemorative rites.

The actual burial chambers were placed at the end of long corridors or sometimes placed deep in the ground behind shafts in the mastabas. Stone plugs,

MASTABAS tombs typical of the Old Kingdom that evolved into the more elaborate structures of later eras.

debris and various traps were incorporated into the design in order to deter thieves and to protect the corpse and the funerary regalia. These burial chambers were normally surrounded by other rooms that served as storage areas.

The use of mastabas in ancient Egypt altered the mortuary processes in time. The bodies originally placed in the shallow graves on the fringe of the desert were preserved by the heat, the sand and the lack of moisture. Placing such corpses inside brick structures altered the natural preservation processes and the priests began to employ embalming. (See MORTUARY RITUALS.)

Matit a lion goddess of HIERANKOPOLIS in ancient Egypt. Her cult was popular at Thinis also. Jars discovered in tombs dating to the Early Dynastic Period bear her image. In some eras she was also considered a guardian of the royal residences.

mau called *ma'au* when large in form, the ancient Egyptian word for cat and the name of the feline deity worshipped at BUBASTIS. Sacred to the goddess Bast, *mau* lived in the mythical PERSEA TREE. The deity guarded RE' at night, cutting off the head of APOPHIS when that symbol of evil tried to attack the god.

Mau-Taui the guardian deity of the Judgment Hall where the goddess MA'AT weighed the souls or hearts of the deceased Egyptian for OSIRIS and his compan-

ion judges. Mau-Taui was considered a theophany or personification of the god THOTH. (See JUDGMENT HALL OF OSIRIS.)

"May the King Make an Offering" a phrase used in ancient Egypt, *Hetep-di-Nesut*, translated as "An Offering Given by the King." The words normally began the funerary texts written on stelae and on the tomb walls of deceased Egyptians. They relate to the custom of the kings, who gave an offering to every important official sometime before his death. In time, the inscription was included in the mortuary formulas. The funerary texts thus referred to ancient tradition and implied that the king, as a son of the god, could and would provide spiritual offerings instead of the material ones brought to the grave sites in early eras. (See MORTUARY RITUALS, PHARAOHS.)

"May My Name Prosper" a mortuary phrase used by the ancient Egyptians and discovered in a text dating to the 6th Dynasty (2323–2150 B.C.). The Egyptians believed that any nameless creature, or a human being that was forgotten, was unable to exist in the afterlife. The gods and mankind had to know the name of the person in order for that man or woman to remain active and vitally sustained in the afterlife. The Egyptians thus asked their families and friends to make their names prosper. Those who could afford to hire priests to perform the MORTUARY RITUALS were ensured of continued remembrance.

The royal cults, naturally, provided hosts of priests for the constant commemorations of dead kings and queens.

Medamud site of an important Old Kingdom (2572–2134 B.C.) temple, located a few miles south of Thebes. The temple had a sacred grove and was surrounded by a wall that was designed with a unique tunnel system. Medamud was dedicated to the god MONT. SENWOSRET III (1878–1841? B.C.) of the 12th Dynasty built a new temple there to honor the deity, and there is some evidence of New Kingdom (1550–1070 B.C.) structures.

medicine the science conducted by the priests of the PER-ANKH, the House of Life. The Egyptians termed it the "necessary art." Because of the mythological aspects attributed to the practice of medicine in Egypt by the Greek historians, scholars have not recognized the importance of that art. The Greeks honored many of the early Egyptian priest-physicians, especially IMHOTEP of the 3rd Dynasty (c. 2620 B.C.), whom they equated with their god Asclepius. When they recorded the Egyptian medical customs and procedures, however, they included the magic and incantations used by the priests, which made medicine appear trivial or a superstitious aspect of Egyptian life. Magical spells were indeed a part of Egyptian medicine, thus the Greeks' disdain was not totally inaccurate. Nevertheless, scholars have long recognized that the Egyptians carefully observed various ailments, injuries and physical deformities, and offered many prescriptions for their relief.

Diagnostic procedures for injuries and diseases were common and extensive in Egyptian medical practice. The physicians consulted texts and made their own observations. Each physician listed the symptoms evident in a patient and then decided whether he had the skill to treat the condition. If a priest determined that a cure was possible, he reconsidered the remedies or therapeutic regimens available and proceeded accordingly. This required, naturally, a remarkable awareness of the functions of the human body. The physicians understood that the pulse was the "speaker of the heart," and they interpreted the condition now known as *angina*. They were also aware of the relationship between the nervous system and voluntary movements. The physicians could identify lesions of the head, fractures of the vertebrae and other complex conditions. Operations were performed on the brain. Skulls recovered from graves and tombs indicate that Egyptian patients lived through such operations and survived for years afterward. The human brain was not saved during the embalming process, deemed unworthy of protection in the CANOPIC JARS. Brains of the deceased were normally destroyed or savaged in the actual embalming procedure.

In treating bone fractures, the Egyptians were remarkably astute. Wooden splints and stiffened linens were placed beside injured bones, or in the nostrils of patients with damaged nasal bones. Gags and wooden tubes were inserted into the mouths of those with jaw injuries or patients in the process of being treated for such. The tubes were used to provide nourishment conveniently and to drain fluids. Brick supports and body casts were employed to keep patients still and upright, and other materials were molded to their bodies to supply clean, sturdy foundations for recovery. Flax and other materials were used to pack wounds in the clinics or in the hospitals, as well as in the treatment of sores or surgical incisions. Bandages were normally made of linen and were applied with the hygienic standards adopted in the nation. The priests also used poultices, adhesive strips and cleansing agents. Other therapeutic procedures included the cauterization of wounds, using fire drills or heated scalpels.

Egyptians of all eras had terrible teeth and peridontal problems. By the New Kingdom (1550–1070 B.C.), however, dental decay was critical. Physicians packed some teeth with honey and herbs, perhaps to stem infection or to ease pain. Some mummies were also provided with bridges and gold teeth. It is not known if these dental materials were used by the wearer while alive or inserted in the embalming process.

The pharmaceuticals of the ancient Egyptian priest-physicians included antacids, copper salts, turpentine, alum, astringents, alkaline laxatives, diuretics, sedatives, antispasmodics, calcium carbonates and magnesia. They also employed many exotic herbs. All dispensing of medicines carefully stipulated in the medical papyri, with explicit instructions as to the exact dosage, the manner in which the medicine was to be taken internally (as with wine or food) and external applications. Some of the prescriptions contained strange and exotic ingredients, and the dosages sometimes included magical spells or incantations as accompanying remedies.

The diseases that afflicted the ancient Egyptians were as varied as those present in the world today, especially in the area of the Mediterranean and African continent. The most common parasite infecting the bodies of the Egyptians was the bilharzia (schistosome), still prevalent on the Nile. The Egyptians suffered from hernias, tumors, arthritis, scoliosis, rheumatism, osteitis, heart trouble, high blood pressure, bronchitis, tuberculosis, pneumonia, appendicitis, kidney stones, abscesses, smallpox, liver problems, cystitis and various ovarian illnesses. They also suffered some forms of poliomylitis and peritonitis. Spinal curvature and meningitis were also evident. Some of the medical texts that have provided information on the Egyptian medical practices are: the Ebers, Edwin Smith, Chester Beatty VI, and Hearst papyri.

Medinet el-Faiyum See CROCODILOPOLIS.

Medinet Habu a site on the western shore of the Nile opposite THEBES where New Kingdom (1550–1070 B.C.) temples were discovered. The temple erected by RAMESSES III (c. 1194–1163 B.C.) of the 20th Dynasty is one of the most completely preserved structures in Egypt. Ramesses surrounded the shrine with walls and made it a vast complex, complete with a fortified gate. Scenes placed on the walls of the temple depict Ramesses' achievements. Also included are important reliefs and inscriptions from the era. A portrait of the god PTAH was incorporated into the design to welcome visitors to the temple. Ptah was believed to carry the prayers of the faithful to the god AMON, who remained hidden in the sanctuary of the complex. This combination of Old Kingdom and New Kingdom gods, actually represented both Upper and Lower Egypt as well as different eras, perpetuating the concept of national unity.

MEDINET HABU the high gates of the great shrine erected by Rameses III.

A temple of TUTHMOSIS III (c. 1479–1425 B.C.) of the 18th Dynasty was also discovered on the site. The temple, dedicated to the god Amon as well, was begun by TUTHMOSIS I and was called "Amon-Is-Splendid-in-Thrones" or the "Splendor-of-the West." HATSHEPSUT, the 18th Dynasty queen-pharaoh (the daughter of Tuthmosis I), directed much of the building work during her reign, but the dedication was made by Tuthmosis III. Medinet Habu was enlarged in the Greco-Roman Period. (See HIGH GATE OF MEDINET HABU.)

Medinet Madi See NARMOUTHIS.

Medir an official of the 3rd Dynasty, serving in the region of DJOSER (2630–2611 B.C.). Medir was governor of certain territories in Upper Egypt. When the Nile failed to rise and inundate the land for a number of years, Djoser consulted with Medir and with his vizier of Memphis, IMHOTEP, seeking remedies from them both. The two counselors advised Djoser to visit the ELEPHANTINE Island, because he had seen the god KHNUM in one of his dreams. Khnum's cult center was on the Elephantine. Djoser visited the shrine and made certain repairs and additions, and the Nile flooded the land soon after.

Medjay the name given to units of the Nubian forces long in service in Egypt, particularly under Kamose of the 17th Dynasty (c.1550 B.C.), when he began his campaigns to oust the HYKSOS from the northwestern territories of ancient Egypt. Kamose's father, Sekenenre'-Tao' II, had started the war against the Hyksos king, Apophis. The Medjay, famed as warriors of cunning and stamina, served as scouts for the Egyptians on the marches or at the oases of the Libyan Desert. In actual battle they formed light infantry units and rushed to the front lines, delighting in hand-to-hand combat and in slaughter of the enemy.

When Ahmose I, the brother of Kamose and the founder of the 18th Dynasty and the New Kingdom (c. 1567 B.C.) assaulted the Hyksos capital of Avaris, the Medjay were again at his side. When the war ended successfully, the Medjay became the backbone of the newly formed state police. Some of their members, men such as DEDU, distinguished themselves and were given high political and governmental posts. Tuthmosis III (c.1479–1425 B.C.) built a temple to DEDUN, the Nubian god who was probably a patron of the Nubian troops. The Medjay are associated with the PAN-GRAVE people in southern Egypt and in Lower NUBIA. Indications are that these troops served as occupation forces and garrisoned some fortresses for the Egyptians during the New Kingdom.

Mefdet   See MAFDET.

Megiddo   See TUTHMOSIS III'S MILITARY CAMPAIGNS.

Mehen   a great mythical serpent that figured in ancient Egyptian cosmogonic and religious texts. Mehen was carried through the sky each day by divine bearers. The creature surrounded the solar bark of the god RE', preserving the deity in its coils. In some versions Mehen had a head on each end of his body, so as to bring greater protection to Re' on his travels. (See BARKS OF THE GODS.)

Mehurt   listed as Mehueret in some records, the celestial cow that gave birth to the sky according to ancient Egyptian legends. Her name meant "flooding waters." Mehurt represented the spiritual river of the heavens. She was normally associated with the cult of ISIS and was considered a protectoress of the deceased in the various halls of trial and judgment.

Mehy   an official of the 19th Dynasty, serving in the reign of SETI I (1306–1290 B.C.). Mehy's rank and role remain a mystery because many of his mortuary reliefs and images were struck by the agents of RAMASSES II, Seti's successor. It is obvious that Mehy was a warrior. He was normally depicted in princely trappings and appeared on Seti's war reliefs. Some of the love songs of the era mention Mehy as a romantic hero. Some records indicate that Mehy was a commoner by birth, and he was possibly a favorite of Seti. In either case he earned the enmity of Ramesses II, Seti's son and natural heir.

Meidum   a site south of Memphis dominated by a two-tiered pyramid started by HUNI (2599–2575 B.C.) and completed by SNOFRU (2575–2551 B.C.), the last ruler of the 3rd Dynasty.

The pyramid stood on a prepared earthen platform, with an entrance constructed on the northern side some distance from the ground. The passage to the chambers located inside of the pyramid opened onto a vertical shaft. The burial chamber was lined with limestone, and the remains of a wooden coffin were discovered in the room. The MASTABA of a famous Egyptian couple, Prince RE'HOTPE and his wife, NOFRET, is located beside the Meidum Pyramid. The royal pair were celebrated by a unique portrait-style painted statue group. The statues and remarkable 4th Dynasty paintings are in the Egyptian Museum, Cairo.

Meir   a necropolis site south of HERMOPOLIS. Tombs from the First Intermediate Period (2134–2040 B.C.) and the Middle Kingdom (2040–1640 B.C.) were discovered in the area.

mekes   the ancient Egyptian name for the royal sceptre having one flat end. It was a symbol of kingly power and was used in many eras.

Meket-Aten   a princess of the 18th Dynasty, a daughter of AKHENATEN (Amenhotep IV) and Queen NERFERTITI, (1353–1335 B.C.). Paintings depicting the royal couple mourning her also portray a nurse holding a baby, leading to the speculation that she died in childbirth. She was buried at 'AMARNA, but her tomb was vandalized.

Meketre'   an official of the 11th Dynasty, serving in the reign of Mentuhotpe II (2061–2010 B.C.). Meketre' was the chancellor and chief steward of the nation, living long enough to hold various offices in the reign of MENTUHOTPE III as well. Meketre's tomb, located near DEIR EL-BAHRI on the western shore of Thebes, is world famous for its wooden replicas depicting the daily life and activities of his era. Painted miniature figurines, including soldiers, ships, farm workers, overseers, even cattle, were placed in the tomb beside miniature buildings and gardens. Meketre''s tomb was linked to that of Inyotef, probably his son and heir.

Mekhenet   a name for the ancient Egyptian solar bark of the god RE'. (See MANDET, MESEKET and BARKS OF THE GODS.)

Memnon   See COLOSSI OF MEMNON.

Memphis   the capital of ancient Egypt from the Early Dynastic Period, continuing as a seat of political power even when the kings maintained a capital in another region. Originally named Hiku-Ptah, or Hut-Ra-Ptah, the "Mansion of the Soul of Ptah," Memphis was located on the western side of the Nile, south of modern Cairo. The first capital of the first NOME of Lower Egypt, Memphis was supposedly founded by 'Aha, (2920 B.C.). Legends state that the king altered the course of the Nile in order to clear the plain for his capital. This plain, on the western side of the Nile, was some four miles wide, and its western end sloped upwards to the cliffs of the Libyan Desert. The distinctive white walls of Memphis were made of mud and mud bricks, overlaid and then painted.

In some eras the city was called Ankh-Tawy, "the Life of the Two Lands." When the capital was offi-

cially at HERAKLEOPOLIS, IT-TAWY, THEBES or PER-RA-
MESSES in later eras, the affairs of state were conducted in part in Memphis, and most dynastic clans
spent a portion of each year in residence there. The
city remained great throughout the nation's history.
The modern name derives from the period of the 6th
Dynasty in the Old Kingdom, when Pepi I (2289–
2255 B.C.) built his beautiful pyramid at Saqqara. That
mortuary monument was called Men-nefer-Mare' the
"Established and Beautiful Pyramid of Men-nefer-
Mare'." The name soon came to designate the surrounding area, including the city itself. It was called
Men-nefer and then Menfi. The Greeks, visiting the
capital centuries later, translated the name to Memphis.

A temple of PTAH once dominated the capital, but
only the precinct walls of that structure can be seen
today in modern Mit Rahina. There are also remains
of shrines dating to the reigns of SETI I (c. 1306–1290
B.C.) of the 19th Dynasty and Ramesses II (1290–1224
B.C.). Merneptah (1224–1214 B.C.) also built on the
site. The necropolis area of Memphis was divided
into six sections, including Saqqara, with its remarkable collection of tombs from the Archaic Period and
the Old Kingdom. Nothing remains today except
archaeological sites and a museum. (See EGYPT and
STEP-PYRAMID.)

menat   a form of ancient Egyptian AMULET heavily
weighted and used to counterbalance the heavy collars worn by the rulers and members of the aristocracy. The *menat* was attached to the back of such
collars to keep them in place. As an amulet the *menat*
was painted or carved with spells, prayers and divine
images. Made of stone, faience or metal, it was worn
with strands of beads when not used as a counterbalance.

Mendes   an ancient Egyptian cult center at modern
Tell el-Rub'a. The name was derived from the Mendes
ram god, called BA'EB-DJET, or Ba'eb Djedet. Mendes
was the chief town of the 16th nome of the northern
territories of Lower Egypt. It was a shrine of the ram
cult and was graced by a temple of the god, which
included a monolithic granite sanctuary.

Menes   the legendary unifier of ancient Egypt, now
thought to be the first king of Egypt, 'AHA (2920 B.C.),
whose *nebti* name was Men. The unification was not
completed by 'Aha or by his immediate successors.
Some regions remained independent until the reign
of Kha'sekhemwy (c. 2660 B.C.).

Menhet   a famous royal wife of the 18th Dynasty,
married to TUTHMOSIS III (1479–1425 B.C.). It is be-

MENAT an amulet often used as a counterbalance for the
heavy golden collars of the Egyptians.

lieved that Menhet was the daughter of a Syrian
chief, given to Tuthmosis in marriage along with her
two sisters, MERTI and MENWI. She was buried in the
WADI GABBANET EL-KURRUD, called the Valley of the
Tombs of the Monkeys, with her sisters. Each of

them received identical mortuary regalia and funerary offerings, to ensure equal honors in the tomb.

Menkaure' (Mycerinus) the fifth king of the 4th Dynasty (2490–2472 B.C.), the son of KHEPHREN and probably Queen Per(senti?). The Greek historians, relying on legends, labeled Menkaure' as "pious," especially in comparison with his dynastic predecessors. He built his pyramid at GIZA; it is smaller than the other two (those of KHUFU and Khephren) but was to be covered with costly Aswan granite. A basalt SARCOPHAGUS within the pyramid contained fine panel decorations, examples of the age's sureness and skill. Statues and other art works give testimony to his patronage of the arts during his reign. His principal queen was KHAMERERNEBTY II, who bore him a son, Khunere, who did not live to succeed him. Another son, apparently not Khamerernebty's, was SHEPSES-KAF.

Menkauhor the seventh king of the 5th Dynasty (2396–2388 B.C.). He is not well known. A small alabaster figure of him is in the Egyptian Museum in Cairo, and his pyramid is in DASHUR. He is recorded as having sent a mining expedition into the SINAI to obtain materials for his tomb. The pyramid is believed to be in ruins a short distance from the North Stone Pyramid on that site.

Menkhaf a prince of the 4th Dynasty, the son of KHUFU (2551–2528 B.C.) by a lesser wife. He became a vizier for KHEPHREN, a custom of the 4th Dynasty, in which the various members of the royal family served in the important administrative capacities.

Menkheperresenb an official of the 18th Dynasty, serving TUTHMOSIS III (1479–1425 B.C.) as high priest of AMON and as chief architect. Menkheperresenb also controlled the "Gold and Silver Houses," a poetic term for the royal residence at THEBES. He was buried on the western shore of the river opposite the capital. (See PERO.)

Menna an official of the 18th Dynasty who served TUTHMOSIS IV (1401–1391 B.C.). Menna was attached to the temple's assessment program, working in the various NOMES to tally harvests and to gather up the crop tithes. His mortuary stela announced his close relationship to the local farmers. He was buried at Thebes. (See AGRICULTURE.)

Mentuemzaf (Djed' ankhre') listed as a late king of the 13th Dynasty, number 32c, (date unknown). His monument was discovered at DEIR EL-BAHRI, and

Menkauhor, depicted in an Old Kingdom relief.

another at Gebelein. Mentuemzaf's son is recorded as having lived at AVARIS, the capital of the HYKSOS in the eastern Delta. These Asiatics eventually took control of MEMPHIS, the capital, and in Mentuemzaf's reign they apparently influenced much of Egyptian royal affairs.

Mentuhotpe II (Nebheptre') (2061–2010 B.C.), the fourth king of the 11th Dynasty, the son of INYOTEF III and Queen AOH. In 2040 B.C., Mentuhotpe's armies took the city of Herakleopolis, which had served as the capital of the kings of the rival 9th and 10th Dynasties. This victory not only established the 11th Dynasty from Thebes as the rulers of a united Egypt but put an end to the historical First Intermediate Period, ushering in the Middle Kingdom. Mentuhotpe consolidated Egypt's borders, fought against the Libyans who had infiltrated the Delta, and against

Mentuhotpe II, from a Middle Kingdom statue.

the Asiatics in the SINAI. He is also recorded as having conducted expeditions in NUBIA, where he levied tributes. This king had Nubian and Lybian units in his army.

DEIR EL-BAHRI was the site of his mortuary complex, erected on the western shore of the Nile across from Thebes, his clan home. The funerary temple is now almost completely destroyed but was originally designed with columned porticoes, terraces and courtyards, where sycamore and tamarisk trees complemented statues of the king. A sloping passage led to a burial chamber, made of blocks of sandstone and containing an alabaster sarcophagus. Mentuhotpe's several wives and consorts, as well as members of his court were buried at Deir el-Bahri. The COFFINS, SARCOPHAGI and other funerary regalia have provided important information about the Egyptian language at the close of the First Intermediate Period. His queen was Neferu, but his heir, MENTUHOTPE III, was the son of another consort, Tem.

Mentuhotpe II's Army   a remarkable collection of bodies discovered at DEIR EL-BAHRI beside the mortuary complex of the king. Almost 60 soldiers were entombed there in ritual burial. All of them had died

of battle wounds, and they wore shrouds marked with the cartouches and seals of Mentuhotpe II. The tomb was robbed during the Second Intermediate Period (1640–1532 B.C.) but then covered by a landslide, which sealed it effectively.

Mentuhotpe III (S'ankhkare')   (2010–1998 B.C.), the fifth king of the 11th Dynasty, the son of MENTUHOTPE II and Queen TEM. Apparently, he ascended the throne at an advanced age. A veteran of his father's campaigns, Mentuhotpe did not have to undertake vigorous military campaigns, dedicating himself instead to patronage of the arts and rebuilding. He opened trade with the Red Sea region and was involved with the WADI HAMMAMAT quarrying operations. His mortuary temple, built near his father's complex at DEIR EL-BAHRI, was not finished, but he also built a temple to the god THOTH, or a festival shrine of some sort, on a high hill overlooking the Nile on the western shore. The letters of an official named Hekanakhte, in service as a mortuary priest in the tomb of a vizier at Thebes, provide considerable information about this period. Mentuhotpe's heir was born to Queen Imi, a lesser ranked consort.

Mentuhotpe IV (Nebtawyre')   (1998–1991 B.C.) the sixth king of the 11th Dynasty, the son of MENTUHOTPE III and Queen Imi. During his reign he initiated expeditions to mines and quarries and had an immense SARCOPHAGUS lid quarried in WADI HAMMAMAT and then sailed down the Nile to his tomb site. He founded a harbor town (KUSER) on the Red Sea for the shipbuilding operations conducted by the Egyptians in preparation for journeys to PUNT. Many of these projects were conducted by Mentuhotpe's vizier, Amenemhet, who succeeded him.

Menwi   a famous royal wife of the 18th Dynasty, married to Tuthmosis III (1479–1425 B.C.). Menwi was a daughter of a Syrian chieftain, given to the pharaoh along with her two sisters, MENHET and MERTI. The three were buried in the WADI GABBANET EL-KURRUD, in identical tombs with sumptuous grave goods.

Menyu   a god of ancient Egypt, the lord of the desert. Menyu was believed to be the son of ISIS, and was revered at COPTOS, called the Neb-Semt, or desert deity. He was depicted in some eras as a warrior bull god. Menyu was also a god of generation. He was listed on the PALERMO STONE.

Menzala   a lake in the Delta region of ancient Egypt. (See LAKES.)

Mereneith a queen of the 1st Dynasty, believed to be the wife of WADJ (date unknown) and probably the mother of DEN, although she could have served only as his regent during his minority. Mereneith did rule Egypt for a brief period. Her mortuary complexes at SAQQARA and ABYDOS attest to her standing. Some 20 Egyptians were buried as part of her funerary regalia, including artisans and craftsmen. It is not known if these people were slain or buried when they died naturally. A stela erected in her honor has her name entwined with the SEREKH symbol, a royal insignia. Her coffin also bore royal emblems.

Mereruka an official of the 6th Dynasty, serving TETI (2323–2291 B.C.) as vizier. Mereruka married Princess Shesheshet, a daughter of the king, and he supervised the construction of Teti's mortuary complex. His own magnificent tomb at SAQQARA is famous for its elaborate reliefs and for the statue of Mereruka as a KA entering through a false door.

Meresankh I a queen of the 3rd Dynasty, a lesser ranked consort of HUNI (2599–2575 B.C.), who bore the heir, SNOFRU, the founder of the 4th Dynasty.

Meresankh III a queen of the 4th Dynasty, wife of KHEPHREN (2520–2494 B.C.), and the daughter of Prince KEWAB and HETEPHERES II. She was the mother of Prince NEBMAKHET. Her mortuary complex at GIZA, a beautifully sculptured and painted rock-cut tomb, was prepared for her by her mother. She died in the reign of SHEPSESKHAF, and her son was buried nearby.

Meresger a goddess of ancient Egypt's Theban necropolis. She is called the Lady of Heaven and the PEAK OF THE WEST in Egyptian religious texts. Meresger was noted as a goddess who chastised the evildoer. The Egyptians depicted her as a "savage lion" to all who performed sinful acts until they called upon her name for forgiveness. The goddess lived on the rocky spur of Sheik Abd-el-Gurneh, at the necropolis site of Thebes, where she was called the Lover of Silence; an allusion to her mortuary role. She was popular throughout many eras of Egyptian history.

Meri an official of the 12th Dynasty, serving Senwosret I (c.1971–1926 B.C.). Meri was the supervisor of the king's pyramid at LISHT, overseeing the construction of the mortuary complex. He also governed the pyramid area. His funerary stela, now in the Louvre, gives an account of his career and honors.

Merikare' a king of the Herakleopolitan 10th Dynasty (date unknown), probably the son of KHETY III, who was honored by the *Instructions for Merikare'*, a didactic text. Khety wrote about the events of his reign, a period in which the Inyotefs of Thebes were beginning their assault on the Herakleopolitans. Khety regrets many of the events that took place, and he speaks of the ideals of Egypt and the spirit which king and subject should adopt in order to attain spiritual maturity. Merikare' appears to have been middle aged when Khety bequeathed him the Herakleopolitan throne. He faced growing tensions with Thebes in an uncertain period. He died before the armies of MENTUHOTPE II, advanced on his capital and ITY was his successor. His mortuary pyramid was constructed near Memphis.

Meriptah an official of the 18th Dynasty, serving in the region of Amenhotep III (1391–1353 B.C.). The high priest of the god AMON, Meriptah conducted the major religious festivals in the Theban court. He also witnessed the rise of the god ATEN, who was to play a major role in the life of Egypt during the reign of AKHENATEN (Amenhotep IV). Meriptah was buried at Thebes.

Merit-Amon a queen of the 18th Dynasty, the wife of AMENHOTEP II (1427–1401 B.C.), and the daughter of TUTHMOSIS III and Queen MERYT-RE'-HATSHEPSUT. She was depicted on reliefs at DEIR EL-BAHRI in the company of her father. Her CARTONNAGE COFFIN is prized for its workmanship and beauty and

Queen Merit-Amon's cartonnage mask from Thebes, one of the most beautiful surviving mortuary pieces.

is in the Egyptian Museum, Cairo although the portrait mask does not seem to be accurate, as it does not match her mummified remains. (See BENIMERYT.)

Meritites   a queen of the 4th Dynasty, the wife of KHUFU (2551–2528 B.C.). She is believed to have been the mother of Prince KEWAB and Queen HETEPHERES II, and it is possible that she was also the mother of HARDEDEF and BAUFRE'. She was probably set aside upon the death of Khufu, when RA'DJEDEF murdered Kewab and assumed the throne.

merkhet   an astral gauge used by the ancient Egyptians for architectural surveys and construction projects. Much like the modern plumb line, the *merkhet* provided relatively accurate measurements, something required for the construction of the massive monuments that not only had to be based on secure foundations but were positioned according to astronomical configurations.

Merneptah   (Baenre'hotephirma'at)   (1224–1214 B.C.) the fourth king of the 19th Dynasty, the son of RAMESSES II and Queen ISTNOFRET. He was apparently the 14th son of Ramesses, the others having died before they could succeed their long-lived father. Active militarily while a prince, Merneptah was in his fifties when he came to the throne. The borders of Egypt were troubled and the army in a state of neglect. The Libyans, driven by famine in their own land, came into the Delta, and Merneptah finally faced a coalition of Libyans and SEA PEOPLES, tribes which had come from as far away as Asia Minor and the Aegean Sea. A Libyan prince led the invasion, which included the families of the Sea Peoples and their household furnishings. Merneptah supposedly consulted the oracle of AMON at Thebes and then saw the god PTAH in a dream, both urging his military action. He met the invaders at a western frontier site called Pi-yer, where he slew over 6,000 of them and took their families captive. The Libyan prince, Mauroy, fled to his homeland but was overthrown there. The war with the Libyans was recorded at KARNAK and on a stela from Athribis.

Another stela, called the Israel Stela, is associated with Merneptah. The monument declares Merneptah's victories on all sides, with lavish pride for his military prowess, and it mentions Israel. A revolt in Palestine had brought Merneptah and his armies to the scene. This is the only mention in Egyptian monuments of Israel, and it would appear to confirm the fact that the Israelites were established in their own domain during Merneptah's reign. He lived to the age of seventy two, and his mummified remains

MERNEPTAH   the warrior son of Ramesses II.

give evidence of his age. Merneptah was bald, corpulent and stood 5 feet 7 inches tall. The mummy shows signs of calcification of the arteries as well as arthritis. The king's poor teeth bore evidence of dental surgery having been performed while he was still alive. His tomb was constructed in the VALLEY OF THE KINGS, on the western shore opposite Thebes. Carved into the cliffs, the tomb contained a giant SARCOPHAGUS.

Merti   a famous royal wife of the 18th Dynasty, one of three Syrian chieftain's daughters who were given to Tuthmosis III (1479–1425 B.C.). She was buried with her sisters, MENWI and MENHET, in identical tombs in the WADI GABBANET EL-KURRUD, the Valley of the Tombs of the Monkeys.

Meryre' I an official of the 18th Dynasty's 'AMARNA Period, he served AKHENATEN (Amenhotep IV—1353–1335 B.C.) as the high priest of the god ATEN. He bore the title of Great Seer of Aten when Akhenaten decided to share priestly powers toward the end of his reign. Meryre' conducted the affairs of the temples at 'Amarna, but the death of Akhenaten and the subsequent removal of the capital by his successors to Thebes, where they accepted the dominance of the god Amon gain, put an end to the Aten cult and destroyed his power. 'Amarna was abandoned and later demolished by HOREMHAB, the last king of the dynasty. Meryre' and his wife, Tener, disappeared. His beautifully adorned tomb at 'Amarna was found in an unfinished state.

Meryre' II an official of the 18th Dynasty's 'AMARNA Period, serving AKHENATEN, Amenhotep IV, (1353–1335 B.C.) as a superintendent of Queen NEFERTITI's royal household and affairs. Meryre' watched with his father, the high priest of Aten, as 'Amarna and the cult of the new god collapsed. He disappeared when the successors of the Akhenaten moved to Thebes and embraced the worship of Amon again. Meryre's unfinished tomb was discovered in the cliffs at 'Amarna.

Meryt-Amon also called Meryt-Aten, a queen of the 18th Dynasty, the wife of SMENKHKARE', (1335–1333 B.C.). Meryt-Amon was the daughter of AKHENATEN (King Amenhotep IV) and Queen NEFERTITI. When Nefertiti left Akhenaten's palace in 'Amarna and took up residence in her own mansion, Meryt-Amon became queen in her place, even though she was married to Smenkhkare'. The death of Akhenaten in c. 1335 B.C., brought about Smenkhkare' 's coronation. He had been Akhenaten's attendant for two years and had assumed many administrative duties. Smenkhkare' and Meryt-Amon returned to Thebes, anxious to placate the priests of Amon and the military faction, led by General HOREMHAB. Smenkhare' was dead or deposed one year later, however, and Meryt-Amon disappeared.

Merytamon a queen of the 19th Dynasty, the eldest daughter of RAMESSES II (c.1290–1224 B.C.) and Queen NEFERTARI. When Nefertari died or retired to the harem palace near the FAIYUM, Merytamon became a queen, ranking second to BINT-ANATH, her sister. A third queen, MA'AT HORNEFRURE, was a Hittite royal princess, given in marriage to Ramesses.

Merytatum a prince of the 19th Dynasty, the son of RAMESSES II (c. 1290–1224 B.C.) and Queen NEFER-TARI. Merytatum went on one campaign to the SINAI with his father. He then became the high priest of RE' at HELIOPOLIS.

Meryt-Re-Hatshepsut a queen of the 18th Dynasty, the wife of TUTHMOSIS III (c. 1479–1425 B.C.). She was a Memphite with no royal claims but as the mother of Tuthmosis' heir, AMENHOTEP II, Meryt-Re-Hatshepsut was honored in her son's reign. She outlived Tuthmosis and was buried at Thebes.

Meseket the sacred bark used by the god RE' in his nightly descent from the heavens. Re' rode on the MANDET in the morning according to the ancient mythology concerning his cult. (See BARKS OF THE GODS.)

Mesentiu name of an ancient Egyptian group of people from Edfu who figure in the early legends about the unification of the kingdom. They were supposedly skilled in metallurgy as well as battle.

Mesenty an ancient Egyptian term that meant the "Lord of all Creation," a particular name applied to the god PTAH.

Meshkent a goddess; patron of birth in ancient Egypt, she was identified in some eras with HATHOR.

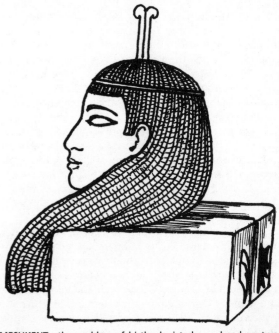

MESHKENT the goddess of birth, depicted as a head on two birthing stones.

The goddess was portrayed as two bricks with a human head, signifying the special seat used by Egyptian women during the last stages of childbirth. The goddess was also an attendant in the JUDGMENT HALLS OF OSIRIS, where she supposedly pleaded on behalf of the Egyptian deceased so that they could enter paradise.

Meshwesh   a people who dominated LIBYA in the Ramessid era. They led an army into the Delta of Egypt in the reign of RAMESSES III (1194–1163 B.C.) in the 19th Dynasty. On two occasions the Egyptians defeated the forces of the Meshwesh. With the fall of the New Kingdom in 1070 B.C., however, the Libyans grew in strength and eventually formed their own dynasty in Egypt.

Mestha   See PALETTE.

Mesthi-Imsety   See CANOPIC JARS and IMSETY.

Mesu-heru   the canopic guardians, when addressed as the four sons of the god HORUS. The sons presided over the organs of the deceased in the tomb in the CANOPIC JARS.

mesut   an ancient Egyptian word for evening, which actually means the "time of birth." It was believed that the stars were swallowed by a divine sow each sunrise. They were given birth by the sow each evening.

metals   the mining operations of the Egyptians were extensive, and they started expeditions in the Early Dynastic Period (2920–2575 B.C.) to explore the availability of natural resources. This practice was continued throughout the pharaonic period.

Gold, called *nub, nub nefer* (when of the finest grade) or *tcham* (electrum), the combination of gold and silver used in the war helmets of the imperial pharaohs, was mined in such areas as the Wadi Alaki, Wadi Miah and at Nubian sites.

Silver, called *hedj* (white gold), was scarcer in Egypt, and higher in value than gold until the Middle Kingdom. Copper was not available in quantity in Egypt but was mined in the WADI MAGHARA of the SINAI. Copper was called *hemt* or *baa en pet*, when it was discovered in meteorites. Lead was called DEHETY, and iron was called *baa* and *baa-en-pet* when discovered in meteoric form. Iron was common in Egypt, as was lead, and both were prized.

In the SINAI the Egyptians had to fight Asiatic nomads defending their lands and harrassing caravans and military units sent to begin mining operations. The Sinai was a continuing source of copper, and in the New Kingdom the mines at Timna were in use. It is probable that the Egyptians employed defeated Asiatics in the mines. The eastern desert was an important source of gold. The Wadi Abbad, east of Edfu, had mining operations in the Ramessid era, and SETI I (1306–1290 B.C.) dug wells there and built a complex and a temple for the workers on the site.

In the Nubian territories below the cataract at AS-WAN, the Egyptians were able to conduct two types of mining operations. In the area around BUHEN and KERMA they were able to recover gold from riverside deposits. The WADI-ALAKAI-Wadi Gabgaba complex provided gold in shallow surface workings, and probably copper as well, as slag heaps were discovered near the ancient fort at Kubban. Wadi Hudi was also a source of gold and amethyst. The inscriptions in this region date to the Middle Kingdom (2040–1640 B.C.). The area at Dal Island contain some Old Kingdom inscriptions concerning mining operations.

Metjen   (Methen in some lists) an official of the 3rd Dynasty, serving DJOSER (2630–2611 B.C.) in a number of capacities. Metjen, however, is famous as a biographer of the era. The reliefs in his SAQQARA mastaba provide detailed portraits of the political, social and religious aspects of the beginning of the Old Kingdom. Metjen began his career as a scribe, becoming the governor of the Delta lands. In time he ruled the eastern section of the FAIYUM and another NOME for the king. He was buried beside Djoser, signifying his rank and honors. His father, Anubisemonkeh, was a scribe and judge.

military   an institution that evolved over the centuries as a result of Egypt's expansion and contact with outside elements. Egypt's military forces had a definitive role in maintaining the sovereignty of the country and in obtaining natural resources and new lands.

Predynastic Period

Internal warfare led to the provisional unification of Egypt in 3000 B.C. SCORPION, NA'RMER and their military predecessors conducted campaigns in Lower Egypt in order to establish a cohesion of independent regions and provincial clans. The palettes and maceheads which document the period portray the legendary unifiers in personal combat, and images of fallen foes and divine intervention place their military activities in the context of national unification.

Warfare must have been a continuing process

throughout the predynastic period, as conflicting groups carved out their territories and established the perimeters of their influence. It is interesting that the totems of many of the Upper Egyptian NOMES were depicted in documents about Na'rmer, indicating that these warrior groups were already established to some extent and used as military units.

Early Dynastic Period

The early kings of Egypt did not preside over a united land in the 1st Dynasty (2920–2770 B.C.). There is evidence of resistance on the part of various regions. 'AHA recorded adding territories in the south (probably the area between Gebel es-Silsileh and Aswan). DJER (c. 2900 B.C.) recorded a campaign against the Asiatics in the eastern desert. PERIBSEN, at the beginning of the 2nd Dynasty (2770 B.C.) made raids into Palestine, probably exploratory expeditions or raids for cattle and other loot. KHA'SEKHEMWY (2649 B.C.), the last king of the 2nd Dynasty, secured Egypt's unification, indicating continual or at least intermitant warfare on the Nile up to that point. It is possible that the first settlement at BUHEN in NUBIA was made in his reign, as Kha'sekhemwy and his successors had started to penetrate the territories below the First Cataract of the Nile.

Old Kingdom

The rulers of the Old Kingdom were militarily active. The Egyptian interest in the SINAI territory led them to conduct punitive expeditions against the local *Bedwi*, the Asiatic nomads who roamed the region and resented Egyptian efforts to set up mines and quarries there. In the reign of SNOFRU at the start of the 4th Dynasty (2575–2551 B.C.), Egypt had a rather large fleet of naval vessels as well, supposedly sent to the Levant on trading expeditions.

Buhen, at the Second Cataract of the Nile in Nubia, became a base for southern trade, and was fortified with stone walls and a dry moat. All of the kings of Snofru's dynasty, including the pyramid builders of GIZA, are represented at Buhen by seals. Snofru is said to have conducted a massive raid in the vicinity of Buhen and it is probable that other Nubian settlements were begun in this period.

The kings of the 5th Dynasty continued the warfare. In that era the Egyptian army is recorded as having penetrated the Plain of Sharon. WENIS, the last king of the 5th Dynasty, claimed to have made five expeditions into Syria and Canaan. Reliefs from the 6th Dynasty depict assaults on Palestinian walled cities, and a true military leader other than the pharaoh emerged from this period: General Weni, in service to PEPI I (2289–2255 B.C.).

Weni, as commander of the royal armies, levied troops from the local nomes when any military campaign seemed imminent. Nomarchs were responsible for a certain number of troops, to be supplemented by Nubian mercenaries under command of caravan leaders or trade supervisors. Many of these troops were veterans of militia training or active duty in previous campaigns. The basic unit of the army at the time was the battalion, although its exact size and functions are not documented. The militia-levy system had its obvious drawbacks. Troops brought from the various nomes held allegiance only to their own leaders. The extra levies used as support for the militias were even less nationalistically oriented. For this reason there must have been some core units of the Egyptian army that were maintained as a regular force. There is evidence of so-called "household" units at the time. Weni commanded a well-trained military force, which suggests the presence of a regularly maintained core unit responsible for training the nome recruits. Weni's position was that of commander of troops, but he also performed other tasks for the king. Some generals served as caravan leaders as the expansion of trade warranted a military presence in remote regions. These positions appear to have been hereditary, the beginnings of a military caste. Ordinance and other logistical and provisionary departments were already functioning, and there were reserves and supplies mandated for the military units.

In Nubia there was a decided shift in Egyptian activities. Men like Weni used Nubian mercenaries, particularly when he served as the governor of Upper Egypt, but trade was the key to Egypt's relationship with Nubia. HARKHAF and his famous expedition for the child king PEPI II (2246–2152 B.C.) indicate a limited role in Nubia, mostly economic, not military. Buhen and the other forts were no longer invested with troops, and Nubia was comparatively free of Egyptian forces.

The soldiers of the Old Kingdom were depicted as wearing skull caps and carrying clan or nome totems. They used maces with wooden heads or pear-shaped stone heads. Bows and arrows were standard gear, with square-tipped flint arrowheads and leather quivers. Some shields, made of hides, were in use but not generally. Most of the troops were barefoot, dressed in simple kilts or naked.

First Intermediate Period

With the collapse of the Old Kingdom in 2134 B.C., military activities in Egypt were confined once again to the regions within the nation's borders. The KHETY clan of HERAKLEOPOLIS moved against their northern and western neighbors to carve out a new royal realm. The kings of the 9th and 10th Dynasties (2134–2040 B.C.) were vigorous warriors, added by nome allies. They could not penetrate into Upper Egypt because of the Theban resistance, and eventually the Thebans attacked their southern outposts and began marching on their capital. Nubian troops were employed in the battles taking place. In 2040 B.C., the armies of MENTUHOTPE II took Herakleopolis, and the internal wars of Egypt were coming to a close.

The Middle Kingdom

The fall of Herakleopolis ended the 10th Dynasty and started the Middle Kingdom. The land was united, but there were standing armies in some nomes, and aristocrats did not hesitate to use their forces to exact vengeance or to consolidate holdings. Such nobles were free to act on their own behalf as long as they provided the required number of troops to the royal campaigns. Such petty feuds between the nomes were ended in the 12th Dynasty.

There was a standing army in this period, composed of conscripts. There was a minister of war and a commander in chief of the army, or an official who worked in that capacity. Frontier units were on duty at the borders and troops accompanied many of the mining and quarrying expeditions.

Mentuhotpe and his successors continued vigorous campaigns against Libya and the Sinai, and are reported as having expanded their operations even into Syrian lands. The kings of the 12th Dynasty (1991–1783 B.C.), the Amenemhets, started their reigns with military campaigns. AMENEMHET I was a usurper and was skilled in military affairs, having served in martial and administrative affairs for the last Mentuhotpe. Upon staking his claims, he took an armada of ships up and down the Nile to discourage any rebellions from nome clans. He also erected a series of garrisoned fortresses on the northern borders, called the WALL OF THE PRINCE. When Amenemhet I died, his son and heir, SENWOSRET I, was on a campaign in Libya, having a small unit of bodyguards with him.

A vast army of scribes and administrators served the military forces of Egypt in this period. The frontier fortifications were manned, and there were even "shock troops" used in campaigns. There are some indications that professional soldiers were in the ranks of the Egyptian army at this time, called the "Brave" or the "Valiant." Officers could be denoted in reliefs by the feathers which they wore in their caps.

In Nubia the Middle Kingdom had considerable impact. The Mentuhotpes continued their raids, and the Amenemhets made the policy of fortifying settlements part of their dynastic goals. Senwosret I (1971–1926 B.C.) erected several fortresses and kept them fully staffed with troops. Ikkur, Aniba and Quban date to this era, and the region around Buhen was more stiffly fortified. Forts may have been erected by the 12th Dynasty kings as far south as SEMNA.

The term Kush came into being here, to designate a region of Nubia that had its capital at Kerma. During the last part of the Old Kingdom and the First Intermediate Period, the Nubians had built a relatively strong state in the region. SENWOSRET III completed the pacification of the area and established the southern borders of Egypt as far south as Semna and Uronarti.

The military gear of the Middle Kingdom was much the same as that of the Old Kingdom, although troops now carried axes and copper blades, bound to wooden hafts with leather thongs. A long bronze spear became popular, and the soldiers wore leather shirts and kilts.

The Second Intermediate Period

There was warfare throughout much of Egypt during the period following the collapse of the Middle Kingdom in 1640 B.C. Asiatics began to consolidate their holdings, after having penetrated Egypt and establishing their own domains. The HYKSOS, as these Asiatics were called, introduced the horse into the Nile Valley, using the animals to pull chariots and to carry loads. The horses of that era were not actually heavy enough to carry the weight of a man for long distances, something that the Egyptians remedied rather quickly.

After a brief period of tolerance, the Thebans began to assault the southern outposts of the Hyksos, as Sekenenre'-TA'O II (c.1560 B.C.) began a full-scale war to oust the aliens from the Nile. When he died, his son KAMOSE took the field in his place. Under his command the Egyptians fielded cavalry units, having lightened the Hyksos chariot and having trained special units for such tactics. He also commanded an unusual fighting force, called the MEDJAY, a group of Nubians who had allied themselves with Egypt's cause. The Medjay served as scouts for the main units and then as light infantry. Kamose used the Libyan desert OASES as effective hiding places in his assaults on the Hyksos, and he was within striking distance of AVARIS, the Hyksos capital, when he died or was slain in battle.

'AHMOSE I (1550–1525 B.C.), his younger brother, took up the cause and surrounded Avaris, using both land and sea forces. The Hyksos were forced to withdraw from Egypt, and the New Kingdom began. The army was no longer a confederation of nome levies but a first-class military force. The king was the commander in chief, but the vizier and another administrative series of units handled the logistical and reserve affairs. Apparently the senior officers of the army could debate campaign events with the king while on tours, and others were consulted for their experience.

The army was organized into divisions in the New Kingdom, both chariot forces and infantry. Each division numbered approximately 5,000 men. These divisions carried the names of the principal deities of the nation. When Egypt was not at war the army served as a reserve force, stationed in both Upper and Lower Egypt.

The chariot force was divided into squadrons of 25 men each, and the infantry contained two types of soldiers, the veterans and the conscripts of the campaign. The kings had their own elite corps, serving as bodyguards and special shock troops. There were alien mercenary units in the army in this period as well. Some, like the Sherden Pirates, were pressed into service after capture, and others, like the Libyans and Nubians, were long-established units of mercenaries. A definite officer corps existed, with the lowest grade commanding 50 men and the highest, led by the "standard-bearers," amounting to as many as 250 men. The troop commander was in charge of several brigades or commanded entire fortresses. Above this level were the various administrative officer staffs. In many instances the princes of Egypt led units into action, as in the case of two of Ramesses II's sons, who went to war in Nubia while still lads.

Pack animals were used for the various supplies, but boats were important in this period as well. A great naval station was located at PERU-NEFER, near Memphis. AMENHOTEP II, the son of TUTHMOSIS III (1479–1425 B.C.), commanded that depot and ship-building site while still a prince. Ox-drawn carts were also used in the field.

The pharaohs of the New Kingdom started with the war against the Hyksos and continued campaigns throughout that period. 'Ahmose's successor, AMENHOTEP I, maintained the military structures, but it was TUTHMOSIS I (1504–1492 B.C.) who took the armies of Egypt to the Euphrates River and began the empire. His grandson, Tuthmosis III, fought at MEGIDDO and then conducted 20 more campaigns in order to put down rebellions among the occupied or vassal states of the Mediterranean region. Tuthmosis III also took hostages from the royal families of conquered states and cities and trained them in Egypt so that they were ready to rule in their own time as allies.

In Nubia, meanwhile, tribes had risen again, and 'Ahmose I and his successors had to campaign there. Under Tuthmosis I the Egyptian fleet made its way south and established at fort a TOMBOS, which enabled the Egyptians to assault the regions easily. Tuthmosis I went as far as the Fourth Cataract. When he withdrew to Egypt, the body of the king of the warring tribe hung upside down on the prow of his ship. The interest in Nubia was mostly economic, and Egypt did little to respect the ways of the Nubians.

HOREMHAB, the last king of the 18th Dynasty (1319–1307 B.C.) was a trained military commander. He conducted campaigns to maintain the empire, which had diminished during the 'AMARNA period and with the fall of the Mitannis, Egypt's allies. Before he died he placed RAMESSES I on the throne, a military comrade in arms, and the Ramessids began their military exploits.

The Ramessids, experts in campaigns and enthusiastic about the empire, warred constantly to maintain a balance of power. They faced the mighty Hittites, and in the battle of KADESH, both the Egyptians and Hittites escaped disaster narrowly. An alliance was the result of the conflict, which divided lands between them. The great military leader of Egypt in this period was RAMESSES II (1290–1224 B.C.). His son, MERNEPTAH, had to fight the SEA PEOPLES and the Libyans, and conducted his campaigns with cunning and fervor.

The last great warrior pharaoh of this era was RAMESSES III, who maintained Egypt's military prowess, which gave way eventually to dynastic weakness and the avarice of the priests of AMON, which brought an end to the New Kingdom. (See EGYPT.)

Min the Greek form of the Egyptian *Menu*, a god of travel in the desert and the guardian of fertility and harvests. Min was worshipped at COPTOS and at Akhmin from the earliest eras. The god was represented as a man with an erect penis, wearing a plumed crown with a streamer, or as a mummy, adorned with a plumed crown and carrying a flail. LETTUCE was a symbol of Min, who was honored with festivals and riotous celebrations. In time he was incorporated into the AMON cult and was also worshipped in some areas as Min-Horus.

Min an official of the 18th Dynasty, serving TUTHMOSIS III (1479–1425 B.C.) as the mayor of Thinis and overseer of the priests of ANHUR. His most important position, however, was as the archery instructor of AMENHOTEP II, Tuthmosis' son and heir. A veteran of military campaigns, Min supervised the prince's military training. He was buried with honors at Thebes.

Mitry an official of the 5th Dynasty, serving in the early periods of that royal line as a provincial administrator of royal territories. Mitry was also one of the MAGNATES OF THE SOUTHERN TEN, a high-ranking position as counselor and judge. His tomb at Saqqara contained 11 wooden statues, extremely rare in ancient Egypt, life-sized portraits of the official and his wife. (See GOVERNMENT and LEGAL SYSTEM.)

Mnevis a bull sacred to HELIOPOLIS. The animal was considered a THEOPHANY of the god RE'. Because of the solar aspects of the bull's cult, AKHENATEN allowed the ceremonies of Mnevis to continue during the 'AMARNA Period. Mummified Mnevis bulls have been discovered, attesting to the fact that the animal was afforded the cultic rituals conducted for APIS and the other bulls. Mnevis had to have a black coloring, without markings, with tufts of hair on its body and tail. The animal was provided with a sanctuary and with companion cows and calves. Mnevis was normally depicted as a bull with the sun disk and the uraeus on its horns. (See BUCHIS.)

mokattem a site south of modern Cairo, the source of fine quality limestone, used in the construction of the STEP PYRAMID at SAQQARA.

Mongoose called Ichneumon by the Greeks, a divine being of ancient Egypt, which was considered a theophany of the god ATUM of HELIOPOLIS in early times. Revered because of its assault on serpents, and because it ate crocodile eggs, the mongoose was also associated with Re'. In some statues the mongoose is shown carrying weapons, and in most depictions the animal has a solar disk on its head.

Mont the ancient Egyptian god worshiped at ERMENT (Hermonthis). Mont was a sun god, dating to the earliest eras in the vicinity of Thebes in the Upper Kingdom, and an ancient warrior god, related to the Horus cult. He was depicted as a man with a hawk's head, wearing plumes and a sun disk. The kings of the 11th Dynasty (2134–1991 B.C.) especially honored Mont. The bull called BUCHIS was his theophany.

months the ancient Egyptian periods of 30 days each, incorporated into the CALENDAR by the priest in early eras. These months were part of three seasons and are as follows:

ICHNEUMON the mongoose deity, with the sun disk. The animal was honored because of its ability to slay serpents.

Season of *akhet*—the inundation—winter
  Thoth
  Paopi
  Athyr
  Khoiak
Season of *proyet* or *peret*—the sowing—spring
  Tybi (or Tobe)
  Mekhir
  Pnamenoth
  Pharmuthi
Season of *shemu* or *shomu*—the harvest—summer
  Pakhons
  Paoni
  Epep
  Mesore

MONTHS   a god of a day of the month in the Egyptian calendar.

The use of only 30 days in each month caused a gradual alteration between the true rotation of the earth and the seasons, based on a lunar calculation. The Egyptians attempted to remedy that situation by adding EPAGOMENAL DAYS at the end of the year.

mortuary rituals   the ceremonies and protocol involved in the burial of ancient Egyptians. Such rituals and traditions were maintained throughout the nation's history, evolving over the centuries as various material and spiritual needs became manifest. In the predynastic periods the Egyptians, following the customs of most primitive cultures, buried their dead on the fringes of the settlement region, in this case the surrounding deserts. This custom was maintained for a long time in Upper Egypt, but in Lower Egypt the people appear to have buried their dead under their houses as well.

Cemeteries in the MA'ADI cultural sequence (3400–3000 B.C.) contained human and animal graves. Unborn babies' remains were found in graves inside the settlements. In the BADARIAN period (4500–4000 B.C.), the graves were oval or rectangular, roofed, and contained food offerings. The corpses of this period were covered with hides or reed mattings. Rectangular stone palettes, part of the grave offerings, were accompanied by ivory and stone objects in the Badarian grounds. In the NAQADA II sites (3500–3000 B.C.) there is evidence of definite mortuary cults, as funerary pottery is evident. The graves were linked

with wooden planks in some instances, plastered and painted, with niches designed to hold the ritual offerings.

The corpses of the predynastic periods were normally placed in the graves on their left sides, in a fetal or sitting position. The religious texts of later eras continued to exhort the dead to rise from their left sides and to turn the right to receive offerings. The graves were also dug with reference to the Nile, so that the body faced the West, or Amenti.

By the time Egypt was unified after 3000 B.C., the people viewed the tomb as the instrument by which death could be overcome, not as a mere shelter for cast-off mortal remains. The tomb became a place of transfiguration. The *akh*, the transfigured spiritual being, emerged from the corpse as a result of religious ceremonies. The *akhu*, the deceased, soared into the heavens as circum-polar stars, with the goddess Nut. As the PYRAMID TEXTS declared later: "Spirit to the sky, corpse into the earth." All of the dead were incorporated into cosmic realms, and the tombs were no longer shallow graves but the "houses of eternity."

With the first dynasties of Egypt came sophistication about death and the rituals of preparation. The need for a receptacle for the KA, the astral being that accompanied the mortal body throughout life, led the Egyptians to elaborate on burial processes and rituals. They began to speak of death as "going to one's *ka*." The dead were "those who have gone to their *kas*." Through the intercession and guidance of these astral beings, the dead changed from weak mortals into unique immortal spiritual beings, exchanging life on earth for the perfect existence of eternity.

The cult of OSIRIS also began to exert influence on the mortuary rituals and the ideals of contemplating death as a "gateway into eternity." This deity, having assumed the cultic powers and rituals of other gods of the necropolis, or cemetery sites, offered human beings salvation, resurrection and eternal bliss. Osiris would remain popular throughout Egypt's history. His veneration added moral impetus to the daily lives of the people, common or noble, because he demanded, as did RE' and the other deities, conformity to the will of the gods, a mirroring of cosmic order, and the practice of MA'AT, a spirit of quietude and cooperation throughout life.

The impact of such philosophical and religious aspirations was great. The shallow graves, dug under the houses or in the fringe areas of the desert, were abandoned. MASTABAS, the tombs made out of dried brick, were devised to provide not only a burial chamber but a place for offerings and rituals. Mas-

MORTUARY OFFERINGS Sennefer and his sister, Merit, view mortuary offerings in his tomb at Thebes, part of the elaborate rites accompanying burial.

tabas offered not only a safe receptacle for the corpse but a home for the *ka*, and for the BA, which accompanied it through eternity. The necropolis sites of the Early Dynastic Period were filled with mastabas that had upper, ground-level chambers, shafts and hidden burial rooms. The mortuary liturgy began to evolve at the same time, and offerings were provided and gifts laid in front of the deceased each day, especially when the corpse was of royal status.

The desert graves had provided a natural process for the preservation of the dead, something which the mastabas changed. Corpses placed away from the drying sands, those stored in artificial grave sites, were exposed to the decaying processes of death. The commoners and the poor, however, conducted their burials in the traditional manner on the fringes of the desert. The priests of the various religious cults providing funerary services and rituals discovered the damage that was being done to the corpses and instituted customs and processes to alter the decay, solely because the *ka* and the *ba* could not be deprived of the mortal remains. In some instances, believing that both spirits wandered at times, reserve heads (stone likenesses of the deceased) were placed just outside the tombs so that the spirits could recognize their own bodies and return safely, and so that a head would be available if the real one was damaged or stolen.

The elaborate mastabas erected at Saqqara and in other necropolis sites and the cult of Osiris, the Lord of the Westerners, brought about new methods of preservation, and the priests began the long mortuary rituals to safeguard the precious remains. In the early stages the bodies were wrapped tightly in resin-soaked linen strips, which resulted only in the formation of a hardened shell in which the corpses eventually decayed. Such experiments continued throughout the Early Dynastic Period, a time in which the various advances in government, religion and society were also taking place. Funerary stelae were also introduced at this time. During the Early Dynastic Period the tombs of the kings and queens were sometimes surrounded by the graves of servants as well, as courtiers may have been slain to accompany the rulers into eternity. Such burials took place in the cemeteries around tombs, such as the tomb of Mereneith, an important woman of the era. The custom was abandoned rather abruptly.

The process of embalming, taken from the Latin word meaning "to put into aromatic resins," was called *ut* by the Egyptians. The word "mummy" is from the Persian, meaning pitch or bitumen, which was used in embalming during the New Kingdom. In later eras corpses were coated or even filled with molten resin and then dipped in bitumen, a natural mixture of solid and semisolid hydrocarbons, such as asphalt, normally mixed with drying oil to form a paint.

In the beginning, however, the processes were different. Corpses dating to the 4th Dynasty, those of Queens HETEPHERES II and MERESANKH III, for example, show indications of having been embalmed in the old way.

In order to accomplish the desired preservation, the early priests of Egypt turned to a natural resource readily available and tested in other ways: NATRON, called *net-jeryt* as it was found in the Natron Valley (or WADI NATRON), near modern Cairo. That substance was also called *hesmen*, after the god of the valley, or *hesmen tesher*, when used in the red form. Natron is a mixture of sodium bicarbonate and sodium carbonate or sodium chloride—sodium salt. It absorbs moisture and is also antiseptic. The substance had been used as a cleansing agent from early eras on the Nile.

The priests washed and purified the bodies and then began to prepare the head of the corpse. The brain was sometimes left intact in the skull but more often the priests inserted hooks into the nose, moving them in circular patterns until the ethmoid bones gave way and allowed an entrance into the central cavity. A narrow rod with a spoon tip scooped out the brains, which were discarded.

In some eras the brain was surgically removed from the bodies, a rather sophisticated operation because it involved the atlas vertebrae and entrance through the neck. Once cleared of brain matter, by use of the hook or by surgical means, the skull was packed with linens, spices and Nile mud. On at least one occasion (as exemplified by a mummy available for modern forensic research) the head was packed with too much material and was swollen and split apart. The mouth was also cleansed and padded with oil-soaked linens, and the face was covered with a resinous paste. The eyes were covered with linen, one pad on each eyeball, and the lids closed over them. The corpse was then ready for the "Ethiopian Stone," a blade made out of obsidian.

Peculiarly enough, the mortuary priest who used the blade was reportedly shunned by his fellow priests and embalmers. He was trained to cut from the left side of the abdomen in order to expose the cavity there. Puncturing the diaphragm he pulled out the lungs and the liver, leaving the heart in the body, an essential aspect of the mortuary rituals in all ages. The mortuary spells and rituals demanded a union between the heart and the body. Care was taken to preserve the heart from injuries and to keep it in its

Anubis, a vital participant in the mortuary rituals, is depicted caring for the mummified corpse in a Theban funerary text. Many deities were associated with the funerary rites, a ceremony considered important to the Egyptians of every period.

rightful place. When a heart was accidentally moved or damaged, the priests stitched it carefully again. Mummies studied have shown evidence of such surgical care. All of the other organs in the abdomen (with the exception of the kidney, which was normally left intact and in place) were removed. The lungs were placed in a CANOPIC JAR protected by Hapi. The stomach was placed in a canopic jar protected by Duamutef, the intestines given to the care of Qebhsennuf, and the liver placed in the jar assigned to Imsety.

Each period of ancient Egypt witnessed an alteration in the various organs preserved. The heart, for example, was preserved in some eras, and during the Ramessid dynasties the genitals were surgically removed and placed in a special casket in the shape of the god Osiris. This was performed, perhaps, in commemoration of the god's loss of his own genitals or as a mystical ceremony. Throughout the nation's history, however, the canopic jars (so named by the

Greeks of later eras) were under the protection of the Mesu heru, the four sons of Horus. These jars and their contents, the organs soaked in resin, were stored near the SARCOPHAGUS in the special containers. The reason that the priests cleansed the abdomens of the corpses so quickly was that decay and putrefaction started there instantly. With the organs removed, the cavity could be cleansed and purified, handled without infection and embalmed with efficiency. The use of natron was involved in the next step of the process. The Greeks reported that the mummies of the ancient eras were soaked in a bath of natron. It has been established, however, that the liquid form of the crystals would not only hinder the drying process but would add to the bloating and decay. The bodies were buried in mounds of natron in its dry crystal form. When the natron bath had dried the corpse sufficiently, the nails were tied on and finger stalls placed on the corpse. The natrion bath normally lasted 40 days or more, producing a darkened, withered corpse. The temporary padding in the cavities was removed and stored in containers for use in the afterlife.

The corpse was washed, purified and dried, and then wads or pads of linen, packages of natron or sawdust, were used to fill the various empty portions of the body. Aromatic resins were also used to make the corpse fragrant. The outer skin of the mummy, hardened by the natron, was massaged with milk, honey and various ointments. The embalming incision made in the abdomen was closed and sealed with magical emblems and molten resin. The ears, nostrils, eyes and mouth of the deceased were plugged with various wads of linen, and in the case of royal corpses the tongue was covered with gold. The eyes were pushed back with pads and closed, and the body was covered with molten resin.

The cosmetic preparations in some instances accomplished after that included the application of gold leaf, the painting of the face and the restoration of the eyebrows. Wigs were placed on some corpses, and they were dressed in their robes of state and given their emblems of divine kingship. In some eras the bodies were painted, the priests using red ochre for male corpses and yellow for the women. Jewels and costly amulets were also placed on the arms and legs of the mummies.

The actual wrapping of the mummy in linen (called "yesterday's linen" in the case of the poor, who could only provide the embalmers with used cloth), took over two weeks. This was an important aspect of the mortuary process, accompanied by incantations, hymns and ritual ceremonies. In some instances the linens taken from shrines and temples were provided to the wealthy or aristocratic deceased, in the belief that such materials had special graces and magical powers. An individual mummy would require approximately 445 square yards of material.

Throughout the wrappings semiprecious stones and AMULETS were placed in strategic positions, each one guaranteed to protect a certain region of the human anatomy in the afterlife. The linen bandages on the outside of the mummy in later eras were often red in color. Later eras provided royal bodies with glass net coverings or beaded blankets. The mummy mask and the royal collars were placed on the mummies last. The mask, called a "CARTONNAGE," developed from earlier eras. Linen sheets were glued together with resins or gum to shape masks to the contours of the heads of the corpses, then covered in stucco. These masks fitted the heads and shoulders of the deceased. Gilded and painted in an attempt to achieve a portrait, or at least a flattering depiction of the human being, the masks slowly evolved into a

CAT MUMMY   one of thousands found in Egyptian shrines.

coffin for the entire body. The entire process took from 70 to 90 days, although one queen of the Old Kingdom was recorded as having been treated for 272 days. When it was ended, the body was placed within its coffin, and the funerary rituals could begin.

The funeral processions started from the VALLEY TEMPLE of the king or from the embalming establishment early in the morning. Professional mourners, called KITES, were hired by the members of the deceased's family to wear the color of sorrow, blue-gray, and to appear with their faces daubed with dust and mud, signs of mourning. These professional women wailed loudly and pulled their hair to demonstrate the tragic loss which the death of the person being honored caused to the nation. Servants of the deceased or poor relations, headed the funeral procession. They carried flowers and trays of offerings, normally oils and foods. Others brought clothes, furniture and the personal items of the deceased, while the SHABTIS and funerary equipment were carried at the rear. The *shabtis* were small statues in the image of the deceased placed in the tomb to answer the commands of the gods for various work details or services. With these statues available the corpse could rest in peace.

Boxes of linens and the clothes of the deceased were also carried to the tomb, along with the canopic jars, military weapons, writing implements, papryi etc. The TEKENU was also carried in procession. This was a bundle designed to resemble a human form.

Covered by animal skins and dragged on a sled to the place of sacrifice, the *tekenu* and the animals bringing it to the scene were ritually slain. The *tekenu* would have symbolized the actual courtiers and servants sacrificed in the mortuary rituals of the Early Dynastic Period royal clans. The *sem* or mortuary priest followed next, dressed in a panther or leopard skin and wearing the traditional white linen robe of his calling. The *sem* priest would be accompanied by a retinue of other priests, such as the *ka* priests and others, the actual embalmers. The coffin and the mummy arrived on a boat, designed to be placed on a sled and carried across the terrain. When the coffin was to be sailed across the Nile to the necropolis sites of the western shore, two women mounted on either side. They and the *kites* imitated ISIS and

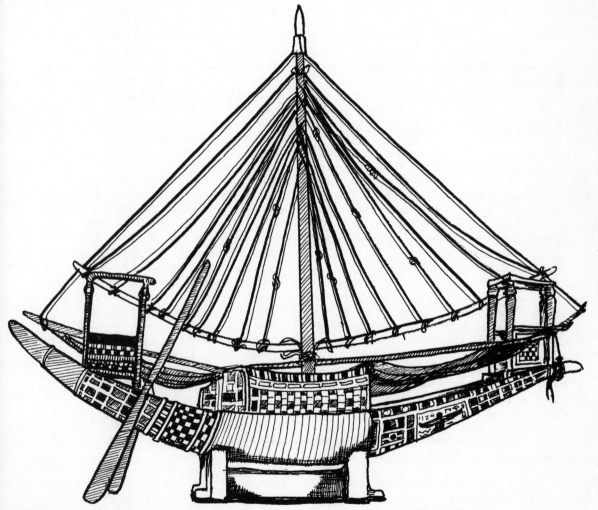

MORTUARY BOAT   a replica of the actual Nile vessels, duplicated for tombs of the 4th Dynasty. The tombs of the royal kings of Egypt had vast pits in which such vessels, life-size, were stored for eternity. Some tombs had ships made out of bricks.

NEPHTHYS, who mourned the death of Osiris and sang the original Lamentations.

The family and friends of the deceased, an entire populace if the mummy was that of a king or queen, followed on land or on separate barges across the river. The hearse boat used for the crossing had a shrine cabin adorned with flowers and with the palm symbols of resurrection. During the crossing the *sem* priest incensed the corpse and the females accompanying it. The professional mourners sometimes rode on top of the cabin as well, loudly proclaiming their grief to the neighborhood.

The procession landed on the opposite shore of the Nile and walked through the desert region to the site, where the *sem* priest directed the removal of the coffin so that it could be stood at its own tomb entrance for the rituals. In later eras a statue of the deceased was used in its place. A *ka* statue was often used in the same ceremony, an image of the deceased with upraised arms extending from the head. The priest touched the mouth of the statue or the coffin and supervised the cutting off the leg of an ox, to be offered to the deceased as food. All the while the MUU DANCERS, persons who greeted the corpse at the tomb, performed with harpists, the *hery-heb* priests and *ka* priests, while incensing ceremonies were conducted.

The mummy was then placed in a series of larger coffins and into the sarcophagus, which waited in the burial chamber inside. The sarcophagus was sealed, the canopic jars put carefully away, and the doors closed with fresh cement. Stones were sometimes put into place, and seals were impressed as a final protection. A festival followed this final closing of the tomb.

These rituals did not apply to all Egyptian burials. The poor conducted similar ceremonies on the desert fringes, sometimes using cliff sites for tombs. Another custom that originated in the Early Dynastic Period and remained popular throughout Egypt's history was the burial at ABYDOS, the city of the god of the dead, Osiris.

Once the body was entombed, the mortuary rituals did not end. The royal cults were conducted everyday, and those who could afford the services of mortuary priests were provided with ceremonies on a daily basis. The poor managed to conduct ceremonies on their own, this being part of the filial piety which was the ideal of the nation. A daily recitation of prayers and commemorations was based on the Egyptian belief that any nameless creatures, unknown to the gods or people, ceased to exist at all. Thus the name of the deceased had to be invoked on a daily basis in order for that person to be sustained even in eternity.

Documents dating to the Middle Kingdom indicate that members of the royal family and the nome aristocrats endowed mortuary priests for rituals to be conducted on a perpetual basis at their tombs providing stipends and expense funds. Entire families or clans of priests conducted such services, particularly in the pyramidal complexes of the kings. Such pyramid rituals were paid by the state, as part of the royal cult. Mortuary offerings were brought everyday. These gifts were listed first in the LIST OF OFFERINGS, started in the Old Kingdom, and evolved into the LITURGY OF OFFERINGS. In return, the priests performing these rites were given estates, ranks and honors and could not be turned over to other priests, except in the case of a son inheriting his father's priestly rank and position. A legal system emerged from these contracts, which protected the deceased against rivalry or disputes among the priests endowed to perform perpetual offerings. If a mortuary priest sued another for more rights or properties, he lost every rank and honor that he possessed. If a particular priest stopped the mortuary services requested and paid for, his order instantly assumed all of his benefits and material goods.

A symbol of the contracts made by the mortuary priests and the deceased were the TOMB BALLS, discovered in ancient Egyptian burial chambers. Such balls, made of bits of papyrus and linen, were marked with the hieroglyph for "seal" or "contract." They are believed to be symbols of the contracts drawn up between the priests and the family of the deceased or the corpse himself. They were deposited by the priests as tokens of good faith, binding their agreements by placing them before the *ka* of the dead.

The daily mortuary liturgies that were performed each morning by the priests, in keeping with their contracts, involved a greeting of the deceased. The mummy, or in most cases a statue, was placed on a small stand. The Opening of the Mouth ceremony was then performed. This involved touching the lips of the deceased with a special instrument designed to emit magical properties, the *ur-heka*. The statue was then purified and given gifts of food and adornments. The Liturgy of the Offerings contained more than 114 separate ceremonies. The purpose of the ritual was to change meat, bread and wine into divine, spiritual substances for the deceased and the gods. This transmutation of offerings was documented in tombs as far back as the 5th Dynasty (2465 B.C.). It was also believed that the ritual could revitalize the senses and the various organs of the deceased. All was based on the resurrection of Osiris and on the basic creed that no human life was obliterated at the moment of death but transformed into shapes that accommodated the eternal environment

The ritual of mortuary sacrifice followed, as food and drink were offered to the *ka* and *ba* of the deceased. This followed the custom of the early eras, when the king was obliged to present such an offering for each citizen.

The mortuary rituals thus embraced all aspects of death among the Egyptian people. The preparation for the tomb, in keeping with spiritual aspirations and religious doctrines, provided each Egyptian with the necessary physical properties to ensure eternal bliss. The funerary rituals were conducted with great dignity and earnestness, in order to deliver the corpse to the appointed site, where transformations could take place. The mortuary ceremonies secured for the Egyptians a guarantee that they would not be forgotten.

mummies See MORTUARY RITUALS.

musical instruments recreational and religious implements integrated into every aspect of Egyptian life. The god Iby was considered the patron of such

Female musicians, a popular part of festivals, banquets and temple rituals

instruments, but other deities, such as HATHOR, were involved in the playing of music in all eras. Hymns and processional songs were part of all religious rituals, and the Egyptians enjoyed musical groups and bands at festivals and at celebrations. On certain feasts the queens and royal women, accompanied by musicians and dwarfs, danced and sang to the god or to the king.

In the Old Kingdom and probably in predynastic times, flutes and clarinet-type instruments were played. Males played small versions of the harp, an instrument which eventually evolved into immense and highly decorated pieces. The first harps were held in the hand, later harps were freestanding and weighty. Trumpets appeared in the Old Kingdom as well.

In the Middle Kingdom harps were accompanied by the SISTRUM. Rattles, tambourines, clappers and a type of guitar were played as well. Cymbals and castanets remained popular from the Old Kingdom onward. The lute and the lyre appeared during the Second Intermediate Period era of HYSKOS domination (1640–1532 B.C.) and were probably introduced by these Asiatics when they invaded the Nile region. New Kingdom tombs have reliefs depicting the use of such instruments. The angular and arched harps were in vogue during the empire, as well as the large and small drums and oboe pipes. Other instruments came into Egypt as a result of the various foreign invasions after the fall of the New Kingdom.

Mut   an ancient Egyptian goddess, considered a divine consort of AMON at Thebes. She was depicted as a woman with a human head, wearing the double crown and with the feather of MA'AT at her feet. Her theophany was the vulture. Her name meant mother, and she was honored with a temple at Thebes, complete with a sacred lake.

The mythology of her cult taught that Mut was a sky goddess who took the form of a cow when Amon emerged at HELIOPOLIS. Amon mounted her back and rode her to his divine destination. Mut adopted KHONS and became part of the sacred triad at Thebes.

Mutemwiya   a queen of the 18th Dynasty, the wife of TUTHMOSIS IV (1401–1391 B.C.). She is considered by some scholars to have been a Mitanni princess, given to the king as a tribute. The mother of the heir, AMENHOTEP III, she was honored by the Egyptians. Mutemwiya was buried at Thebes.

Mutnodjmet   a queen of the 18th Dynasty, the consort of HOREMHAB (1319–1307 B.C.). She was mentioned in 'Amarna reliefs and must have had royal

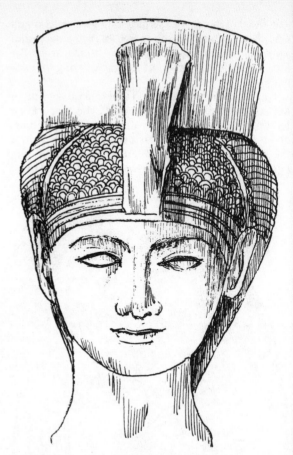

MUTNODJMET   the consort of Horemhab, as depicted in a Theban statue.

connections. Mutnodjmet was depicted on Horemhab's coronation reliefs, where an account of their marriage was given. A black granite statue of her, with Horemhab, is in Turin.

Mutnofret   a queen of the 18th Dynasty, the mother of TUTHMOSIS II (1492–1479 B.C.). Mutnofret was a lesser-ranked wife of TUTHMOSIS I, but appears to have had some royal titles in her own right.

Muu Dancers   a group of professional women who waited at the grave sites to greet the funeral processions with song. The necropolis areas served as the stages for their renditions. The Muu Dancers were normally accompanied by a small orchestra when they performed.

Muyet   a royal female of the 11th Dynasty, in the reign of MENTUHOTPE II (2061–2010 B.C.). Muyet was only five years old when she died and was buried in the tomb provided for her in the king's vast mortuary complex at DEIR EL-BAHRI. She was buried with five necklaces of great beauty and value. Her limestone sarcophagus did not proclaim her actual status, and it is assumed that she was an intended bride of the king.

Mycerinus   See MENKAURE'.

Myrrh   called *anti* by the ancient Egyptians, the aromatic plant brought to Egypt from PUNT. The trees were planted on temple grounds and the gum resin product of the plant was used in rituals as incense and as a perfume for the gods.

Mysteries of Osiris   See OSIRIS.

N

Nakht an official of the 18th Dynasty, serving in the reign of Tuthmosis IV (1401–1391 B.C.). Nakht was a priest-astronomer, one of the trained sky watchers of the temple who was responsible for giving the charts and information about the various orbits of the heavenly bodies as they affected the seasonal changes of the earth. He was buried at Thebes, and his tomb is famous for the depiction of the blind harper on its walls. (See ASTRONOMY, PRIESTS.)

Nanefer-ka-ptah a prince of the 19th Dynasty, the son of Merneptah (1224–1214 B.C.), made famous by Egyptian magical tales. The prince is supposed to have discovered the magical books of the god THOTH. He made a copy of the book, washed it away with beer and then drank the beer, expecting to have digested all of the printed material as a result. He was buried at COPTOS. (See MAGIC.)

naos the enclosed shrine areas that were reserved for statues in ancient Egyptian temples.

Napata a site below the Third Cataract of the Nile, now the region of local tribes, where a mountain was dedicated to the god AMON. The river loops at this point, and a flat-topped peak was the dominant part of the landscape there. The Egyptians called it the "Table" or the "Holy Mountain."

Naqada a site north of THEBES, where predynastic burials were discovered. It also served as a necropolis area for the 1st Dynasty (2900 B.C.). The name of the site lends itself to the period of social and cultural growth in the Nile Valley. The site contained vast amounts of pottery, and cylinder seals as well as tomb sites were discovered there, marked with the names of NA'RMER, 'AHA and others. A trapezoid step pyramid was discovered near Naqada, without a temple or hall. Thick coats of masonry layers formed the facade of the pyramid, which had a base approx-

imately 60 feet in each direction. (See EGYPT, PREDYNASTIC PERIOD.)

Na'rmer one of the last predynastic kings, associated with the unification of Upper and Lower Egypt (3000 B.C.). Na'rmer is believed to have come from HIERAKONPOLIS, a capital and shrine city of Horus in the predynastic eras of Egypt. He followed in the footsteps of SCORPION and others who tried to subdue the Delta. The actual unification of Egypt was not accomplished until the close of the 2nd Dynasty (c. 2640 B.C.).

A palette discovered at Hierakonpolis depicts Na'rmer's efforts. A ceremonial mace-head, also discovered in that city, depicts Na'rmer as capturing 120,000 men, 400 oxen, 1,422,000 goats, and the standards of the Delta NOMES. After his victory, Na'rmer is believed to have married a Memphite aristocrat in order to consolidate his gains. Queen Neithotpe was possibly that noble heiress. She is named in some lists as the mother of 'Aha (called Menes), the first king.

Na'rmer sent an expedition into the eastern desert, and his inscription was discovered on the rocks of the WADI EL-QASH, on the Coptos trade route. He is believed to have been buried at Saqqara, or possibly in the necropolis at Tarkhan. A cenotaph bearing his insignia was discovered in ABYDOS. (See NA'RMER PALETTE.)

Na'rmer Palette called Na'rmer's Victory Palette, it was discovered in Hierakonpolis. The palette was designed for ceremonial use. On it Na'rmer is depicted in the war crown of Upper Egypt and in the red wicker crown of Lower Egypt, signifying that he conquered that territory. Na'rmer is also shown as a bull (a royal symbol), destroying a city with its horns and trampling the enemy troops under its hooves. On the reverse side of the palette two fallen figures lie before him. The god HORUS is shown coming to the king's aid by bringing prisoners to him. The palette, made of schist, is an important historical and artistic document. (See ART AND ARCHITECTURE.)

Narmouthis called Narmonthis (modern Medinet Madi) in some records, a village on the edge of the FAIYUM region which contains a 12th Dynasty temple (1991–1783 B.C.). Rectangular in design, the shrine is graced by a hypostyle hall with papyrus columns, a vestibule and a three-compartment sanctuary.

natron called *net-jeryt, hesmen* or *hesmen desher* by the Egyptians, a substance found in the Natron Valley near modern Cairo. *Net-jeryt* meant "belonging to the god"; *hesmen* was the name of the valley deity; and *hesmen desher* denoted a red variety of natron. The Valley of Natron, or WADI NATRON, provided a substance which was a mixture of sodium bicarbonate and sodium carbonate or sodium chloride—sodium salt. Its chief property was its ability to absorb moisture, and it was mildly antiseptic.

Natron was used as a detergent in early eras in Egypt and then adopted as the main preserving agent for the MORTUARY RITUALS. In time it became the vital element for the embalming processes, used as a steeping substance to dry out the corpses and to prevent decay. Natron was used in its dry crystal form for embalming, although some linen wrappings appear to have been steeped in a solution of the crystals.

Nauri Decree a document issued by SETI I (1306–1290 B.C.) of ancient Egypt's 19th Dynasty in the fourth year of his reign. The decree was promulgated on behalf of the workers at OSIRIS' holy city of ABYDOS, where the king was in the process of building his great mortuary complex. The Nauri Decree incorporated prior legal codes, serving as a charter for the temple and for its various estates, and was designed to ensure the maintenance of the king's mortuary cult after his death. The workers were subject to a stern code of behavior while they built the tomb, with penalties for crimes clearly delineated. The Decree points to the troubled era of Seti's reign. Normally, workers on the mortuary complexes of the kings would not have required warnings or threats in order to regulate their behavior. Construction sites of the early periods were places of spirituality and dedication. During Seti's reign, however, conformity to the ideals of the nation had partially lessened and the impact of the mortuary rituals had declined.

navy See MILITARY and PERU-NEFER.

neb a hieroglyphic sign that is translated as "all" and used on AMULETS and the ANKH insignias. The *neb* was also the symbol of obeisance or prostration performed by the ancient Egyptians in the presence of a king or a deity.

Nebamun an official of the 18th Dynasty, serving TUTHMOSIS IV (1401–1391 B.C.) and AMENHOTEP III (1391–1353 B.C.). He was a commander of the Theban state police force, composed normally of the famed MEDJAY troops. Nebamun was buried on the western shore of Thebes.

Nebamun an artisan of the 18th Dynasty, serving AMENHOTEP II (1427–1401 B.C.) as a sculptor and as a supervisor of many royal building projects. He shared a tomb with IPUKI on the western shore of Thebes near Deir el-Bahri.

Nebemakhet a prince of the 4th Dynasty, the son of KHEPHREN (2520–2494 B.C.) and Queen MERESANKH III. Nebemakhet did not succeed his father but became a priest for the royal cult. His tomb was built in the royal cemetery, and he is also depicted in his mother's elaborate rock-cut tomb at GIZA.

Nebenteru an official of the 19th Dynasty, serving SETI I (1306–1290 B.C.) and RAMESSES II (1290–1224 B.C.) as high priest of AMON. Nebenteru was a NOME aristocrat who was appointed high priest in the 17th year of Ramesses reign. He was a descendant of the KHETY clan of the 9th and 10th Dynasties. Nebentery's son, PASER, became vizier in the same era.

Nebetku an official of the 1st Dynasty, serving DEN (date of reign unknown). Nebetku's tomb was built in SAQQARA but was altered on two occasions. It was obviously started as a PYRAMID but eventually became a simple MASTABA, indicating a certain architectural daring that could not be sustained by the artisans of his period.

Nebetu'u a goddess of ancient Egypt, considered a form of HATHOR. She was worshipped at Esna, where she was called the "Mistress of the Territory."

Nebhepetre' See MENTUHOTPE II.

Nebireyeraw (Swadjenre') the sixth king of the 17th Dynasty (date unknown). He is credited with a stela erected at KARNAK that commemorates the sale of an hereditary governorship at el-Kab (Nekheb). Nothing else is known of his life.

Nebseni's Papyrus an Egyptian mortuary document, older than the famous ANI PAPYRUS. Now in the British Museum, Nebseni's Papyrus is 76 feet by 1 foot. It is a mortuary commemorative, a revised version following the Theban changes of the later periods. The texts included in the papyrus are sometimes outlined in black. An address of the god HORUS to his father, the god OSIRIS, is also included in the document.

Nebt a noblewoman of the 11th Dynasty, the heiress of the estates of the ELEPHANTINE Island at Aswan. The mother of Princess NEFERUKAYT, Nebt held a unique position in her own right. She was a patroness of the arts and retained librarians and scholars in her service. She held the rank of a NOME princess and was commemorated on a stela erected in her territory.

nebti **name** See ROYAL NAMES.

Nebt-tawya a royal wife of the 19th Dynasty, married to RAMESSES II (1290–1224 B.C.). Nebt-tawy was a minor queen and was buried in the Valley of the Queens. Her tomb was very large and beautiful and provides striking documentation of the era.

Nebwawi an official of the 18th Dynasty, serving in the reigns of TUTHMOSIS III (1479–1425 B.C.) and AMENHOTEP II (1427–1401 B.C.). Nebwawi was the high priest of OSIRIS at ABYDOS. He served HATSHEPSUT but managed to stay in favor with her successors. On occasion Nebwawi was summoned to the court to serve as a counselor. His mortuary stela provides details of his life, and a statue was also erected at Thebes in his honor.

Nebwenef an official of the 19th Dynasty, serving in the reign of RAMESSES II (c. 1290–1224 B.C.). He was a high priest of Amon and the king's first prophet of HATHOR and ANHUR. His mortuary temple was built near the tomb of SETI I, whom he had served at the beginning of his career. His tomb depicted Ramesses II and Queen NEFERTARI making the announcement of his appointment as high priest.

nefer the ancient Egyptian word meaning good, beautiful, complete, or perfect. *Nefer* AMULETS were used in mortuary rituals, and the word was applied to the gods and to holy objects. Amulets of the *nefer* were placed on the stomachs and windpipes of the deceased in order to protect those organs in the afterlife. The stomach was normally put into CANOPIC JARS for preservation, but the *nefer* amulets guarded the area of the body where the stomach would be restored in eternity. The *nefer* was also used as an insignia of happiness and good fortune, representing all things beautiful, both in a material and in a spiritual sense.

Neferhetepes a princess of the 5th Dynasty, the daughter of KAKAI (2446–2426 B.C.). She married an official named Ti. The sons of this union were allowed to inherit the rank of prince as a special royal favor.

Nefer-hor an ancient Egyptian form of the god PTAH, worshipped at MEMPHIS as the "Fair of Face." The name was applied to other deities in some eras.

Neferhotep I (Kha'sekhemre') (c. 1741–1730 B.C.) the 22nd king of the 13th Dynasty. He was not of royal blood, and his father appears to have been a priest in ABYDOS, which benefited from his royal patronage. His name was discovered in Byblos, and he ruled all of the Delta with the exception of XOIS and the HYKSOS-held AVARIS. A stela discovered at Abydos and an inscription cut into the rocks at Aswan document his reign. His wife, Senebsen, was mentioned on a stela.

Neferhotep III (Sekhemre's'ankhyawy) (date unknown) one of the last kings of the 13th Dynasty. A stela discovered at KARNAK mentions his aid to Thebes. He is supposed to have worn the *khepresh*, the war CROWN made of ELECTRUM. This appears to be the first reference to that particular style of royal headdress. Neferhotep III conducted military campaigns against the HYKSOS, but the Asiatics were in firm command of their Delta territories.

Neferhotep an official of the 18th Dynasty, serving AYA (1323–1319 B.C.) and HOREMHAB (1319–1307 B.C.) as a scribe of AMON and as a superintendent of royal lands. His tomb in the Theban cliffs is noted for its graceful depiction of MORTUARY RITUALS.

Neferma'at a prince of the 4th Dynasty, the son of SNOFRU (2575–2551 B.C.) and Princess Nefertkau. Nefertkau was Snofru's daughter. Neferma'at's wife was the Princess Itet; their son was HEMIUNU, the vizier of KHUFU. Neferma'at was buried near his father at MEIDUM. The beautiful relief of the geese of Meidum were discovered in the tomb of Itet.

Neferpert an official of the 18th Dynasty, serving 'AHMOSE I (1550–1525 B.C.) as the superintendent of royal building projects. He supervised the construction of the temples of PTAH and AMON for the king. His tomb at Thebes is famous for its reliefs, which depict the transportation of immense stones from various quarries.

Nefertari   (Nefertari-Mery-Mut in some lists) a queen of the 19th Dynasty, the wife of RAMESSES II (1290–1224 B.C.). She is mentioned on a stela dating to the first years of Ramesses' reign, and is believed to have been the daughter or a relative of BAKENKHONS, a prominent official. She was a favorite wife of the king, holding the rank of consort or great wife. Her

Queen Nefertari, as depicted in her tomb in the Valley of the Queens at Thebes, one of the largest.

brother was Amenmose, the mayor of Thebes at the time. Her sons were Prince Amonhirwonmef and Prince Prehirwonmef. Her other children were Princess MERYTAMON and Princess Mertatum.

A small temple built at ABU SIMBEL was dedicated both to the goddess HATHOR and to Nefertari. She disappeared from the scene soon after the dedication of that temple, either dying or retiring to the harem complex near the Faiyum. Her tomb in the VALLEY OF THE QUEENS is one of the largest and most beautifully decorated grave sites discovered.

Nefertem   the ancient Egyptian god of the sun, the son of the god PTAH and the goddess SEKHMET. He is also listed as a son of BASTET at HELIOPOLIS. Nefertem was depicted as a young man wearing an open lotus flower crown, with feathers and ornaments. In other eras he was represented by a lion. A staff was part of his representation. Perfumes were sacred to Nefertem, who is supposed to have brought a fragrant flower to the god RE' to soothe him during a time of suffering. Nefertem thus had a cosmogonic role in the LOTUS legends.

Neferti   (Nefero-rohu in some lists) a lector-priest at Bubastis in the reign of AMENEMHET I (1991–1962 B.C.) of the 12th Dynasty who wrote a pseudo-prophetic account supposedly dating to the 4th Dynasty. Neferti claimed that a sage in the reign of SNOFRU predicted the coming of Amenemhet. The writings were discovered in the Leningrad Papyrus.

Nefertiti   a queen of the 18th Dynasty, the wife of AKHENATEN (1353–1335 B.C.). Her name means "the beautiful woman has come," and she is one of the most beloved and famous of all ancient Egyptians. Her bust in the Egyptian Museum, Berlin, is one of the best known of all Egyptian treasures. Little is known about her origins, although there has been a great deal of speculation. In the fourth year of Akhenaten's reign she appeared with him at the site of Akhetaten (el-'AMARNA), the new city dedicated to the god ATEN. In the sixth year, Nefertiti's name was changed to Nefernefruaten, which means "Beautiful in beauty is Aten."

Nefertiti lived with Akhenaten in 'Amarna, where he conducted religious ceremonies to Aten. They raised six daughters there, but no sons. One of the daughters, Maketaten, died, and the couple's grief is depicted in wall paintings. Nefertiti disappeared from the court after that. There is some evidence that she remained at 'Amarna, living in a villa called Hataten, but her daughter replaced her as the king's principal wife. Smenkhkare', who became Akhena-

World-famous painted limestone bust of Queen Nefertiti in the Egyptian Museum, Berlin, originally from el-'Amarna.

ten's successor in 1335 B.C., reportedly assumed Nefertiti's religious name. Her body has never been discovered.

Neferu an official of the 12th Dynasty, serving SENWOSRET I (1971–1926 B.C.) as overseer of transportation and trade in NUBIA, particularly in the region surrounding the fortress at BUHEN, south of the First Cataract of the Nile. Buhen was fortified and served as an important garrison for protecting the expanding trade of the Middle Kingdom. His mortuary stela, which gives information about this era, is in the British Museum.

Neferu a queen of the 12th Dynasty, the consort of AMENEMHET I (1992–1961 B.C.). Amenemhet I was not of royal blood, being a commoner of partial Nubian descent who usurped the throne upon the death of the last king of the 11th Dynasty, whom he had served as vizier. It is not recorded whether Neferu was a princess of a royal clan, but it can be assumed that Amenemhet married her in order to strengthen his claims to the throne. She would have had to be an heiress of a considerable domain in that case, bringing the king needed power and prestige. She was buried in a small pyramid near the king's tomb.

Neferukheb a princess of the 18th Dynasty, the daughter of TUTHMOSIS I and Queen 'AHMOSE (1504–1492 B.C.). Supposedly the elder sister of HATSHEPSUT, Neferukheb died before she could inherit the throne. She was buried at Thebes.

Neferukhayt listed as Neferu-kayt in some records, a queen of the 11th Dynasty, probably the wife of King MENTUHOTPE II (2061–2010 B.C.), and the daughter of Princess NEBT, the heiress of the Elephantine. A learned woman, Neferukhayt maintained a library and collected papyri and various artworks in a vast museum.

Neferu-Re' a princess of the 18th Dynasty, the half-sister and possibly wife of TUTHMOSIS III (1479–1425 B.C.). The daughter of TUTHMOSIS II and HATSHEPSUT, Neferu-Re' played an important role during the reign of her mother. For a long time scholars believed that she died before she could become the ranking consort, but a tablet discovered in the Sinai in recent years styles her "King's Daughter, King's Wife." Neferu-Re' 's statues, showing her in the arms of Senenmut, attest to the fact that Senenmut and 'Ahmose Pen-Nekheb were her official tutors, an honorary title. Senenmut was also named her steward and her "Great Father Nurse."

When Hatshepsut assumed the throne in her own right, Neferu-Re', supposedly assisted her in the empire's affairs. Tuthmosis was relegated to a lesser role during Hatshepsut's reign, but Neferu-Re' remained at the palace. Hatshepsut depended more and more upon her over the years, and when Neferu-Re' died in the eleventh year of her mother's reign, the queen-pharaoh's strength ebbed. Senenmut died about the same time, thus making Hatshepsut too feeble to contain Tuthmosis and his allies.

Nefru-Sobek (Sebek'kare') a queen-pharaoh of ancient Egypt, the eighth ruler of the 12th Dynasty (1787–1783 B.C.). She was probably the daughter of AMENEMHET III and the half-sister of AMENEMHET IV, whom she succeeded. She was mentioned in the Karnak, Saqqara and Turin king lists. A sphinx and three statues of her were found in the Delta.

Nefrusy a site north of HERMOPOLIS. The HYKSOS and their Asiatic allies had fortified the city during their period of domination. KAMOSE (1555–1550 B.C.) of the 17th Dynasty of Thebes attacked the fort with MEDJAY troops and with a cavalry of Egyptian chariots. The defenders, shocked by the sight of the Nubian mercenaries, who were renowned for their ferocity and cunning, and by the Egyptian use of the horse and chariot, abandoned the site and fled north-ward, with the army of Kamose in hot pursuit.

Negative Confessions (now called the Declarations of Innocence) part of the mortuary rituals of ancient Egypt, a text developed by priests to aid the deceased when in the presence of the FORTY-TWO JUDGES in the JUDGMENT HALLS OF OSIRIS. The Confessions were to be recited to establish the moral virtue of the deceased and his or her right to eternal bliss.

The Negative Confessions detail some of the ethical and moral concerns of the various eras of Egypt, expressing the aspirations and the acknowledgment of personal responsibility for actions. The Confessions included:

I have not stolen.
I have not plundered.
I have not slain people.
I have not committed a crime.
I have not stolen the property of a god.
I have not said lies.
I have not cursed.
I have not copulated with another man.
I have not copulated with another man's wife.
I have not caused anyone to weep.
I have not eaten my heart (indulged in despair).
I have not led anyone astray.
I have not gossiped.
I have not slandered.
I have not been contentious in affairs.
I have not caused terror.
I have not become heatedly angry.
I have not eavesdropped.
I have not made anyone angry.
I have not made anyone hungry.

Such confessions covered the scope of the average person's life in Egypt in all eras. The regulation of personal conduct, including admonitions against petty acts and minor bad habits, were probably considered important to the social and religious well-being of the nation. The spirit of cooperation and quietude are also evident in the Confessions. The length of the Negative Confessions varied, and in some periods each one of the affirmations was accompanied by an address to a particular judge. (See RELIGION and MORTUARY RITUALS.)

Nehem Auit a goddess associated with HATHOR and with THOTH. She was called the "Deliverer from Violence" and the "One Who Serves the Deprived." The SISTRUM was her favorite instrument, and she was depicted as a woman wearing a sistrum crown or the pillar of Hathor on her head. The goddess was invoked by people in all eras as one who could repel evil spirits and curses. She was particularly beneficial to the living.

Nehes a form of the sun god, called the "Awakened One" or the "Awakening." The ancient Egyptians believed that this deity was a companion of RE'.

Nehesy an official of the 18th Dynasty, serving in the reign of HATSHEPSUT (1473–1458 B.C.). Nehesy belonged to the group of counselors and able statesmen supporting Hatshepsut during her reign. He served as chancellor and as a treasurer of Amon. Nehesy was buried at Thebes.

Nehi an official of the 18th Dynasty, Viceroy of Nubia under TUTHMOSIS III (c. 1479–1425 B.C.). His title was "King's Son of Kush," and he was stationed at the ELEPHANTINE Island at Aswan, where he governed the territories below the First Cataract of the Nile. Nehi brought tribute annually to the king. On a stela of victory, raised for Tuthmosis III at the WADI HALFA, Nehi praised his own fidelity and continued service. (See GOVERNMENT AND VICEROY.)

Neith the Greek name for the Egyptian Nit, a goddess whose cult dated to predynastic times. SAIS was the site of her original cult, but it soon extended through the Delta and Faiyum regions. SOBEK, the crocodile god, was represented in some eras as her son, hence some statues depict her nursing a crocodile. She was called the patroness of the Libyans. Neith was depicted as a woman wearing the crown of Lower Egypt and holding bows and arrows. Her hieroglyphic sign was that of crossed arrows. In later eras the hieroglyph was believed to represent the weaving shuttle, and Neith became the patron of the weavers of Egypt and the patroness of hunting and warfare. In hymns and prayers Neith was addressed as the "Opener of the Ways."

Nekaure' a prince of the 4th Dynasty, the son of Khephren (2520–2494 B.C.). Nekaure' was a mature adult when he died, and inscribed a will on the walls of his tomb at GIZA that announced that while "living on his two feet, without ailing in any respect" he was stating his testament for his death. This phrase was the equivalent of the modern term "being of sound mind and body." The will bequeathed towns and estates to his daughter, but her premature death made it revert to him again and eventually to his wife. Other properties were given to the mortuary priests in order to secure an endowment for his own funerary cult. (See MORTUARY RITUALS.)

Nekhebet the ancient Egyptian goddess personified by the vulture, worshipped at el-Kab (Nekheb) and the patroness and guardian of the Upper Kingdom from earliest times. Royal reliefs depict the vulture soaring above the head of the king. In some eras Nekhebet was considered a wife of the Nile god, but she was also addressed as a "daughter of the sun." She was shown at times as a woman with the white crown or as a woman with the head of a vulture. Her name meant "She of Nekheb."

In the mortuary literature, Nekhebet has a part in the birth of OSIRIS and inhabits the primeval abyss (the waters of chaos) before creation. In this capacity she was also considered a patroness of nature and childbirth. A water lily with a serpent entwined in the stems adorned her pictures in some cult centers, a reference to her role in the creation.

Nekhebu an official of the 6th Dynasty, serving in the reign of PEPI I (2289–2255 B.C.). Nekhebu was an architect and construction superintendent for the royal projects and built canals and temples throughout Egypt for Pepi. His tomb was discovered at GIZA.

Nekhen See HIERAKONPOLIS.

Nekhen Souls See SOULS OF NEKHEN.

Nekonekh an official of the 5th Dynasty, serving in the reign of USERKHAF (2465–2458 B.C.). A nobleman associated with the court and the throne, Nekonekh received endowments from Userkhaf, probably in return for long and faithful service. The nobleman's tomb inscriptions provided an account of his rewards.

Nekure' See NEKAURE'.

nemes the unique striped cloth headdress worn only by the kings of ancient Egypt, usually mounted with the uraeus.

Nemtyemzaf the third king of the 6th Dynasty (2255–2246 B.C.), the son of PEPI I and Queen ANKHNES-MERY-RE' I. His reign was brief. Nemtyemzaf's wife was Queen Nit. A daughter of Pepi, she married PEPI II after she was widowed. The king was buried in a pyramid at Saqqara.

Nenkhsekhmet an official of the 5th Dynasty, serving in the reign of SAHURE' (2458–2446 B.C.). A physician to the royal court, Nenkhsekhmet was in the service to the king for a long period. The physician was honored by the king and provided with limestone and a false door for his tomb. Sahure' commanded his own workmen to gather the materials. A stela discovered at Saqqara commemorates Nenkhsekhmet's singular rewards.

Nenwef called Nen-waf in some records, an official of the 18th Dynasty, serving in the reign of King TUTHMOSIS III (c. 1479–1425 B.C.). Nenwef was a military commander for this great warrior pharaoh, active in the newly formed cavalry units. Such units were greatly feared throughout the Mediterranean area and were professionally trained and deadly in battle. Nenwef and his family were commemorated in a mortuary stela.

Neper an ancient Egyptian god of the harvest and grain, worshipped in predynastic eras but later incorporated into the cult of OSIRIS.

Nephthys the Greek name for the ancient Egyptian goddess Nebt-Hut. Nephthys was the sister of ISIS and OSIRIS and the wife of the god SETH. She was addressed in most eras as the "Lady of the Castle," and reliefs depicted Nephthys as a woman, wearing the hieroglyphs for palace on her head.

Nephthys tricked Osiris into siring her son, ANUBIS, whom she promptly abandoned to the care of Isis. When Osiris was slain, however, Nephthys aided Isis in restoring him, after mourning his death in the famed LAMENTATIONS. She was associated with the mortuary cult in every era and was part of the ancient worship of MIN. The desert regions were dedicated to her, and she was thought to be skilled in magic.

Neshmet See BARK OF THE GODS.

Nessumontu an official of the 12th Dynasty, serving in the reign of SENWOSRET I (1971–1926 B.C.). Nessumontu began his career in the reign of AMENEMHET I and became a military commander. He led a campaign against the Asiatic Bedouins of the SINAI, probably leading Nubian mercenaries into battle. His mortuary stela, now at the Louvre, gives an account of his career.

netcher the ancient Egyptian name for the pennants used on temples to display the symbols of the god in residence. Flagstaffs and pennants were part of all religious buildings on the Nile, dating to the time when the local NOME and cult totems were placed in the courts of the primitive shrines.

neter the ancient Egyptian word meaning god.

neterui   the sacred mortuary ritual used in the ceremonies of the "Opening of the Mouth" in some rituals, alongside the *ur-heka*. The symbol, which was a simple angle in stone or metal, was used in the mummy wrappings in order to provide the protection of the gods, who could be summoned by the *neterui*.

Net Spells   ancient Egyptian magical formulas provided to each corpse in the BOOK OF THE DEAD for protection on the deceased's last journey into Tuat or the Underworld. The Net Spells kept demons away from the dead and placated He-Who-Looks-Behind-Himself, the ferryman on the Lake of Eternity. (See ETERNITY and MORTUARY RITUALS.)

Nibamon   called Nibamun and Nebamon in some records, an official of the 18th Dynasty, serving in the reign of TUTHMOSIS III (c. 1479–1425 B.C.). Nibamon started his career as a court official, becoming the steward of one of Tuthmosis' lesser wives and a captain in the royal naval fleet. His mortuary stela was discovered at Thebes. (See MILITARY.)

Nile   the world's longest river and the source of all life and abundance in ancient Egypt. The Nile flows approximately 4,665 miles out of Africa's heart on a unique northward journey to the Mediterranean Sea. The Nile taps two separate climatic resources in order to come bounding into Egypt: the summer monsoons of Ethiopia and the Sudan, which feed the river with storm waters, and Central Africa's two annual rainy seasons, which nurture the Nile with gentle downpours and overflowing lakes.

The Nile flows from two sources. The White Nile rises from the deep pools of equatorial Africa, and the Blue Nile sweeps down from the Abyssinian highlands. These combine with many tributaries, including the Atbara, which joins the Nile at the Fifth Cataract, bringing vast quantities of affluvium and red mud.

The cataracts of the Nile, the progression of 10 rocky, white-rapid regions, formed the southern border of ancient Egypt. The First Cataract at ASWAN, demarcated the border of Egypt for centuries. The other cataracts provided rocky peaks upon which the Egyptians built a series of fortresses and garrisoned trading posts and towns to command traffic on the Nile.

Just above Aswan, at Edfu, the great Nile Valley begins. Limestone cliffs parallel the river for more than 400 miles, marching beside the shoreline, sometimes close to the water and sometimes swinging back toward the deserts. The cliffs reach heights of 800 feet in some areas, with mesas and plateaus glistening against the sky. The cliffs on the west stand like sentinels before the Libyan Desert, and the eastern slopes withdraw into the Arabian or Red Sea Desert. This valley provided a true cultural and geographical shelter for the emerging people of the region.

The Delta of Lower Egypt is a watery fan of seven major tributaries emptying into the Mediterranean Sea: the Pelusiac, Tanite, Phatnitic (Damietta), Sebennytic, Bolbitinic (Rosetta), Mendesian and Canopic branches.

The waters of the Bahr Yusef, a stream dedicated to Joseph (an Islamic hero and not the Biblical patriarch), flow out of the Nile and into the Faiyum; a natural depression alongside the river about 65 miles south of modern Cairo, at ASSIUT. They are trapped in the depression. Thus a rich marshland region of wetlands and moist fields was made available to the ancient Egyptian farmers. The site was also inhabited by CROCODILES, which were honored with a shrine.

The river's annual floods deposited a ribbon of fertile soil along its banks. In time, the Egyptians would use canals, irrigation ditches and sophisticated hydraulic systems to reclaim lands and expand their agricultural base. When the Nile inundated the land the benefits were twofold. The river not only left rich deposits of mud and fertile silt but leached the soil of harmful salts as well. When the Nile began to recede at the end of the inundation, the Egyptians used dams and reservoirs to store water for the dry seasons of the year. The inundation of the river was gradual, heralded by the arrival of Sopdu, the Greek Sirius or Dogstar, in the sky. By July the first waters came rushing into the land, increasing every day until the fields and orchards were flooded. The inundation lasted through October, when the Nile receded again. It is estimated that Egypt received as much as 30 feet of mud as a result of each annual inundation. For this reason the Egyptians called their land Khem, the Black Land. The deserts on either side of the river were called the Deshret, the Red Lands. The stark contrast between the two regions is still evident.

Along its banks the Nile sustained a variety of fish and fowl. Ducks, geese, waterbirds and nesting birds could be caught in the marshes with clap nets or with throwing sticks. The Nile nurtured the sacred lotus, reeds and the papyrus plant, which scribes used to make papyri. The river was endless in its bounty, and the people sang its praises continually. They understood from the charts of the astronomer-priests when to anticipate the rising floods, taking appropriate steps to prepare for the inundation and

The Nile river, depicted as twin gods—benefactors of Egypt (the Two Lands).

to celebrate the religious significance of the event. Nile festivals remained popular in every era.

The river was always the "Father of Life" to the ancient Egyptians, or the "Mother of all Men" to some generations. The Nile was also the manifesta-tion of the god HAPI, the divine spirit that unceas-ingly blessed the land with rich silt deposits from the continent's core.

The religious texts of ancient times link the Nile to a celestial stream which emptied out of the heavens at the Elephantine, or in the caves thought to be in that region. The annual flooding in Hapi's hands was thus called the "Libation," made in the honor of HORUS in the south and in honor of SETH in the Delta.

The name for the river is Greek in origin, a version of the Semitic NAKHAL, or river. The Egyptians called the river Hep-Ur, Great Hapi, or "sweet water." Each generation addressed the Nile with its own special name and hymn of praise. The river was Egypt's life blood, not only did it sustain the people, but it imposed on them a sense of stewardship and a seasonal regimen, prompting the spirit of cooperation that was to become the hallmark of the nation.

Nile festivals   celebrations of the river and the god Hapi, its divine manifestation, in ancient Egypt, held throughout all historical periods. The Night of the Tear was the June holiday, dedicated to the goddess ISIS as the beginning of the annual inundation. It was believed that the goddess Isis shed tears over the body of her husband, OSIRIS, and these tears multiplied and caused the Nile to overflow its banks. The Night of the Tear honored Isis as the goddess of nurturing and mortuary powers, associating her with the basic life-giving function of the river.

The Night of the Dam or the Night of the Cutting of the Dam, was celebrated when the inundation had reached its highest levels. Earthen dams were built to measure the height of the water, and then the upper levels were thinned and broken by boats. The ceremony signified the completion of the river's nurturing duties. The festival remained popular in all eras, and a version was performed in modern times at various sites in Egypt until the building of the dam at ASWAN. (See NILE.)

Nile level records   inscriptions marking the heights of various inundations of the Nile River, discovered on the rocks at SEMNA and dating to the reign of AMENEMHET III of the 12th Dynasty (1844–1797 B.C.) and continuing through the close of the 17th Dynasty (1550 B.C.). These were part of the annual recording of the river's inundation levels, similar to the NILO-METERS.

Nilometers   pillars or slabs that were positioned at various strategic locations on the river to determine the height of the annual inundations or floods. It was important for the Egyptians to determine the flow of the river each year, so they positioned the pillars far south of the First Cataract at Aswan to give early warning of any variation in the Nile's flood levels. Such information was sent to the king by messenger and to the various regional governors, so that any necessary preparations could be made for the event. Two such measuring devices were used, in the Delta and at the First Cataract, in ancient times, and subsidiary pillars were positioned in the Second and Fourth Cataracts during the empire.

The pillars were inscribed with a scale cut into cubit measurements: 1 cubit equals 2⅓ inches. Other measurements were inscribed on later pillars. The Nilometers not only provided information on the level of the floods but allowed the priests and governors to determine the crops which would thrive as a result of the amount of silt being deposited. Prospective harvests were thus assessed and the tax bases of the crops determined in advance. (See AGRICULTURE, ELEPHANTINE and NILE.)

Nine Bows   a term used by the ancient Egyptians to signify the subdued enemies of the nation. The Nine Bows became a symbol of empire and was reproduced on statues and even on the slippers of the kings, so that when he walked he symbolically trampled his enemies underfoot.

Ninetjer   the third king of the 2nd Dynasty of ancient Egypt (date unknown). He is recorded as having built temples and celebrated festivals in Memphis. Ninetjer is supposed to have ruled approximately 38 years.

Niuserre   See IZI.

Nofret   a princess of the 4th Dynasty, the wife of Prince RE'HOTPE, the son of SNOFRU (2575–2551 B.C.). Statues of the royal couple were discovered in their twin mastabas at MEIDUM and are now on display at the Egyptian Museum in Cairo.

nomarchs   the hereditary aristocracy of the Egyptian nomes, or provinces. These nobles raised their own armies, served as the representatives of the kings and defended their own borders. Some, such as the nomarchs of Assiut or Beni Hassan, were famed for their military prowess. In times of weak kings, the nomarchs became more independent and involved themselves in provincial feuds. Most nomarchs were hereditary princes or "counts."

nome   from the Greek *nomos*, a province or administrative region of ancient Egypt, called *sepat* in Egyptian. Some nomes date to predynastic times, and all were governed by an *heri-tep a'a*, a "great overlord," a hereditary title roughly equivalent to prince or count. Such overlords were responsible for military levies demanded by the kings, and for the taxes and tributes assessed for their regions. Each nome had a capital city and a cult center dedicated to the god of the territory, but these changed in the course of Egyptian history. The number of nomes was altered as well, standardized only in the Greco-Roman period.

The nomarchs and their extended families maintained their own life-styles and traditions even in periods of strong centralized rule. During the Intermediate Periods, eras of dynastic weakness, the nomes asserted their independence and competed with each other. The cliff tombs of ASSIUT and BENI HASAN and other monuments testify to the continuing strength and dynamism of the nomes.

Nubia the land below the First Cataract of the Nile, called Ta-seti, Wawat and Kush in reference to specific regions. The area was of vital concern to Egypt in all eras, and as early as the 1st Dynasty (2920–2770 B.C.) Egyptian kings were active there. 'AHA recorded the taking of two villages below GEBEL ES-SILSILA during his reign, and DJER's name appears in a mutilated battle scene at the WADI HALFA. Trade with Nubia was considered essential. The Egyptians exchanged pottery and stone for ivory, gold, ebony, ostrich feathers and eggs, leopard skins, copper, amethyst, carnelian, feldspar, oils, gum resins, cattle, dogs, and a variety of exotic wild animals. In time the Nubians manufactured goods in wood, leather and metal to trade as well, and accepted copper tools, jewelry and AMULETS.

At the end of the 2nd Dynasty, KHA'SEKHEMWY led a military campaign into Nubia, starting colonies around the major mining sites and fortifying the trading posts already in existence. The Egyptians maintained these posts but did not attempt to penetrate into the hinterland. The first such trading settlement known was at BUHEN, near the Second Cataract, founded as early as the 2nd Dynasty. SNOFRU, in the 4th Dynasty (2575–2551 B.C.) invaded Nubia and reported bringing back prisoners and cattle. The gold and copper mines of the region were probably being worked by then, and FORTRESSES and garrisoned positions were becoming more extensive. Nubians were already serving as mercenaries in the Egyptian army. General WENI, the commander of the military forces for PEPI I (2289–2255 B.C.), attached whole units of Nubians to his forces.

The extent of Egyptian activity in Nubia during the First Intermediate Period (2134–2040 B.C.) is in question to some extent, but MENTUHOTPE II (2061–2010 B.C.) of the 11th Dynasty is credited with reconquering Nubia after uniting Upper and Lower Egypt in 2040 B.C. In the Middle Kingdom the term Kush identified the lower territories of Nubia, a designation used throughout the New Kingdom as well.

During the Middle Kingdom, the QUARRIES and mining operations were reopened, and caravans from southern domains traded with the Egyptians at fortresses. These fortresses stretched along the Nile from cataract to cataract, with each garrison positioned to send messages north or south in case of Nubian troop movements or widespread migrations.

When the Middle Kingdom collapsed, the Egyptians withdrew from Nubia, and the region around KERMA became a capital for the people of Kush. The Kushites, however, were not able to assist the HYKSOS or Asiatics when the kings of the 17th Dynasty at Thebes began their northern assault (c. 1560 B.C.). KAMOSE, the last king of that line, and the older brother of 'AHMOSE, the founder of the New Kingdom, appears to have had a Viceroy of Nubia. He may have taken possession of the former Egyptian territories before marching against APOPHIS and the Hyksos foes.

When he did go into battle he used the MEDJAY, Nubians who had taken up residence in large numbers in the Egyptian Eastern Desert. The Medjay are believed to be the PAN-GRAVE people. Their grave sites appear in southern Egypt at this time, as well as in Lower Nubia. The Medjay remains found below the First Cataract probably belonged to those troops who served as an occupying force for the Egyptians there.

'Ahmose I (1550–1525 B.C.) had Viceroys of Nubia and rehabilitated the fortresses there. In time the Egyptians would control the Nile down to the Fifth

Nubians bearing tribute, from a Theban relief.

Cataract. They did not venture inland at any given point but were content to conduct extensive trading operations, along with their usual mining and quarrying operations. During this period the Egyptians displayed little interest in the customs, religion or national ideals of the Nubian people. Their god, DEDUN, received some royal patronage, as during the reign of TUTHMOSIS III (1479–1425 B.C.), but in general the region was viewed simply as an occupied territory and was extended none of the courtesies offered the Levantine city-states.

Nubia was administered by Egyptian officials according to accepted procedures. It was divided into an Upper Nubia and a Lower Nubia, each under the control of a governor. The northern province probably including the lands as far south as Semna, was called Wawat and was administered at Aniba. Upper Nubia was governed from Amara West, at least during the 19th Dynasty (1307–1196 B.C.). The fortresses and garrisons were under a single commander, assisted by the usual assortment of Egyptian officials, scribes, bureaucrats and agents.

Nubkhas a queen of the 11th Dynasty, the consort of MENTUHOTPE II (2061–1010 B.C.), whose tomb was discovered at DEIR EL-BAHRI. The site was surrounded by masonry and enclosed by boulders and rubble, probably the result of a landslide.

Nubti an ancient Egyptian name for the god Seth in Upper Egypt.

Nun a being of ancient Egypt, believed to represent the primeval watery abyss of the cosmogonic texts out of which the god arose. Nun was thought to inhabit every watery darkness; thus he was confronted in deep wells or in caverns. He was also associated with the Nile at the time of inundation.

Nut an ancient Egyptian goddess of the sky. The wife of GEB and his sister, Nut was separated from him by the command of RE'. SHU raised her up so that Geb could not touch her, and a ban was put on her time of bearing children. The EPAGOMENAL DAYS were the only period of the year in which Nut could conceive. During that time Nut gave birth to OSIRIS, HORUS (the old), SETH, ISIS and NEPHTHYS.

Nut is depicted as a woman stretched over the horizon, with stars and celestial lights forming her garb. She was depicted on occasion as a heavenly cow or as the sow that ate the stars each morning and then gave birth to them at twilight. When she was shown as a woman, she wore a round vase on her head, the hieroglyph of her name. Nut figures in many religious legends. In some she is the cow that Re' mounts when he emerges from the abyss at the moment of creation. In the mortuary rituals she protects the deceased, who rise into her heavenly abode as stars. Nut did not have a temple or a cult dedicated to her worship. In some texts she was called *Kha-bewes*, "one with a thousand souls."

O

oases   important sites in ancient Egypt located in the western desert. They served as trade links to more distant regions and as outposts against periodic invasions. Called *wehat*, meaning a garden or a green and fertile region, the oases were a source of crops such as dates and grapes. Oases were also places of refuge. When KAMOSE (1550 B.C.) of the 17th Dynasty began his military campaigns against the alien HYKSOS in the northern territories, he and his armies used the various oases as hiding places. They were able to move within striking distance of the enemy without being detected.

The major oases of ancient Egypt were:

Siwa   incorporated into Egypt in the Late Period, when it was known as Jupiter Ammon and revered as a religious site by pilgrims, especially those coming from Libya.

Bahariya   the northern oasis, used by Kamose and others in military campaigns, also a wine-producing region.

Farafrah   called Ta-ahet in some eras, a cattle-raising region from early times.

el-Dakhla   called Tchesti, or the Inner Oasis, temple ruins and Old Kingdom settlement remains have been discovered there.

Kharga   called Uaht-rest, the Outer or Southern Oasis, it was used as a trading outpost and was the site of HIBIS.

obelisks   large upright stone beams with four sides and a tapering end carved into the form of a pyramidion, used as religious symbols in ancient Egypt. Called *tekhenu* by the Egyptians, the obelisks were given their modern name by the Greeks, who believed their shape resembled small spits. Obelisks were considered sacred to the god RE' and to other solar deities, and the ancient texts describe their particular role. According to the old mythology, obelisks came in pairs; two were in heaven and two were on the earth in every age.

Heliopolis boasted obelisks from the early eras of the nation, and they were also raised at THEBES and at MEMPHIS. The temples of THOTH, AMON, ISIS, KHNUM, OSIRIS, NEITH, PTAH and other gods normally had obelisks. During the New Kingdom era, the time of empire, obelisks came to be an architectural element of the great temples. The kings of the 18th Dynasty used them to adorn KARNAK and other religious sites at Thebes, and the Ramessid kings had obelisks fashioned for their new capital in the Delta.

During the New Kingdom the stone pillars were endowed with supernatural significance. They were believed to be inhabited by the gods or by the spirits of the deity. They thus merited offerings and special ceremonies. TUTHMOSIS III (1479–1425 B.C.) instituted such practices for the obelisks that he erected at Karnak. A new feast and new liturgies were adopted for the offerings made to the god, as the obelisks were believed to have a real solar significance. They were positioned according to the traditional patterns. The rising and the setting of the sun were honored by these pillars, and they had to conform to specifications as to height and location.

Most of the obelisks erected in ancient Egypt were of granite, quartzite or basalt. At the Aswan quarry, a favorite source of stone for obelisks during the imperial period, granite was heated by bonfires and then cooled by water until the stone split; wooden spikes drove passageways into the desired sections. Workmen cleared a path to the stone, marking the length, which was of about 100 feet. Using tools made of hard stones, the workmen began to fashion the sides of the pillar, crawling in and around the obelisk to complete their section of the monument. The obelisk was supported by stones so that it would not crack as the workmen leveled the sides and completed the surface carving.

When the pillar was carved to satisfaction, ropes were slung around it and the stone was raised and placed on a heavy sledge. It took several thousand

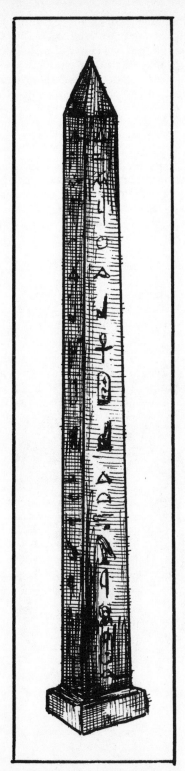

An obelisk, one of Egypt's most enduring art forms.

workmen to pull the sledge to the banks of the Nile. There, vessels waited in dry docks specially designed to allow safe loading of the pillars. The unique aspect of this loading process is that the boats remained in dry dock until the pillars were safely on board. Then the vessel and the sacred cargo were slowly floated on water emptied into the dock. When the ship and the pillar were stabilized, the dock gates were open and the vessel made its way out onto the Nile.

Nine galleys, each with more than 30 rowers, towed the vessel and the obelisk to Thebes, where a ceremonial ritual and vast crowds awaited their arrival. A ramp was prepared in advance, and the pillar was pulled to the incline. The unique part of the ramp was a funnel shaped hole, filled with sand. The obelisk was positioned over the hole and the sand was emptied, thus lowering the pillar into place. When the obelisk had been positioned on its base and fastened there, the ramp was removed and the priests and royal household arrived to take part in dedication rituals and in ceremonies in honor of the god of the stone.

Obelisks are characteristically Egyptian but have been honored by all civilizations since the fall of the New Kingdom. Few of the original pillars remain in Egypt. Several capitals around the world boast at least one of these graceful emblems of faith. They remain insignias of another time and place.

Ogdoad   the eight gods worshipped at HERMOPOLIS, and first mentioned in the Middle Kingdom. These deities were believed to have been the first creatures to emerge from the watery chaos before creation. The Ogdoad was also believed to constitute the soul of the god THOTH. The male members of the Ogdoad (four in number) were always depicted as having frog heads. The female divinities (four consorts) were serpent-headed.

The original gods of the Ogdoad were Amon and Amaunet, Nun and Naunet, Heh and Hehet, Kaku and Keket, and they were believed to have caused the Nile to flow and the sun to rise over Egypt each day. Amon gained prominence in Thebes during the Middle Kingdom and in the imperial period. Heh became the symbol of ETERNITY, and was thus honored in the various eras. Nun, endowed with particular cosmogonic importance, was worshipped in his own right.

oils   substances prized by the ancient Egyptians and used for various rituals and ceremonies, mummification and cosmetics. Tablets with basins of alabaster have been discovered, clearly designed to hold oils.

The Egyptians availed themselves of a variety of oils. The ceremonial perfume used to anoint the god and to make the sanctuary of the temple fragrant for holy feast days was known as *hekenu*. Syrian balsam, salves, anointing oils, cedar and Libyan oils were all part of the temple ceremonies, and other oils were used in religious services throughout Egypt and in embalming to make the limbs of the mummies supple.

Ombos   called Nubty, The Golden, by the ancient Egyptians, a site south of COPTOS on the western shore of the Nile, that was noted for its gold mines. Obmos was inhabited from predynastic times, and was dedicated to the god SETH. A temple was found on the site, which was a rival to DENDERA in some eras. (See METALS.)

On   See HELIOPOLIS.

"on the bricks"   an ancient Egyptian term for giving birth. Women sat on specially designed brick daises in the last hours of labor. MESHKENT, the goddess of birth, was depicted with two bricks in her insignia.

Onouphis   See A'A-NEFER.

Onouris   See ANHUR.

Opet   originally a goddess of ancient Egypt, the patron of a section of eastern Thebes, which contained special shrines to the god AMON. (See LUXOR.)

oracles   famed throughout ancient Egypt's historical periods and part of all cult centers, even in the Libyan OASES, especially SIWA. Oracles were always popular with the people, who had an innate curiosity about the future and daily affairs. They were used in conjunction with lucky or unlucky days and were deemed messengers of the divine.

On festival days the statues of the gods were carried through the streets of the cities or floated on barges to the local shrines or necropolis regions. The people flocked to the processions, anxious for the statues to reach the stations that were erected on street corners. There the statues were asked questions about the future and received ritualized and traditional responses. The statue of the god moved on its pedestal or in its shrine, or the entire shrine swayed to one side or the other when questions were posed it. A negative response to a question was indicated by movement in one direction and a positive response by movement in another. In some cult centers the statues "spoke" to the faithful. The sacred bulls of Egypt were also used as oracles. An animal was led into a vast hall crowded by faithful onlookers. The people asked their questions and the bull was loosed. Two doors opened onto chambers containing the bull's favorite food. One door signified a negative answer to the questions and the other a positive reply. The bull entered one chamber, thus rendering its divine judgment.

Orbiney Papyrus   a text of the 19th Dynasty, dating to the reign of SETI I (c. 1306–1290 B.C.) and supposedly a copy of an earlier document. The papyrus contained the TALE OF THE TWO BROTHERS, the legend of good and evil in ancient eras. The Orbiney Papyrus is in the British Museum.

Orion   See ASTRONOMY.

Osireion   the name given the cenotaph of SETI I (c. 1306–1290 B.C.) at Abydos, erected behind his vast mortuary temple in OSIRIS' holy city. The struc-

OSIREION   one of the pillared chambers from Seti I's cenotaph at Abydos.

ture was unfinished at the time of Seti's death. His grandson MERNEPTAH (c. 1224–1214 B.C.) completed it in his honor. The walls were covered with passages from the BOOK OF THE DEAD, the Book of Gates, astronomical and other texts. A unique feature of the Osireion was an island surrounded by canals. The false sarcophagus of the king rested on the island.

Osiris one of the most popular and enduring gods of ancient Egypt, whose cult dates to the Old Kingdom and continued into the Greco-Roman Period. Osiris' earliest manifestation was Asari, a man-headed god of agriculture. Andjeti was another fertility god who, united with Khentiamenti of ABYDOS in agricultural celebrations, was absorbed into the Osirian cult in time. Possible *DJED* pillar symbols date to the 1st Dynasty (2920 B.C.) at Helwan, and the cult is mentioned in the 5th Dynasty (2465–2323 B.C.). Osiris appears to have been part of the Heliopolitan pantheon and was mentioned in the PYRAMID TEXTS. His cult gained early acceptance at Abydos and at BUSIRIS. He was addressed as *Wen-nefer*, the "Beautiful One," and then became Khentiamenti, the "Foremost of the Westerners," as Amenti, the West, always represented death and the grave to Egyptians.

The myth of Osiris was the basis for the god's cult, and this legendary account of his life is given in the Pyramid Texts. Osiris was slain by his brother deity, SETH, and discovered by ISIS and NEPHTHYS. The goddess stopped the corruption of his flesh and brought him to life twice because Seth attacked the body again. A heavenly trial resulted, with Osiris accusing Seth of the murderous acts before the gods. Osiris was praised by the gods, who condemned Seth.

The death of Osiris and his resurrection played an important part in the cult that became symbolic of the kings of Egypt in time. The dead pharaohs of Egypt were considered embodiments of Osiris, having been equated with HORUS, Osiris' son, while on the throne. Other aspects of Osiris' cult include his dismemberment by Seth and his rule in an ideal time before the start of the nation.

The earliest representation of Osiris dates to the 5th Dynasty, when he was depicted as a man with a divine wig. In subsequent eras he kept his mortal appearance, but always in a mummified form, which was part of his funerary role. In the Middle Kingdom Osiris was depicted wearing the white helmet of Upper Egypt, perhaps to designate the god's origins. In time he was normally depicted wearing the *atef* crown, the elaborate plumed headdress. In his hands he carries the crook and flail.

In the MORTUARY RITUALS, Osiris is the paramount

Osiris, pictured in a unique double robe, wearing the white helmet of Upper Egypt and holding the crook and flail.

judge of the non-royal Egyptians, who had to appear in his JUDGMENT HALLS to face him and his companions, the FORTY-TWO JUDGES. The mortuary rituals in most eras revolved about this role of Osiris, and the BOOK OF THE DEAD offers various accounts of the trial and the weighing of the hearts of the dead. The god, however, represented more than fertility and judgment. Much of his appeal was based on his embodiment of cosmic harmony. The rising Nile was his insignia, and the moon's constant state of renewal symbolized his bestowal of eternal bliss.

In time Abydos became the center of his cult, and pilgrims made their way there for various celebrations. The deceased longed to be buried beside the god, and if such a burial was not possible, the relatives of the dead person placed a mortuary STELA in Abydos so that the individual could share in Osiris' bliss. Other cultic observances were conducted in the name of Osiris. (See below.)

Osiris' Bed a unique mortuary offering discovered in tombs of the 18th Dynasty (1550–1307 B.C.). These were boxes fashioned out of wood or pottery normally in the shape of the god. Osiris' Beds were often hollow, planted with Nile mud and corn. The boxes were then wrapped as mummies and placed in the tomb. The corn was expected to sprout as a symbol of Osiris' resurrection. Some boxes did contain actual evidence of growth when they were unwrapped centuries later.

Osiris' festivals religious celebrations conducted in honor of the god in all eras of Egyptian history. One festival, held in November (according to the modern calendar) celebrated the beauty of the god. A second festival, called the Fall of the Nile, was a time of mourning. As the Nile receded, the Egyptians went to the shore to bestow gifts and to show grief over Osiris' dying another time. The Nile represented Osiris' capacity to renew the earth and to restore life to the nation.

When the Nile began its steady rise toward the flood stage, Osiris was again honored. Small shrines were cast adrift on the river, and priests poured sweet water into the Nile, declaring that Osiris was found again. Mud and various spices were often formed into the shape of the crescent moon to honor Osiris' return. The festival honoring the DJED Pillar was celebrated by the royal court each year, with songs and dances in honor of the coming harvests.

Osiris' mysteries ceremonies held in honor of the god, dating to the 12th Dynasty (1991–1783 B.C.), and staged in ABYDOS. Dramas were performed with the leading roles assigned to high-ranking community leaders or to temple priests. The mysteries recounted the life, death, mummification, resurrection and ascension of Osiris, and the dramas were part of a pageant that lasted for many days. Egyptians flocked to the celebrations. After the dramas a battle was staged between the "Followers of Horus" and the "Followers of Seth." This was a time-honored rivalry with political as well as religious overtones. Part of the pageant was a procession in which a statue of Osiris, made out of ELECTRUM, gold or some other precious material, was carried from the temple. An outdoor shrine was erected to receive the god and to allow the people to gaze upon the "Beautiful One." There Osiris was again depicted as rising from the dead and ascending to his heavenly realms. Other mysteries honoring other deities were held in HELIOPOLIS, BUSIRIS, BUBASTIS, MEMPHIS and THEBES.

ostraka fragments or slabs of stone or pottery used for writing or sketching by the ancient Egyptians. They were used much like modern paper, for memos and letters. Ostraka were often provided to student scribes for practicing writing by copying literary texts. They are much more numerous in archaeological sites than papyri. The ostraka discovered by modern excavation of Egyptian sites bear copies of truly ancient texts, artistic renderings, examples of the use of the canon of art and other information.

Overthrowing Apophis an unusual text dating to the Ramessid period but part of a religious mythology known from ancient times in Egypt. Apophis was a serpent that assaulted the god Re' nightly, according to Heliopolitan religious traditions. In some eras Apophis was deemed a manifestation of the god SETH. Apophis had to be overthrown through prayers. The ritual of overthrowing the serpent included recitation of a list of the serpent's "secret" names and a selection of hymns to be sung on the occasion of his destruction. According to the ritual, the serpent had been previously annihilated, hacked to pieces, dismembered, flung into the abyss. This treatment of Apophis, however, did not deter him from making another attack upon Re' the following night. The Egyptians assembled in the temples to make images out of the serpents in wax. They spat upon the images, burned them and mutilated them. Cloudy days or storms were signs that Apophis was gaining ground, and solar eclipses were particular times of terror for the Egyptians, as they were interpreted a sign of Re' 's demise. The sun god emerged victorious each time, however, and the people continued their prayers and anthems.

Oxyrhynchus the modern el-Bahnasa, once called Harday. The capital of the 19th NOME of Upper Egypt, the site contained the mummified remains of dogs. OSIRIS was favored in this region, where more Greek papyri have been found than in any other site in Egypt.

oxyrhyncus the Nile fish believed to have eaten the phallus of the god OSIRIS when SETH dismembered him and cast his body parts into the river. Out of devotion to Osiris, in some nomes the fish was considered forbidden food.

P

paddle dolls   flat, painted wooden dolls deposited in the tombs of the Middle Kingdom. These figurines, crude by the artistic standards of the Egyptians, had elaborate hairstyles, composed of strings of mud and faience beads, which were laced with bits of straw. The design obviously mimicked the elaborate wigs worn in all eras. Paddle dolls were discovered in 11th Dynasty tombs. Their inclusion among the mortuary regalia is not fully understood. Some sources indicate that the dolls were provided as sexual companions or servants for the deceased.

A paddle doll from an Egyptian grave site.

pa-duat   the ancient Egyptian name for a narrow tomb chamber designed to honor the particular god of the structure. Within the *pa-duat* the statue of the god was dressed and adorned with scented oils, probably as part of the daily MORTUARY RITUALS conducted by the priests. At DEIR EL-BAHRI the *pa-duat* was discovered in the upper court of Mentuhotpe II's elaborate mortuary complex.

Pakhenty   a site south of Thebes that was dedicated to the god AMON and contained a vast shrine for rituals.

Pakht   a lion goddess believed to guard both the living and the dead in ancient Egypt. Her shrine, built by HATSHEPSUT (1473–1458 B.C.) and completed in the 19th Dynasty, was located at BENI HASAN. The Greeks named the temple the Speos Artemidos, associating Pakht with their own goddess Artemis. Originally a huntress of the deserts and known for ferocity against the enemies of Egypt, Pakht was often depicted in statues that guarded the gates of temples and royal residences of the nation.

Palermo Stone   a fragment of diorite (or some other dark stone) containing information from the early dynasties. The largest piece of the stone is in Palermo, hence its name. A second piece is in the Egyptian Museum in Cairo, and a smaller section is in the University College of London. The Palermo Stone was broken out of the center of a slab believed to have been approximately 7 feet long and 2 feet high, if stood on its long edge. Inscribed on both sides with details about the predynastic kings and those of the Early Dynastic Period and Old Kingdom through the middle eras of the 5th Dynasty, the Stone provides a king list dating to predynastic times. Some 120 kings ruling in Upper and Lower Egypt before the unification in 3000 B.C. are named.

palette called a *mestha* by the ancient Egyptians, vessels put to everyday and ceremonial use during all eras. Most of these vessels were made of wood or stone, and were of varying size. In some palettes there were oval hollows, designed to hold cosmetics, inks or paint. Writing needs were held in the center grooves of the palettes of the scribes, with sliding wooden covers. Others used slats of wood glued across the groove to hold the reeds in place. The palette of Na'rmer, and the Libyan (or "Cities") Palette, provide information about the late Predynastic Period.

Panehsi a clan of public officials in the New Kingdom, probably members of the same family, listed in some records as Panhey. The first Panehsi was an official of the 18th Dynasty, serving in the reign of AKHENATEN (1353–1335 B.C.). He was a member of the temple of ATEN during the 'AMARNA period. His tomb portrait depicted him as an elderly, heavy-set man. The second Panehsi was an official of the 19th Dynasty, serving RAMESSES II (1290–1224 B.C.) as a scribe and director of the nation's gold stores. He was superintendent of the gold shipments from Nubia. This Panhesi was buried at Thebes.

The last Panehsi, an official of the 20th Dynasty, served RAMESSES XI (1100–1070 B.C.). He was the viceroy of NUBIA, involved as well in military affairs. When a revolt against the high priest of AMON took place in Thebes, Panehsi gathered up army units and marched to the old capital. There he put down the rebellion, dismissing the truant prelate. Returning to his administrative center at the ELEPHANTINE, Panhesi left one of his officers in charge of the city. This man, HERIHOR, made himself the high priest of Amon and usurped the throne, putting an end to the New Kingdom.

pan-graves Upper Nubian burial sites found throughout southern Egypt, dating to the time by the 17th Dynasty of THEBES (1640–1550 B.C.). These graves are closely related to the MEDJAY units employed by KAMOSE when he began his assaults on the HYKSOS and their Asiatic allies, c. 1555 B.C.

The shallow graves (from 10–15 inches to 6 ft) are normally oval or circular in design—pan-like. The bodies placed inside were found clad in leather garments and bearing primitive jewelry. Pottery included in the graves was of the C-Horizon (Nubian) variety—rough brown with patterns of oblique lines or undecorated. Painted skulls of horned animals were placed in nearby offertory pits, and the graves also held Egyptian axes and daggers.

The pan-graves found in Lower NUBIA date to the same period and are believed to have been dug by immigrants to the region or by the Medjay who settled in the territory as Egyptian allies or as an occupation force there. Pan-grave pottery has also been found in el-Kab and Quban, an indication that the Medjay units garrisoned these positions for the Egyptians. There was some conflict between the Medjay and the local populations in Nubian territories in the past, and the troops would have been a reliable occupation force.

papyrus *cyperus papyrus*, a plant once common throughout the Nile Valley and now rare. The ancient Egyptians called the plant *djet* or *tjufi*. The Greeks gave the world the modern name. When papyri was formed in rolls, it was called *djema*.

The stem of the papyrus plant was cut into thin strips, which were laid side by side in a perpendicular fashion. A solution of resin from the plant was laid down, and a second layer of papyrus was put into place, horizontally. The two layers were then pressed and allowed to dry. Immense rolls of papyrus could be made by joining the single sheets. One roll, in the British Museum, measures 135 feet long. The common size, however, was from 9 to 10 inches by 5 to 5½ inches.

Papyri were originally made for religious documents and texts, with sheets added to the rolls as needed. The sides of a papyrus are the *recto*, where the fibers run horizontally, and the *verso*, where the fibers run vertically. The *recto* was preferred, but the *verso* was used for documents as well, allowing two separate texts to be included on a single papyrus. Papyrus rolls were protected by the dry climate of Egypt. One roll discovered in modern times dates to c. 3500 B.C. (See SMA-TAWY.)

papyrus scepter an AMULET of ancient Egypt, called the *wadj* or *uadj* in some records, believed to impart strength, abundance and virility to the wearer.

Par a personification of AMON when that god was called the Lord of the Phallus. Par was the representation of the god in fertility rituals in THEBES and in the surrounding area.

Paser an ancient Egyptian line of officials, probably connected to the same NOME clan. One Paser served AMENHOTEP II (1427–1401 B.C.) in the 18th Dynasty as a military commander. A second Paser served SETI I (1306–1290 B.C.) and RAMESSES II (1290–1224 B.C.) as vizier. This Paser was mentioned in ancient papyri. The third Paser was in the service of Ramesses IX (1131–1112 B.C.) of the 20th Dynasty as the mayor

Aten cult. He retained his religious office during the subsequent brief reigns and then served under the last king of the 18th Dynasty, HOREMHAB.

Pawara an official of the 18th Dynasty, serving AKHENATEN (1353–1335 B.C.) during the 'Amarna Period. The legate of Egypt to the city-state of Amurru, Pawara witnessed the decline of Egyptian power in the area because of Akhenaten's refusal to totally defend his nation's allies and territories. Pawara was slain in Amurru, and his successor was forced to

PAPYRUS   a plant now rare in Egypt.

of the eastern shore of Thebes. He was involved in the TOMB ROBBERY TRIAL, bringing charges against PAWERO and other high officials.

Patenemheb an official of the 18th Dynasty during the 'AMARNA period, serving in the reign of AKHENATEN (1353–1335 B.C.). Patenemheb was a high priest of RE' who witnessed the fall of 'Amarna and the

Bronze mirror shaped as a papyrus scepter with the head of Hathor.

leave the area, surrendering the city-state to its own ruler as the Egyptians withdrew.

Pawero an official of the 20th Dynasty, serving RAMESSES IX (1131–1112 B.C.) as the mayor of the western shore of Thebes. Pawero, an hereditary prince and count and the chief of the necropolis police, was involved in the great tomb robbery scandal of that era. The outcome of his trial, which was held in accordance with the law, is unknown. The mayor of eastern Thebes, a man named PASER suffered abuse and threats from Pawero but continued to demand an end to the wholesale robberies which were being conducted. Pawero and his gang were involved with many high officials, and the discovery of their invasion of the royal tomb sites on the western shore was a serious scandal. The Abbot and Amherst Papyri give accounts of this affair.

Pay Lands mythological sites believed to have been created by the gods of the PRIMEVAL MOUND at the dawn of time. The lands were formed by the sacred utterings of the gods and were called the Blessed Islands. The falcon or hawk was the lord of these mystical abodes. The various Pay Lands created by the gods included the Mansion of Isden, the Island of RE', the DJED Pillar of the Earth, and Behdet (Edfu). Other Pay Lands believed to have been formed at the moment of creation were the Great Seat, the Great Place and the Throne. They were held to be gardens and marsh areas, free of the watery chaos and sacred to all Egyptians as the seats of the gods. (See COSMOGONY and RELIGION.)

Peak of the West the ancient Egyptian site on the western shore of THEBES, on the hill of Sheikh Abd-el-Gurneh, the abode of the goddess MERESGER, who was called the Lady of Heaven. The Peak of the West is a spur on the hill that faces Thebes.

pectoral a necklace made out of stone, faience or other materials. The pectoral was normally glazed blue or blue-green. Pectorals were worn by the royal clans in all eras of Egypt and were very popular among all classes in the New Kingdom.

Pe-Hathor See GEBELEIN.

Penno called Penni and Penne in some records, an official of the 20th Dynasty, serving RAMESSES IV (1156–1151 B.C.). Penno was one of the Egyptian authorities in the lands below the First Cataract, the governor of the region called Wawat, and director of the quarry operations in that area. He erected a statue of Ramesses IV and received silver urns from the king in return.

Pentaur, Poem of a hieroglyphic text discovered on the walls of the temple of Luxor and dating to the reign of RAMESSES II (c. 1290–1224 B.C.). Considered one of ancient Egypt's most important historical documents, the account was written by one of the king's companions on the military campaign against Kadesh. A short form was found in the Sallier Papyri.

The battle of Kadesh was decisive in returning to Egypt the international stature which it had enjoyed during the 18th Dynasty, establishing Ramesses II as one of the nation's great pharaohs and Egypt as a military power among its contemporaries. Pentaur described the campaign in poetic terms, providing a sense of drama to the scene when the king realizes that he has been ambushed. Ramesses II rallies his forces, which include the Regiments of Re', Ptah, Sutekh and Amon. With the king in the lead, the Egyptians battle their way free. The Hittites and their allies had hoped to destroy Ramesses at Kadesh but were forced to sue for peace and for an alliance with Egypt as a result of the battle.

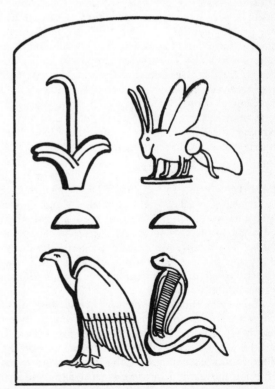

Symbols of Upper and Lower Egypt in hieroglyphs, used in all temple and royal reliefs.

Pentu an official of the 18th Dynasty during the 'AMARNA period, serving in the reign of AKHENATEN (c. 1353–1335 B.C.). Pentu served as the royal physician at 'Amarna. His tomb discovered near the ruined city depicts his career and honors.

Pepi I (Meryre') the third king of the 6th Dynasty, ruling from 2289 to 2255 B.C. in Memphis. The son of Teti and Queen Ipwet, Pepi was an innovative military leader. He abandoned the defensive posture that had marked Egypt's border campaigns early in his reign. His general WENI, using Nubian troops brought up from below the cataracts, attacked the Sinai and southern Palestine, going as far as Mount Carmel to pursue rebellious Bedouins. Pepi was supposed to have trapped an enemy army by landing troops on the Palestine coastline. Weni and Pepi I also led a campaign in Nubia to establish garrisons and trading posts.

His pyramid, Men-nefer-Mare', was an impressive mortuary complex which in time lent its name to the surrounding area, including the capital. Originally called Hiku-Ptah (or *Hat-Ku-Ptah*), the Mansion of the soul of Ptah, the capital was named Men-nefer, then Menfi. The Greeks transliterated it as Memphis in later eras. Rare copper statues of Pepi I and one of his royal sons were discovered in HIERAKONPOLIS and are in the Egyptian Museum of Cairo. Such metal statues were rare in ancient Egypt, vulnerable to decay. Pepi I also constructed temples at Tanis, Bubastis, Abydos, Dendera and Coptos. His first wife was involved in a harem plot, which was investigated by General WENI. She disappeared soon after, and Pepi married the two daughters of a local nomarch, naming them both ANKHNES-MERY-RE'. One bore NEMTYEMZAF and the second was the mother of PEPI II.

Pepi II (Neferkare') (2246–2152 B.C.) the fifth king of the 6th Dynasty. The son of PEPI I and Queen ANKHNES-MERY-RE'II, he was only six years old when he came to the throne as the successor of NEMTY-EMZAF. His mother served as his regent. His uncle, the vizier DJAU, Ankhnes-Mery-Re' 's brother, was also involved in administrating the nation during Pepi's minority.

While still a child, Pepi received word from one of his officials, a man named HARKHAF, that a dwarf had been captured and was being brought back to MEMPHIS. He dispatched detailed instructions on the care of the small creature, promising a reward to his official if the dwarf arrived safe and healthy. He also notified the various governors of the cities en route to offer every possible assistance to Harkhaf on his journey. The letter stresses the importance of 24-hour care, lest the dwarf be drowned or injured.

During his reign Pepi II sent trading expeditions to NUBIA and PUNT. He had a vast fleet at his disposal, and he was interested in establishing new trade. He is reported as having ruled Egypt for 94 years. His wife was Queen Nit, the widow of Nemtyemzaf. He also married Ipuit, the daughter of his predecessor. Another wife was Queen Ankhnes-Pepi, whose son or grandson began the short-lived 8th Dynasty. Yet another wife was Queen Wedjebten. Pepi II's pyramid was built in southern Saqqara, formed of masonry and limestone and decorated with PYRAMID TEXTS.

Pepy-Nakht a nobleman of the 6th Dynasty, serving in the reign of PEPI II (2246–2152 B.C.). Pepy-Nakht was the Old Kingdom equivalent of the viceroy of Nubia, serving as the governor of the lands below the First Cataract. His cliff tomb at ASWAN gives detailed information about his expeditions into Nubia to put down a rebellion of local tribes there. He slew princes and nobles of the Nubian tribes and brought other chiefs back to MEMPHIS to pay homage to the king. Pepy-Nakht also traveled to the Red Sea to bring back the body of an official slain in the coastal establishment (possibly Kuser), where the Egyptians had ships built for expeditions to PUNT. KUSER was the port used by the Egyptians in most eras.

Per-Ankh the "House of Life," an institution that served as a scriptorium or a depository for texts. The first reference to the Per-Ankh dates to the Old Kingdom (2575–2134 B.C.). Some mention of the institution can be found in Middle Kingdom (2040–1640 B.C.) records but the main evidence dates to the 19th Dynasty and later (1307–1196 B.C. and onward). Two officials from the Per-Ankh were involved in the conspiracy against RAMESSES III (1194–1163 B.C.), part of the HAREM plot.

In the past the Per-Ankh was described by writers as a primitive university and educational center for the Egyptians, but this is no longer considered a valid description. Research was conducted in the House of Life because medical, astronomical and

per-nefer the "house of beauty," the ancient Egyptian term for the various mummification sites. Such places were established for commoners, who were not embalmed at their tombs. The term *per-nefer* also designated one of the chambers in the valley temples of the royal mortuary complexes where corpses of the kings were embalmed.

mathematical texts perhaps were maintained there and copied by scribes. The institution served as a workshop where sacred books were composed and written by the ranking scholars of the times. It is possible that many of the texts were not kept in the Per-Ankh but discussed there and debated. The members of the institution's staff, all scribes, were considered the learned men of their age. Many were ranking priests in the various temples or noted physicians and served the various kings in many administrative capacities. The Per-Ankh probably existed only in important cities. Ruins of one House of Life were found at 'AMARNA, and one was discovered at ABYDOS. Magical texts were part of the output of the institution, as were the copies of the BOOK OF THE DEAD.

Peribsen   the fourth king of the 2nd Dynasty (date unknown), who was not the immediate succesor of NINETJER. He may have been an outsider or even a usurper. He used the SETH designation in his titles, a change in kingly symbols in that era. Peribsen is known for a mortuary complex in Abydos. Nothing else of his reign is documented.

pero (or *per-a'a*)   the ancient Egyptian name for the palaces or royal residences of the kings. The term meant "great house" and designated not only the royal residence but also the official government buildings in the palace complexes. Such centers were called the "Double House" or the "House of Gold and House of Silver," an allusion to Upper and Lower Egypt. The administration of the two sections of Egypt were conducted in their respective buildings. These royal residences of the kings were normally made of bricks, and thus perished over the centuries, but the ruins of some palaces, found at 'AMARNA, DEIR EL-BALLAS, PER-RAMESSES, etc., indicate the scope of the structure and the elaborate details given to the architectural and artistic adornment. In the reign of TUTHMOSIS III of the 18th Dynasty, the term *pero* began to designate the king himself, and later kings employed the word in *cartouches*.

Per-Ramesses (or Pa-Ramesses)   the royal complex of the kings of the 19th and 20th Dynasties, founded by RAMESSES II (c. 1290–1224 B.C.). Located in the northeastern Delta, Per-Ramesses was called the House of Ramesses, Beloved of Amon, Great of Victories. It was sometimes abbreviated Great of Victories. It comprised a vast palace, private dwellings, temples, a military base, administrative buildings, harbors, gardens, vineyards and orchards. The site

of Per-Ramesses is near Qantir on the banks of the Pelusiac branch of the Nile, a suburban district of the ancient AVARIS, the HYKSOS capital of the Second Intermediate Period.

The Ramessids were from that part of the Delta and returned there to establish their capital. The area was used for royal ceremonies and pageants. Temples and stages for various festivals of the king's cult were discovered there. The original royal residence erected by Ramesses is believed to have covered an area of 4 square miles.

Persea tree   a sacred tree celebrated in ancient Egyptian mythology. The Persea was associated with the cat, originally in HELIOPOLIS, where it resided and slew APOPHIS, the legendary serpent.

Peru-Nefer   the principal naval base of ancient Egypt's New Kingdom. The base was located near MEMPHIS and was a ship dock and repair complex for the fleets of Nile and Mediterranean-going vessels employed in the trade and military campaigns of the period. AMENHOTEP II (1427–1401 B.C.) was in command of the naval station prior to his accession to the throne. (See MILITARY.)

pet   the ancient Egyptian name for the sky, also called *hreyet*. The *pet* was supported by four pillars, depicted as mountains or as women with their arms outstretched. Many texts allude to the pillars, associated with the solar bark of the god RE' in which he sailed across the sky. The goddess NUT personified the sky as well.

pharaoh   the Greek form of *pero* or *per-a'a*, originally the Egyptian word for royal residence. The term became associated with the king and eventually designated both the residence and the ruler. It is of Hebraic origin.

With the provisional unification of Upper and Lower Egypt in 3000 B.C., the first dynasties appeared. Dynastic rulers were placed within the context of a state royal cult that equated them with the gods and with specific tasks to be conducted on behalf of the people. The royal cult dates to the earliest dynastic period in Egypt, and from the start it supported the concept of the king as the "good god," the incarnation of HORUS, the son of RE', and the intermediary between the people and all divine beings. When the king died, he was thought to become OSIRIS in Tuat or the Underworld.

The kings of Egypt were normally the sons and heirs of their immediate predecessors, either by the Great Wife, the chief consort, or by a lesser-ranked

A pharaoh in a festival robe, from a New Kingdom Period relief.

New Kingdom the kings did not hesitate to name commoners as their Chief Wife, and several married foreign princesses.

The kings of the Early Dynastic Period (2920–2575 B.C.) were monarchs who were intent upon ruling a united land, although the actual process of unification was not completed until 2649 B.C. There is evidence that these early kings were motivated by certain ideals concerning their responsibilities to the people, ideals which were institutionalized in later eras. Like the gods, who created the universe out of chaos, the pharaoh was responsible for the orderly conduct of human affairs. Upon ascending the throne, later kings of Egypt claimed that they were restoring the spirit of MA'AT in the land, cosmic order and harmony, the divine will.

Warfare was an essential aspect of the king's role from the beginning. The rulers of the predynastic eras, later deified as the SOULS OF PE and NEKHEN, had fought to establish unity, and the first dynastic rulers had to defend borders, put down rebellions, and organize the exploitation of natural resources.

Government was in place by the dynastic period, the nation being divided into provincial territories called NOMES. Royal authority was imposed by an army of officials, who were responsible for the affairs of both Upper and Lower Egypt. The law was the expression of the king's will, and all matters, both religious and secular, were dependent upon his assent. The entire administration of Egypt, in fact, was but an extension of the king's power.

By the 3rd Dynasty DJOSER (2630–2611 B.C.) could command sufficient resources to construct his vast mortuary complex, a monumental symbol of the land's prosperity and centralization. The STEP PYRAMID, erected for him by IMHOTEP, announced the powers of Djoser and reinforced the divine status of the kings. Other Old Kingdom (2575–2134 B.C.) pharaohs continued to manifest their power with similar structures, culminating in the great PYRAMIDS at GIZA.

In the First Intermediate Period (2134–2040 B.C.) the role of the pharaoh was eclipsed by the dissolution of central authority. Toward the end of the Old Kingdom certain powers were delegated to the nome aristocracy, and the custom of appointing only royal family members to high office was abandoned. The 7th and 8th Dynasties attempted to reinstate the royal cult, but these did not stave off the collapse of those royal lines. In the 9th and 10th Dynasties, the KHETYS of Herakleopolis assumed the role of pharaoh and began to work toward the reunification of Egypt, using the various nome armies as allies. The rise of the INYOTEFS of Thebes, however, the 11th Dynasty,

wife. Some, including Tuthmosis III (1479–1425 B.C.) of the 18th Dynasty, were the offspring of the pharaoh and HAREM women. In the early dynasties the kings married female aristocrats to establish connections to the local nobility of Memphis, the capital. In subsequent periods many married their sisters or half-sisters, if available, and some, including AKHENATEN, took their own daughters as consorts. In the brought an end to the Khetys' designs. MENTUHOTPE II (2061–2010 B.C.) captured Herakleopolis and reunited Upper and Lower Egypt.

The Middle Kingdom emerged from Mentuhotpe's victory and Egypt was again united under a central authority.

When the Middle Kingdom collapsed in 1640 B.C., Egypt faced another period of turmoil and division. The 13th through 16th Dynasties vied for land and power, and the HYKSOS dominated the eastern Delta and then much of Lower Egypt. It is interesting that these Asiatic kings, especially those among them called the "Great Hyksos," aped the royal traditions of Egypt and embraced all of the titles and customs of their predecessors. In Thebes, however, another royal line, the 17th Dynasty, slowly amassed resources and forces and began the campaigns to expell the Hyksos. KAMOSE, the last king of this line, died in battle, and the assault on AVARIS, the Hyksos capital, was completed by 'AHMOSE I, who founded the New Kingdom (1550–1070 B.C.). This was the age of the Tuthmossids, followed by the Ramessids, Egypt's imperial era. Military activities characterized the period, and many of the kings were noted warriors. The prestige of the king was greatly enhanced; Amenhotep III and Ramesses II had themselves deified.

The New Kingdom, as other dynastic eras in Egypt, drew to a close when the kings were no longer able to assert their authority, and thereby galvanize the nation. The New Kingdom collapsed in 1070 B.C.

phoenix a sacred symbol in ancient Egypt. The sun god RE' manifested himself as the phoenix, which was associated with resurrection and rebirth, like the BENNU.

Pillar of His Mother priestly caste of the HORUS cult of ancient Egypt, supposedly open only to royal princes. TUTHMOSIS III (1479–1425 B.C.) of the 18th Dynasty was recorded as being a member of this priesthood when he was chosen as the heir to the throne.

pillow amulet a carving of the ancient Egyptian HEADREST used as an AMULET. This magical talisman was believed to assure the deceased that his or her head would be resurrected in the afterlife.

Piramesse See PER-RAMESSES.

pirates See SEA PEOPLES.

Plain of Salt a region near the WADI NATRON in the western Delta, used as a natural resource in all eras of Egyptian history.

Poem of Pentaur See PENTAUR, POEM OF.

police the units serving the kings of Egypt that kept the peace in a specified region. One of the oldest police groups was a border unit stationed in various forts of garrisons on the western, eastern and southern frontiers of Egypt during every era. Members of the Bedouin tribes of the SINAI were part of this border patrol in some eras. The WALL OF THE PRINCE, instituted by AMENEMHET I (1991–1962 B.C.) in the 12th Dynasty, aided the border units by providing them with garrisons on the eastern and western borders. The string of fortresses below the First Cataract also served to house these units.

A state police was developed after the Second Intermediate Period, composed of the famed MEDJAY warriors. There had been other state units in the past, but this new police team maintained the capital and served the king personally. The backbone of the state police, the Medjay were Nubian warriors who served with Kamose (1550 B.C.) and 'Ahmose I (1550–1525 B.C.) when they campaigned against the HYKSOS invaders and drove them out of Egypt.

The temple police units were normally composed of priests who were charged with maintaining the sanctity of the temple complexes. The regulations concerning sex, behavior and attitude during and before all ritual ceremonies demanded a certain vigilance, and the temples kept their own people available to insure order and a harmonious spirit.

Police units were stationed at the borders to watch over caravans and trading expeditions and to maintain order among the foreigners who came with their own goods to conduct business within Egyptian territory. Police also guarded over the various cemeteries of Egypt, particularly having royal tombs. Mortuary complexes had to be watched by priests and police, and the vast tombs of the Theban western shore had to be patroled on a daily basis. Other units functioned under the direction of the NOME chiefs in the various regions of Egypt. Still other units, mostly military, functioned in the quarry and mining sites in the deserts.

posesh-khef a mortuary instrument of ancient Egypt, fashioned as a slightly forked tool. Made of horn or granite, the instrument was discovered in the tomb of MENTUHOTPE II of the 11th Dynasty at Deir el-Bahri (2061–2010 B.C.).

Prehirwonnef a prince of the 19th Dynasty, the son of RAMESSES II (1290–1224 B.C.) and Queen NEFERTARI. Prince Prehirwonnef was active in the military campaigns of his father. He died before he could inherit the throne.

priests over the centuries, the main function of priests appears to have remained constant; they kept the temple and sanctuary areas pure, conducted the cultic rituals and observances, and performed the great festival ceremonies for the public.

Soon after the unification of Upper and Lower Egypt in 3000 B.C., the priests were in service in major religious centers throughout the nation. Cultic rituals had been conducted in all regions before the unification, but the centralization of government allowed them to flourish and to influence the cultural development of the whole kingdom. The priesthood did not emerge as a class, however, until the New Kingdom.

HELIOPOLIS was an early center for the solar cult in honor of RE' and Atum. The high priest of Heliopolis was called the Great One of the Seers and held many responsible positions in Early Dynastic Period and Old Kingdom administrations. In some eras the head of the Heliopolitan cult was a member of the royal family, but most often the position was in the hands of a dedicated and talented commoner. The high priest of MEMPHIS, dedicated to the god PTAH, was sometimes called the Great One Who Rules The Artificers, and many gifted men served in this capacity, including IMHOTEP, the builder of the STEP PYRAMID for DJOSER.

In the New Kingdom, the high priest of AMON in Thebes held even greater powers. He was called the chief prophet of Amon-Re'. Other temples of Egypt came under his jurisdiction at this time. Eventually the priests of Amon would usurp the throne of Egypt and cause the downfall of the New Kingdom. Before that, however, the Amonite priests were normally men dedicated to the service of their god and nation in an administrative capacity. MENKHEPERRESENB, the high priest of Amon during the reign of TUTHMOSIS III (1479–1425 B.C.), for example, was an architect and the head of the palace and city of Thebes.

Priests officiating in smaller temples were called *web* or *wab*. The *web* priest also served as a purificator during rituals and cultic rites. The *sem* priests were mortuary ritualists. The *hem-ka* priests performed funerary rites and the *hem-neter* assisted in the temples. The *kheri-heb* priest was the lector, the master of mortuary rituals for the royal clans, and was attended by the *heri-shesheta*, the head of mysteries (called *kheri-shesheta* in some lists). Other high-ranking priests of lesser temples were called *uab-a'a amihru, ur hekau* or *neter atef*, depending upon their role and their cult. In the Old and Middle Kingdoms there were some

A priest in the service of the royal clan, from an Old Kingdom relief.

priestesses, associated with goddess cults, but during the New Kingdom their role was reduced to singing. There is no evidence of temple prostitution in ancient Egypt, despite its existence in other contemporaneous societies.

In most periods the priests of Egypt were members of a family long connected to a particular cult or temple. Priests recruited new members from among their own clans, generation after generation. This meant that they did not live apart from their own people, and thus maintained an awareness of the state of affairs in their communities.

Most priests in Egypt married and were succeeded by their children. Regulations concerning sex, however, were very stringent in every era, and priests were also obliged to fast before and after ceremonies and to maintain regularity in their own life-styles and in their dress. Priests wore white linen in the temple and sandals, common only to the nobility or temple servants in each historical period. Leopard skins, pendants and plaited hair pieces denoted their ranks and offices.

Temples were the center of each town or village, but they were not open to the public except on certain feast days. The priests alone entered the temples, and worked in a series of chambers of increasing seclusion. The rank of the priest determined his access to interior sanctuaries.

During training priests were taught quietude, modesty and self-sacrifice, and a spirit of dedication to the god and to the nation was cultivated. Each morning the priests dressed, incensed and anointed the statue of the god with oils. The interior shrine was then closed and sealed against intruders. At noon purifying water was added to the holy fonts, and the sanctuaries were swept and washed again. At night more offerings were made, but the sanctuary was not opened. On certain days, in some eras several times a month; the god was carried on arks or ships into the streets or set sail on the Nile. There the oracles took place and the priests answered petitions.

In time the priests would witness the downfall of their own shrines and temples, and others of their ranks would enter the political world with ambitions. Even the role of the priesthood would be bartered away or squandered for gain. From the earliest eras, the spiritual aspirations of the Egyptian people were given expression by the priests, who maintained their cults and generally performed their religious obligations with loyalty and scrupulous dedication.

Primeval Mound   the site of creation claimed by all temples and recorded especially in the temple of

EDFU in ancient Egypt, called in some eras the "High Dune." These islands rose out of the watery chaos, offering the gods the sacred DJEBA or perch, the seat of creation. The Primeval Mound at Edfu was guarded by two lords, called the Companions of the Most Divine Heart. (See COSMOGONY, PAY LANDS and TEMPLES.)

prince   See PHARAOHS.

princess   See QUEENS.

Prisse Papyrus   a document dating to the reign of Izezi (2388–2356 B.C.) of the 5th Dynasty. The papyrus is now in the Louvre, with another copy in the British Museum. The writings of the 5th Dynasty sage PTAH-HOTEP are contained in this document. (See LITERATURE.)

proyet (or *peret*)   the second SEASON of the year in ancient Egypt. This period, composed of four MONTHS, was dedicated to "growth," as its name implies. *Proyet* followed the season of *akhet,* the time of the inundation of the Nile. The season was followed, in turn, by *shomu,* the time of harvest.

Ptah   the god of ancient Egypt in MEMPHIS, called Ptah-Sokar in a double form and Ptah-Sokar-Ausar in the triune style. Ptah dates to the earliest dynastic eras of Egypt, and perhaps beyond. A sophisticated theology made Ptah somewhat obscure to the average Egyptian. The Memphite teachings concerning Ptah were discovered on a stela, which explained the cosmogony of the cult and the region. Accordingly, Ptah was the only true god, the creator, and all others, divine and human, emanated from his will. The cosmogonic groups of other cities were supposed to have been devised by Ptah. This deity was also the source of the ethical and moral orders in the world, and he was called the Lord of Truth in all historical periods. He was deemed capable of bringing forth life with words, as the tongue announced what the god's heart experienced. MEMPHIS, the cult center of Ptah was called Hiku-Ptah or Hat-Ka-Ptah, the mansion of the soul of Ptah. Statues and reliefs depicting the god showed him as a man with very light skin, mummy wrappings and an immense collar with the MENAT. Most such depictions of Ptah were designed as pillars, emblems of justice. Called the First of the Gods, Ptah was a patron of the great architectural monuments that began in the Old Kingdom. As Tatenen he was revered as the creative urge, both for the world and for the individual works of art. Despite his involved theology, Ptah remained

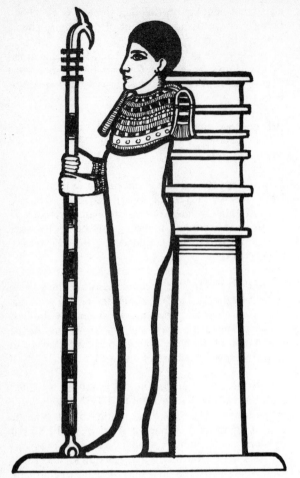

Ptah, the deity, in his mummy wrappings, beside the *djed* pillar.

popular in Egypt, and was honored especially in the great temple complexes of AMON.

Ptah-hotep a sage of ancient Egypt, serving Izezi in the 5th Dynasty (2388–2356 B.C.). The maxims of Ptah-hotep are contained in the PRISSE PAPYRUS in the Louvre and in another copy in the British Museum. Ptah-hotep exhorted his fellow Egyptians to conduct their affairs with quietude and righteousness. He urged them to be truthful and to treat their neighbors and fellow countrymen with kindness and tolerance. He was especially concerned with the weak and the oppressed. (See LITERATURE.)

Ptahshepses an official of the 4th Dynasty, serving in the reign of SHEPSESKHAF (2472–2467 B.C.) and marrying Princess Khama'at, a daughter of the king. Ptahshepses was raised in the palace of Menkaure' called Mycerinus, and remained in service through the 4th Dynasty and into the early years of the succeeding royal line. He was buried at Saqqara.

Ptah-Sokar-Osiris Figures mortuary statues designed like SHABTIS and highly prized in ancient Egypt for their magical powers. Fashioned out of wood, painted and gilded, the figures were placed in tombs. Ptah was the guardian of all creation, and Osiris and Sokar were related to the mortuary cults of the nation.

Punt a semimythical land, Punt is believed to have been located in Eastern Sudan or Ethiopia, reached by the Egyptians through the WADI TUMILAT and the Bitter Lakes in the eastern Delta on their way to the Red Sea. Other expeditions to the Red Sea went through the Wadi Hammamat, on the Coptos Road. The city of Kuser on the coast offered shipbuilding facilities, and expeditionary fleets were outfitted on the Red Sea each year. Punt was visited by the Egyptians from the early eras. A 4th Dynasty relief (2575–2465 B.C.) depicts a Puntite in the company of the one of KHUFU's royal sons. A 5th Dynasty document attests to the fact that kings of every period sent ships to Punt for myrrh and other exotic commodities.

Reliefs in the temple of HATSHEPSUT (1473–1458 B.C.) of the 18th Dynasty depict a family that was brought back from Punt by one of the expeditions of the time. A chief is shown with his wife, two sons and a daughter. These same reliefs portray Egyptian fleets sailing to and from the fabled land, a convention that continued in the Ramessid era.

Punt held a fascination for the Egyptians, who valued the land's products, especially myrrh trees, which were planted in the temple compounds and produced a high-grade incense used in religious festivals and rites. Other products brought back by the expeditions included ebony, ivory, wild animals, skins, spices, gold, resins, gums, woods and cosmetics.

Puyemre' an official of the 18th Dynasty, serving HATSHEPSUT (1473–1458 B.C.), as a high-ranking priest of the temple of AMON. It is, however, as an architect that he is principally remembered. He created the beautiful shrine of MUT that Hatshepsut had erected, and he was consulted on other royal building projects. Puyemre' survived Hatshepsut and was accepted by her successor, TUTHMOSIS III. The king's KARNAK schemes were influenced by his designs. Puyemre' was buried with honors at Thebes.

pylon the majestic gateway leading to Egyptian temples, dating to the 18th Dynasty (1550–1307 B.C.).

Pylons are large, slightly battered (inclined) structures with overhanging cornices, cut with reliefs and containing grooves for flagstaffs, which were placed in front of every religious building in ancient Egypt. (See ARCHITECTURE, KARNAK.)

pyramids   called *mr* by the Egyptians, a monument erected as a tomb and stage for mortuary rituals. The pyramid was considered the place of ascent, the point of departure for the royal deceased on his journey to eternity, and were normally given special names to signify their special status as tombs of the kings. Architecturally, the pyramid represented the culmination of the mortuary structures elaborated from the Early Dynastic Period (2920–2575 B.C.).

The MASTABAS, the brick tombs of the early historical era, were provided with burial and offertory chambers, and represent the original mortuary buildings of Egypt. Some, such as those erected for the kings and queens at SAQQARA and ABYDOS, were designed with facades having recessed and projecting walls, after the palaces of the era, and became known as "mansions for eternity." One such mastaba, that of an official in the reign of DEN in the 1st Dynasty named NEBTKU, started out to resemble a pyramid but was then altered to its traditional form.

In the reign of DJOSER (2630–2611 B.C.), in the 3rd Dynasty, IMHOTEP placed a series of stone mastabas atop one another in a graduated design, forming the STEP PYRAMID at Saqqara. The Step Pyramid was originally 204 feet high, composed of six separate layers or "steps", each one successively smaller in size. The base measured 358 feet by 411 feet. The layers of the pyramid were faced with limestone and were surrounded by a vast complex of buildings, replicas of those erected to celebrate *sed* festivals, and a wall, which was carved in relief to resemble a palace facade. The entire enclosure measured 1,800 by 900 feet and was paved with limestone. The walls contained 211 bastions and 14 gateways.

The Step Pyramid contained a 90-foot shaft that led to underground chambers and passageways. The burial vault was 13 feet high, encased entirely in granite, with a plug to seal the entrance made of the same material. The eastern section of the pyramid contained tombs of Djoser's wives and sons. Eleven shafts have been discovered, sunken to almost 100 feet. The enclosure around the pyramid contained shrines, altar chambers, courts, a *heb-sed* hall, storerooms and the tombs of Djoser's courtiers. The site was actually a miniature city, with its own priests and liturgical schedules. Other step pyramids were started soon after Djoser's reign. Some have been discovered at Seila, Zawiyet el-Mayitin, el-Kula, Edfu

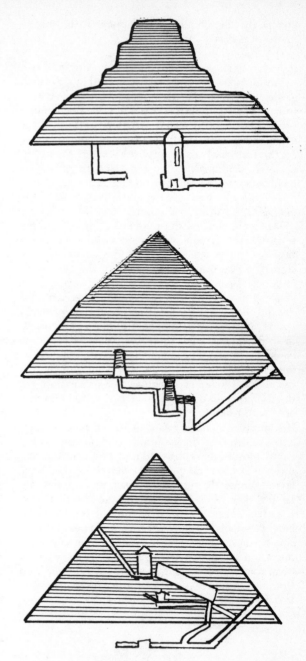

PYRAMIDS the top figure represents the shape of the step pyramids of the Old Kingdom's Third Dynasty that were the forerunners of the true pyramid. Burial chambers were incorporated into the design in subterranean levels.
The middle figure is of the Bent Pyramid of the Fourth Dynasty, erected at an angle when the architects could not manage the height and steep angle of a true pyramid. The burial chambers in this pyramid are more elaborate and protected by corridors, traps and plugs.
Finally, the true pyramid, from the Fifth Dynasty, shown with its grand gallery, double burial chambers and false corridors.

and at the Elephantine; they appear to be mostly tombs of nobles.

The true pyramid appeared in the 4th Dynasty, in the reign of SNOFRU (2575–2551 B.C.), who built two pyramids at Dashur and finished his father's pyramid at Meidum. The traditional pyramidal complex evolved from that tomb, which contains the various components that were considered necessary to the purpose of the monument. The first attempted pyramids rose on the fringes of the desert area west of Memphis, between Meidum and Abu Rowash. The great pyramids at GIZA are best known today, but there are 70 other such monuments stretching the length of the Nile as far south as the Sudan.

The centerpiece of the pyramid complex was the pyramid. The pyramid was a solar symbol, stemming from the cult at HELIOPOLIS. Its four sides were designed to face the cardinal points of the earth. The entrance was normally on the north side, sometimes above ground level and sometimes level with the ground. Beside the pyramid was placed an offertory shrine, a chapel for holding mortuary rites and rituals in commemoration of the royal cult. This building contained ceremonial chambers and the mandatory false door for the use of the KA ("soul") of the deceased king. Religious insignias and statues adorned the chambers, and the walls were inscribed and covered with reliefs.

A mortuary temple was constructed near the pyramid, with an elaborate entrance corridor and central court. Most of these have disappeared over the centuries, but when the pyramids were built they were lavish shrines, with offertory chambers, rooms containing altars, storage rooms and the traditional SERDAB. The serdab contained statues of the deceased king, positioned so that their eyes could peer through slits in the wall to view the daily ceremonies conducted in the deceased's name and memory. Nonroyal tombs also contained serdabs. A causeway led from this temple to a VALLEY TEMPLE on the banks of

the Nile or at a distance in the desert. The walls of the causeway were elaborately decorated, and originally they had stone roofs. Valley temples were the sites of initial funerary observances. They comprised various chambers designed to accommodate the priests involved in the obsequies.

Less elaborate pyramids and tombs were also built for queens and for favored nobles and certain members of the royal family. These were constructed near the main pyramid. Solar barks or mortuary boats were also brought to the complex. Some, fashioned out of wood and gold, were buried in deep pits in 4th Dynasty Pyramids. The pyramid of KHUFU at Giza was provided with two boat pits. The entire pyramid complex was surrounded by walls, a tradition dating to the great limestone enclosure that surrounded the Step Pyramid at Saqqara. Private tombs and the burial places of lesser members of the royal clan or of the court were placed just inside these walls.

The construction of the pyramid was an involved and lengthy process. For example, some estimate that the Great Pyramid of Khufu required the full-time labor of thousands of workers over a 20-year period. A site was chosen for a monument by architects and artists based on the type of ground available. The desert fringes, with rocky cores and outcroppings, normally offered the firmest base for the weight of the construction. An appropriate site would be levelled by workmen, and then the foundation dug out of the ground according to the design and architectural plan. The foundation was extremely important, and most pyramids contain foundation stelae and other commemorative inscriptions, much like the cornerstones of modern buildings. When the dedication rituals were completed, workmen began to dig out the various chambers, corridors and passageways for the subterranean level of the monument.

Some unfinished pyramids, such as the pyramids at Abu Rowash and Zawiyet el-Aryan, have magnificent underground chambers and hallways. Stairways, passages, ramps, portcullis (stone slabs lowered into place to block halls at critical junctures, especially in the 4th Dynasty pyramids), traps and stone plugs were installed beside the burial rooms and storage areas. Large ramps for lowering the granite or alabaster sarcophagi were also erected, sometimes with staircases on either side.

Construction on the pyramid would then start. Some had solid stone cores, much like the mastaba levels of Imhotep's Step Pyramid, but others had initial walls, filled with rubble, mud and sand. Layers of masonry supported the walls, and these were encased in fine stone and then capped by the pyr-

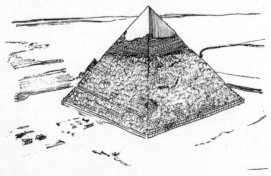

KHEPHREN'S PYRAMID   the great tomb at Giza.

amidion. It is thought that ramps were built to each level as the construction continued; so that the stones could be moved into place. As the pyramid grew in height, the appropriate ramps would be heightened. There is some debate about whether ramps were used. It is possible that mounds were built and attached to the sides or fashioned on the ascending levels. Such conveniences were removed when the casings were being applied.

When the structure was completed, with the chambers painted and inscribed and the casing put into place so that the stone shimmered and glistened in the sunlight, the funeral of the deceased commenced at the site. The SARCOPHAGUS was lowered into the burial chamber, where rituals were also conducted. Some chambers were carved out of a single piece of stone. Once firmly in place, the burial chamber was sealed and plugged, and the corridors leading away from it were also blocked by various means. When the funeral cortege was outside, the doorway of the pyramid was sealed by moving stones into place to complete the wall. The entrance was thus concealed and the tomb secured.

The Great Pyramid at Giza, erected by Khufu, (2551–2528 B.C.) is the most outstanding example of the genre, the only surviving wonder of the ancient world. The base of the pyramid covers 13 acres, and a total of 2,300,000 yellow limestone stones are believed to have been used in its construction. The pyramid was called the Horizon of Khufu and was positioned in keeping with the astronomical and religious traditions of the era. Originally part of a vast complex, the pyramid now stands amid only two other great pyramids and various smaller tombs of queens and other royal member of the royal family.

pyramidion   See BENBEN.

Pyramid Texts   the oldest religious literature in ancient Egypt, taking the form of inscriptions on the walls of the pyramids of the 5th and 6th Dynasties (2465–2150 B.C.). Magical spells, incantations, religious beliefs and myths were incorporated into the Pyramid Texts. The priests of HELIOPOLIS are credited with their origin, prompted by a desire to provide the royal deceased with the knowledge of Taut or the Underworld. The texts include prayers and admonitions concerning the afterlife. The Pyramid Texts gave way to the COFFIN TEXTS in the First Intermediate Period (2134–2040 B.C.).

Q

Qa'a the seventh king of the 1st Dynasty (c. 2065 B.C.). Little is known of his reign, but he is mentioned in the Abydos, Saqqara and Turin KING LISTS. Stone vessels bearing his insignia were discovered under the pyramid of DJOSER.

Qantir once part of RAMESSES II's (1290–1224 B.C.) capital PER-RAMESSES, in the eastern Delta at AVARIS, the HYKSOS capital of the Second Intermediate Period (1640–1532 B.C.). This site was once heavily populated and the setting for magnificent buildings and monuments.

Qarta an official of the 6th Dynasty, serving PEPI I (2289–2255 B.C.) as chancellor of the court. Qarta was also a priest and a noted librarian or archivist. He was honored by the king while he lived and was given a tomb in the area set aside for nobles in SAQQARA.

Qarun See FAIYUM.

Qau the name given to the ancient Egyptian road that led to the quarries in the northern Sinai.

Qebehsenuf one of the divine sons of the god Horus, associated with mortuary rituals. Qebehsenuf was the guardian of the intestines of embalmed Egyptians. He was depicted with a hawk's head on the CANOPIC JARS used to store such preserved organs in the tombs.

Qebhet a goddess of ancient Egypt, considered the daughter of the god ANUBIS and the personification of "cool water," one of the vital elements required in the mythological eternal paradises. She was originally a serpent goddess, whose cult was restricted to a few NOMES. In some eras Qebhet was associated with various solar and Nile cults.

Quban a fortress opposite el-Dakka, occupying a strategic position just south of the First Cataract in NUBIA. Quban was protected by three circular walls with rounded bastions. The fortress dates to the 12th Dynasty (1991–1783 B.C.), probably erected by Senwosret I. It was refurbished by the Ramessid pharaohs when they garrisoned northern Nubia. (See FORTRESSES.)

quarries the geological conformation of ancient Egypt, especially its southern regions, was characterized by sandstone cliffs. Limestone, favored by the Egyptians for the casings of pyramids, was abundant at various sites throughout the Nile Valley. Granite was found at Aswan in two varieties: the red, called *syenite* by the Greeks (after Syene, Greek for Aswan), and the black. Basalt, calcite, diorite, obsidian, porphyry, quartzite and serpentine were among the minerals quarried. A variety of semiprecious stones was also mined.

Quarries of the Nile Valley included Tura, a site opposite GIZA, where fine limestone was extracted; Gebel el-Ahmar, northeast of modern Cairo, which yielded quartzite; Bersha, near Tura and known for limestone; and Gebel el-Silsila, north of Aswan, which was a source of sandstone. Hatnub, near 'Amarna, was quarried for alabaster, and Ibhet, south of Aswan, contained black granite, with red granite available from other quarries in the region.

NUBIA was an important source of hard stone and minerals, and quarries were established there in periods of dynastic strength. Mines in the western desert provided diorite gneiss and possibly carnelian, and the Wadi el-Hudi yielded amethysts.

queens with few exceptions, the consorts of the kings of ancient Egypt derived their rank and powers from their husbands. These women were themselves often the daughters of kings, but they could be aristocrats or even commoners. In some instances women of the harem, or lesser wives, attained the rank of queen by giving birth to an heir.

In the cartouches of royal Egyptian women, the designations "King's Daughter," "King's Wife," or "King's Mother" were carefully applied. Though many princesses of the royal line did not marry their brothers or half-brothers, the firstborn royal daughter often did. As queens, royal wives administered the palace and the harems and had some say in the affairs of the nation or the capital. Queen mothers (whether royal or commoner), those who had given birth to an heir, were elevated in the reigns of their sons and given additional honors.

In some periods the kings married their daughters also. AKHENATEN, for example, married several of his daughters, and RAMESSES II made his daughters con-

A queen of Egypt, bearing lotus blossoms.

sorts after their mothers died or retired. AMENHOTEP III was encouraged by his queen, TIY, to marry their daughter, Princess SITAMUN, probably in the hopes of increasing the number of heirs to the throne.

Some queens were from foreign lands. KIYA, the wife of AKHENATEN, was believed to be a Mitanni princess, and MA'AT-HORNEFRURE, wife of RAMESSES II, was probably the princess mentioned in the BEN-TRESH STELA. TUTHMOSIS III had three Syrian wives, daughters of chieftains, who were buried in separate tombs and provided with duplicate funerary regalia. Amenhotep III married a princess from Babylon.

Egyptian princesses were not given in marriage to cement foreign alliances, no matter how persistent the requests. To enhance his prestige, one Asiatic ruler wrote that he would accept any Egyptian woman of high birth as his bride, knowing that he could pass her off as a princess to his own people. Those princesses who did not marry heirs to the throne wed officials or remained at court unmarried. Princess SIT-HATHOR-YUNET, whose dazzling mortuary regalia is indicative of the esteem in which she was held by three generations of kings, did not marry.

There were queens who usurped the throne or held political power temporarily as regents for their minor sons. Regents include MERENEITH of the 1st Dynasty, believed to have been the wife of WADJ and the mother of DEN, and ANKHNESMERY-RE' II of the 6th Dynasty, who served as coregent, with her brother, the vizier DJAU, for PEPI II. In the New Kingdom two female regents assumed the throne themselves: HAT-SHEPSUT of the 18th Dynasty and TWOSRET of the 19th Dynasty. A woman ruler ended the 6th Dynasty, according to some lists, and another, NEFRUSOBEK, closed the 12th Dynasty.

The queens, whether in command of Egypt or serving as a consort to the kings, remain fascinating facets of Egyptian history for the modern world. Some of them left an imprint on their own times, and others stand as exotic examples of feminine charms on the Nile. Some of the most notable through the ages were:

Early Dynastic Period—Mereneith, probably only a regent, had two mortuary complexes built at ABY-DOS and SAQQARA, using the royal insignias. Neith-otpe, the possible mother of 'AHA, the first king of Egypt, was honored with similar mortuary monuments, one containing the seals of the fabled NA'RMER.

Old Kingdom—The two queens named HETE-PHERES left relics of their existence; one in tomb furnishings that had to be moved because of grave robberies, the second as a witness to royal dynastic feuds. The KHAMERERNEBTY queens have left their own mark. The second one, the wife of KHEPHREN,

Queen Teo, the mother of Tuthmosis IV, from a Theban statue.

Neferhent, a Middle Kingdom queen.

is remembered by a beautiful statue that shows her beside the king in a remarkable display of equality and familiarity. KHENTKAWES, the wife of SHEPSES-KHAF, is called the Mother of the 5th Dynasty. The two Ankhnes-Mery-Re's, both given to PEPI I in marriage, bore him heirs and one served as regent for her son, Pepi II.

The Middle Kingdom—A bevy of women accompanied MENTUHOTPE II in his tomb at DEIR EL-BAHRI, and on the SARCOPHAGI of many of them the world is told that the inhabitant was the "Sole Favorite of the King." The mother of AMENEMHET I, a usurper, was honored by her son when he had cemented his claims to the throne. Nefrusobek, the last ruler of the 12th Dynasty, was a woman who maintained her reign for only four years.

The New Kingdom—Because it is better documented, this period of Egyptian history provides a roster of vivacious women. TETISHERI, the commoner wife of TA'O I of the 17th Dynasty, was the grandmother of 'AHMOSE, the founder of the New Kingdom, and she lived to an old age with him in the

palace with Queen AHHOTEP. 'Ahmose was married to 'AHMOSE-NEFRETIRI, who gained prominence by appearing with the king at public functions and by having her name mentioned in public records.

Hatshepsut, the daughter of TUTHMOSIS I, claimed the throne after serving as the regent for Tuthmosis III and ruled Egypt, building a temple at Deir el-Bahri and sending expeditions to PUNT and other sites in continued trade. TIY, the commoner wife of Amenhotep III appeared in public records and in foreign correspondence. NEFERTITI, the commoner wife of Akhenaten, stands unrivaled as an example of grace and loveliness from that age. Kiya, the foreign born second wife of Akhenaten, is depicted with her own exotic charms.

In the Ramessid era women such as NEFERTARI, whose loveliness graces shrines on the Nile, including the temple built in her honor at ABU SIMBEL, speak of a cultured era. Twosre, who served as a regent for a time, took the throne with her foreign vizier, BAY, at her side.

The following queens are discussed in this book:

QUEENS OF EGYPT

DYNASTY	NAME	ROLE	DESCENDANTS
1st	Neithotpe	Mother of 'Aha, husband unknown but possibly Na'rmer	
	Berenib	Wife of 'Aha	
	Hent	Lesser wife of 'Aha	Mother of Djer
	Herneith	Wife of Djer	
	Merneith	Probably wife of Wadj	Regent (and possible mother of Den)
	Betresh (or Tarset)	Wife of Adjib	Mother of Semerkhet
2nd	Hapnyma'at	Wife of Kha'sekhemwy	Mother of Djoser
3rd	Heterphenebty	Wife of Djoser	
	Meresankh I	Wife of Huni	Mother of Snofru
4th	Hetepheres I	Wife of Snofru	Mother of Khufu
	Nefertkaw	Daughter and wife of Snofru	Mother of Prince Neferma'at
	Meritites	Wife of Khufu	Mother of Prince Kewab and Princess Hetepheres II & Princess Hardedef and Baufre'.
	Henutsen	Wife of Khufu	Mother of Prince Khufukhaf and possibly Khephren
	Kentetenka	Wife of Ra'djedef	
	Hetepheres II	Wife of Kewab and Ra'djedef	Mother of Meresankh III
	Per(senti?)	Wife of Khephren	Mother of Menkaure' and Prince Nekaure'
	Hedjhekenu	Wife of Khephren	Mother of Prince Sekhemkare'
	Meresankh III	Wife of Khephren	Mother of Prince Nebemakhet
	Khamerernebty I	Wife of Khephren	Mother of Khamerernebty II
	Khamerernebty II	Wife of Menkaure'	Mother of Prince Khunere'
	Khentkawes	Wife of Shepseskhaf Possible wife of Userkhaf	Mother of Kakai? Possibly mother of Sahure'
	Bunefer	Wife of Shepseskhaf	
5th	Neferhetepes	Mother of Userkhaf (unknown husband)	
	Reputneb	Wife of Izi (Niuserre')	
	Khentikus	Wife of Izi (Niuserre')	
	Nebet	Wife of Wenis	Mother of Prince Wenisankh
	Khemut	Wife of Wenis	
6th	Ipwet	Wife of Teti	Mother of Pepi I
	Khuit	Wife of Teti	
	Amtes	Wife of Pepi I	(In harem scandal)
	Ankhnesmery-Re' I	Wife of Pepi	Mother of Nemtyemzaf
	Ankhnesmery-Re' II	Wife of Pepi	Mother of Pepi II
	Nit	Wife of Nemtysemzaf and wife of Pepi II	
	Ankhnes-Pepi	Wife of Pepi II	
	Iput	Wife of Pepi II	
11th	Neferukhayet	Wife of Inyotef II	
	Aoh	Wife of Inyotef III	Mother of Mentuhotpe II
	Henite	Wife of Inyotef III	
	Henhenit	Wife of Mentuhotpe II	
	Neferu	Chief wife of Mentuhotpe II	
	Kawit	Wife of Mentuhotpe II	
	Tem	Wife of Mentuhotpe II	Mother of Mentuhotpe III
	Sadek	Lesser wife of Mentuhotpe II	
	Ashait	Wife of Mentuhotpe II	
	Nubkhas	Wife of Mentuhotpe II	
	Kemsit	Wife of Mentuhotpe II	
	Neferukayt	Wife of Mentuhotpe II	
	Imi	Wife of Mentuhotpe III	Mother of Mentuhotpe IV
	Amunet	Wife of Mentuhotpe III	
12th	Nefret	Mother of Amenemhet I	
	Nefrutoten	Wife of Amenemhet I	Mother of Senwosret I
	Dedyet	Wife of Amenemhet I	
	Nefrusobek	Wife of Amenemhet I	
	Neferu	Wife of Amenemhet I	
	Nefrusheri	Wife of Senwosret I	Mother of Amenemhet II
	Mereryet I	Wife of Amenemhet II	
	Kemanub	Wife of Amenemhet II	
	Hent	Wife of Senwosret II	
	Sebekshedty-Neferu	Wife of Senwosret III	Mother of Amenemhet III
	Mereryet II	Wife of Senwosret III	
	Merseger	Wife of Senwosret III	
	Neferkent	Wife of Senwosret III	

DYNASTY	NAME	ROLE	DESCENDANTS
12th **(cont.)**	Merysankh	Wife of Senwosret III	
	Neferu	Wife of Senwosret III	
	A'at	Wife of Amenemhet III	
	Nefruptah	Wife of Amenemhet III	
	Kemanut	Wife of Amenemhet III	
	Nefrusobek	Queen-Pharaoh	
13th	Ana	Wife of Sobekhotep I	
	Senebsen	Wife of Neferhotep I	
17th	Sobekemsaf	Wife of Inyotef V	
	Tetisheri	Wife of Ta'o I	Ta'o II and Princess Ahhotep I
	Ahhotep I	Wife of Ta'o II	A'hmose, Kamose and 'Ahmose-Nefretiry
18th	'Ahmose Nefretiry	Wife of 'Ahmose	Amenhotep I, Prince 'Ahmose Sipar, Ahhotep II and several daughters
	Inhapi (perhaps Thent Hep)	Wife of 'Ahmose I	Princess Hent-Tenemu
	Kasmut	Wife of 'Ahmose I	
	Ahhotep II	Wife of Amenhotep I	Prince Amunemhet and Princess A'hmose Tumerisy
	'Ahmose Merytamon	Wife of Amenhotep I	
	Senisonbe	Mother of Tuthmosis I (Husband unknown)	
	'Ahmose	Wife of Tuthmosis I	Hatshepsut and Princess Amonmose and Wadjmose and Princess Neferukheb
	Mutnofret	Wife of Tuthmosis I	Tuthmosis II
	Hatshepsut	Queen-Pharaoh and wife of Tuthmosis II, a temporary regent for Tuthmosis III	Princess Neferu-Re'
	Isis	Lesser wife of Tuthmosis II	Mother of Tuthmosis III
	Meryt-re-Hatshepsut	Wife of Tuthmosis III	Mother of Amenhotep II
	Ahset	Wife of Tuthmosis III	
	Teo	Wife of Amenhotep II	Mother of Tuthmosis IV
	Mutemwiya	Wife of Tuthmosis IV	Mother of Amenhotep III
	Tiy	Wife of Amenhotep III	Mother of Akhenaten, and Princesses Sitamun, Baketamon, Ast, Hentmereb and Hentaneb
	Sitamun	Daughter/wife of Amenhotep III	
	Nefertiti	Wife of Akhenaten	Mother of Meketaten, Meryaten, Ankhesenamon and other daughters
	Kiya	Wife of Akhenaten	Sons and daughters unknown
	Meryt-Amon	Consort of Akhenaten	
	Ankhesenamon	Wife of Tut'ankhamun	
		Wife of Aya	
	Tey	Wife of Aya	
	Mutnodjmet	Wife of Horemhab	
19th	Sitre	Wife of Ramesses I	Mother of Seti I
	Tuya	Wife of Seti I	Mother of Ramesses II and Princesses Tia and Hentmire
	Nefertari	Wife of Ramesses II	Princes Amonhirwonmef and Prehirwonmef and Princesses Merytamon and Mertatum
	Isnofret	Wife of Ramesses II	Merneptah and Prince Khaemweset, and Princess Bint-Anath
	Ma'at Hornefrure'	Wife of Ramesses II	
	Bint-Anath	Daughter/wife of Ramesses II	
	Merytamon	Daughter/wife of Ramesses II	
	Nebt-tawy	Wife of Ramesses II	
	Isetnofret	Wife of Merneptah	Mother of Seti II
	Takhaet	Wife of Amunmesse	
	Baktwerel	Wife of Amunmesse	
	Tia	Wife of Amunmesse	Possible mother of Siptah
	Twosre	Queen-Pharaoh and wife of Seti II	Regent for Siptah
20th	Tiye	Wife of Ramesses III	
	Ta-Opet	Wife of Ramesses IV	Mother of Ramesses V
	Nubkhesed	Wife of Ramesses V	

Qurna site, on the western shore of Thebes, of a temple of SETI I (c. 1306–1290 B.C.) of the 19th Dynasty. RAMESSES II, Seti's heir, completed the structure, adding a colonnaded court, a hypostyle hall and rows of pillars. The shrine contained a precinct for the sacred bark of AMON. Another colonnade was dedicated to the sun cult, and a chapel area was erected in memory of the founder of the dynasty, RAMESSES I. (1307–1306 B.C.). Tombs from the 18th and 19th Dynasties were also discovered at Qurna, alongside Middle Kingdom necropolis areas.

Qurnet Murai a necropolis site on the eastern hill of Deir el-Medineh, on the western shore of the Nile opposite Thebes. Tombs from the 18th Dynasty and the Ramessid era were discovered there. (See DEIR EL-MEDINEH.)

R

Ra'djedef   third king (2528–2520 B.C.) of the 4th Dynasty of ancient Egypt, the son of KHUFU and one of his lesser wives. It is believed that Ra'djedef murdered his brother, Prince KEWAB, who was the rightful heir to the throne. He did bury Khufu, however, and presided over his mortuary rites. He married Queen HETEPHERES II, the widow of Kewab, and his chief wife was Kentetenka. Ra'djedef's reign ended abruptly. His pyramid was discovered at ABU ROWASH.

Ramesses I (Menpehtire')   the first king of the 19th Dynasty (1307–1306 B.C.). The son of a military veteran commander named Seti, Ramesses was born in the city of AVARIS, where the Hyksos and their Asiatic allies had founded their capital during the Second Intermediate Period. He entered military service and worked his way up through the ranks. During his military career, Ramesses fought at the side of the future king HOREMHAB in the closing decades of the 18th Dynasty.

He was a commander of troops, the superintendent of the Egyptian cavalry, a royal envoy and the superintendent of the "Mouths of the Nile" (the Delta branches of that river), with the rank of general. In time he became Horemhab's vizier, and then the Primate of Egypt, the high priest of AMON in charge of all other temples in the nation. When Horemhab died childless, Ramesses was named Deputy of the Throne, the hereditary prince and heir. His wife was Queen Sitre, mother of SETI I. He was an elderly man at the time, his son, Seti I, was already a military commander and an advocate of the return to empire.

Ramesses means "Re' fashioned him," and his throne name, Menpehtire, was translated as "Enduring is the might of Re'." This title was taken by Ramesses as a tribute to 'AHMOSE I, the founder of the New Kingdom (1550 B.C.). Ramesses honored 'Ahmose and considered him the ideal pharaoh.

One of his first acts as king was to restore and

Ra'djedef of the 4th Dynasty, from an Old Kingdom statue.

refurbish the great temple of Amon at KARNAK. He then named SETI as his co-regent and died only 16 months after his coronation.

Buried in the Valley of the Kings on the western shore of Thebes, near the tomb of Horemhab, Ramesses' body was vandalized and later placed in Deir el-Bahri by the priests who feared for the corpse's safety.

Ramesses II (Userma'atre'setepenre')   the third king (1290–1224 B.C.) of the 19th Dynasty, one of the longest lived pharaohs of Egypt. The son of SETI I and Queen TUYA, Ramesses was introduced early to military campaigns. He accompanied his father in Libya at the age of 14 or 15. Ramesses II also went on campaigns in the Mediterranean and Palestinian regions. He was named co-ruler of Egypt in Seti's seventh year, taking the name Userma'atre', which translates as "Strong in right is Re'." At the age of 22 he undertook a campaign in Nubia, accompanied by two of his own sons. All three participated in a ferocious chariot charge at the enemy.

With his father, Ramesses II began vast restoration programs and building projects up and down the Nile. They built a palace at AVARIS, where RAMESSES I has started a new capital, and opened or refurbished wells, quarries and mines. Ramesses assumed the throne upon Seti's death in 1290 B.C. He was intent on restoring Egypt's empire and began a series of wars against the Syrians, fighting at the Battle of KADESH, which was immortalized by the POEM OF PENTAUR. This poem was inscribed on Ramesses' temple walls.

Ramesses built a vast tomb at Thebes, two temples at Abu Simbel, one to Ptah in Memphis, and restored other shrines and complexes throughout Egypt. The hypostyle hall at Karnak was completed in his reign. He also maintained the Osirian tradition by building a mortuary complex at Abydos, as well as his famed RAMESSEUM. He lived to the age of 96 and had 200 or more wives and concubines, siring 96 sons and 60 daughters. Ramesses outlived his sons, with the thirteenth surviving long enough to be his heir.

His chief queen and consort at the start of his reign was NEFERTARI, who bore him children. When she died or retired, Queen ISTNOFRET became his companion and consort. When she died or retired, the daughters of Ramesses BINTH-ANATH and MERYTAMON, took her place. With them, the Hittite princess, renamed MA'AT HORNEFRURE', shared the highest rank of royal wife.

The mummified remains of Ramesses II indicate that he stood 6 feet in height, had a jutting jaw, a long and thin nose, small, close-set eyes, thick lips and large ears. His muscles had atrophied before he died, and he did show other signs of advanced age. His genital organs were removed during the embalming process and placed in a special casket in the form of Osiris. He had suffered from smallpox, had poor teeth and degenerative forms of arthritis. There were also signs of arteriosclerosis in his legs. Ramesses II is called "The Great."

Ramesses II Cycle a text found on a stela in the temple of Khons at Thebes. The story of the Bekhten Princess was included in the document. (See BENTRESH STELA.)

Ramesses III (Userma'atre'meryamun) the second king (1194–1163 B.C.) of the 20th Dynasty. Ramesses III was the last great pharaoh of the New Kingdom. The son of SETHNAKHTE, the founder of the 20th Dynasty, Ramesses served as his co-ruler and later inherited the throne. (Sethnakhte reigned only three years.)

Ramesses fought the Libyans, led by the MESHWESH, in the fifth and eleventh years of his reign. In the eighth year he defended Egypt against an invasion of the SEA PEOPLES, using an army composed of trained mercenary units. When the Sea Peoples (the Sherden Pirates), a group of raiders who sailed up and down the Mediterranean coast assaulting city-states, entered the Delta, Ramesses set up a series of traps and ambushes in the Delta and caught the pirates during one of their attacks. He slew many of

Ramesses II, wearing the war crown of electrum, from a 19th Dynasty statue.

Ramesses III, shown with the goddess Isis in a mortuary temple from the 20th Dynasty.

the brigands and pressed the rest into military service. Successful in securing the borders of the nation, he turned his attention to rebellious Palestinian tribes. Again he was victorious.

Attacking Nubia to put down rebellions there, Ramesses continued the custom of receiving tribute from territories conquered by Egypt. Such offerings and gifts had flowed into Egypt during the Tuthmossid period. He campaigned again in Palestine when the tributes stopped.

Internally, however, Egypt was experiencing a steady decline. Workers in Thebes had to strike in order to get their normal pay, and unrest was evident among all social classes. A HAREM revolt took place, with a subsequent trial, which implicated many royal women and dignitaries and led to the death of the conspirators.

Monuments from Ramesses reign include the great mortuary complex at MEDINET HABU, on the western shore of Thebes, three shrines at KARNAK, dedicated to the gods Amon, Mut and Khons, and a beautiful palace at Leontopolis (Ausim), north of modern Cairo. Ramesses died at the age of 65 and was buried in the Valley of the Kings.

Ramesses IV (Hegama'atre'setepenamun)   the third king (1163–1156 B.C.) of the 20th Dynasty. He was in line for the throne of his father, RAMESSES III, and he survived the turmoil of the HAREM conspiracy, which was designed to foil his claims. Burying his father, Ramesses IV placed a document in his tomb, known today as the Papyrus Harris I. This text provides an elaborate commemorative of the reign of Ramesses III and is a fitting tribute.

Ramesses IV was in his forties when he came to the throne. His reign was brief but eventful. He sent an expedition to the quarries in the Wadi Hammamat and controlled Nubia with a firm grip. His Viceroy of Nubia was Penno, who raised up a statue in his honor. In return, Penno received two silver vases from the king. Ramesses also completed the shrine of KHONS in KARNAK and erected a temple at Asasif on the western bank of the Nile at Thebes. Ramesses' tomb was built in the Valley of the Kings on the western shore of Thebes. His mummified remains indicate he was a small man with a bald head, good teeth and a long nose.

Ramesses V (Userma'atre'sekheperenre')   fourth king (1156–1151 B.C.) of the 20th Dynasty. The son of Ramesses IV and Queen Ta-Opet, he died prematurely after a reign of only four years. It is believed that he died of smallpox at the age of 35. His tomb was completed by his successor and then usurped.

Ramesses IV, as depicted in a 20th Dynasty relief.

All that remains of his reign is a stela, discovered at Gebel Silsilh.

Ramesses VI (Nebma'atre'meryamun)   the fifth king (1151–1143 B.C.) of the 20th Dynasty. The uncle of RAMESSES V, and a son of RAMESSES III, he usurped the throne and the tomb of his predecessor. He did allow various mortuary observances to continue for Ramesses V, however. Ramesses VI usurped cartouches of previous kings for economy, and left his name on inscriptions in the Sinai. His statues were discovered in Bubastis, Coptos, and at Karnak, as well as in Nubia. His wife was Queen Nubkhesed, and his daughter was Isis or Idet. Ramesses' mummy was so badly damaged that after finding the tomb desecrated the priests had to pin the corpse to a board in order to provide the remains with a decent burial.

Ramesses VII (Userma'atre'setepenre'meryamun)   the sixth king (1143–1136 B.C.) of the 20th Dynasty, probably the son of RAMESSES VI. He built a tomb in the Valley of the Kings but left no other monuments. Some papyri mention him. He had a son who did not live to succeed him.

Ramesses VIII (Userma'atre'akhenamun) the seventh king of the 20th Dynasty (1136–1131 B.C.), probably a son of RAMESSES III. All that remains of his reign is an inscription at MEDINET HABU and some plaques, and a modest tomb. His mummy has vanished.

Ramesses IX (Neferkare'setenre') the eighth king (1131–1112 B.C.) of the 20th Dynasty. This is the king involved in the tomb robbery scandal in the Theban necropolis. His reign also witnessed the campaigns of the Libyan bandits. His son, Montuherkhopshef, did not live to succeed him. Ramesses IX was buried in the Valley of the Kings.

Ramesses X (Khenerma'atre'setepenre') the ninth king (1112–1100 B.C.) of the 20th Dynasty. Few of his monuments survive. During his reign there were strikes called by unpaid workers, who left a tomb in the Valley of the Kings.

Ramesses XI (Menma'atre'setepenptah) the tenth and last king (1100–1070 B.C.) of the New Kingdom and the 20th Dynasty. Not a vital or energetic ruler, Ramesses XI's reign was a period of turmoil. PANEHSI, viceroy of Nubia, went from the Elephantine to Thebes to put down unrest arising from contention over the Theban region between the high priest of Amon and others. A famine took place at the same time, giving rise to the designation "Year of the Hyena." HERIHOR, left in Thebes by Panehsi to keep control of affairs there, soon assumed the role of the high priest of Amon and eventually became vizier as well, after bringing about Panehsi's downfall. Panehsi, in turn, rebelled and brought an end to Egypt's domination in NUBIA. Herihor, joined by SMENDES in the north, soon administered the affairs of Egypt, as Ramesses XI remained in seclusion. When Ramesses died, Herihor and Smendes divided Egypt between them.

Ramesses a prince of the 19th Dynasty, the first-born son of RAMESSES II (1290–1224 B.C.) and Queen ISTNOFRET. While a child he rode in a chariot attack against rebellious Nubians on a campaign with the king. He became a general and was heir to the throne, but he died before his father.

Ramesses Nebweben a prince of the 19th Dynasty, the son of RAMESSES II (1290–1224 B.C.). This Ramesses was a hunchback and died at the age of 30. It is believed that he spent most of his life in retreat in the palace of the harem near the Faiyum.

Ramesseum the temple of RAMESSES II (1290–1224 B.C.) at Thebes. The Ramesseum was a mortuary temple, including a palace and an administration center. Some of the most important documents of the era were found within its confines. The site was called "The House of Ramesses in the House of Amon." A papyrus discovered there contained the Tale of the Eloquent Peasant. That document is now in a Berlin museum.

Pylons were erected as gateways in the Ramesseum to commemorate Ramesses' battle at KADESH. The complex also boasted courts, a hypostyle hall and a throne room. A colossal statue of the king, measuring over 55 feet high, was in the first court. One unique chamber of the Ramesseum was the Astronomical Room. Medical texts concerning the treatment of stiffened limbs were also discovered in the Ramesseum.

Ramose an official of the 18th Dynasty, he served AMENHOTEP III (1391–1353 B.C.) and AKHENATEN (1353–1335 B.C.). Ramose was vizier of Egypt during the transitional years before the 'AMARNA Period. He witnessed the growth of the new religion of Akhenaten but died before the new capital at 'Amarna was constructed. Ramose was buried in Thebes, on the western shore, but his tomb, famed for its reliefs, appears not to have been used by him. Some records indicate that Ramose was a relative of AMENHOTEP, SON OF HAPU.

Ramose an official of the 19th Dynasty, serving in the reign of RAMESSES II (c. 1290–1224 B.C.) as a chief administrator and as a scribe in the various temple bureaus. He was the son of a court official who began his career in the reign of TUTHMOSIS IV of the 18th Dynasty.

Ra'neferef the fifth king of the 5th Dynasty of ancient Egypt (2419–2416 B.C.). Virtually nothing is known of his reign.

Ranofer an official of the 5th Dynasty (2465–2323 B.C.), he was a priest of the temples of PTAH and SOKAR. Ranofer was made famous by statues of painted limestone which are now in the Egyptian Museum in Cairo. The statues, life-sized, were found in his tomb at Saqqara.

rastau the ancient name for the passages built into Egyptian tombs to lead the dead to the other world, TUAT. Originally this term was used to designate the necropolis area of Memphis, Saqqara, but came into signify other regions as well.

Rawer an official of the 5th Dynasty, serving in the reign of KAKAI (2446–2426 B.C.) as a ritual priest. A mortuary stela relates that Rawer was accidentally struck by the king during a religious ceremony but sustained no injury. He was favored after the accident.

Re′ the solar god of the ancient Egyptians, whose cult at HELIOPOLIS or HERMOPOLIS developed in the Early Dynastic Period. Re′ was the most popular solar deity of Egypt, and his cult incorporated many of the attributes and mythology of various other temples. Re′ appeared on the ancient pyramidal stone in the Phoenix Hall at Heliopolis, as a symbol of rebirth and regeneration. Re′ 's cult concerned itself with material benefits: health, children, virility, etc.

The sun was called Khepri at dawn, Re′ at noon, and Atum at night. As Atum the god was depicted as a human with a double crown upon his head. As Khepri he took the form of the sacred beetle. As Re′ the god was depicted as a man with the head of a falcon (or hawk), surmounted by the cobra and the uraeus. He was also identified with Horus, then called *Re′-Horakhty*, Re′-Horus. In this form he was the horizon dweller. At dawn Re′ came across the sky in his solar bark, called the "Boat of Millions of Years," accompanied by lesser divinities of his train.

Re′ appeared as Atum in the cosmogony of Heliopolis. PTAH is supposed to have shaped the egg out of which Re′ arose. In other cosmogonic tales Re′ rose as a LOTUS flower from the waters of the abyss. In turn he begat GEB, the earth, and NUT, the sky. Of these were born OSIRIS, SET, ISIS and NEPHTHYS. The waxing and waning of the moon was the monthly restoration of the Eye of Re′ by the god THOTH. This eye, alongside the Eye of Horus, became one of the holiest symbols of ancient Egypt.

Re′ was the Living King, as OSIRIS was the Dead

SOLAR CULT Re′ Horakhty watching the sun appear at the eastern gate of heaven, from an inscription.

King. During the Old Kingdom the concept of the kings assuming the powers of Re' took root. The kings became the physical sons of the deity, a concept which would remain constant throughout Egyptian history. Even Alexander the Great after he conquered Egypt with his Greek armies centuries after the fall of the New Kingdom, journeyed to the OASIS of Siwah in the Libyan or western desert to be adopted as a son of the god Re' and given the powers of the true kings of the Nile. During the New Kingdom the god AMON was united to Re' to become the most powerful deity in Egypt.

Records of Restoration   a document dating to the 20th Dynasty (c. 1065 B.C.), when HERIHOR, the usurper high priest of Amon, oversaw the reburial of SETI I and RAMESSES II. Their tombs were discovered to have been violated. The record gives an account of the royal corpses and their new graves. (See TOMB ROBBERY TRIAL.)

Redesiyeh   a temple site located 5 miles north of modern Edfu, dating to the reign of SETI I (1306–1290 B.C.) of the 19th Dynasty. Inscriptions on the walls of the temple concern the king's accomplishments.

Redji   a princess of the 3rd Dynasty, thought to be the daughter of DJOSER (2630–2611 B.C.). She was immortalized by a diorite statue discovered at Saqqara and now in Turin.

Re'emkuy   a prince of the 5th Dynasty, the son of IZEZI (2388–2356 B.C.). When he died at a young age he was placed in the MASTABA of a certain judge of the royal courts, Neferiryetnes. Re'emkuy had served as a priest in various capacities and as a counselor to the king. The reliefs and decorations of the mastaba were altered to salute the prince upon his burial.

Re'hotpe   a prince of the 4th Dynasty. The son of SNOFRU (2375–2551 B.C.), Re'hotpe served as high priest at HELIOPOLIS. He married Princess NOFRET, and their twin mastabas were built near the MEIDUM pyramid. In this tomb were found their famous limestone statues, which are now in the Egyptian Museum in Cairo. The figures, in a seated position, are lifelike and display the skill of the artisans of that era.

Rehu-erdjersenb   called Rehu'ardjersen in some records, an official of the 12th Dynasty, serving AMENEMHET I (1991–1962 B.C.) as chancellor of the court. His tomb at el-LISHT was built near the royal pyramid. The walls of the gravesite are famous for the elaborate

reliefs, which depict the chancellor hunting in the Nile marshes. A stela proclaiming his deeds and listing the members of his family was found in ABYDOS.

rekhet   a hieroglyph in the form of a lapwing used to represent certain tribes of ancient Egypt. This symbol appears on the mace-head of the SCORPION King in the predynastic period. The significance of the tribes is uncertain.

Rekhmire'   an official of the 18th Dynasty, serving as vizier to TUTHMOSIS III (1479–1425 B.C.). The son of a priest of AMON, Nefer-weben, and the nephew of the vizier Woser, Rekhmire' became the most powerful commoner in the land during Tuthmosis' reign. His Theban tomb contains autobiographical material and scenes showing him and his wife, Meryt, partaking in the joys of eternity. The tomb also holds the decrees given by the king concerning Rekhmire''s role as vizier, making it an invaluable reference concerning the political, legal and social aspects of the New Kingdom and the empire. (See GOVERNMENT.)

Rekh-nesu   the ancient Egyptian term for the companion of the king, the "One Whom the King Knows," a title originally given to the counselors who con-

REKHMIRE' the Theban vizier Rekhmire' and his wife, Meryt, from a tomb wall painting.

ducted the affairs of the palace and state. In time the title became honorary. (See GOVERNMENT.)

religion ancient Egyptians had no word or single hieroglyph to denote religion. Their spiritual ideals permeated every aspect of their lives. Predynastic cultural sequences give evidence of one of the earliest inclinations of Egyptian religion—the belief in an afterlife. Animals were carefully buried alongside humans in the prehistoric eras, and the color green, representing resurrection and regeneration, figured prominently in grave rites. Fertility goddesses from the NAQADA I and II cultural sequences attest to the rudiments of cultic practices. A young male fertility god was also evident, as were indications of the emerging rites of various deities—NEITH, MIN, HORUS, among others. AMULETS, slate palettes, block figures with religious associations, and the Horus and SETH symbols were also found.

With the unification of Egypt in the Early Dynastic Period, the various local deities assumed regional importance. Horus became the patron of the kings, alongside Seth, in the eastern Delta. PTAH became the principal deity of Memphis, the first capital, and the cult of RE' flourished at HELIOPOLIS. SOKAR was evident in royal ceremonies, according to the PALERMO STONE and other documents from that era. NEKHEBET and WADJET had already been designated as the patrons of Upper and Lower Egypt. WEPWAWAT, THOTH, ANUBIS and the APIS bull were accepted as part of the Egyptian pantheon.

The royal cult was a special aspect of religion from the early period, associated with Horus and OSIRIS. The concept of the King as intermediary between the divine and the human was firmly in place by the time of the Old Kingdom (2575–2134 B.C.). From the 5th Dynasty pharaohs were addressed "the son of Re'." Dead rulers were identified with Osiris.

Festivals and rituals played a significant part in the early cultic practices in Egypt. Every festival celebrated a sacred or mythical time of cosmogonic importance (honoring the SOULS OF PE and Nekhen for example), and upheld religious teachings and time-honored beliefs. Such festivals renewed the awareness of the divine and symbolized the powers of renewal and the sense of the "other" in human affairs.

From the Early Dynastic period a tendency to henotheism is evident in Egypt, especially in hymns and didactic literature. Creation was explained in complex cosmogonic texts, and the presence of several, conflicting explanations of how the world began did not present a problem for Egyptians.

Egyptians did not demand a system of logical de-

Djoser, shown celebrating royal anniversary rites, from Saqqara.

velopment of their religion. All that was necessary were the observances of the cultic rites and the festivals so that the people could mirror the divine order as interpreted by the PRIESTS. While the cults and celebrations represented regional or national preoccupation with particular deities, the individual Egyptians were quite free to worship a god according to their own inclinations. The people exercised free will in this regard, which led to an awareness of social and religious obligations, especially in the observance of the spirit of MA'AT.

Surrounded by a variety of gods, Egyptians still maintained belief in one supreme deity who was self-existent, immortal, invisible, omniscient, the maker of heaven and earth and the Underworld, Tuat. The various gods assumed the supreme rank as the sole deity when addressed by their particular worshipper.

Re' was credited with having announced that all men were the equal recipients of sunlight, air, water and harvests. Re' also instructed all men to live as brothers and to think on the West, AMENTI, the symbol of the grave and the afterlife. Amon was believed capable of nurturing and protecting each Egyptian as an individual, while he sustained the creatures of the field and the river and led the nation's military and cultural advances.

Religious beliefs were not codified in doctrines, tenets or theologies. Most Egyptians did not long to explore the mystical or esoteric aspects of theology. The celebrations were sufficient, because they provided a profound sense of the spiritual and aroused an emotional response on the part of adorers. Hymns to the gods, processions and cultic celebrations provided a continuing infusion of spiritual idealism into the daily life of the people.

In the First Intermediate Period (2134–2040 B.C.) following the fall of the Old Kingdom, the local or regional gods reassumed importance because of the lack of a centralized government. The god of the capital region usually assumed leadership over the other gods and assimilated their cults. Although Re', Horus, Osiris and Isis held universal sway, and Ptah remained popular, other deities began to assume rank. MONT of Hermonthis, AMON of Thebes, SOBEK in the Faiyum, and other local deities drew worshippers. The COFFIN TEXTS emerged at this time, making available to non-royal personages the mortuary rites once exclusive to the kings.

When MENTUHOTPE II put an end to the Herakleopolitan royal line in 2040 B.C., ushering in the Middle Kingdom, the religious life of Egypt was altered. Mentuhotpe and his successors strengthened the solar cult, which had implications for the royal cults as well, the king being the model of the creator god on earth. Also during the Middle Kingdom ABYDOS became the focal point of OSIRIS MYSTERIES, and pilgrims flocked to the city. Osiris was identified with the dead pharaoh, the ruler of the realm of the dead. Those judged as righteous by Osiris and his underworld companions were entitled to paradise.

The Second Intermediate Period (1640–1532 B.C.) did not have a tremendous impact on the religious life of the nation because the HYKSOS, who dominated the Delta regions, and the Thebans, who controlled Upper Egypt, stayed constant in their observances. To enhance their legitimacy the Hyksos and their Asiatic allies were quick to assume the cultic observances of the previous kings. When 'AHMOSE I ousted the Hyksos and ushering in the New Kingdom (1550–1070 B.C.), the royal cult again predominated, but alongside it Amon the god of Thebes assumed importance. The brief 'AMARNA period, in which AKHENATEN tried to erase the Amonite cult and replace it with that of the god ATEN, was too short-lived to have had lasting impact. Akhenaten, Aten and the temporary capital at el-'Amarna were obliterated by later kings. HOREMHAB (1319–1307 B.C.) went so far

as to date his reign, which followed the 'Amarna episode, from the close of AMENHOTEP III's reign, so as to eradicate all traces of Akhenaten and his three successors.

The Ramessid kings upheld the royal cult and the established pantheon. PER-RAMESSES, the new capital in the eastern Delta, was a great congolmeration of temples and stages for cultic festivals. Until the New Kingdom collapsed in 1070, the spiritual traditions were maintained, and later eras saw again the same religious patterns along the Nile.

One last aspect of Egyptian religion which needs to be understood is the use of animal figures or animal heads in the portrayals of the divine beings in Egypt. The various depictions of such creatures in the ruins of the temples and shrines have given rise to exotic interpretations and to esoteric explanations of those images. The current understanding of the use of such animals is that these creatures were viewed as THEOPHANIES, images that were devised to represent the gods in different manifestations or forms. The Egyptians lived close to nature, surrounded by animals, birds, insects, serpents and fish. Some of these were used as representations of the local NOME gods before the unification of Upper and Lower Egypt in 3000 B.C. Serving as the local fetish or totem, they disappeared or were absorbed into the cults of the various gods in time. The Egyptians did not worship animals or serpents but relied upon their familiar forms to demonstrate what they believed to be spiritual truths. (See GODS AND GODDESSES, MORTUARY RITUALS, RESURRECTION, SOLAR CULT, TEMPLES and PRIESTS.)

ren   the ancient Egyptian word for name. It was considered vital to an individual's identity on earth and in the afterlife. A nameless being could not enter into the realms of gods—in fact, could not exist at all. The duty of each family member, therefore, was to perpetuate the names of their ancestors in cultic ceremonies. The names of the deceased were recited aloud each day, long after they had been buried. Those who could afford to do so hired mortuary priests to recite the daily liturgies in honor of the dead, so as to assure their eternal bliss. The dead were also believed to benefit from the recitation of the royal or divine names, which made the kings and the gods happy to intercede on their behalf.

Re'neb   the second king (date unknown) of the 2nd Dynasty. He is believed by some scholars to have been a usurper. His royal seals were discovered at Saqqara and near Erment (Hermopolis).

Renenet (or Renenutet)   the goddess of good fortune in ancient Egypt, often associated with ISIS. Her temple was erected in the FAIYUM during the Middle Kingdom. She was associated with HATHOR and other goddesses and took on roles concerning harvests, fate, happiness and childbirth.

Renni   an official of the 19th Dynasty, serving AMENHOTEP I (1525–1504 B.C.). Renni was the mayor of EL-KAB and the overseer of the priests of various temples. His tomb at Thebes is famous for its reliefs, which contain scenes of agricultural life, banquets and funerary rites.

Renpet   a goddess of the ancient Egyptian year, and the Egyptian word for year. Renpet was very popular in the late periods of Egypt. She was depicted as a woman wearing various symbols of crops and harvests. In some eras she was associated with the solar cult of SOPDU, the star called Sirius, the Dogstar, by the Greeks, that signaled the coming inundation of the Nile.

Report of Wenamon   See WENAMON.

Reserve Heads   ancient Egyptian busts created as portraits of the deceased. The heads frequently had broken ears and marks of scoring. It is believed that this damage was caused by the artisans when they broke the molds made out of linen and thin plaster. The damage could have taken place at that instant. For some reason the heads were not repaired or restored. Reserve Heads were placed outside of the

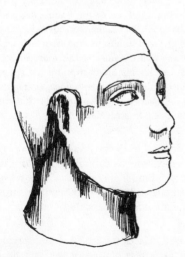

Reserve Head with damaged ears, from an Old Kingdom necropolis.

tombs in the necropolis sites of the nation so the *ba* would recognize the site as its own, and to serve as an extra head in case the human one was lost. Many such heads were discovered in the Egyptian cemeteries of the Old Kingdom.

Restoration Stela   See TUT'ANKHAMUN.

Resurrection   the Egyptians believed firmly that souls never died but achieved renewed existence in eternity when mortal remains were prepared and placed in appropriate tomb sites. Every religious ceremony conducted in connection with the funerary and mortuary rites was designed to foster that belief. In the cult of OSIRIS an important aspect was the god's resurrection and ascension into heaven, with the promise that all mortals could share in his eternal bliss after being judged by him beyond the grave. (See BENBEN, BENNU, BOOK OF THE DEAD, JUDGMENT HALLS OF OSIRIS, MORTUARY RITUALS and RELIGION.)

Ret   an ancient Egyptian goddess, considered the consort of RE' and the mother of all the gods of the nation. Called Re-et in some lists, she was considered the female sun. She was worshipped at HELIOPOLIS and was depicted normally as a woman wearing horns and the solar disk.

Rhind Papyrus   a document dating to the 17th Dynasty of the Second Intermediate Period (1640–1550 B.C.). The papyrus was copied by a Theban scribe of later eras and deals with the mathematical knowledge of the era. Fractions, calculus and other aspects of mathematics were discussed in the text.

rishi pattern   the name given to the feathery design found on the ancient Egyptian sarcophagi of the 17th and early 18th dynasties. The pattern imitated the Horus wings. The body of the deceased within the sarcophagus was enfolded within the protective wings of the god. The pattern was common in Theban tombs.

Rite of the House of Morning   a solemn ceremony conducted each day in ancient Egyptian palaces. The king's levee was a great event. Priests and courtiers attended him, ready to assist in bathing and dressing. He washed in water from the local temple lake to symbolize his primordial rebirth. The water represented the watery abyss of the god NUN. The king was then anointed, robed, invested with the royal insignias and praised by priests wearing masks depicting the gods Horus and Thoth. If the king was not in residence at the time, a substitute official or a member of the royal family was given similar honors in his stead. In some eras the kings also chewed bits of NATRON, another symbol of rebirth and resurrection.

River of Heaven   called the Celestial Stream or the Celestial River in some records, that part of the Nile that Egyptians believed entered the earth at the ELE-PHANTINE, after flowing down from the sky.

Ro-an   called Roen and Ra-an in some records, an official of the 18th Dynasty who served TUTHMOSIS III (1479–1425 B.C.) as a mortuary priest, supervising the rituals at the tomb of Queen Ahhotep. Ahhotep was the mother of 'AHMOSE, the founder of the dynasty. Tuthmosis III erected a temple in honor of Queen Ahhotep.

Roset   a site in the cliffs near ABYDOS, once considered entrance to Tuat or the underworld during some eras of ancient Egypt.

Rosetta   See NILE.

Rosetta Stone   a portion of a large black basalt stela, which was discovered in August 1799 near the Rosetta branch of the Nile by a Frenchman, an engineer attached to Napoleon's army during the Egyptian campaign, named Bouchard or Boussard. When the French surrendered Egypt in 1801, the stone passed into the hands of the British, who placed it in the British Museum in London. The Rosetta Stone measures 3 feet 9 inches by 2 feet 4¼ inches and is inscribed with 14 lines of hieroglyphs, 32 lines of demotic symbols and 54 lines of Greek. These inscriptions, apparently written by the priests of Memphis in the reign of Ptolemy V Epiphanes (205–180 B.C.), commemorate his accession and his patronage. The importance of the stone was immediately recognized because the Greek inscriptions provided a key to the translation of the Egyptian hieroglyphs.

The decipherment of the hieroglyphs was accomplished by an Englishman, Thomas Young, and by Jean-François Champollion of France. Young, recognizing the cartouche form, decided that the names of Ptolemy and Cleopatra would be written in symbols with phonetic values that would correspond to those names in Greek. He managed to assign accurately the correct values to six signs and partially correct values to three more. Young also recognized the direction in which the texts should be read by

ascertaining the way birds in the inscriptions were facing.

In 1821, Champollion took up the task and published memoirs on the decipherment of both the hieroglyphic and the hieratic form of the Egyptian language. He recognized that some signs were alphabetic, some syllabic and some determinative. He also established the fact that the Egyptian inscriptions were a translation from the Greek. His work inspired many Egyptologists.

royal cults   the veneration of Egyptian kings as the intermediaries of the gods. The focus of early Egyptians on the divine nature of the kings is exemplified by the ROYAL NAMES, monuments, CROWNS and elaborate tombs. The cult was furthered as well by the MORTUARY RITUALS observed at the tomb sites of the kings and queens, some maintained over centuries. (See DAILY ROYAL RITES, PHARAOH and RELIGION.)

royal names   the titles comprising five elements used by the kings of Egypt, denoting their connection to the gods, their divine purpose and function. The royal names included the following:

Horus name   the first of the royal names, usually written in a SEREKH alluding to the king as the true representative of the god HORUS on earth.

NEBTI *name*   signifying the king's rule over Upper and Lower Egypt.

Golden Horus name   depicting the royal person as the "gold of the gods," the earthly manifestation of the divine ones and their beloved representative.

NISUT-BIT *name*   the title prefaced by two words meaning king: the Lord of the South, *Bit*, and Lord of the North *Nisut*. This name, considered a king's *prenomen*, was given to him at his coronation. The *prenomen*, or first CARTOUCHE name, is the most important and frequently used name. In inscriptions the appearance of the PRENOMEN alone indicates which king is meant.

Son of Re' name   the king's actual birth name, denoting his inclusion in a royal line.

Royal Wadi   the desert road leading from el-'AMARNA, AKHENATEN's capital, to the tombs of officials and royal family members. These royal tombs were ransacked, and neither Akhenaten's nor NEFER-TITI's mummies has been located.

Rudjek   an official of the 5th Dynasty, serving KHUFU (2551–2528 B.C.) as a counselor and as the head of the priests who took care of the royal mortuary complex at GIZA, the site of the Great Pyramid of KHUFU and those of his successors. (See MORTUARY RITUALS, PRIESTS and REN.)

Ruia   the father of Queen TUYA, the wife of SETI I (1306–1290 B.C.). Tuya was a commoner, married to Seti before HOREMHAB designated RAMESSES I (Seti's father) heir to the throne. Ruia, commander of chariots in the Egyptian army, a force reinstated and strengthened by Horemhab after the 'AMARNA Period, was a veteran campaigner. He and his wife, Raia, were buried at Thebes.

S

sa   the Egyptian word for protection, used as an amulet in its hieroglyphic form.

Sa-Ankh   See DAILY ROYAL RITES.

Sabaf   an official of the 1st Dynasty, serving in the reign of QA'A, (c. 2760 B.C.). Sabaf was a counselor of the court, given special recognition as the king's companion. His mortuary stela, discovered at ABYDOS, lists his ranks and honors. (See FRIENDS OF THE KING.)

Sabni   an official of the 6th Dynasty, serving PEPI II (2246–2152 B.C.) as a crown governor for the territory of ASWAN. He directed quarrying operations for the formation of two OBELISKS for the cult center at HELIOPOLIS. A descendant of a military commander, Sabni was buried at Aswan.

Sabu   officials of the 5th and 6th Dynasty, serving WENIS (2356–2323 B.C.) and TETI (2323–2291 B.C.). Ibebi Sabu began his career in the service of Wenis and then became the high priest of PTAH at Memphis when Teti founded the new royal line. His mastaba at Saqqara contains details of the king's coronation rituals. Thety Sabu, the son of Ibebi, inherited his father's role as the high priest of Ptah and conducted affairs so well that it was decided that he did not need a co-priest to manage the god's estates and ceremonies. Prior to Thety's term of office, the role of high priest had been shared by two men. Thety Sabu had the story of his life and honors placed on the false door of his tomb at Saqqara. The door is now in the Egyptian Museum in Cairo.

Sacred Book of the Temple   See SATRAPE STELA.

sacred lakes   a feature of some TEMPLES in ancient Egypt, symbolizing the primordial waters before the moment of creation. Whenever the king was in residence the water from the temple's sacred lake was used to wash him each morning in a spiritual baptism.

Sadeh   a princess of the 11th Dynasty, either the daughter or concubine of MENTUHOTPE II (c. 2061–2010 B.C.). She was listed as a "Sole Favorite of the King," a term used to denote a lesser-ranked wife in that era. There are some indications that she was a daughter of Queen ASHAIT, another lesser-ranked royal woman of Mentuhotpe's reign.

saff tombs   from an Arabic term meaning row, a particular type of ancient Egyptian tomb. Such tombs were cut into the cliffs at Beni Hasan and Thebes from the 11th Dynasty onward.

Sages of Meheweret   ancient Egyptian mythological beings depicted at the temple of Edfu. The Sages were believed to have dictated all wisdom to the god THOTH. They came from the moment of creation, and their adages and admonitions supposedly provided the early Egyptians with the basis for a steadily evolving moral code.

sah   the ancient Egyptian name for the spiritual body that was expected to emerge after death. When embalming was performed, the mortal remains were changed into the *sah*. This spiritual being was empowered to exist throughout eternity. (See MORTUARY RITUALS, RESURRECTION.)

Sahure'   the second king (2458–2446 B.C.) of the 5th Dynasty, possibly the son of Queen KHENTKAWES. Sahure' is credited with having established the Egyptian navy, which he engaged in a punitive expedition along the Mediterranean coast. Sahure' sent a fleet to PUNT and traded with Palestine. He also had diorite quarried in the desert west of ABU SIMBEL. As a military commander, he took an active role in fighting the Libyans in the western desert.

Sahure' began the royal cemetery at ABUSIR, south of SAQQARA, with his pyramid complex there. It was designed with colonnaded courts and reliefs depicting his military campaigns. It is considered a model of 5th Dynasty funerary architecture, using not only basic building materials from the local region but fine limestone from the Tura quarry as well. Sahure''s desert hunting expeditions and his naval fleet are depicted on the walls of the pyramid. The scenes are in low relief and were once painted. His mortuary temple had rain spouts shaped as lion heads, forerunners of Gothic gargoyles. Copper-lined basins and lead plugs were also discovered in the complex.

Sai Island site, near the Third Cataract of the Nile, of New Kingdom inscriptions. (See NUBIA.)

Sais modern Sael-Hagar in the western Delta, the chief city of the fifth NOME of ancient Egypt. Sais was a cult center for the goddess NEITH. In the 26th Dynasty the capital of Egypt was located in that city.

Salitis the first king (c. 1640 B.C.) of the 15th Dynasty, of the HYKSOS, Asiatics who entered the Delta during the end of the Middle Kingdom who eventually set up their own dynasty. He is called "sultan" in some lists, and his Asiatic name was probably Sharek or Sharlek. Salitis and his successors are referred to as the "Great Hyksos." He took the capital of MEMPHIS during his reign, placing the kings of the contemporaneous 13th Dynasty under his control as vassals.

Saqqara a plateau overlooking the ancient capital of MEMPHIS, which served as a necropolis site for the early dynasties of Egypt. The plateau is divided into two main areas. The northernmost region is dominated by the STEP PYRAMID, built by IMHOTEP for DJOSER (2630–2611 B.C.) of the 3rd Dynasty. Beyond that is the pyramid of WENIS (2356–2323 B.C.) of the 5th Dynasty, which was the first to contain the PYRAMID TEXTS incised on its walls and painted reliefs designed to represent wall hangings. This pyramid originally had a vast causeway leading to the Nile. Around these royal tombs were many belonging to nobles and private persons of various eras. Beyond them are the Step Pyramid of Hetepsekhemwy (c. 2770 B.C.) of the 2nd Dynasty, and the pyramids of USERKHAF (2465–2458 B.C.) of the 5th Dynasty and TETI (2323–2291 B.C.) of the 6th Dynasty. These were also surrounded by the tombs of nobles and court officials.

STEP PYRAMID Imhotep's magnificent structure, with adjoining buildings.

Also discovered in the area were the cenotaphs of 1st and 2nd Dynasty rulers, including 'AHA, DJER, DEN and QA'A, and the vast complex of Queen MERENEITH. The SERAPEUM, the burial place of the sacred bulls of APIS and other animal cemeteries complete the findings available in the north.

The southern region of Saqqara contains the pyramid of PEPI II, called *Men-nefer-Mare'*, which eventually lent its name to the entire region, including the capital, titled Memphis, the Greek form of the Egyptian Men-nefer or Menfi. Beyond that are the pyramids of Izezi (2388–2356 B.C.) and Nemtyemzaf (2255–2246 B.C.). The southernmost part of Saqqara contains the pyramids of PEPI II (2246–2152 B.C.) and Shepseskhaf (2472–2467 B.C.). This last pyramid is known as the Mastabat el-Faraun. Other notable discoveries of the area include the statue of the Old Kingdom official known as Sheik-el-Beled (called the Ka'aper Statue) and the tomb of HOREMHAB, the last king of the 18th Dynasty (1319–1307 B.C.). (See KA'APER STATUE.)

Saqqara List See KING LISTS.

Salamuni the necropolis area for the ancient Egyptian city of AKHMIN, including an 18th Dynasty temple. The necropolis was dedicated to the god MIN, as the entire region was the deity's cult center.

Sallier Papyri a collection of documents dating to the New Kingdom. The papyri contained accounts of the campaigns of RAMESSES II (c. 1290–1224 B.C.) of the 19th Dynasty and the tale of the confrontation between Sekenenre'-TA'O II of the 17th Dynasty (c. 1560 B.C.) and his HYKSOS contemporary, APOPHIS of the city of AVARIS in the northeastern Delta. That confrontation led to the Theban campaigns against the Hyksos and their eventual expulsion. Also included in the collection is a copy of the POEM OF PENTAUR, an account of the battle of KADESH. The SATIRE ON TRADES is part of this collection as well.

sarcophagus from the Greek term meaning "eater of flesh," the stone receptacles for the mummified remains of ancient Egyptians. The Greek term supposedly referred to a type of limestone that was believed to dissolve human remains. Stone sarcophagi used in the 5th Dynasty (2465–2323 B.C.) had intricate patterns resembling the facades of palaces, and these patterns sometimes included painted replicas of the colored materials used on palace facades. These sarcophagi were so heavy and large that they had to be placed inside the burial chambers before funerals because of the labor and time involved in setting them in place. It is believed that the sarcophagus of KHUFU (2551–2528 B.C.) was actually incorporated into the pyramid in the process of constructing that monument.

Stone sarcophagi became rare by the Middle Kingdom (2040–1640 B.C.), used exclusively for royal or noble burials. Their decoration was austere, but some, like the ones discovered at DEIR EL-BAHRI, in the mortuary complex of MENTUHOTPE II (2061–2010 B.C.), were covered with painted reliefs. The New Kingdom form of sarcophagus was either rectangular or anthropoid. The sarcophagi used for non-royal persons as early as the 18th Dynasty and in the Ramessid era sometimes represented the deceased in daily attire. The royal sarcophagi were rectangular, carved with the figures of deities and embellished with bands of religious texts. Sometimes the sarcophagi had rounded heads, which gave them the appearance of royal CARTOUCHES. At the start of the 19th Dynasty the custom developed of carving the form of the king in high relief on the outer lid. The inner and outer surfaces were painted with mortuary texts. Sometimes a picture of the goddess NUT, the sky deity, lined the interior. With the close of the New Kingdom, the sarcophagi lost popularity until after 650 B.C., when the royal families again adopted their use.

Sarenpet an official serving SENWOSRET I (1971–1926 B.C.) of the 12th Dynasty as mayor of Khnum. He also oversaw the priests of the local temples. Sarenpet's tomb in ASWAN is noted for its lovely scenes of bullfights and fishing and a portrait of Sarenpet and his dog.

saru See GOVERNMENT and LEGAL SYSTEM.

Satis Satet in some records, a goddess of ancient Egypt, associated with the god KHNUM at Aswan. She was normally depicted as a woman wearing the horns of a cow and a conical crown and carrying bows and arrows, and was associated with the falling waters of the Nile and the hunt. Upper Egypt was called Ta-Satet, the "Land of Satet."

Satire on Trades called the Instructions of Dua-Khety in some lists, a text known from the Sallier Papyrus II, the Papyrus Ananastsi VII and various OSTRAKA. The text stresses the disadvantages of most professions or labors when compared to that of the scribe. The satire takes the form of a scribe addressing his son, who is neglecting his studies. The life of a scribe is called "the path of the god." The text is also called the Hymn in Praise of Learning in some records, and probably dates originally to the Middle Kingdom. It appears to refer to an earlier work.

Satirical Papyrus a document dating to the 20th Dynasty (1196–1070 B.C.), the papyrus is a unique collection of artistic works satirizing the state of the nation during the reigns of the last Ramessid kings. Charming animal figures demonstrate the peculiar reversal of roles taking place in that historical era. A mouse is being shown pampered and served by cats. A baby mouse is even shown in the arms of a loving cat nurse. As the social order of the nation eroded, the satirical drawings served as a warning and as an incisive commentary on the breakdown of the society. The Satirical Papyrus is now in the Egyptian Museum in Cairo.

Satrape Stela a document which listed the mythical shrines and cult centers of ancient Egypt. In some records it was called the Sacred Book of the Temples and was used as a reference work by priests and archivists.

scarabs ancient Egyptian amulets in the form of the *Scarabeus sacer* beetle. Probably dating to the Old Kingdom, these amulets were very popular throughout Egypt's history. They were also called *khepror* and were carved from stone, gold, semi-precious stones, gems and faience. The scarab beetle was associated with the life-giving and ever-present sun because of its activities. The insect pushes a ball of dung into a hole and lays its eggs in the warm substance, thus providing its offspring with security and food. The Egyptians related the activities of the beetle to the solar cult stories about the rebirth of the sun. The scarab was believed to roll the sun across the sky each day.

Scarabs bore the CARTOUCHES of the various Egyptian kings. After his reign, the cartouche of TUTHMOSIS III (1479–1425 B.C.) was used in scarabs. Heart scarabs were placed on mummies for protection and

SCARAB   the sacred insignia of ancient Egypt.

to guarantee favorable judgments in Osiris' Halls. AMENHOTEP III (1391–1353 B.C.) also used large scarabs as commemoratives of his marriage to TIY.

scepter   the ancient Egyptian royal symbol, called the *hekat* when it was in the shape of a shepherd's crook and *waset* when it represented the head of the god SETH.

scorpion   a symbol associated with the goddesses SELKET and ISIS. Seven scorpions accompanied Isis as her protectors when she searched for the body of her husband, the god OSIRIS. The Egyptians believed that scorpions would not sting women because of Isis' goodness.

Scorpion King   the legendary predynastic warrior who began the assault on the northern lands in order to unite Upper and Lower Egypt. He is called Zekhen in some lists. Scorpion is identified by a ceremonial mace-head discovered at HIERAKONPOLIS (modern Kom el-Ahmar). The mace head depicts a temple-founding ceremony with Scorpion (the sign for the insect is next to the king's face) digging the first trench. The mace-head is now in the Ashmolean Museum, Oxford.

scribes   the literate elite of ancient Egypt which assumed a variety of functions in the various historical periods in governmental and religious institutions. Some scribes attained high rank and honors, and the profession was always esteemed. In one ancient document the life of the scribe is called the "path of the god." Literacy was the prerequisite for any higher secular or religious office.

Scribes were exclusively males, and were recruited from all classes of society, as literacy and loyalty were the two basic qualifications. They were educated by priests and encouraged to develop their skills in specialized recordkeeping or in temple and governmental affairs. Scribes were assigned to government or estate offices or to the various bureaus of temples after receiving training in reading, writing and in the basic tenets of law, temple lore and administrative procedures. They had to have command of the nearly 800 hieroglyphs of Middle Egyptian, and of additional signs when they were added to the language in the Ramessid era. Scribes were normally attached to the various temples they served, but in the New Kingdom, when the religious complexes grew larger and more sophisticated, lay scribes were hired. Scribes were also required to have knowledge of the classical texts and mathematics. Initially they performed routine tasks, normally record keeping.

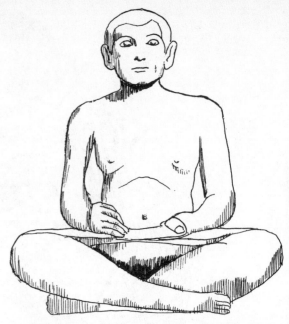

A scribe in a typical working pose, from a 5th Dynasty statue.

The best-known symbol of the scribe was the kit or palette, which contained slates, inks, smoothing stones for papyri and reed brushes, which were kept firm by chewing the end of the fibers. The kits, rectangular cases with indentations on one side for small cakes of ink, were attached to a cord. The ink was of lamp-black or any carbonized material mixed with gum and water by the scribe. Brushes were held in the center cavity of the box, which had small pieces of wood glued across the opening or a sliding cover to keep them in place. Brushes could be fine or heavy, depending upon their use and age.

In the larger temples scribes worked as archivists or as librarians. They kept the census, recorded tax assessments, measured the rise of the Nile and generally maintained the vast religious and governmental correspondence. Some accompanied military expeditions or local government officials to the mines and quarries to record the annual findings there. Many important inscriptions and documents of the military exploits of the New Kingdom, especially the campaigns of TUTHMOSIS III and RAMESSES II, were the work of scribes.

Sea Peoples   a term denoting a confederation of roving brigands, listed as Sherden, Sheklesh, Lukka, Tursha and Akawasha, who attacked settlements on the Mediterranean coast during the 20th Dynasty. The Hittite and other states of the region were under constant assault by these bands which specialized in swift raids along the shoreline. When the Sea Peoples, who are believed to have come from Asia Minor or the Aegan, began to raid Egypt's Delta, RAMESSES III (1194–1163 B.C.) set traps and ambushes in its intertwining waterways. He caught vast numbers of the brigands and slew more. Those taken prisoner were pressed into the Egyptian army and navy.

The term Sea Peoples is also used to denote the brigands who struck at Egypt's northwestern territories in the reign of MERNEPTAH (1224–1214 B.C.) of the 19th Dynasty. These were allies of the Libyans, who combined their forces to invade the Delta, bringing loads of household goods with them in the hope of settling in the region on a permanent basis. Merneptah is recorded as having sought advice from the oracles of the gods before gathering an army to deny the Sea Peoples access to Egypt. He brought units of archers and cavalry to the region, meeting the enemy at a site called Pi-yer. The Egyptians defeated the invaders, slaying more than 6,000 and taking Libyan royal family members captive.

seasons appearing in their written form in the Early Dynastic Period (2920–2575 B.C.), there were three seasons of four months each, with 30 days in each month. The symbol for the entire year was a sprouting bud, and the word for year was *renpet*. The year began with the season of *akhet*, the time of the inundation of the Nile, starting approximately the third week of July according to modern calculations. *Akhet* was followed by *proyet* (or *peret*), the time of sowing. The last season, *shomu* or *shemu*, was the time of the harvest. Each season had its own festivals and cultic celebrations.

Seat of the First Occasion the ancient Egyptian term for a TEMPLE site. These buildings were believed to rest upon the original location of the gods' entrance into the world. (See COSMOGONY, PRIMEVAL MOUNDS and PAY LANDS.)

seb a feast associated with the first day of harvest. The entire royal court attended celebrations in the fields, and processions and festive rituals were held. The FESTIVAL ended with the king and his retinue sailing on the Nile or on one of the sacred lakes of the temples.

sebayet the ancient Egyptian word for "teaching" or "instruction," used to describe the didactic LITERATURE handed down through the generations.

Sebekamzaf I (Sekhemre'-wadjkha'u) the third king of the 17th Dynasty at Thebes, the royal line

that ruled from 1640–1550 B.C. The date of his reign is unknown. He left an inscription at the Wadi Hammamat, and his name appears on monuments at Abydos, Thebes and the Elephantine.

Sebekamzaf II (Sekhemre'-shadtawy) the 10th king of the 17th Dynasty at Thebes, the royal line that ruled from 1640–1550 B.C. The date of his reign is unknown. His name appears on a monument at Medamud, and at Wadi Hammamat. He is listed as having ruled for 16 years, and was called "great" by his contemporaries. Sebekamzaf began construction projects at Thebes and at Abydos.

Sebekhotpe I (Ka'ankhre') the 12th king of the 13th Dynasty (c. 1750 B.C.); his reign is obscure. CYLINDER SEALS and SCARABS bearing his CARTOUCHE are all that remain of his rule.

Sebekhotpe II (Sekhemre'khutawy) the 16th king of the 13th Dynasty (date of reign unknown). He made additions to the temples at DEIR-EL-BAHRI and at Medamud. His statue was found at Semna. Sebekhotpe II is thought to have ruled for only four years.

Sebekhotpe III (Sekhemre'swadjtawy) the 21st king of the 13th Dynasty (c. 1745 B.C.), a commoner whose parents were listed in a temple inscription. His monuments were discovered at el-Kab and Lisht, and his name is inscribed on an altar at Sehel Island. Sebekhotpe is mentioned in the Bulaq Papyrus.

Sebekhotpe IV (Kha'neferre') the 24th king (c. 1730–1720 B.C.) of the 13th Dynasty, a commoner whose statue was found at the Third Cataract. Another statue was discovered in Tanis. The HYKSOS, the Asiatics who entered the Delta and consolidated their power there as the 15th and 16 Dynasties (contemporaneous) founded the capital of AVARIS during Sebekhotpe IV's reign (See EGYPT, *Second Intermediate Period*.)

Sebekhotpe V (Kha'hotepre') the 25th king (c. 1720–1715 B.C.) of the 13th Dynasty. He was a native of Thebes and left a stela at Karnak. Nothing else is known of his reign.

Sebek-khu an official of the 12th Dynasty, he served SENWOSRET III (1878–1841? B.C.) as a military commander. He led an expedition into Syria, a journey of some historical importance to the era. He also conducted military campaigns in NUBIA. Sebek-khu served Senwosret's successor, AMENEMHET III, in the same capacity. The details of his career were found on a mortuary stela in Abydos.

Sebni an official of the 6th Dynasty, serving PEPI II (2246–2152 B.C.) as an expeditionary leader. He was the son of an official murdered on the coast of the Red Sea. Sebni's grandfather had also been slain while serving in NUBIA. Sebni gathered up his father's body, saw to his proper burial and then took command of the expedition. His mortuary inscriptions gave a vivid account of the sacrifices of his family for Egypt.

Sebu'a, el- a site near the First Cataract of the Nile where Ramesses II (1290–1224 B.C.) built a temple in honor of the gods Amon and Re'-Harakhty. The gateway of this temple led to a court, which contained sphinxes and colossal monuments. A pylon gate opened onto another court, which had more sphinxes. A third court, chapels and storage rooms with columns were built on an underground level of the temple.

sed an ancient Egyptian royal FESTIVAL that began in predynastic times and remained popular throughout Egypt's history. The festival was a symbolic renewal of the king's physical and magical powers. It was usually celebrated in the 30th year of a king's reign and every three years thereafter. Details of the *sed* are obscure because the festival changed over the eras. The hieroglyph for *sed* is an image of an open-sided pavilion with a column and two thrones.

It is believed that the *sed* festival became a substitute for the death of the king, allowing him a ceremonial foretaste of his rule in the afterlife. During the celebration the king visited the shrines of the various gods, dressed in a short garment that completely enveloped his torso and arms. He performed the rite of "going around the wall," ran, danced and jumped in order to demonstrate his rejuvenation.

Sehel Island a site between the First and Second Cataract of the Nile, where ancient Egyptian fortifications and inscriptions were discovered. The Famine Stela, erected in the Ptolemaic period, commemorated the visit of DJOSER (2630–2611 B.C.) of the 3rd Dynasty to the shrine of KHNUM, thus ending a period of drought. A canal was built alongside the rapids at this point in the early dynastic era in order to aid transportation. (See CANAL OF SEHEL and SENWOSRET III.)

Sehetepibre' an official of the late 12th Dynasty, probably serving SENWOSRET III (1878–1841? B.C.) and AMENEMHET III (1844–1797 B.C.) as treasurer. He is

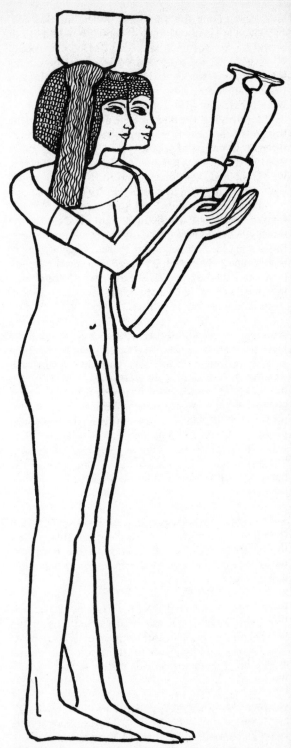

Asiatic princesses celebrating the anniversary of Amenhotep III's coronation.

known for his Loyalist Instructions, in which he advised the Egyptians of his era to obey the king in all things, behavior by which they could attain high office. A copy of this text was found on an Abydos stela and in other documents.

Seker Boat (Hennu and Sokar Boat)   a bark used in religious rites in Memphis, dating to the 1st Dynasty (2920 B.C.). Elaborately adorned with carvings, the bark had a funerary chest and three ornamental oars. When the vessel was used to honor Ptah-Sokar, the combined form of the deity, it was attached to a large sleigh.

sekhem   the word used to denote the power of a god in ancient Egypt or the vital principle of a human being. A *sekhem* scepter was kept in the shrine of OSIRIS at Abydos, supposedly inlaid with faience and precious stones, and with a human face molded in gold at the tip.

Sekhemkhet   the third king (2611–2603 B.C.) of the 3rd Dynasty. His name was inscribed on a cliff near Wadi Maghara. He built a pyramid at Saqqara that was never finished but contained an alabaster coffin.

Sekhmet   a goddess of ancient Egypt, the female counterpart of PTAH at Memphis. Lion-headed in most depictions, she was associated with fires and plagues. Her image on the walls of Sahure' 's temple was venerated as a source of healing in some eras. In some depictions Sekhmet wore a sun disk on her head, and in this form she was a warlike manifestation of the sun, causing flames to devour the enemies of Egypt.

Selket (also called Serqet)   a goddess of ancient Egypt, associated early with the god NUN and originally adored in the southern lands. She was absorbed into the cult of HORUS in time and then became a guardian of the dead. The SCORPION was her theophany, and in TUT'ANKHAMUN's tomb she was beautifully depicted standing guard over the CANOPIC JARS of the mummified king.

sema   an ancient Egyptian AMULET used as a protective shield for the windpipe. The amulet was used by the living, and it was placed in the mummy wrappings to protect the deceased.

Semerkhet   the sixth king of the 1st Dynasty (dates of reign unknown), the son of 'ADJIB and Queen Bentrest. A black quartz stela bearing his name was

SEKHMET   a New Kingdom statue of the goddess, from Karnak.

Selket, the divine guardian of the canopic chest of the tomb.

discovered. He is supposed to have ruled for over eight years.

Semna an important site at the southern end of the Second Cataract in NUBIA, where the Egyptians erected a FORTRESS and a temple complex. Semna marked the southern border for Egypt during much of the Middle Kingdom (2040–1640 B.C.). A stela discovered on the site records that the original fortress was built by SENWOSRET III (1878–1841? B.C.). Semna had served as a trading settlement in previous eras. A second stela, discovered in the temple complex, dedicated the shrine to the Nubian god DEDUN. KHNUM, an Egyptian deity, was also venerated at Semna.

Semna's fortress overlooked the Semna Gorge and was opposite the fortress of Kumma. In time a second fortress, called Semna South, was erected in the region. Detailed reports were sent to Thebes, called the Semna Dispatches, about tracking operations. The MEDJAY, some of whom were in the service of the Egyptians, were kept under surveillance by the commanders of the fortresses.

Sen Ba Stela supposedly belonging to DJER, the second king of the 1st Dynasty, it is considered one of the most beautiful stone monuments of the era, setting the standard for later hieroglyphic mortuary texts.

Sendjemib a clan of ancient Egypt's Old Kingdom. An official named Inti Sendjemib, the first known clan member, an administrator for IZEZI (2388–2356 B.C.), built a small lake for the king's pleasure. His son, Mehi, built a tomb for his father at Giza and carried on the family tradition of government service.

Senenmut an official of the 18th Dynasty, counselor to HATSHEPSUT (1473–1458 B.C.). He was the tutor of Princess NEFERU-RE' and provided support for Hatshepsut when she assumed the throne in her own right, setting aside TUTHMOSIS III. Senenmut was also honored for his architectural skills. He was involved in the various building projects of Hatshepsut, including the temple at DEIR EL-BAHRI on the western shore of the Nile at Thebes and the KARNAK temple.

He amassed 80 separate titles as an official and administrator in the royal court and worked with HAPUSENEB and other supporters of Hatshepsut's reign. Many legends concerning Senenmut have arisen over the years. The many titles and favors bestowed upon him having given rise to much speculation. What is known is the fact that Senenmut dared to attempt to link his own tomb with that of the Queen-Pharaoh. His tomb and his images were also destroyed with a definite ruthlessness by the agents of Tuthmosis III, Hatshepsut's heir, who had been set aside by her claims to the throne.

When Senenmut died in the 19th year of her reign (or possibly before) Hatshepsut was left vulnerable. Contemporary portraits of Senenmut show him with a long nose and a rather cunning face. His tomb was beautifully designed and furnished. Among his funeral offerings was the body of a horse.

Sen-nefer an official of the 18th Dynasty, serving in the reign of AMENHOTEP II (1427–1401 B.C.). Sennefer was the mayor of Thebes, and his wife was a royal nurse. They were both buried in a tomb that appears to have been built originally for TUTHMOSIS II, the grandfather of Amenhotep II. The tomb was on the western shore opposite Thebes.

Senwosret I (Kheperkare') the second king (1971–1926 B.C.) of the 12th Dynasty, the son of AMENEMHET I and Queen Nefrutoten. He served as co-ruler with Amenemhet for more than a decade and was reported as being on a campaign when word reached him that his father was dead. The circumstances of the death are an important plot element in the Tale of Sinuhe, a popular literary work dating to that period.

Senwosret returned to the capital, then located at ITH-TAWY, on the border between Upper and Lower Egypt, and began his reign. He was militarily active as a king, campaigning in NUBIA and extending Egypt's borders to the area between the Second and Third Cataract. KERMA and other fortresses were erected in this period. The fortress at SEMNA was also established by him. Gold, copper, granite and other natural resources were mined and quarried, and Senwosret maintained the mines in the Sinai with a firm hand.

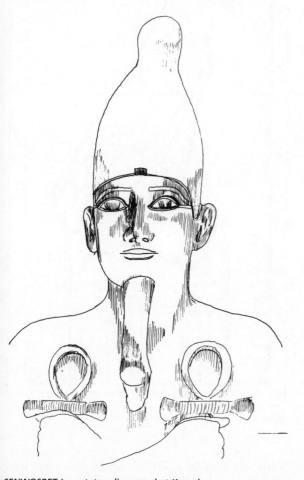

SENWOSRET I   a statue discovered at Karnak.

Amenemhet I supposedly dictated his Instructions to Senwosret, warning him of the perils faced by a weak monarch. With the borders of Egypt secured and the availability of natural resources ensured, Senwosret turned his attention to internal affairs. He raised buildings up and down the Nile and adorned numerous existing shrines and temples. His most significant monument was a funerary complex at LISHT. The PYRAMID constructed as his tomb consisted of separate compartments filled with sand and rubble and then covered with limestone. A second layer of fine stone completed the structure. The tomb and mortuary temple are notable for their beautiful reliefs and statues. Senwosret I died in the 45th year of his reign. His son, AMENEMHET II, served as co-ruler before he died.

Senwosret II (Kha'kheperre') the fourth king (1879–1878 B.C.) of the 12th Dynasty, the son of AMENEMHET II, he served as co-ruler before his father died. Senwosret II began the reclamation projects in the FAIYUM, transforming thousands of acres of marshland into fields, establishing a sound economic base.

He conducted campaigns in NUBIA, enclosing the fortress at 'Aniba with walls and extending Egypt's borders there. He protected the mines in Nubia and the SINAI and maintained the extraction of natural resources. Senwosret II received tributes from Syria. His pyramidal complex was built at Lahun at the mouth of the FAIYUM. RAMESSES II (1290–1224 B.C.) plundered the site for building materials.

Senwosret III (Kha'kaure') the fifth king (1848–1841? B.C.) of the 12th Dynasty, the son of SENWOSRET II. He is one of the most famous kings of the Middle Kingdom. He limited the power of the noble families of the NOMES and supported the rise of a middle class composed of artisans, merchants, traders and farmers. He was also active militarily, especially in NUBIA, where he consolidated Egyptian holdings. In order to transport troops to Nubia, he restored or restructured the canal near the First Cataract. With his troops he extended Egypt's grip in Nubia to WADI HALFA. A great hymn commemorating his campaigns has survived from his reign.

His wives included queens Mereryet, Neferhent, Neferu, Merseger and Merysankh. Queen Sebek-shedty-Neferu was the mother of his heir, AMENEMHET III. Senwosret III's mortuary complex at Dashur contained tombs for his daughters as well as his queens. He was depicted in contemporary sculptures, considered masterpieces of the Middle Kingdom, as grim and somber faced. (See SEHEL ISLAND.)

Senwosret III, from a 12th Dynasty statue.

Serabit el-Khadim a site in the SINAI where the ancient Egyptians conducted mining operations. SEN-WOSRET I of the 12th Dynasty (1971–1926 B.C.) sent an armed expedition to the area to extract turquoise. A temple to the goddess HATHOR as the "Lady of Turquoise," was erected at Serabit el-Khadim. Stelae discovered at the site depict a Palestinian prince, an ally of the Middle Kingdom rulers.

Serapeum a Late Period necropolis for the bulls of APIS and MNEVIS at SAQQARA and elsewhere. The original vaults for the bodies of the Apis bulls date to the New Kingdom and were incorporated into a cultic complex. Gigantic granite, basalt and limestone sarcophagi held the animal remains; some were dug out of caves. The site at Saqqara dates from the Second Intermediate Period but did not attain its cultic fame until later.

serdab a chamber provided in ancient Egyptian tombs for the statues of the deceased. The word is Arabic for "cellar." Sculpted statues representing the deceased were placed in the *serdab*, which had a window at eye level so that the dead could witness the offerings being conducted as part of the com-memorative tomb rituals. (See MORTUARY RITUALS and TOMBS.)

serekh a building associated with royalty from the early periods following the unification of ancient Egypt (3000 B.C.). Most had elaborate paneled fa-cades, two towers and recessed entrances. They were made of wood and served as royal residences in the Early Dynastic Period (2920–2575). The *serekh* was adapted by Wadji the third king of the 1st Dynasty, as the symbol of the king and appears on a STELA. It also appears on sarcophagi and on the false doors of tombs. A king's name was written above the *serekh* symbol in a rectangle topped by HORUS' symbol of the hawk or falcon. (See ROYAL NAMES.)

Serekh of King Wadj of the 1st Dynasty.

Serpent's Head a phallic AMULET used to protect the living from snakebite in ancient Egypt. When used in the MORTUARY RITUALS the amulet was designed to protect the corpse from worms and serpents in the tomb.

Servants of the Place of Truth called the Servitors of the Place of Truth in some records, the ancient Egyptian name for the artisans involved in the royal tombs in the Valley of the Kings. These artisans lived in settlements near the royal necropolis on the western shore of the Nile opposite Thebes. DEIR EL-MEDINEH was one such example settled in the 18th Dynasty, known for its exquisite tombs, many of which are intact. The artisans were allowed to decorate their own tombs, and in so doing displayed great skill.

Seshat the ancient Egyptian goddess of writing. The wife of the god THOTH, Seshat was associated with the sacred PERSEA TREE, upon which the royal names of the king were written at the time of his coronation. She was depicted with plumes in some eras, but normally as a woman with a star on a pole. The plumes identified her as the recorder of deeds. As the Mistress of Books, Seshat was the goddess who measured time. She became the Mistress of Architects in some eras. Seshat was the divine being who recorded all of the wares brought back to Egypt from PUNT in the reign of HATSHEPSUT (1473–1458 B.C.). Writing was attributed to her as the wife of THOTH.

Seshseshet a princess of the 6th Dynasty, the daughter of Teti (c. 2323–2291 B.C.). She was married to the official, Mereruka, whose tomb at SAQQARA has become famous because of its remarkable false door, which depicts the vizier himself walking through it as a *ka*.

Setau an official of the 19th Dynasty, serving RAMESSES II (1290–1224 B.C.) as the viceroy of NUBIA and then as high priest of AMON at Thebes. Setau repaired the great temple at ABU SIMBEL after an earthquake caused damage to the site. His mortuary stela is in the British Museum.

Seth the Greek rendering of the Egyptian Sutekh, translated as "instigator of confusion," the "destroyer," and accompanied by the TYPHONEAN ANIMAL when inscribed in hieroglyphs. Seth dates to the Early Dynastic Period of Egypt (2920–2575 B.C.), and in the PYRAMID TEXTS of the Old Kingdom he was listed as both a friend and an enemy of the god HORUS. In some eras he was associated with the slaying of APOPHIS, the wicked serpent that made nightly attempts to destroy the god RE'. During the Ramessid era he was viewed as the god of foreign lands and he was supposedly married to the goddess

TYPHONEAN ANIMAL a mythical creature sacred to Seth found in pectorals and tomb inscriptions throughout Egypt.

NEPHTHYS. As a love god he was often invoked with AMULETS and charms. He is best known, however, for his part in the Osirian cult. Seth murdered OSIRIS and set his coffin adrift. When ISIS found the body and restored it, Seth cut the flesh to pieces and hid them. Isis found all of Osiris except for his phallus and brought about his resurrection. Horus, the son of Osiris, then set about seeking revenge, and Osiris pleaded a case against him before the gods.

Cult centers for Seth were located along caravan routes and in the western oases. He was elevated to a national god when RAMESSES II (1290–1224 B.C.) honored him at the new capital, PER-RAMESSES, in the eastern Delta. In time the dominant Osirian cult led to a decline of the Seth cult.

Sethnakhte (Userkha'ure'meryamun) the first king (1196–1194 B.C.) of the 20th Dynasty. He dated the commencement of his reign to the end of SETI II's rule (1204 B.C.), refusing to acknowledge the last monarchs of the 19th Dynasty. His origins are unknown, but he took charge of Egypt's frail government as an old man and accomplished a restoration of peace and order in a short time. He is mentioned in the Harris Papyrus. Sethnakhte started his royal tomb complex before he died, but it was not finished in time. Some records indicate that his body was placed in a tomb originally prepared for TWOSRE. He was succeeded by his son, RAMESSES III, considered the last great pharoah of the New Kingdom.

Seti I (Menma'atre') the second king (1306–1290 B.C.) of the 19th Dynasty. The Egyptians viewed his reign as a new beginning after the difficult period of the late 18th Dynasty. The son of RAMESSES I and Queen SITRE, he was a military commander as his father had been, and he set his sights on the restoration of the vast empire carved out by the Tuthmossids almost a century before.

Campaigning in Asia, a military exploit depicted on the walls of KARNAK, Seti I took three divisions of 20,000 men each into battle. He plundered Palestine and entered Syrian territory, reoccupying abandoned Egyptian posts and garrisoned cities. He then came to terms with the Hittites, who were emerging as the most powerful military state in the region, and wrested control of coastal areas along the Mediterranean. He fought across Palestine and brought Damascus back into the Egyptian fold. A second campaign set him against Kadesh, where he put up a stela commemorating his victory there. RAMESSES II, his heir, campaigned with him.

Within Egypt Seti I undertook many building projects, including one at Karnak, where he completed his father's plan to convert the court between the second and third pylons into a vast HYPOSTYLE HALL.

Seti I, from a relief in his Abydos temple.

Ramesses II was co-ruler at the time. During the same period Seti built his vast ABYDOS mortuary complex and made provisions for the miners and the quarry workers in the eastern desert. He set up a series of regulations about the mines and their products, and built a chapel at Buhen. Returning the capital to Memphis, Seti spent a part of the year in Thebes and time in the eastern Delta, at AVARIS, his home region. In Thebes, he began work on his vast tomb, situated in the VALLEY OF THE KINGS on the western shore. It is the largest tomb in the area, cut 300 feet into the cliffs. Passages and elaborate chambers were incorporated into the design, each one covered with painted reliefs. The hall and burial chamber were provided with vaulted ceilings with astronomical signs and a depiction of the Am Tuat, a version of the BOOK OF THE DEAD.

His queen, TUYA, probably married him before he became a prince of the realm. She was the mother of Ramesses II. They had two daughters as well, Tia and Hentmire. Seti I's mummy was discovered at DEIR EL-BAHRI, and gives evidence that he was a handsome man in his sixties when he died. Buried with him in his original tomb were over 700 SHABTI figures, made of faience, stone or wood. His original tomb was vandalized, as were so many other pharaonic grave sites, and his body was reburied at Deir el-Bahri.

Seti II (Userkheprure'setepenre') the fifth king (c. 1207–1202 B.C.) of the 19th Dynasty. He was the son of MERNEPTAH and Queen ISETNOFRET. Only minor monuments remain from his reign, and he was possibly unseated by Amunmesse, who usurped the throne. Seti II is recorded as having ruled for six years in a troubled era. His mummified remains indicate that he suffered from arthritis, but he had good teeth, something unusual in that period. His wife TWOSRE also usurped the throne during the reign of SIPTAH, his successor. A son, Seti-Merneptah, died young.

Seven Hathors divine beings of ancient Egypt who were precursors of the Fates of Greece. These beings could tell the future and knew the moment of death for each Egyptian. Because a person's destiny depended upon the hour of his or her death and the luck of ill-fortune connected with it, the Seven Hathors were believed to exchange any prince born under unfavorable auspices with a more fortunate child, thus protecting the dynasty and the nation. The Egyptians were greatly concerned with the lucky or unlucky fate of individuals. (See CAIRO CALENDAR and FATE.)

Sewew   the ancient Egyptian name for the coastal region of the Red Sea, opposite COPTOS on the WADI GASUS. This area was used as a port, probably KUSER, and as a shipbuilding site for expeditions to PUNT.

Sha'at   a site on Sai Island, occupied by the VICEROY OF NUBIA in the 19th Dynasty. When SETI I (c. 1306–1290 B.C.) put down a rebellion there, the viceroy Amenemope erected two stelae to commemorate the victory.

shabti   called *shawbti* and *ushabti* in some lists, the ancient Egyptian funerary figurines which were called "The Answerers." These statues were so named because they were designed to accompany the deceased into the various levels of paradise, to comply with requests from the gods. The statues, some of which were beautifully carved and detailed, were made from wood in the early eras and then fashioned out of stone, metal, terracotta or faience.

shaduf   an ancient Egyptian irrigation device still in use on the Nile, introduced into the nation by the HYKSOS, or Asiatic invaders of the Second Intermediate Period (1640–1532 B.C.). The *shaduf* is a simple wooden instrument consisting of a pole with a bucket on one end and a weight on the other. The *shaduf* enabled a farmer, working alone, to raise water from the Nile and to deposit it in the appropriate canal or irrigation ditch. The use of the device after the Hyksos period increased Egypt's agricultural output. Some scholars estimate that the *shaduf* increased the land cultivation by more than 10 percent. The device was just one of many contributions made by the Hyksos during their occupation of the eastern Delta. (See AGRICULTURE.)

Shai   an ancient Egyptian goddess associated with the mortuary cult and the JUDGMENT HALL OF OSIRIS. She was considered the guardian of fate, or *shoy*, as were the SEVEN HATHORS. Shai was one of the attendants of the scales upon which the goddess Ma'at weighed the souls or hearts of the deceased Egyptians. (See FATE, MA'AT.)

Shed   a god of ancient Egypt whose cult originated in Thinis. He was depicted as a young prince on the hunt. In time he became the lord of the deserts and paradise, and was hence called the "Savior." He hunted serpents, scorpions and crocodiles, thus benefiting Egyptians in all eras.

Sheik Abd-el-Qurna   See QURNA.

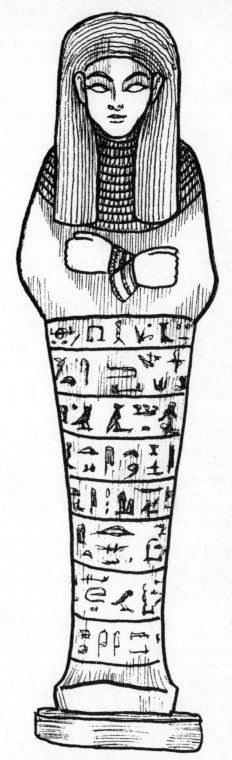

SHABTI the figures placed in all Egyptian tombs to perform duties in Tuat or the underworld.

Sheik el-Beled See KA'APER STATUE.

Sheik Said a site near Hatnub where tombs of local Old Kingdom monarchs were discovered.

shenu the insignia used by the kings of Egypt to enclose their ROYAL NAMES. The *shenu* was an oval frame encircling the royal names of the kings. The symbol represented the eternal powers of the god Re', dedicated in every generation to the protection of the kings of the Nile. (See CARTOUCHE.)

Shepseskhaf the sixth king (2472–2467) of the 4th Dynasty. The heir of MENKAURE', Shepseskhaf ruled Egypt at a time of religious discontent and NOME assertiveness. He completed his predecessor's monuments but then quarreled with the priests of the various temples over spiritual concerns. Some records indicate that he was not of royal blood.

His queen was possibly Khentkawes, (who may have been his daughter), the "Mother of the 5th Dynasty." Another queen was Bunefer. Shepseskhaf built a mastaba in southern Saqqara, which bears the modern name of Mastabet Fara'un. The MASTABA contained a rectangular SARCOPHAGUS.

Sherden Pirates See RAMESSES III and SEA PEOPLES.

Sheshi the second king (1640–1532 B.C.) of the 15th Dynasty, designated "Great HYKSOS" after the Asiatics who entered the Delta region and founded their own capital at AVARIS. The actual dates of his reign are unknown. Seals bearing his ROYAL NAMES were discovered in a fortress at the Third Cataract, at the Elephantine and at Deir el-Bahri.

ships See MILITARY.

Shipwrecked Sailor See TALE OF THE SHIPWRECKED SAILOR.

shomu (*shemu* in some lists) a season of the ancient Egyptian calendar. *Shomu* was the time of harvest, comprising four months of 30 days each. The last season of the Egyptian year, *shomu* was preceded by *proyet*, the time of sowing, and followed by *akhet*, the period of inundation by the Nile. (See CALENDAR and MONTHS.)

shoy See FATE.

Shu an ancient Egyptian god of the air who separated the earth and the sky—the god GEB and the

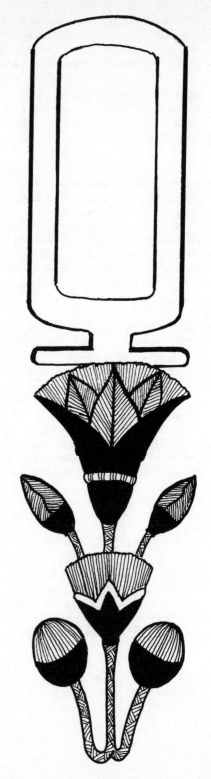

Shenu with lotus adornments.

goddess NUT. He was sometimes depicted with a solar disk on his head, alluding to his place in the solar cult, and he was also worshipped in the leonine form in some cult centers. His primary role, however, was his membership in the ENNEAD in the city of HELIOPOLIS. He and his twin sister, Tefnut, formed the space between the heavens and the earth. The god RE' was the one who commanded Shu to raise Nut into the heavens.

Shunet el-Zebib a site near ABYDOS where a spectacular necropolis, dating to the Early Dynastic Period (2920–2575 B.C.), was discovered. The kings of the first dynasties built mortuary complexes on the fringe of the desert there. The region was a popular area for such structures, being near Abydos, center of the OSIRIS cult. The modern Arabic name, meaning "Storehouse of Dates," alludes to the necropolis discovered there, which includes two walled fortresses.

Sihathor an official of the 12th Dynasty, serving AMENEMHET II (1929–1892 B.C.) as a supervisor of Egyptian mines in the SINAI and in the region below the cataracts. He was considered an expert on turquoise, the stone prized by the Egyptians and favored by the goddess HATHOR. He took part in the construction of the pyramid of Amenemhet II at Dashur, and supervised the building of ten statues for the mortuary complex. Sihathor's stela, which gives an account of his career and his era, is in the British Museum.

Silsila See GEBEL SILSILEH.

Simontu a 12th Dynasty official serving AMENEMHET II (1929–1892 B.C.). Simontu was the "Chief of Works" for the court and a royal scribe, and appears to have held administrative duties in the king's own HAREM. His mortuary stela, now in the British Museum, gives an account of his life.

Sinai the mineral-rich peninsula on ancient Egypt's eastern border where copper, malachite, turquoise and other stones were mined. Turquoise found in predynastic graves indicates that Egyptians either had access to the turquoise mines in the Sinai or traded with the Bedouins of the region.

In the Early Dynastic Period (2920–2770 B.C.) the Egyptians entered the Sinai to start their own mines and quarries. The Old Kingdom rulers also profited from other resources in the region. DJOSER (2630–2611 B.C.) left an inscription in Sinai. Others of his royal line conducted campaigns and military expeditions to enforce the nation's control of the mines

and quarries there. In the 4th Dynasty, SNOFRU (2575–2551 B.C.) suppressed an uprising of Bedouins on the peninsula, which his royal successors and the kings of the 5th Dynasty had to do periodically.

PEPI I (2289–2255 B.C.) of the 6th Dynasty, and his military commander, General WENI, attacked the Bedouins in a series of aggressive campaigns, not content with punitive expeditions. Weni claimed to have chased one tribe of Sinai Bedouins all the way to Mount Carmel to punish them for hindering Egyptian activities in their home territories. When the Old Kingdom collapsed, however, the Asiatics of the Sinai and beyond joined with other nomadic people to enter Egypt. The borders had fallen, and there was no central authority to prevent their entry. These Asiatics lived in comparative peace in the northeastern Delta until the Mentuhotpes of the 11th Dynasty (2134–2040 B.C.) united the NOMES of Egypt and routed all aliens.

The founder of the 12th Dynasty, AMENEMHET I (1991–1962 B.C.), fought the Asiatics when they tried to enter Egypt again and erected the WALL OF THE PRINCE, a series of fortresses and garrisons extending across the border regions. The great copper mines in the Sinai were in full operation during this time. When the Middle Kingdom collapsed, the HYKSOS came into Egypt. They were from an area which was reported as covering much of northern Sinai and part of Palestine. These Asiatics ruled portions of Egypt for almost a century, establishing a capital in the northeastern Delta. They were driven out of Egypt by the armies of 'AHMOSE I of the 18th Dynasty (c. 1532 B.C.). From that point on there was little resistance on the part of the local Bedouins of the Sinai, because Egypt had become too powerful militarily.

Many of the New Kingdom rulers left inscriptions in the Sinai, including HATSHEPSUT (1473–1458 B.C.). In the 19th Dynasty a temple dedicated to HATHOR was erected by RAMESSES II (1290–1224 B.C.) at the copper mines. These pits, and the valued quarries of the region, did not remain in Egyptian hands long after the reign of RAMESSES III of the 20th Dynasty (1194–1163 B.C.). Ramesses IV attempted to regain control of the Sinai, but he died before he could accomplish this task. His successors lacked the resources and the will to reestablish Egypt's former glory.

Sinuhe the Sailor one of the most interesting literary texts of the ancient world; a tale of adventure from the Middle Kingdom (12th Dynasty) discovered in a Berlin Papyrus. The story concerns Sinuhe, a retainer of SENWOSRET I (1971–1926 B.C.) at the time of the murder of his father, AMENEMHET I. The prince is campaigning in Libya, and Sinuhe, apparently fearful for his life, leaves Egypt, beginning a series of adventures. He fights against a giant, much like in the story David and Goliath, visits the courts of Palestine and Syria, and finally returns to Egypt, where he is received by a forgiving pharaoh and by his family. (The tale may have been the inspiration for Sinbad the Sailor as the taking of the city of Joppa by the agents of TUTHMOSIS III [1479–1425 B.C.] may have influenced the story of Ali Baba and the Forty Thieves.) The text provides considerable detail and insight about life in Middle Kingdom Egypt.

Sinu site in the eastern Delta where in ancient times the waters of the Nile entered the Mediterranean Sea. The Greeks called the place Pelusium.

Siptah (Akhenre'setepenre') the seventh king (1204–1198 B.C.) of the 19th Dynasty. A minor of unestablished royal parentage, possibly related to SETI II in some fashion, he inherited the throne. He was very young, and Queen TWOSRE, the widow of Seti II, was named his regent. She was aided by a counselor named BAY. Siptah either died or was removed from the throne by Twosre and Bay. Before he disappeared, however, he is recorded as having conducted a Nubian campaign. This military expedition was probably sent in his name, not requiring his youthful presence on the field of battle. His tomb in the VALLEY OF THE KINGS was eventually usurped by another king.

sistrum called the SESES (or *shesheset*) by the ancient Egyptians, a musical instrument that was popular in the cult of the goddess HATHOR. The sistrum was formed as a sticklike wooden or metal object, with a frame and small metal disks that rattled when the instrument was shaken by a hand. The head of Hathor was often depicted on the instrument or the horns of a cow incorporated into its design. The sistrum was a favored instrument in the cultic rites in Egypt's temples and shrines and was used in religious processions. The sistrum took the form of a CARTOUCHE and was honored for this coincidence.

Sitamun a princess of the 18th Dynasty, the daughter of AMENHOTEP III and Queen TIY (1391–1353 B.C.). Records indicate that Queen Tiy urged Amenhotep to accept Sitamun as a consort. Tiy probably wanted to ensure the birth of other royal heirs. Sitamun is believed by some to be the mother of SMENKHKARE' and TUT'ANKHAMUN as a result of this marriage, as the young kings were brothers. She was buried at Thebes.

SISTRUM a favorite musical instrument, associated with the goddess Hathor.

Sit Hathor-Yunet a princess of the 12th Dynasty, the daughter of SENWOSRET II (1897–1878 B.C.). She was buried at LAHUN, where a cache of her jewelry and mortuary regalia was discovered, indicating her royal rank and the favor of the entire royal clan.

SIT HATHOR-YUNET a 12th Dynasty princess, shown in her actual wig.

Sitre a queen of the 19th Dynasty, the wife of RAMESSES I (1307–1306 B.C.). She was the mother of SETI I. Sitre married Ramesses long before he was proclaimed heir by HOREMHAB.

Siwa an OASIS in the western or Libyan desert. Siwa was a famed religious site in many eras and was visited by pilgrims consulting the oracles there. The region was also noted for its wines and dates, grown and processed by the local inhabitants. During the Roman occupation of Egypt the Siwa was called Jupiter Ammon. It was also visited by Alexander the Great, who consulted the oracle. (See ORACLES.)

sma-tawy (or *sema-tawy*) the insignia of the unification of Upper and Lower Egypt, an entwined PAPYRUS and LOTUS. It appeared on thrones, festival boats and in the palaces and temples.

Smendes called Nesbaneb-Djedet in some records, an official of the 20th Dynasty in the reign of RAMESSES XI (1100–1070 B.C.) who usurped the throne of Egypt. Smendes began his career in Tanis. He became the high priest of Amon and the viceroy of Lower Egypt, working with HERIHOR, also high priest of Amon and the viceroy of Upper Egypt. Together the two men kept Ramesses XI secluded on his estates. When Ramesses died, Smendes and Herihor divided Egypt between them, initiating the 21st Dynasty.

Smenkhkare' ('Ankhkeprure') the 11th king (1335–1333 B.C.) of the 18th Dynasty and the heir of AKHENATEN at el-'AMARNA. Married to Princess MERYTAMON, who replaced NEFERTITI as Akhenaten's consort, Smenkhkare' was depicted in reliefs as Akhenaten's companion. He also appears to have assumed the religious title of Nefertiti, leading to speculation about him and his role in 'Amarna. When Akhenaten died in 1335 B.C., Smenkhkare' assumed the throne. Pressured by the priests of Amon and the military advisors, he returned the capital to Thebes and ruled from the city for two years. His mummified remains indicate that he died at the age of 25. The cause of his death remains a mystery as his corpse displays no physical evidence of diseases.

Sment the goose kept in the temple of Amon at Thebes, associated with the COSMOGONY of Egypt in all eras. (See GEB and GREAT CACKLER.)

Smith Papyrus, Edwin an 18th Dynasty (1550–1307 B.C.) text, which may have originated in the 3rd Dynasty (2649–2575 B.C.). Concerned with the medical practices of the priest-physicians of Egypt, the document contains 48 separate sections that discuss symptoms of diseases, diagnostic traditions and treatment—all aspects of ancient Egyptian MEDICINE. The Edwin Smith Papyrus is one of the texts which enabled modern scholars to assess medical knowledge in pharaonic Egypt.

Snofru the first king (2575–2551 B.C.) of the 4th Dynasty, probably the son of HUNI and Queen MERESANKH I, although some records indicate that he came from Menat-Khufu, near Beni Hasan. Snofru's reign opened an era of military and artistic endeavors in Egypt. He took an active part on the battlefield. The PALERMO STONE gives an account of his military campaigns against the Nubians and the Libyans. He also started trade with the Mediterranean nations and began a series of building projects throughout Egypt. To provide the nation with natural resources,

Smenkhkare' from an el-'Amarna relief.

particularly wood, he sent a fleet of 40 ships to Lebanon and left monuments there to commemorate the event.

Snofru built his mortuary complex at DASHUR, and he finished the pyramid at MEIDUM, which had been started by Huni. The pyramid at Dashur is viewed as an architectural link between the STEP PYRAMID of SAQQARA and the true pyramids, which his son KHUFU and other successors would raise up at GIZA. Snofru actually erected two pyramids at Dashur, one rhom-

boidal in style, indicating an inability on the part of its architects to achieve their original goal. The second pyramid was a true one. Snofru was deified by the kings of the 12th Dynasty, and many rulers of that line chose to erect their own mortuary complexes beside his. Snofru's queen was HETEPHERES I, the mother of Khufu.

Sobek a god of ancient Egypt whose cult center was in the FAIYUM. Sobek, depicted either as a man with a crocodile's head or as a crocodile, was the patron deity of the 13th Dynasty (1783–1640? B.C.). Many kings of that line bore his name in their royal titles. Sobek was mentioned in the PYRAMID TEXTS as a son of NEITH. He was considered one of the beings thought to have emerged from the watery chaos at the moment the world began. The Faiyum and the city of CROCODILOPOLIS were his sacred abodes, and a temple was built for him on the banks of the Nile in Upper Egypt in later eras. Sobek was also associated with 'AHA, the legendary first king of Egypt. The god was equated in some NOMES with SETH, and there the animals were ritually slaughtered. In other regions, crocodiles were venerated.

Sokar (also Seker) an ancient Egyptian god of the Memphite necropolis from predynastic times. He was originally a spirit guardian of the tombs but was elevated in rank after 3000 B.C. He was united with PTAH and depicted as having come from that deity's heart and mind as a force of creation. When the cult of OSIRIS developed, a triune deity, Osiris-Ptah-Sokar, emerged. That trinity is called Ptah-Seker-Asar in some lists.

Sokar's theophany was the hawk, and his shrine and sacred bark date to the period before the 1st Dynasty. He is represented in reliefs as a pygmy with a large head and heavy limbs. He wore a beetle on his head and stood on a cabinet, with hawks in attendance. One of his litanies was included in the Rhind Papyrus.

Sokar boat See SEKER BOAT, BARKS OF THE GODS.

solar boat crafts meant to convey the kings to paradise, buried in great pits beside PYRAMIDS; also, Re''s bark, used in his daily travels. (See BARKS OF THE GODS and SUN'S BOAT.)

solar cult the state religion of Egypt, which can be traced to predynastic times, adapted over the centuries to conform to new beliefs. RE', the sun god, accompanied by HORUS, the sky god, constituted the basis of the cult, which emerged in HELIOPOLIS. Other

SOKAR   the Memphite deity of creation.

Egyptian deities were also drawn into the solar religion: Thoth, Isis, Hathor and Wadjet. In time Osiris was linked to the cult as well.

The kings of the 4th and 5th Dynasties particularly revered the cult, and erected many sun temples in that period. From the reign of Ra'djedef (2528–2520 B.C.), kings declared themselves the "Sons of Re'," and the solar disk, emblem of the sun became the symbol of the kings.

The social implications of the cult were evident in the Pyramid Texts, which date to the 5th and 6th Dynasties (2465–2150 B.C.). In them Re' calls all Egyptian men and women to justice, equality, and to the understanding that death awaits them all in time. Even into the New Kingdom, the Ramessids bore names meaning "Re' fashioned him."

solar disk   See SOLAR CULT.

Son of Re' Name   See ROYAL NAMES.

Song of the Harper   See LAY OF THE HARPER.

Sopdu (also Sopdet)   an ancient Egyptian god and the star known to the Greeks as Sirius, the Dogstar. The appearance of Sopdu signaled the beginning of *akhet*, the season of the inundation of the Nile. Sopdu was also a divinity of the eastern desert and the god of the four corners of the earth, with HORUS, SETH and THOTH. When associated with Horus, the god was called the "Sharp Horus." The star was sometimes represented in a feminine form and was then associated with the goddess HATHOR.

Souls of Nekhen   mythical predynastic kings of HIERAKONPOLIS, believed to have become celestial beings in the afterlife; the guardians of Upper Egypt, as the SOULS OF PE (BUTO) were the guardians of Lower Egypt. The Souls were thought to walk as spirits beside the king on certain festivals and had to be greeted at each CORONATION ceremony. They were deemed the true ancestors of the pharaohs and had their own ritual centers in the capitals.

Souls of Pe   mythical predynastic kings of BUTO, thought to have become celestial beings imbued with powers and magical abilities. The Souls of Pe guarded Lower Egypt, as the SOULS OF NEKHEN protected the southern domain of Upper Egypt. The Souls of Pe and Nekhen were always visited and invoked at CORONATION ceremonies and during certain FESTIVALS. They had their own chamber in the capital and were held in high esteem as the founders of the nation.

SOLAR BOAT a typical representation of the sun god in his heavenly bark.

Speos Artemidos The Greek name given to the chapel constructed in a wadi near Beni Hasan in honor of the ancient Egyptian goddess PAKHT. HAT-SHEPSUT started the shrine, which was completed by TUTHMOSIS III (1460 B.C.) and refurbished by later kings. The shrine appears to have been connected to a previous structure of the goddess' cult; there is mention of the chapel having been restored. The Greeks associated Pakht with their own goddess Artemis, hence the name.

sphinx the form of a recumbent lion with the head of a royal personage. The sphinx emerged in the 4th Dynasty (2575–2465 B.C.). Later it was associated with the god Horemakhet (Horus of the Horizon), Harmachis in Greek, and remained popular throughout Egypt's history as the symbol of the king's power.

The Great Sphinx, measuring 75 feet from base to crown, is 150 feet in length. A text also associated with the Great Sphinx, the Inventory Stela, now in the Egyptian Museum in Cairo, describes the construction of the sacred figure. It is a crouching lion with outstretched paws and a human head, clad in the *nemes*, the striped head covering reserved for the kings in the early historical eras. KHEPHREN (2520–2494 B.C.) built the Great Sphinx at Giza. It was repaired by TUTHMOSIS IV of the 18th Dynasty (1401–1391 B.C.), who stopped there to rest while hunting in the region. A prince at the time, Tuthmosis had a dream in which the sphinx complained about its deteriorated condition and told him that he would become king when he restored the statue. The site was cleared of sand, and a stela was placed between the paws of the sphinx to commemorate the dream and the restoration. The Great Sphinx is currently being repaired.

One of the most unusual forms of sphinx is associated with Tanis, and depicts the creature with a rough mane and prominent ears. Such sphinxes date from the Middle Kingdom but were usurped by the Ramessids and taken to Tanis. Ram-headed sphinxes line the avenue leading to the first pylon at KARNAK.

stations of the gods the highly decorated stands, stages or daises built in the cities and towns of ancient Egypt to serve as resting places for the deities. When arks, statues, portable shrines and barks were carried through the streets of these cities on FESTIVAL days, priests could halt the processions at the stations, allowing the people an occasion to look upon the sacred objects. Purification and other ceremonies were conducted at each site, and in some cases the gods could be consulted by the faithful. In major cities of Egypt the patron deity was carried through the streets many times each month as part of the liturgical calendar.

stela the Greek word for a pillar or vertical tablet inscribed or decorated with reliefs. Such monuments were called *wedj* or *aha* and were used as mortuary or historical commemoratives. Stelae were made of wood in the early eras, but as that material became scarce and the skills of the artisans increased, stones were used. They were normally rounded at one end, but a stela could be made in any style.

In the tombs the mortuary stelae were placed in prominent positions. In most cases the stela was incorporated into the false door of the tomb. Others were free-standing pillars or tablets set into the tomb walls, listing the achievements of the inhabitant of the grave site. Stelae were used to designate boundaries, as in the city of el-'AMARNA, or specify partic-

SPHINX   symbol of ancient Egyptian royalty.

ular roles of temples and shrines. They have provided the world with detailed information about the historical eras of ancient Egypt.

Step Pyramid   the tomb at Saqqara of DJOSER (2630–2611 B.C.) of the 3rd Dynasty attributed to IMHOTEP, the king's vizier. It was the first Egyptian pyramid and the earliest stone building of its size in the world.

Originally conceived as a MASTABA, the usual form of tomb in that era, Imhotep instead fashioned a tower of mastabas in six levels, diminishing in size to form a pyramid. This layered structure reached 190 feet when completed. The base measured 350 feet from north to south and 400 from east to west.

Subterranean passages and chambers were adorned with fine reliefs and with blue faience tiles made to resemble the matted curtains of the royal residence at Memphis. The great shaft of the structure, leading to the burial chamber, was 92 feet long. The chamber at the bottom was 13 feet high, encased in granite. A granite plug sealed the passageway to the actual tomb. Mazes were also incorporated into the design in order to foil potential robbers. The pyramid stands in the center of a vast mortuary complex, enclosed

by walls that measured 1800 by 900 feet. The walls, carved to resemble the paneled facade of the royal residence, were covered with limestone and contained 211 bastions and 14 entrances. The main gateway led to an entrance hall 175 five feet long, decorated with columns. This hall, in turn, opened onto a vestibule with four pairs of columns. Another court held stones for the SED FESTIVAL.

A special chamber was designed to honor the patroness of Lower Egypt, with statues of cobras and appropriate reliefs. That chamber led to a chapel, which contained a false tomb, complete with a shaft, glazed tiles and inscriptions, followed by another court. A room of special interest incorporated into the complex was the *serdab*, the slitted chamber which contained a statue of Djoser, positioned so that the figure could witness the mortuary rituals being conducted in his honor by the funerary priests of the royal cult. This statue was the first life-sized representation of the human form in Egypt.

Two other buildings represented the Upper and Lower Kingdoms in the complex, which also contained smaller pyramids for queens and princes. Eleven shafts, some measuring up to 98 feet, were dug below these tombs, with connecting corridors measuring the same length. These pyramids and the great Step Pyramid were covered in limestone. Saqqara was in effect a miniature city, and priests and custodians served there for decades after the pharaoh was entombed.

steps   an ancient Egyptian symbol representing the staircase of ascension and the throne of the god OSIRIS. As amulets the steps were worn by the living and placed with the mummified remains of the deceased to assure their resurrection and entry into Osiris' eternal domain. (See LADDER.)

sun boat   by an early Egyptian cosmogonic myth, the mode by which the god RE' or the sun itself traveled through the sky into the realms of the night. The sun deity, whether personified as Re' or in its original form, was thought to travel across the sky on a ship. Sometimes this vessel was shown as a double raft. On his journey, Re' was accompanied by the circumpolar stars or by his own double. Sometimes he rowed the boat himself; sometimes he moved by MAGIC. *Heka*, magic, accompanied the sun in most myths.

The ENNEAD of HELIOPOLIS were gods who also accompanied the sun in its daily journey. The SOULS of NEKHEN and PE were mentioned in some myths as riding in the boat daily. In one early depiction the sun boat was a double serpent, its two heads forming the prow and the bow. The sun boat had many adventures during the day, and at night it faced all of the terrors of the darkness, when the dead rose up to tow the vessel through the waters. When the sun became Re', the boats were given specific names.

Sun's Eye   a symbol of all things good and beautiful in ancient Egypt. This insignia denoted the fact that all life along the Nile emanated from the sun. (See AMULET.)

Sun's Well   a pool in ancient HELIOPOLIS where the god RE' was supposed to bathe. It was the site of the original creation, where the deity rose as a LOTUS, a symbol of creation. (See COSMOGONY.)

Sutekh   an ancient Egyptian god, normally considered a form of the god SETH. RAMESSES II (1290–1224 B.C.) of the 19th Dynasty, a devotee of Sutekh, beseeched the god for good weather when the Hittite delegation arrived in Egypt to cement the alliance between the two nations.

Sweet Water Canal   the ancient Egyptian name for the canal dug in early times to link the Nile at Bubastis with the Wadi Tumilat, then to the Bitter Lakes and on to the Red Sea. There is evidence that this canal was in use before the New Kingdom, perhaps during the Middle Kingdom Period.

sycamore   a tree considered sacred in all eras by the Egyptians. The sycamore grew at the edge of the desert near Memphis in the Early Dynastic Period (2920–2575 B.C.) and was venerated as an abode of the goddess HATHOR, the "Lady of the Sycamore." Some religious texts indicate that a legend or myth had been developed concerning the tree. The souls of the dead were believed to take wing and rest in the sycamore. The tree was also involved in the cults of RE', Hathor, MUT and ISIS.

Syene   See ASWAN.

Tabuba (or Tabubna)   an ancient Egyptian literary character, supposedly the daughter of a Bastite priest in the reign of RAMESSES II (1290–1224 B.C.) of the 19th Dynasty. She was beautiful enough to ensnare a royal prince but then subjected him to unspeakable torments. (See TALE OF PRINCE SETNA.)

Tadhukipa   a Mitanni princess who was sent to marry AMENHOTEP III (1391–1353 B.C.) of the 18th Dynasty and who is believed by some to be Queen KIYA, the wife of AKHENATEN. The niece of the Mitanni princess Khirgipa, who had married Amenhotep earlier, Tadhukipa was sent to Thebes and arrived either shortly before or after Amenhotep's death. She is mentioned in a letter from Queen Tiy as having been married to Akhenaten.

Tait   an ancient Egyptian goddess, the patroness of linen weaving, honored in AKHMIN, the center of such industry. When the goddess was associated with the cult of OSIRIS, she was called Isis-Tait. She was supposed to have aided ISIS in wrapping the body of the god when SETH slew him. Tait was depicted as a beautiful woman carrying chests of mortuary linen. (See BYSSUS.)

Tale of the Doomed Prince   a New Kingdom story found in the Papyrus Harris 500, in the British Museum. The tale concerns a prince who is warned of his fate. He is to be attacked by a serpent, and other creatures sent by divine powers. The prince goes in search of his fate, aided by a maiden. Love and loyalty are the key elements of the story, two virtues much admired by the Egyptians throughout their history. The conclusion of the story, however, is missing.

Tale of the Eloquent Peasant   See ELOQUENT PEASANT.

Tale of Khufu and the Magicians   a literary text discovered in the Westcar Papyrus, including the prophecy of the rise of the 5th Dynasty. The tale concerns KHUFU of the 4th Dynasty (2551–2528 B.C.) and his companions, who exchange stories about their own era and the reign of SNOFRU, Khufu's father. Mysterious and exotic, the stories include descriptions of pleasure boats and maidens clad only in fish nets.

Tale of Prince Setna   a text from Ptolemaic and Roman papyri concerning a son of RAMESSES II of the 19th Dynasty (1290–1224 B.C.) who sees a woman named Tabuba (or Tabubna), daughter of a Bastite priest. She is so beautiful that he loses his heart to her, unaware of the fact that she has cast a spell over him. Eventually the prince is forced to slay his children for her love and to endure other torments and shame before wakening to realize that the agony he has experienced is only a dream.

Tale of the Shepherds (or Herdsmen)   a fragmentary tale preserved in the Egyptian Museum, Berlin, which relates the experience of an Egyptian shepherd on the banks the Nile. Beside the river the shepherd confronts a goddess, who hides from his prying eyes in a shrub.

Tale of Sinuhe the Sailor   See SINUHE THE SAILOR.

Tale of the Shipwrecked Sailor   discovered in a papyrus from the Middle Kingdom, the story of an expedition returning by sea from the southern domains. On board, a sailor recounts his adventures when his boat is damaged and sunk during a storm and he alone survives the ordeal, swimming to an island. A gigantic hooded snake rules the island, the only survivor of an attack by comets or a falling star. The serpent counsels the sailor and inspires in him patience and valor. When a ship comes within sight of the island, the serpent restores him to his fellow men with gifts of ointments, myrrh, animals and other precious objects, all of which the sailor delivers to the king. The papyrus upon which the tale was copied is preserved in the Hermitage collection in Leningrad.

Tale of the Two Brothers   from the 19th Dynasty Papyrus Orbiney in the British Museum, considered one of the finest examples of Egyptian narrative literature. The story is an account of the adventures of two gods. Anup, believed to represent ANUBIS, and BATA or Batu, a predynastic god, are caught in a triangle when Anup's wife tries to seduce Bata and fails. In revenge she claims that he assaulted her. Anup sets out to kill Bata, who flees. The god Shu, seeing what evil is taking place, separates the two brothers by a stream filled with crocodiles, and there Batu explains what really happened. Anup, ashamed, goes home to kill his wife and to throw her body to the dogs. Bata goes on a journey and has many adventures, finally siring the future king of Egypt. His journey is religious in nature and much loved by the Egyptians for its didactic overtones. The tale was reported to be in the library of SETI II of the 19th Dynasty (1214–1204 B.C.).

Tangur   a site above the Second Cataract of the Nile, where an inscription dating to the reign of TUTHMOSIS I (1504–1492 B.C.) of the 18th Dynasty was discovered. The VICEROY OF NUBIA in that era put up the inscription to commemorate an expedition to the site.

Tanis   the modern San-el-Hagar, called Djananet by the ancient Egyptians, an enormous mound in the eastern Delta. The city was once sacred to SETH and was a NOME capital. Its location on the shores of Lake Menzala made it an important port. At one time the city was inhabited by the HYKSOS and their Asiatic allies, who entered Egypt during the Second Intermediate Period. A temple was discovered on the site, surrounded by double walls and rows of obelisks. The shrine had three pylons and a hypostyle hall. Four colossal statues and a colonnade with palm style columns all bear the seal of RAMESSES II (1290–1224 B.C.) of the 19th Dynasty. Artifacts from the 12th Dynasty (c. 1991–1778 B.C.) were also discovered at Tanis, including sphinxes, placed there by the Ramessids.

Ta'o I (Djehuti'o) (Senakhtenre')   the 13th king of the 17th Dynasty at THEBES, ruling contemporaneously with the Hyksos 15th and 16th Dynasties in

Tanis Sphinx.

the Delta. His queen, a commoner named TETISHERI, would gain lasting fame as the mother of the New Kingdom. Ta'o I probably resided in the palace at Deir el-Ballas, north of Thebes. He was buried in the Theban necropolis. His heir was TA'O II.

Ta'o II (Djehuti'o) (Sekenenre') called "the Brave" by his contemporaries, the 14th king of the Theban 17th Dynasty, ruling Egypt contemporaneously with the HYKSOS 15th and 16th Dynasties in the Delta. The son of TA'O I and Queen TETISHERI, Ta'o II received a message from APOPHIS of the Hyksos capital in AVARIS stating that the hippopotami in the sacred pool at Thebes kept him awake with their snoring. The Thebans took the message as an insult and began a war against the Hyksos. Ta'o II campaigned but died soon after the start of his crusade, either in ambush or in battle. His mummified remains show the evidence of blows by battleaxes, spears and lances. His ribs and vertebrae were fractured and his skull was opened. He was buried in a cartonnage coffin in Thebes rather hurriedly. Ta'o's wife was Queen AH-HOTEP, his sister, who bore him two sons, KAMOSE and 'AHMOSE, and many daughters. When Ta'o died, Kamose inherited the throne and the crusade to oust the Asiatics from Egypt.

Sekenenre'-Ta'o II's cartonnage mask from his Theban tomb.

Tarif a site on the western shore of the Nile opposite Thebes, containing mastabas from the Old Kingdom Period and SAFF tombs and other graves from the 11th Dynasty.

Tarkhan a site on the western bank of the Nile in the region of the FAIYUM. A necropolis there dates to the Old Kingdom. There are also predynastic tombs in the region, containing the names of various rulers, including Na'rmer, and elaborate funerary regalia was discovered on this site.

Tatenen (Tenen) an earth god of ancient Egypt whose name meant "the Risen Land." He was believed to have emerged from the watery abyss at the moment of creation, and is called the "Revered One" in temple texts. Tatenen brought two staffs with him into the world to repel the serpent from the great PRIMEVAL MOUND, as well as a mace, called the "Great White of the Earth Creator" and dedicated to the falcon. The mace was provided with magical powers and was considered in some eras to be a deity in its own right. Tatenen was also credited with bringing the famed DJED pillar into the world, the symbol that would be connected with the cult of OSIRIS throughout Egypt's history.

Taueret also called Taweret (Thueris in Greek), a goddess of ancient Egypt, the patroness of childbirth in most eras. Taueret was depicted as a hippopotamus, sometimes dressed in the robes of a queen, with a lion's mane. Her head was partly a crocodile's, and she had the feet of a lion. She could also appear as a goddess with the body of a hippopotamus but with the head of a lion. Then she carried daggers which were used against the enemy of the Egyptians, spiritual or mortal. She carried a *sa* amulet, a symbol of protection. Thebes was a cult center of the goddess, and in the New Kingdom and later eras she enjoyed popularity.

Tchanuni an official of the 18th Dynasty, serving TUTHMOSIS IV (1401–1391 B.C.). He was a royal scribe and then a military commander. Tchanuni was buried at Thebes.

Tchay an official during the reign of MERNEPTAH (1224–1214 B.C.). Tchay was a royal scribe for the court and for the office of messages. His tomb on the western shore of Thebes is famous for its reliefs of the mortuary texts. The sun bark, baboons, sacred trees and other objects of veneration depict the religious images of his era.

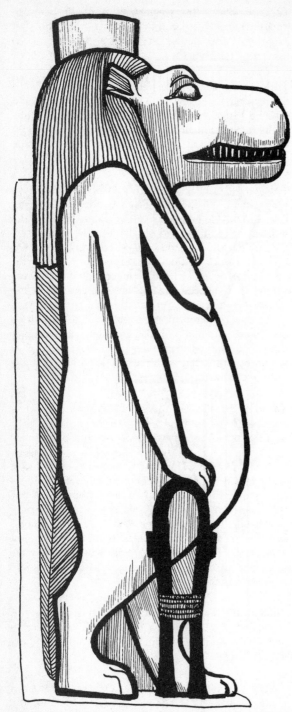

Tauret in the form of the divine hippopotamus, a favorite guise of this Egyptian goddess.

Tefnut an ancient Egyptian goddess, considered originally to be the twin sister of the god SHU. In predynastic times she was the wife of a god named Tefen. In HELIOPOLIS Tefnut was linked to the cre-

ative powers of the god PTAH, serving as a means of bringing life into the world. She also represents the space between heaven and earth. In some eras Tefnut was associated with MA'AT and was viewed as a spiritual power rather than a divine being. She was normally the goddess of the dew or rain, depicted in the form of a lioness or as a woman with the head of a lion, similar to PAKHT. Tefnut supported the sky with Shu and received the newly dawned sun each morning.

tekenu a unique mortuary object used in rituals for the dead. The *tekenu* was made of reeds and other vegetation, shaped into the form of a human being. Dragged on a sled by oxen to the burial site, the *tekenu* was burned ceremoniously. This probably represented the custom of earlier eras when upon the king's deaths their servants and courtiers were perhaps sacrificed in order to accompany the royal personages into the realms of eternal bliss. The *tekenu* assumed the guilt of the deceased and in being destroyed purified the dead for eternity. (See MORTUARY RITUALS.)

Tell-el Yahudiyeh a site in the Delta, some 25 miles northeast of Cairo, which was occupied by the HYKSOS during the Second Intermediate Period. There, a mound has yielded up pottery of Palestinian and Syrian design and even some Minoan ware. The pottery and other artifacts are believed to be evidence of trade between Syria, Palestine, Crete and Egypt during the period of Hyksos domination in the northeastern region of Egypt.

Tem a queen of the 11th Dynasty, married to MENTUHOTPE II (2061–2010 B.C.), believed to be the mother of MENTUHOTPE III. Her tomb at DEIR EL-BAHRI is large and beautifully decorated. The largest of the female graves sites, Tem's burial chamber contained a SARCOPHAGUS made of alabaster and sandstone.

temenos the Greek word for the precincts of the Egyptian temples.

temples religious structures considered the "horizon" of a divine being, the point at which the god came into existence during the creation. Thus, each temple had a link to the past, and the rituals conducted within its court were formulas handed down for generations. The temple was also a mirror of the universe, and a representation of the Primeval Mound where creation began.

Originally the temples were crude huts, copies of the predynastic structures that began to appear in the Nile Valley and in the Delta. The huts were

TEMPLE   the interior of a typical New Kingdom temple.

surrounded by short walls, and the emblems of the god, the totems, were placed on a pole in front of the gateway. Normally, early temples had two poles, bearing flags and insignias. When the Egyptians learned to batter (or gently slope) walls, and to raise up enormous structures of stone, the temples became great monuments of faith. Temples and tombs were the only buildings in ancient Egypt to be made of durable materials. Some temples were created as box-like shrines, with central courts for statues. Some were elaborately columned, particularly the massive temples of the various state gods. Still others evolved out of shrines originally for the BARKS OF THE GODS.

The basic plan of the Egyptian temple, thought to have been devised by the gods themselves, did not vary much in any given area. Most temples had a brick enclosure wall, then a PYLON, the slightly battered or slanted gateway fitted with grooves for the mandatory flagstaffs. The pylons of the larger temples had doors originally made of wood, but in the later eras these were fashioned out of bronze or gold. After the pylon was the forecourt or reception area. When the temple was open for the occasional public ceremony, the people would enter through this court. In the beginning they were simple squares; in time they became great colonnades.

Other vestibules, colonnades, courts and chambers opened onto the front entrance, usually leading backwards at a slight incline. The hypostyle halls that dominated the major shrines such as KARNAK were not inclined but part of the entrance structures. These opened onto the smaller rooms, which were never opened to the public and never used as stages for major cultic rituals. Each new section of the temple was raised higher from the ground so that its rooms became smaller, dimmer and more mysterious. Such chambers were part of an avenue of rooms that led steadily upward to the higher, smaller and darker sanctuaries. Finally one reached the holy of holies, the single room representing the Primeval Mound: remote, shadowy and secure against the curiosity of mankind. Few Egyptians saw such shrines. The gods were hidden from man, and this divine attribute was maintained throughout Egypt's history. Egyptians did not feel compelled to enter the secret rooms or to gaze upon the image of the god. They welcomed the mysterious manifestations of the divine being as they witnessed them in the cultic rites and in the architecture of the temple. The use of aquatic plant designs in the columns and lower wall reliefs alluded to the watery abyss out of which the universe was created. The river, the sun and the verdant earth were all represented in the chambers and courts, making the temple precinct a complete microcosm.

Some alterations in temple architecture were made, but basically it adhered to the general plan. The original shrines of the Early Dynastic Period (2920–2575 B.C.) had three contiguous chambers leading to the sanctuary and hidden shrine of the god. During the Old Kingdom (2575–2134 B.C.) the number of such chambers was increased to five. By the New Kingdom Period the temples could hold any number of rooms. The central shrines in the New Kingdom (1550–1070 B.C.) were box-like, carved out of granite blocks that weighed 50 or more tons. These temples also contained magazines, storerooms, offices for the priests and scribes, administrative bureaus and a brick-lined pit for the barks of the god. The larger temples also contained sacred lakes.

When a new temple was dedicated, a ritual and celebration were conducted, attended by the king or his representative. All of the gods of the past were depicted by priests wearing masks, or by tokens of the divine beings in attendance. Every god of Egypt thus took part in the consecration of the new shrine, as the gods had manifested themselves at the beginning of the world. There were also particular deities who were involved in the creation of new temples and were thus invoked on that solemn occasion. Rituals were held every day in the existing temples of Egypt, and the priests followed a traditional pattern of worship and service, with the accent on cleansing and purification. (See TEMPLE RITUALS, PRIESTS.)

temple models   miniature stone shrines built as offerings to a particular god. One such model was discovered at Tell-el Yahudiyeh, dating to the reign of SETI I (1306–1290 B.C.) of the 19th Dynasty. Temple models were fashioned with pylons, statues, halls and even obelisks, and were placed in real shrines as tributes. The models were inscribed with the name of the donor and were called the "holy of holies." Others were blocks built out of stone, in which holes had been fashioned to allow the devotees to insert obelisks, walls, pylons, statues and other traditional temple adornments.

temple rituals   ceremonies conducted at ancient Egyptian shrines and temples without significant changes over the centuries. Normally the rites began with the offering of incense at the noon hour, although in some eras the rites began early in the morning, especially if attended by the king personally. The incense offered in the morning was myrrh when that substance was available. At night the incense was of a type called *kyphi*. The censor used

NEW KINGDOM TEMPLES

The New Kingdom was the period in which the massive temples so familiar to visitors to Egypt were raised up. Several elements were constant in these temples, all of which served a particular religious purpose and demonstrated the power of the pharaoh and the particular god being honored. These basic elements were:

- a *landing stage* or a small dock directly at the water's edge for the barges that carried the various images of the gods in procession on special festival days. The form of this landing could vary.
- an *avenue of sphinxes,* which led from the landing or to another temple nearby. KARNAK was linked at one time to the LUXOR temple by rows of sphinxes.
- *flagstaffs,* relics of the predynastic shrines, when the totems of the nome family and the nome deity were positioned before the entrances to signal the god being honored. Flagstaffs were tall and were sometimes accompanied by statues of the reigning king or his ancestors.
- *pylons,* slightly battered (or sloping) gateways, stood at the front of the temples. At ABU SIMBEL the pylons were enhanced by magnificent colossal statues of RAMESSES II and NEFERTARI.
- *enclosures,* brick walls, sometimes surrounding gardens or sacred pools.
- *forecourts* were normally constructed just behind the pylons. If there was more than one pylon in the temple, as in the case of Karnak, each such gateway had its own court. Columns and statues adorned these courts.
- *hypostyle halls* adjoining the courts. These vast columned halls, either roofed or open to the air, were part of the main temple. The hypostyle halls were an early type of nave. Some hypostyle halls opened onto special chambers reserved for the barks of the gods.
- the *sanctuaries* of the temples were the furthest back of the inner areas. These were enclosed by walls and contained chapels in which the image of the god was kept. Most sanctuaries had three chapels.

in the ceremony was a bronze pan, which contained pellets burning in a heated dish or bowl.

The dressing and cleaning of the god's statue and shrine were performed each day. Most statues of the gods were clothed in colors deemed appropriate to their particular cult or region. Food was then offered to the god. The trays of vegetables, meat, fruits, breads, cakes etc. were taken the next day to the various mortuary complexes in the region or to the tombs of the deceased Egyptians who had contracted with priests to conduct daily rituals on their behalf.

When the god's meal ended, the temple was swept, scrubbed and then closed. The floors of the temple were normally sanded and washed every day by lesser-ranked priests. At night the god was again saluted and offered gifts and tributes, but the sanctuary, the chamber in which the image of the god rested, was not opened a second time. It was enough for the priests to recite the prayers and hymns in front of his shrine.

When the god was taken out of the temple for a procession or a visit to another temple, the queen or ranking woman of the area escorted or greeted the statue. Sistrums, drums, horns and other musical instruments accompanied the god and were played during rituals.

Teti the founder of the 6th Dynasty (2323–2291 B.C.). The circumstances of his accession to the throne are obscure, but his queen, Ipwet, is believed to have been a daughter of WENIS, the last king of the 5th Dynasty. The historian Manetho claimed that Teti was murdered by his own guards. Many of the court officials of Wenis, however, remained in their positions in Teti's reign.

Teti inscribed his name at Hatnub and granted land to Abydos, but little other documentation survives his reign. His pyramidal complex at SAQQARA, called the "Prison Pyramid" by modern locals, contained a sistrum. A statue, fashioned out of pink and black granite was also found. Perhaps a portrait of Teti, the statue is now in the Egyptian Museum in Cairo. His queens were Khuit and Sesheshet, and Ipwet, probably the ranking consort, gave birth to his heir, PEPI I.

Tetisheri a queen of the 17th Dynasty in Thebes, the commoner wife of TA'O I (date unknown). She was called the "Mother of the New Kingdom" because of her influence over its founders, her son (TA'O II) and grandsons (KAMOSE and 'AHMOSE). From the palace at Deir el-Ballas, Tetisheri raised the warriors who would oust the Asiatics from the Delta. She lived to the age of 70, and decrees were issued

TETISHERI "mother of the New Kingdom," from a statue in the British Museum.

concerning her service to the nation. 'Ahmose granted her a great estate and tomb with priests and servants to conduct mortuary rituals in her honor. A cenotaph was also built for her at Abydos. The British Museum possesses a statue of Tetisheri.

Tety See KHABA.

Thaneni an official of the 18th Dynasty, serving Tuthmosis III (1479–1425 B.C.). A scribe and artistic overseer, Thaneni was entrusted with the inscriptions of the king's annals, detailing Tuthmosis III's wars and the beginning of the empire, on the walls of KARNAK. Thaneni's tomb on the western shore of Thebes gives an account of his deeds and his honors.

Thebes the capital of Egypt during the New Kingdom and the seat of the Theban warrior clans, located on the eastern shore of the Nile, some 400 miles south of modern Cairo. Originally the city was called Uast or Waset, and was built on a flat plain. Thebes was not important as a cult center in the early historical eras. Its present name came from the Greeks, who also called the city Diospolis Magna, the "Great City of the Gods." Homer celebrated it as the city of a hundred gates.

During the Old Kingdom, the city was a minor trading post, but the local clans kept the area secure when the First Intermediate Period saw chaos in the rest of the nation. The Theban lands of that era declared their independence and gave rise to a succession of princes who waged war to unite the nomes and provinces again, with MENTUHOTPE II (2061–2010 B.C.) of the 11th Dynasty capturing the capital of the KHETY clan and putting an end to the civil unrest.

It is believed that Thebes served as a joint capital in that era, but the kings appeared to have taken up residence in a number of locations. The 12th Dynasty, started by another Theban, AMENEMHET I (1991–1962), established a new capital on the border between the Upper and Lower Egypt. Governors were in residence in Thebes, ruling over the southern territories for the throne.

During the Second Intermediate Period (1640–1532 B.C.), when the HYKSOS dominated the Delta territories, the Thebans again stood firm, denying the Asiatics access to most of the southern domains. In the early days there was a truce between the two forces, and the Thebans took their herds into the Delta to graze there without incident. The Hyksos were also able to sail past Thebes to trade with the Nubians below the cataracts. The truce ended with an insult hurled by APOPHIS at TA'O II of Thebes (c. 1560 B.C.). Theban armies began to march on the Hyksos strongholds. When Ta'o died in battle or in an ambush, his son KAMOSE entered the war and rolled back the Hyksos forces. He died and was succeeded by his brother, 'AHMOSE I, who took the city of AVARIS, the Hyksos capital and chased the Asiatics out of the land. He even sent his armies against the temporary stronghold of the Hyksos at Sharuhen in Palestine, once again chasing the Asiatics all the way to Syria.

By this time the god Amon received considerable support from the ruling clan, and the city of Thebes became the deity's cult center. The shrines, temples and buildings erected in the city gave it a reputation for splendor and beauty that lasted for centuries. All other cities were judged "after the pattern of Thebes." The Tuthmossids of the 18th Dynasty (1550–1307 B.C.) lavished care and wealth upon Thebes, making it the nation's capital, although Memphis remained an administrative center of government and a temporary residence of the royal clan. During the era of AKHENATEN (1353–1335 B.C.) Thebes was abandoned for el-'AMARNA, to the north. His death, however, signaled a return to Thebes and a resumption of the building projects and adornment of the temples, shrines and royal residences. The western shore of Thebes became a vast and beautiful necropolis, with stunning mortuary complexes built at DEIR EL-BAHRI (where Mentuhotpe II had erected his mortuary temple in the 11 Dynasty) and in the Valleys of the Kings and Queens.

When the Ramessids came to power, they built a new capital on the site of Avaris, their clan home. Thebes, however, remained popular not only as a residence during certain months of the year but also as the site of the royal burial grounds. Amon remained powerful as well, and the kings continued to adorn the temples and shrines of the god throughout Egyptian history.

Thent Hep   a royal woman of the 18th Dynasty, married to King 'AHMOSE I (1550–1525 B.C.). but holding lesser rank in the court. Thent Hep was the mother of Princess Hent-Temehu.

theophanies   animal or serpent images chosen by the ancient Egyptians to represent the various deities. The animals were chosen for their particular strength, virtue or appearance, considered attributes of the god. Some theophanies date to the predynastic areas and others evolved over the centuries. (See GODS AND GODDESSES, RELIGION, and PRIESTS.)

Theshen   an official of the 5th Dynasty, serving in the reign of SAHURE' (2458–2446 B.C.). Theshen was a treasurer, serving the king also as a counselor and companion. His tomb was prepared for him when he was a small child, as a gift from his father, Zezemonekh. Theshen cherished the tomb and added adornments over his lifetime.

thet or (Tiyet)   an insignia of the cult of ISIS, known as the goddess' girdle. It served as an AMULET for the living and for the dead of ancient Egypt.

Thethi   an official of the 11th Dynasty, serving in the reign of King INYOTEF II (c. 2131–2082 B.C.). Thethi was attached to the royal court at Thebes, when the INYOTEF clan ruled Upper Egypt before the reunification of the lands was accomplished by MENTUHOTPE II. He was the chief treasurer and companion of the king, and he also supervised the building of the king's mortuary complex. Thethi was buried near the monarch on the western shore of Thebes.

Thinis   called Girga in modern times, a city north of ABYDOS that was destroyed over the centuries. A brick mastaba from the 4th Dynasty was discovered nearby. Once the home of valiant warriors, the city gave its name to the first kings of Egypt in the Archaic Period, called the Thinite royal dynasties. A battle was fought at Thinis during the war between the 10th and 11th Dynasties. Prince Herunefer, a royal Theban, died when the city rebelled against Theban domination and had to be subdued and forced into the Upper Kingdom confederation again.

Thinite Period   See THINIS and EGYPT, HISTORICAL PERIODS.

Thoth   the ancient Egyptian god of learning and wisdom, associated with the moon. He was called the "Lord of Heavens," "Beautiful of Night" and the "Silent Being" in various eras. He was normally depicted as a man with the head of an ibis, considered his theophany, although he was also associated with baboons and could take their form. He was honored at first as a scribe god at HERMOPOLIS, and was then given greater cultic prominence, assuming the form of dog-headed apes in many rituals.

Thoth was also a protector of priest-physicians, and was associated in some temples with the inundation of the Nile. His great cultic festival was celebrated at the New Year. He was considered skilled in magic and became the patron of all scribes throughout the nation. Thoth appears in the HORUS legends and was depicted in every age as the god who "loved truth and hated abomination."

Thoth's Book (or the Book of Thoth)   a collection of 42 papyrus rolls, supposedly dictated by the god. Two of the papyri were hymns in praise of Thoth, and four concerned matters of astrology and astronomy, listing the accumulated lore of the priests in these sciences. The skilled astronomers of every temple had to memorize the texts included in these rolls. Ten of the papyri were concerned with religious traditions, and these were consulted for all rituals and festival celebrations, having been handed down from generation to generation. Ten more papyri discussed priestly obligations and regulations.

The actual books concerned philosophy and medicine. All of the others were preliminary texts, given to the priests and scholars to complement the documents. The Book of Thoth was never recovered. It was mentioned only in a few papyri, but the location of the papyri text was not disclosed. Because of its occult and esoteric nature, the Book of Thoth has been prominent in modern interpretations of Egyptian magic, even though the actual texts are not available for study.

Thoth, the god of wisdom and the patron of temple scribes.

throwing sticks   curved hunting weapons used by the ancient Egyptians. The sticks were aimed at ducks and other waterfowl. They were not boomerangs, although they resemble that weapon.

Thuity an 18th Dynasty official serving in the reign of HATSHEPSUT (1473–1458 B.C.) and possibly in the reign of her father, TUTHMOSIS I, as well as during the reign of TUTHMOSIS II. An hereditary nobleman, Thuity succeeded the famous architect Ineni in service to the crown. He also held other court titles and ranks in the temple of the god AMON. He led an expedition to PUNT for Hatshepsut and was involved in her many building projects. Thuity was buried on the western shore of Thebes.

Ti known as Tiy in some records, an official of the 5th Dynasty, serving in the reign of KAKAI (2446–2426 B.C.). Ti's tomb has become one of the most famous sites in Egypt because of its inscriptions and reliefs which are elaborate depictions of daily life and mortuary legends. Located in Saqqara, the tomb also contained a painted statue of Ti, standing almost 6½ feet high. Ti was married to Princess Neferhetepes, the daughter of Kakai. His sons inherited the royal rank.

Tia a princess of the 19th Dynasty, the sister of RAMESSES II (c. 1290–1224 B.C.) and the daughter of SETI I. Princess Tia married an official named Tia, who was a royal scribe. They were buried together at Saqqara, in a tomb near the mortuary complex of HOREMHAB.

Time of the Gods the Egyptian term for the predynastic period. The Time of the Gods referred to the reigns of certain deities, especially those who had relinquished their earthly powers to live in the sky.

Timsah called Timseh in some lists, a lake in the eastern Delta of ancient Egypt, adjacent to the Suez Canal. (See LAKES.)

Tiy a queen of the 18th Dynasty, married to AMENHOTEP III (1391–1353 b). The daughter of Yuia, a provincial priest of Akhmin, and Tuia, a servant of the queen mother, MUTEMWIYA, Tiy probably married Amenhotep while he was a prince. She is believed to have been only 11 or 12 at the time. She was intelligent and diligent, the first queen of Egypt to have her name on official acts, even on the announcement of the king's marriage to a foreign princess.

Giving birth to Akhenaten and a number of royal daughters, Tiy urged her oldest daughter, Princess SITAMUN, to marry the king. It is believed that she did this in order to ensure royal heirs to the throne.

Amenhotep III built a pleasure palace for Tiy and

Queen Tiy, wife of Amenhotep III and mother of Akhenaten, from a Theban statue.

for other members of the royal family at MALKATA, on the western shore of Thebes. He retired to his own palace with his women and allowed her to see to the affairs of state with counselors and officials. Tiy was mentioned by several kings of other lands in their correspondence, having been made known to them in her official dealings. She was widowed at the age of 48. Akhenaten retired to 'AMARNA, and for a time Tiy lived there. Depictions of her show a forceful woman with a sharp chin, deep-set eyes and a firm mouth.

Tiye a queen of the 20th Dynasty, married to RAMESSES III (c. 1194–1163 B.C.). She was involved in the HAREM plot, which sought to assassinate the king and place her son on the throne of Egypt, and was mentioned in the Juridical papyrus of Turin. The plot against the king was discovered, and the queen and other members of the cabal were tried in a royal court. Nothing is known of the fate of Queen Tiye in the affair.

Tjel modern Tell Abu Seifa, a site near el-Qantara, the original northeastern frontier town of ancient

Egypt. It was the start of the military road to Egypt's Palestinian domains. Nine fortified wells dotted the road from Tjel to Rafa, the first Asiatic town, which was located some 120 miles from the Egyptian border.

Tjemehu   a tribe of Libyans depicted in Egyptian reliefs. These people were blond and lived along the western borders of Egypt in many eras. (See LIBYA.)

Tjuroy   an official of the 18th Dynasty, serving 'Ahmose I (1550–1525 B.C.) and probably AMENHOTEP I. Tjuroy was the son of 'AHMOSE-SITAYET, the VICE-ROY OF NUBIA. An hereditary nobleman, he inherited his father's titles and the office of regulating the affairs of the lands below the cataracts.

Tod   a site south of Thebes on the eastern shore of the Nile that contained the remains of a temple dedicated to the god MONT. The shrine dates to the 12th Dynasty and is credited to SENWOSRET I (1972–1926 B.C.). Seals and CARTOUCHES from that dynasty were discovered there, along with cylinders. An earlier shrine from the Old Kingdom (2575–2134 B.C.) was also found at Tod, as well as Greco-Roman monuments.

tomb   the structure built by the Egyptians for their mortuary rituals and for the burial of their dead. The early tombs of the Egyptians, in both the north and south, were dug out of the soil on the fringes of the deserts. Several such burial sites have been discovered, and one entire setting is now in the British Museum. The bodies were laid in the ground with pottery, personal items and weapons, following the customs of other primitive peoples. In time, however, the funerary offerings and the regalia accompanying the corpses demanded more room, as the mortuary rituals became more sophisticated. The Egyptians began building MASTABAS, tombs made out of dried bricks, with shafts and burial chambers dug into the ground. The main level of the mastaba contained a room for ceremonies and then an additional

room, a SERDAB, used to position a statue of the deceased so that his spirit could witness the services being offered in his name.

The STEP PYRAMID at SAQQARA started the phase of royal pyramids, but these vast complexes, some the size of small cities, were reserved only for royalty and their immediate associates. Commoners and the lesser nobles continued to build their tombs at the edge of the desert, although cliff tombs were popular in many NOMES. Others built mastabas in the desert, and these were accompanied by CENOTAPHS, or false tombs, constructed for religious purposes, to honor a particular god or region. Such cenotaphs were discovered in the necropolis areas of ABYDOS and at GEBEL SILSILA

Temples were used in conjunction with tombs at the start of the New Kingdom, and it became evident that such sites were vulnerable to robbers. AMEN-HOTEP I (1525–1504 B.C.) decided to use the cliffs in the VALLEY OF THE KINGS on the western shore of Thebes as his burial site. Others in the dynasty imitated him, and the VALLEY OF THE QUEENS was also opened for the royal women and princes. The tombs of these individuals were maintained by mortuary priests, contracted and supported by the will of the deceased or by royal decree. The priests performed daily rituals of offerings and prayers at these sites, and entire families continued in service at the tombs as hereditary priests. (See MORTUARY RITUALS, PRIESTS, PYRAMIDS; see also ETERNITY.)

tomb balls   clay objects discovered in ancient Egyptian tombs, all marked with the hieroglyph for "contract" or "seal." These balls are believed to have represented the contracts drawn up on behalf of the deceased and his or her family with the mortuary priests. Such priests were contracted to continue daily mortuary rituals at the tombs. Some of the tomb balls contained bits of papyrus and linen. They were probably deposited in the tomb by the priests as insignias of good faith, thus binding the contractual agreement in the presence of the dead. (See MORTU-ARY RITUALS.)

Tombos   a strategically located island north of the Third Cataract of the Nile where TUTHMOSIS I of the 18th Dynasty (1504–1492 B.C.) established a garrison and left a stela to commemorate his victories. Tuthmosis' stela depicted not only his Nubian victories but his military exploits in Asiatic lands, including his visit to the Euphrates River. (See TUTHMOSIS I.)

Tomb Robbery Trial   conducted in the reign of RAMESSES IX (1131–1112 B.C.) of the 20th Dynasty,

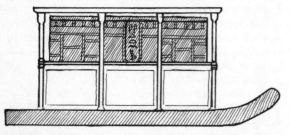

Mortuary sledge, used to transport coffins to the tombs.

and reflecting the decline of the Egyptian government in that era, the trial came about as a result of investigations demanded by PASER, the mayor of Thebes, over vandalized tombs. He suffered abuse and harrassment as a result of his insistence, especially from Prince PAWERO, who was the head of the necropolis sites and the necropolis police of that era. Investigations continued, and eventually the involvement of higher-ranked officials was uncovered. The Abbott Papyrus gives some details about the investigation and about the tombs searched for desecration and vandalism.

totemism See GODS AND GODDESSES.

Tract of Re' an area in the eastern Delta, near the HYKSOS capital of AVARIS, that was the home of the Ramessid clan. It was later honored by many monuments and buildings. (See PER-RAMESSES.)

trade the system of economic and artistic exchange that existed between Egypt and its neighbors from the Predynastic Period through the New Kingdom (1550–1070 B.C.). Such trade dates to the eras before the unification of Egypt, c. 3000 B.C., as evidenced by objects discovered in sites from that time. The NA'RMER PALETTE, for example, with its depiction of monsters and entwined long-necked serpents, is distinctively Mesopotamian in design. Knife handles from the same period demonstrate further Mesopotamian influences, brought about probably by an exchange of trade goods and artistic values. Mesopotamian CYLINDER SEALS were found in NAQADA II sites. It is possible that trade was not the basis for the appearance of such goods in Egypt; there are some who theorize that they were brought into Egypt by migrant Mesopotamians.

Early evidence of actual trade missions to Lebanon, no doubt for wood and cedar oil, dates to the reign of 'ADJIB of the 1st Dynasty (c. 2700 B.C.). Syrian-style pottery has also been found in tombs from this period. Such trade was probably conducted by sea, as the Asiatic Bedouins in the SINAI made land-based caravans dangerous. Egypt was trading with the Libyans in the Early Dynastic Period (2920–2575 B.C.), probably for olive oil. The kings also fought to maintain Egypt's western borders and to subjugate the Libyans, called the Hatiu-a in that period.

NUBIA was an early trading partner. DJER (c. 2900 B.C.), the second king of the 1st Dynasty, is reported to have taken part in a battle at WADI HALFA, where two villages were subdued. KHA'SEKHEMWY, who united Egypt during his reign (c. 2650 B.C.), conducted punitive campaigns there as well, probably

to safeguard the trade centers being operated in the region. Ebony and ivory were prized by the Egyptians, who gave the Nubians copper tools, jewelry and amulets in return. Some local Nubian chiefs appear to have served as trade agents for the Egyptians, no doubt for a percentage of all goods brought to the centers by the outlying natives. These chiefs grew wealthy, as the Nubian Soyala grave sites indicate. The Egyptians established a trading settlement at BUHEN, at the Second Cataract, in the 2nd Dynasty, probably to provide a center for the caravans arriving from the interior regions.

The adventures of HARKHAF in the 6th Dynasty (c. 2245 B.C.) are well documented. He brought back incense, ebony, oils, panther skins, elephant tusks and a marvelous dancing dwarf, which was the delight of the boy-king PEPI II (2246–2152 B.C.).

In the Middle Kingdom, after MENTUHOTPE II had reunited Egypt in 2040 B.C., the trading centers began to flourish again. Expeditions were sent to PUNT in almost every reign, and a shipbuilding operation on the Red Sea was begun to facilitate them. Contact had been made with Punt as early as the 5th Dynasty (2465–2323 B.C.), as reported by the PALERMO STONE. In the Middle Kingdom the Egyptians had contact with many of the Mediterranean nations, perhaps even Crete, called Kheftiu by the Egyptians. Minoan pottery was discovered in Middle Kingdom tombs. In Nubia the major forts were refurbished and new ones erected at critical junctures along the Nile, to facilitate trade and the extraction of natural resources. Egypt conducted trade in the Mediterranean region, and a special relationship was developed with Byblos, where considerable Egyptian influence is obvious.

The New Kingdom (1550–1070 B.C.) was the period in which the armies of the Nile marched to the Euphrates and to the Fifth Cataract, just above modern Khartoum. The expeditions to Punt are well documented in this era, especially those sent by HATSHEPSUT (1473–1458 B.C.). Egyptians were much taken with luxury goods in this period, and the tributes coming from exotic lands (either vassal or client states or from allies) increased their appetite for foreign items.

The Libyans fought against Egypt on several occasions, especially in the 19th and 20th Dynasties, joined by a roving group of brigands called the SEA PEOPLES, but the region was exploited and trade was continued. The Libyan trade, as well as the trade with other regions, appears to have been officially regulated in this period, with tolls, and tariffs. The kings sent out expeditions and fleets regularly, and many officials led the commercial ventures, some coming from the bureau established for foreign trade.

Caravans moved through the Libyan desert oases, and pack trains were sent into the northern Mediterranean domains. It is believed that Egypt conducted trade in this era with Cyprus, Crete, Cilicia, Ionia, the Aegean islands and perhaps even with mainland Greece. Syria remained a popular destination for trading fleets and caravans, where Syrian products were joined with those coming from the regions of the Persian Gulf. The Egyptians received wood, wines, oils, resins, silver, copper and cattle in exchange for gold (which they had in vaster amounts than any other country), linens, papyrus paper, leather goods and grains. Money had not been adopted by the Egyptians, but fixed media of exchange were used so that trade goods could be valued consistently and fairly. Gold, silver, copper and even grain were used as bartering values.

During much of the New Kingdom Nubia was controlled by the Egyptians, who maintained control of the region around the cataracts and conducted mining and quarrying operations. The trade centers flourished, with caravans coming from the south and the interiors. Nubia provided Egypt with ebony, ivory, resins, and exotic wild animals.

Tributes and foreign trade declined after RAMESSES III (1194–1163 B.C.). Expeditions to the mining regions of the Sinai ended after RAMESSES V (1156–1151 B.C.), but there was no drastic end to trade when HERIHOR and SMENDES usurped the throne in 1070 B.C. Egypt was an established trading partner with the world around it, and that tradition was maintained in good times and in bad.

Transmigration of Souls
the belief among the Egyptians that led to the development of particular texts that would enable the deceased to learn the incantations and powers to assume special forms in the afterlife. Some of these spells were included in the BOOK OF THE DEAD.

Travels of an Egyptian
a text that dates to the 19th Dynasty of Egypt and is regarded as an actual account of the journey of an official of that era, much like the REPORT OF WENAMON in the 20th Dynasty. The official traveled through Asiatic countries and endured many hardships.

Tumas
a site located 150 miles south of Aswan, where PEPI I (2289–2255 B.C.) of the 6th Dynasty celebrated a victory over the local Nubians. The king left an inscription noting his victory on the rocks of Tumas.

turquoise
See HATHOR, SERABIT EL-KHADIM and SINAI.

Tuneh el-Gebel
(or Tuna el-Gebel) a site near the city of HERMOPOLIS, near the entrance to the FAIYUM, serving as a necropolis. Hundreds of mummified ibis were discovered there, with human graves that date to the Greco-Roman period.

Tura
(or Turra) a site on the Nile across from Giza, where limestone was quarried by the ancient Egyptians. This quarry was in operation from the earliest dynastic period, and the kings of the Middle Kingdom celebrated its reopening when Egypt was reunited and at peace. (See GEBEL MOKKATEM.)

Turin Canon
a document preserved on a papyrus now in the Egyptian Museum at Turin. The papyrus, a roll of 12 pages, contains a list of ROYAL NAMES with reign dates, starting with MENES and ending with RAMESSES II. The payrus was written in the HIERATIC style and provides an accurate list of the kings of Egypt to the 19th Dynasty. Sent in a crate to the museum, the document arrived in crumpled fragments, but it is considered the most reliable KING LIST, supplementing the other lists available.

Tut'ankhamun
(Nebkheprure') the 12th king (1333–1323 B.C.) of the 18th Dynasty, the most well-known pharaoh in modern times because of the discovery of his tomb. He was the successor of SMENKHKARE', probably only eight or nine at his succession. He was married to ANKHESENAMON, the third daughter of NEFERTITI and AKHENATEN, and for a time the young couple remained at el-'AMARNA. Then they moved to Memphis and refurbished the apartments of AMENHOTEP III at Thebes for their use.

The Restoration Stela, which dates to this period, gives an account of Tut'ankhamun's efforts to stabilize the government and to restore the temples and honors of the old gods of Egypt after the 'Amarna period. He even subsidized new priests and the palace staff from his own pocket. It is believed that AYA was one of his counselors at the time, and he probably suggested the reform measures. Tut'ankhamun had been given the name Tut'ankhaten, but assumed his new name as part of the restoration of the old ways. He also moved some of the bodies of the royal family from 'Amarna to Thebes, as evidenced by a cache of royal jewelry apparently stolen during the reburial and then hidden in the royal wadi area.

In his 19th year, Tut'ankhamun died, apparently from a head wound. The nature of the wound, which

LION   a statue from the tomb of Tut'ankhamun.

Theban line. Tuthmosis had married 'Ahmose, a sister of AMENHOTEP I, and was named heir when the king died childless. 'Ahmose bore Tuthmosis two daughters, Neferukheb and Hatshepsut, and two sons, Wadjmose and Amenmose. These two sons were passed over for Tuthmosis II, born to Mutnofret, a lesser-ranked royal woman and perhaps a NOME heiress.

Assuming the throne, Tuthmosis I began many building projects, including the extension of the great temple of Amon at KARNAK. Aided by INENI, the famed architect of the era, Tuthmosis added pylons, courts and statues to the shrine, setting the standard for the eventual magnificence of the temple. He also led a military campaign into NUBIA, fighting the local warrior clans and penetrating beyond the Third Cataract. Some records indicate that Tuthmosis battled the chief of the Nubians there. A hand-to-hand combat cost the Nubian his life and his territory. Tuthmosis returned to Thebes with the body of the chief hanging from the prow of his ship. After defeating the local inhabitants, Tuthmosis started a new series of fortresses on the Nile and named a new VICEROY OF NUBIA to handle the affairs below the cataracts. His greatest military exploits, however, were conducted in the lands beyond the eastern borders of Egypt. Like others of his line he smarted over the

was in the region of the left ear, makes it likely the result of a battle injury or an accident, and not the work of an assassin. When he was buried in the VALLEY OF THE KINGS, two mummified fetuses were found in coffins sealed with his name. It is believed that they were his children, born prematurely. After his death, Ankhesenamon made the extraordinary offer of herself and the throne of Egypt to the Hittite king Shuppululiumash.

The wealth of Tut'ankhamun's mortuary regalia has mesmerized the modern world. It is believed that his canopic coffinettes were originally Smenkhkare''s. Tut'ankhamun is also credited with a mortuary temple in the area of MEDINET HABU. He had designed colossal statues for this shrine, but they were usurped by his successors.

Tuthmosis I (Akheperkare')   the third king of the 18th Dynasty (1504–1492 B.C.), a commoner by birth, Tuthmosis may have been a distant relative of the king or an heir of the Theban NOME aristocracy. His mother, Senisonbe, is identified only as ''King's Mother,'' which clearly marks her as an aristocrat or even a commoner, perhaps with ties to a connected

Tuthmosis I, the first empire-builder of the New Kingdom, from a Theban temple relief.

recent domination of the HYKSOS or Asiatics in the Delta. He felt the Egyptians needed to avenge themselves for the shame, and Tuthmosis I led an army against the territories in order to subdue tribes and to create buffer states and vassals. He managed to reach the Euphrates River with his armies, erecting a stela there to commemorate his victory. His exploits allowed him to boast that he had enlarged the boundaries of Egypt to match the circuit of the sun. At Karnak, to commemorate his victories and popularity, he had a hypostyle hall built entirely of cedar wood columns and added a copper and gold door, obelisks and flagstaffs tipped with ELECTRUM.

The tomb of Tuthmosis I was begun early in his reign. Ineni supervised the preparation in secret, placing it high in the cliffs overlooking the western shore of Thebes. The king's mortuary temple, now vanished, was located near MEDINET HABU. So popular was Tuthmosis I that his mortuary cult continued into the 19th Dynasty. He brought Egypt reviewed vigor and a sense of continuity and stability. Above all, his military campaigns healed the wounds of the Thebans and set the pattern of empire.

The mummified remains identified as those of Tuthmosis I were found with a cache of bodies in DEIR EL-BAHRI, reburied there when later dynasties discovered the original royal tombs had been vandalized. The corpse of the king was bald, showing signs of arthritis and poor teeth. Tuthmosis I had a narrow face, and an arched nose. There have been questions as to the true identity of the corpse over the years, with some scholars holding the opinion that it is not Tuthmosis'.

Tuthmosis II (Akheperenre') the fourth king (1492–1479 B.C.) of the 18th Dynasty. He was the son of TUTHMOSIS I and MUTNOFRET, a lesser–ranked wife and possibly a NOME heiress of Thebes. There has been considerable doubt about the military capacities of this heir to the throne. Frail and sickly, he was overshadowed by HATSHEPSUT, his queen, throughout his reign. However, it is recorded that he conducted at least one campaign against the Asiatics. One fragmented document states that he even entered Syria with his army and conducted another campaign in Nubia. This campaign, however, is recorded in another place as having been accomplished by others in his name. He is supposed to have come to the area to view the trophies of victory.

Tuthmosis II added to the Karnak shrine but left no other monuments to his reign. He had a daughter, NEFERU-RE', and a son, TUTHMOSIS III, from a harem woman. This son was declared his heir before Tuthmosis II died at the age of 29 or 30. His mummified remains give evidence of a systemic illness, possibly from tooth decay, an affliction quite common in that period. He was heavy-set, without the characteristic Tuthmossid muscular build, but his facial features resembled those of his warrior father.

Tuthmosis III (Menkheperre') the fifth king of the 18th Dynasty (1479–1425 B.C.), the son of TUTHMOSIS II and ISIS, a harem woman. He was named heir before Tuthmosis's death, and on later monuments he inscribed an almost miraculous account of that event. The god Amon was supposed to have forced the bearers of his sacred ark to kneel during a festival celebration. The ark was saluting a novice of the temple, Tuthmosis, serving a type of novitiate reserved for the princes of Egypt. Amon and the bearers of the sacred ark prostrated themselves in front of the prince, and Tuthmosis III rose up as the heir to the throne.

He was, however, too young to rule at the time of his father's death, and HATSHEPSUT, Tuthmosis's queen, was named regent. She allowed Tuthmosis' coronation and perhaps married him to her daughter, NEFERU-RE'. Two years later, however, with the help of her courtiers and the priests of Amon, led by HAPUSENEB and SENENMUT, she took the throne in

Tuthmosis III, Egypt's warrior pharaoh.

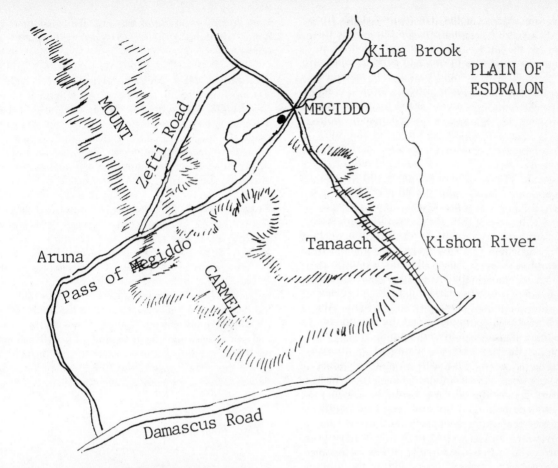

MEGIDDO (Armageddon)   site of the great victory of Tuthmosis III.

her own name, adopting masculine attire, and become queen-pharaoh. Tuthmosis was allowed to wear the robes and crowns of a king, but he was relegated to the background. That situation obtained until c. 1469 B.C., when Neferu-Re' and Senenmut died, leaving Hatshepsut vulnerable. She died or was otherwise removed from power and Tuthmosis came into his own.

He had conducted some military campaigns during Hatshepsut's reign, and he had spent a great deal of time preparing the land and naval forces of Egypt for his own expeditions. He began his reign by attacking the king of Kadesh, a northern Mediterranean region, and his allies. Territories throughout western Asia were in revolt, and Tuthmosis had to combat them in order to reestablish Egyptian suzerainty. He led his own regiments, sending ships to the Palestinian coast to meet him, and faced the army at the fortress of Megiddo, Armageddon. The Asiatics expected that he would attack them directly, but

Tuthmosis turned direction at Aruna and took his troops single-file over Mount Carmel, surprising the enemy from behind. The Egyptian cavalry, much feared in those days, sent the panic-stricken Asiatics fleeing into Medgiddo, to which he laid siege, building a wall around the outer defenses of the city. Tuthmosis left a token force there while he raided the lands of neighboring kings and chieftains. The campaign lasted only a few weeks, and on his return to Thebes Tuthmosis stopped with his troops to harvest the crops of the Asiatics.

He would conduct many military campaigns during his lifetime, many of them against Kadesh, which proved a wily and able adversary. He maintained a standing army, using mercenary regiments, particularly the ferocious Nubian troops that had won the day for his ancestor, 'AHMOSE I. He also held noble children of the conquered territories hostage, raising them in Thebes as Egyptians as a means of ensuring the loyalty of their parents and securing theirs for the future. Egypt was flooded with treasure, tribute and dignitaries from every land and city-state in the region as a result of its imperial statuage.

Tuthmosis regulated the internal affairs in the nation as well, setting the standards for viziers and court officials and using their talent to launch building projects, though many of his agents set about destroying the monuments of Hatshepsut and her cohorts in an effort to erase her memory. The construction boom was related to Egypt's new economic prosperity.

Tuthmosis III was one of Egypt's greatest generals. He conquered lands from the Fifth Cataract of the Nile to the Euphrates River, where he raised a stela, and kept his empire securely under Egyptian control.

He was possibly married to Neferu-Re', who died young, and then to Meryt-Re-Hatshepsut, probably a Memphite heiress. They had a son, AMENHOTEP II, and several daughters. Tuthmosis also had other wives, some from other kingdoms.

Tuthmosis III died in the 55th year of his reign and was buried in a tomb in the VALLEY OF THE KINGS. This tomb was decorated with strange sticklike renditions of the Am Tuat, the New Kingdom version of the BOOK OF THE DEAD. His mummified remains, damaged from vandalism and later reburied in Deir el-Bahri, give evidence of his having been 5 feet tall and of medium build. His statues depict a handsome face, lynx eyes and a hawklike nose. (See TUTHMOSIS III'S HYMN OF VICTORY, TUTHMOSIS III'S INSTRUCTIONS TO HIS VIZIER, TUTHMOSIS III'S MILITARY CAMPAIGNS, TUTHMOSIS III'S NUBIAN ANNALS.)

Tuthmosis III's Hymn of Victory

A black granite document discovered in KARNAK and now in the Egyptian Museum, in Cairo, giving praise to the god AMON for the King's victories and commemorating his having reached the Euphrates River. (See TUTHMOSIS III'S MILITARY CAMPAIGNS.)

Tuthmosis III's Instructions to His Viziers

addressed to REKHMIRE', an official of Tuthmosis' reign and of his successors', and recorded on the tomb of Rekhmire' at Thebes, the instructions are considered remarkable for their detailed description of the functions of government and the standards for the proper administration of national affairs at all levels. (See VIZIER and GOVERNMENT.)

Tuthmosis III's Military Campaigns

recorded on the walls of KARNAK by Thaneni the scribe, a series of records concerning the expeditions conducted by TUTHMOSIS III during his reign. They are filled with detailed accounts of Egypt's military activ-

ities during its imperial era and are considered by some to be among the most important documents of ancient Egypt.

Tuthmosis III's Nubian Annals recorded at KARNAK, they recall Tuthmosis' expedition through the First Cataract, where he cleared the ancient canal. Tuthmosis took 17 towns and districts on this campaign. In another record 115 towns and districts are named, and on yet another list, recorded on a pylon in Amon's temple, the names of 400 towns, districts and regions are cited.

Tuthmosis IV (Menkheprure') the eighth king (1401–1391 B.C.). of the 18th Dynasty. The son of AMENHOTEP II and Queen Teo, Tuthmosis IV saw military duty as a prince and received the title of "Conqueror of Syria" for his efforts. He also fought in Nubia as a young man and proved himself courageous. When he took the throne of Egypt he was faced with rebellions in Syria and in the lands below the cataracts. He was politically involved in the growing rivalry between the emerging state of Hatti and the Mitanni Empire, and sided with the Mitannis, a choice that would plague the 19th Dynasty. He married a Mitanni princess to seal the alliance. When

TUTHMOSIS IV.

Assyria threatened the Mitannis, Tuthmosis IV sent them gold to help pay for their defense.

Peace brought Egypt prosperity, however, and Tuthmosis IV restored and embellished many buildings, including an obelisk of TUTHMOSIS III at KARNAK. The pillar had been lying on its side for three decades; Tuthmosis IV raised it and added an inscription at its base. As a prince, he had so restored the Great SPHINX at Giza, and a legend evolved out of that event.

His wife was Queen Mutemwiya, considered by some to have been a Mitanni princess. His heir was AMENHOTEP III. Tuthmosis IV died at an early age, wasted from some illness. His tomb on Thebes' western shore was a great complex of underground passages, stairways and chambers. The burial hall was designed with pillars and a sunken crypt with a granite sarcophagus. His mummified remains show that he had well-manicured fingernails and pierced ears.

Tuta called Tutu in some records, an official of the 18th Dynasty, serving in the reign of AKHENATEN (Amenhotep IV), 1353–1335 B.C. Tuta was the chamberlain of Akhenaten's court at el-'AMARNA, serving as a legate and diplomat as well. He had charge of the various foreign affairs of the kingdom, and greeted the embassies from other lands. His elaborate tomb at 'Amarna was never finished.

Tuya a queen of the 19th Dynasty, married to SETI I (c. 1306–1290 B.C.). A commoner, the daughter of Ruia and Raia, Tuya had married Seti before he was elevated to royal status. Seti's father, RAMESSES I, had been bequeathed the throne by HOREMHAB when the latter died childless.

Tuya gave birth to a son who died in infancy and then to RAMESSES II. Her daughters were Tia and Hentmire. Queen Tuya lived to see her son reign. He honored her and gave her royal recognition on all occasions. Her tomb in the VALLEY OF THE QUEENS on the western shore of Thebes contained a pink granite sarcophagus.

Two Companions of the Heart divinities of ancient Egypt who figure in the creation myths of the nation. They lived on the original Primeval Mound and their personages were exalted on the walls of the temple at EDFU.

Two Fingers a symbol in the form of the index and medius fingers. The fingers represented Horus' own digits, which he used to help OSIRIS up the LADDER to heaven. The sign was fashioned into an AMULET for both the living and the dead.

Two Ladies the name given to the ancient Egyptian goddesses NEKHEBET and WADJET. They were the protectors of Upper and Lower Egypt and were depicted on the crowns of the kings in every era.

Twosre (Sitre'meritamun) the eighth and last ruler of the 19th Dynasty, a queen-pharaoh (1198–1196 B.C.). The widow of SETI II, Twosre served as the regent for the heir, SIPTAH, but he disappeared after four years and she ruled in her own right, assisted by her counselor, BAY. Her reign did not last long, and the later Ramessids struck her name from the royal rolls. Twosre built a handsome tomb in the VALLEY OF THE KINGS, but SETHNAKHTE, the founder of the 20th Dynasty, usurped it. Several reliefs remain, as well as seals of her reign, but she left no other last monuments.

Typhonean animal the mythical creature associated with the god SETH and depicted in the DASHUR pectoral. (See GODS AND GODDESSES.)

U

uatch (or *wadj*)   the ancient Egyptian name for green stones.

uatcht   ancient Egyptian for an AMULET made out of green stones. These were considered particularly potent with magic.

Uat-Ur (or Wadj-wer)   the ancient Egyptian name for the Mediterranean Sea, which translates as "Great Green." The sea was sometimes depicted as a man, with heavy breasts for nurturing and with skin resembling pattern of waves. He was often shown with images of the Nile.

Uben   the ancient Egyptian name for the celestial bodies who were thought to have brought the light of dawn to the earth each day. The baboon was celebrated in mythological lore as greeting the Uben and the dawn.

udjat   (called *uadjet* or *wadjet* in some lists) the symbol of the Eye of RE' or HORUS. The AMULET form of the symbol was favored in all eras as the bearer of the strength and the protective powers of the sun and the moon, two vital elements in Egyptian mythology. The amulet was worn by the living and placed in tombs as part of mortuary offerings. (See HORUS EYE.)

Uer-khorphemtiu   an ancient Egyptian title for the high priest of PTAH at Memphis, called the Great Chief of the Artificers.

Uer-ma'a (or Wer-ma)   the title borne by the high priest of HELIOPOLIS, known as the Great Seer.

Umm el-Ga'ab (or Umm el-Qa'ab)   the necropolis region of the city of ABYDOS, called the "Mother of Pots" by the local inhabitants. Monuments of all of the kings of the 1st Dynasty (2920–2770 B.C.) were found at the site, as well as the monuments of PER-IBSEN and KHA'SEKHEMWY of the 2nd Dynasty: The superstructures of the tombs have vanished, and only the brick-lined pits are now visible. The kings of the Early Dynastic Period, however, left stone stelae and clay sealings, as well as ivory figurines and some furniture. The tomb of DJER, located at Umm el-Ga'ab, was declared the tomb of the god OSIRIS, and this site received many votive offerings of pottery, especially in the New Kingdom. Umm el-Ga'ab was the site of predynastic burials as well. The area has gained fame for the sounds made by the finely grained sand covering it. The sand makes eolian melodies when the wind blows against the dunes. The ancient Egyptians thought that such sounds were made by the assembling dead.

Unis (Unas)   See WENIS.

Upesh-Pet   See ASTRONOMY.

Upper Kingdom   See EGYPT.

uraeus   the insignia of the kings of ancient Egypt, worn on crowns and regal headdresses. The uraeus was fashioned out of the figure of the cobra, the goddess WADJET, the serpent protectoress of Lower Egypt. The cobra was always depicted with its hood extended, rearing up on crowns on the brows of the kings, threatening the enemies of Egypt as the divine cobra had once terrorized the foes of RE.' The cobra was also linked to the cult of OSIRIS and HORUS. (See ISIS.)

ur-heka   the instrument used by the mortuary priests in the ceremony of the Opening of the Mouth and in other funerary rites. (See MORTUARY RITUALS.)

Urhiya   an official of the 19th Dynasty, serving SETI I (1306–1290 B.C.). Of Hurrian or Canaanite descent,

Urhiya was a military commander who became a general during the campaigns of the king. The fact that he was of alien or foreign descent demonstrates the changes that had come about in Egypt during the previous two dynasties. Urhiya and other foreign-born officials of the 19th and 20th Dynasty served Egypt faithfully.

Uronarti a site near the Second Cataract of the Nile, where SENWOSRET III of the 12th Dynasty (1878–1841? B.C.) erected a FORTRESS during his Nubian campaign. The fortress was built on an island south of SEMNA, another strategic Egyptian stronghold. A rock inscription discovered at Uronarti gives an account of a campaign conducted by AMENHOTEP I of the 18th Dynasty in the same region (1525–1504) B.C.). He and the other kings of his royal line conquered Nubian territories after the close of the Second Intermediate Period. (See MILITARY and NUBIA.)

Userhat an official of the 18th Dynasty, serving AMENHOTEP II (1427–1401 B.C.). Raised in the palace in Thebes, probably as a companion of the prince, Userhat started his career as a scribe, a position that he held throughout his life. He was buried at Thebes, and his tomb is famous for its scenes of hunting, harvests and the daily routines of life along the Nile in that era.

Userhetamon "Mighty of Brow is Amon," the name of the ancient Egyptian bark presented to the god Amon at Karnak by 'AHMOSE I of the 18th Dynasty (1550–1525 B.C.) to celebrate the expulsion of the HYKSOS and their Asiatic allies from the northern territories. (See BARKS OF THE GODS.)

Userkhaf the founder of the 5th Dynasty of ancient Egypt (2465–2458 B.C.). His parentage is obscure, but there is some indication that his mother was Neferhetepes, the daughter of RA'DJEDEF. Userkhaf possibly married Khentkaues to ally himself with the main royal line of the period. His reign is not well documented, but his pyramid, built near the

USERKHAF the founder of the 5th Dynasty.

Step Pyramid of SAQQARA, demonstrates some of the architectural and artistic skills of the era. The pyramid was designed with a mortuary temple and a chapel for offerings. The temple court was surrounded by square granite columns, and reliefs were painted on the walls. Two busts of Userkhaf were recovered from this temple.

ushabti See SHABTI.

V

Valley of the Kings (Biban el-Muluk) the desert necropolis on the west bank of the Nile opposite the ancient Egyptian capital of THEBES. The 18th Dynasty, having cleared Egypt of the HYKSOS, the Asiatic invaders of the Second Intermediate Period (1640–1532 B.C.), began to build elaborate mortuary complexes of great splendor at Thebes. AMENHOTEP I (1525–1504 B.C.) is credited with having devised the plan of separating the royal tombs from mortuary temples, but he was buried probably at Dra'Abu-el-Naga'. TUTHMOSIS I, his successor, was the first king to have a tomb cut into the cliffs of the Valley of the Kings.

The valley has two main branches, the East Valley and the West. The greatest number of tombs are found on the eastern side, and in the west lie the tombs of AMENHOTEP III and AYA. The plan of the royal tomb of this era consists of a long, slightly inclined rock-cut corridor, at the end of which is the burial chamber. The decoration of the tombs was of a religious nature, normally the mortuary texts of the BOOK OF THE DEAD. There are pillars and giant reliefs in some tombs, however, and staircases in others. Tomb plugs and other architectural traps (almost always ineffectual) were incorporated into the design to ward against robbers. The most complex tomb in the Valley of the Kings was constructed for SETI I of the 19th Dynasty (1306–1290 B.C.). The tomb of TUT-ANKHAMUN was discovered in the Valley of the Kings as well.

Valley of the Queens (Biban el-Harim or Biban el-Sultanat) the necropolis on the western shore of Thebes that served as a burial site for the royal women of the 18th, 19th and 20th Dynasties in the New Kingdom (1550–1070 B.C.). Other royal family members were also buried in the Valley of the Queens, especially during the Ramessid period, when princes were entombed in the area. This necropolis is said to hold more than 70 tombs, and many of them are stylish and lavish in their decoration. One of the most beautiful of all is the resting place carved out of the rock for Queen NEFERTARI (1290–1224 B.C.) of the 19th Dynasty. The polychrome reliefs in her tomb are preserved.

valley temples part of ancient Egyptian mortuary complexes. The valley temple was designed as a counterpart to the mortuary vestibule of the temple of the PYRAMID. The mortuary temple stood directly beside the pyramid, and the valley temple, its twin in design, stood on the banks of the Nile, or at a distance in the desert linked to the mortuary temple by gigantic causeways, which were covered and elaborately decorated. Both had T-shaped entrance halls. There is some evidence that the valley temple was the site of embalming rituals and processes in some eras. The royal corpses were brought to the shrine, where special chambers had been designed for the various stages of the preparation and the wrapping of the body. (See MORTUARY RITUALS.)

Viceroy See VIZIER.

Viceroy of Nubia See VIZIER.

Vizier called a *djat* or *tjat* in ancient Egypt, the prime minister of the nation in all eras. In the Old Kingdom the viziers of Egypt were normally kinsmen of the king, members of the royal clan, and thus trusted with the affairs of the court. An exception to this tradition, however, was the best-known vizier of the Old Kingdom, a commoner named IMHOTEP. He built the STEP PYRAMID for DJOSER of the 3rd Dynasty (2630–2611 B.C.). Gradually the office was divided, with one vizier serving as the director of affairs for Lower Egypt and the other governing the territories of Upper Egypt. The vizier of Upper Egypt ruled from the ELEPHANTINE to Assiut, and the other governed all the lands above Assiut.

Viziers heard all domestic territorial disputes,

maintained a cattle and herd census, controlled the reservoirs and the food supply, supervised industries and conservation programs, and were required to repair all dikes. The bi-annual census of the population came under their purview, as did the records of rainfall and the varying levels of the Nile during its inundation. All government documents used in ancient Egypt had to have the seal of the vizier in order to be considered authentic and binding. Tax records, storehouse receipts, crop assessments and other necessary agricultural statistics were kept in the offices of the viziers.

Members of the royal family normally served as assistants to the viziers in every era. The office was considered an excellent training ground for the young princes of each royal line, although many queens and princesses received extensive training and undertook a period of service with the vizier and his staff. Queens HATSHEPSUT and TIY are New Kingdom examples of royal women involved in the day-to-day administration of the nation.

If the capital was in the south, at Thebes, the vizier of Upper Egypt lived there and served also as mayor of the city. Normally he was assisted by a mayor of the western shore, because the vast necropolis sites and the artisans' villages there demanded supervision. The viziers of Upper and Lower Egypt saw the king on a daily basis or communicated with him frequently. Both served as the chief justices of the Egyptian courts, and listened to appeals or decisions from the NOME justices. Other state officials, such as the treasurer, chancellor, keeper of the seal, etc., served under the viziers in a tight-knit and efficient bureaucracy. In the New Kingdom a third governor was added to the force.

'AHMOSE I (1550–1525 B.C.) of the 18th dynasty established the Viceroyalty of NUBIA in order to maintain orders in the rapidly expanding territories below the cataracts. This viceroy was called the "King's Son of Kush," an honorary name, but the normal candidates were hereditary princes and counts of the various nomes. There had always been a governor for the territories below the cataracts, but in the New Kingdom the post was given an official title and rank. Many of these Viceroys of Nubia had to maintain standing armies and military skills. They were used to halt rebellions or to delay invasions until the regular army units could get to the scene. The Viceroys of Nubia served at the Elephantine Island at Aswan. Certain "Governors of the North" were also appointed during the New Kingdom period in order to maintain control of the Egyptian areas in Palestine, Lebanon and Syria during the time of empire.

The most famous vizier of the New Kingdom was REKHMIRE', who served TUTHMOSIS III (1479–1425 B.C.). This able official was buried at Thebes, and on his tomb walls he gave an account of Tuthmosis III's instructions concerning the duties and obligations of a righteous vizier. The commands or instructions are remarkable for their detailed description of the workings of all levels of government. They include a description of the vizier's palace office, the type of reports deemed necessary to maintain communications with other government bureaus, and 30 separate activities that were part of his position. Again and again stress is placed on service to the oppressed or the weak, a theme that dates back to the sages of the Old Kingdom and the ELOQUENT PEASANT of the 10th Dynasty. Normally the viziers of Egypt were remarkable men, astute, well-trained and dedicated to the service of rich and poor alike, in an ideal expression of the spirit of MA'AT, the ethical and moral principal guiding the nation. (See GOVERNMENT and LEGAL SYSTEM.)

W

Wabet the "House of Purification," where the bodies of the deceased were taken for the first stages of the embalming rituals vital to each funeral. In some eras the word was also applied to chambers in the VALLEY TEMPLES of the great pyramids and mortuary complexes of the kings. (See MORTUARY RITUALS and VALLEY TEMPLES.)

wadi an Arabic term for a gulley or dry riverbed, used in modern designations of Egyptian sites.

Wadi Abbad a site east of EDFU, where gold-mining operations were conducted in the New Kingdom era of ancient Egypt. SETI I (1306–1290 B.C.) of the 19th Dynasty erected compounds and dug wells for the benefit of workers there. He also built a temple on the site and directed that the gold be sent to the temple of Abydos.

Wadi Alaki a gold-bearing region in the vicinity of QUBAN near the Second Cataract of the Nile. Under the supervision of the Viceroy of Nubia, who was stationed at the ELEPHANTINE at Aswan, Wadi Alaki was refurbished by the kings of the 19th Dynasty, who set up mining operations there. A well was dug at the mining camp by RAMESSES II (c. 1290–1224 B.C.).

Wadi el-Sebua a site south of the First Cataract where RAMESSES II (1290–1224 B.C.) of the 19th Dynasty built a temple. The shrine was dedicated to the gods Amon and Re'-Harakhty. An avenue of sphinxes and a stone pylon graced the site, which was filled with statues.

Wadi Gabbanet el-Kurrud (or Wadi Qubbanet el-Qirud) a site in the desert on the western shore of the Nile, 2 miles west of the necropolis at DEIR EL-BAHRI, called the Valley of the Tombs of the Monkeys. The three Syrian wives of TUTHMOSIS III (c.

1479–1425 B.C.) of the 18th dynasty were buried there in identical tombs with sumptuous mortuary regalia. They were MERTI, MENWI and MENHET, probably given in marriage to the king by their Syrian chief father as a gesture of loyalty and respect. (See MERTI, MENHET and MENWI.)

Wadi Gasus a site on the coast of the Red Sea, parallel to the ancient Egyptian city of COPTOS. A stela dating to the 18th Dynasty was discovered there, as well as a text from the Middle Kingdom. This site was important to the Egyptians in all eras as the starting point for expeditions to PUNT. The Egyptians lost some officials in the region, victims of hostile attacks, but the wadi and other important sites in the area were kept guarded by Egyptian military units in the New Kingdom. (See KUSER.)

Wadi Halfa an area located at the Second Cataract of the Nile in NUBIA, considered a strategic position by the ancient Egyptians. Inscriptions discovered in the region commemorate the Nubian campaigns of King SENWOSRET I of the 12th Dynasty (1971–1926 B.C.). Another stela, erected in the 19th Dynasty, commemorated the temple of Horus, which was built on the site. In many eras Wadi Halfa was the southern border of Egypt. In other historical periods Egypt extended its control far to the south, and with the close of the New Kingdom relinquished many claims to the region.

Wadi Hammamat one of the important roadways of ancient Egypt in all eras. This dried river gulley began at COPTOS, where the Nile swerves closest to the Red Sea, and stretched across the eastern desert to the seacoast. Caravans traveled by this route in all periods, and it is believed that some of the inhabitants of Upper Egypt entered the area in this fashion in the predynastic times. (SEE KUSER, TRADE.)

Wadi Hudi also Wadi el-Hudi, a site 6 miles southeast of modern Aswan noted for amethysts. A copper-mining operation was founded there by SENWOSRET I of the 12th Dynasty (1971–1926 B.C.). The Middle Kingdom rulers sent expeditions there to locate natural resources.

Wadi Maghara a site on the Sinai peninsula of ancient Egyptian copper and turquoise mines. Inscriptions from the reign of AMENEMHET III of the 12th Dynasty (1844–1797 B.C.) were discovered there. He sent an expedition to the region in search of copper and malachite.

Wadi Mia also Wadi Miah, a rocky site near EDFU that led to gold mines some 35 miles inland from the river. SETI I (1306–1290 B.C.) of the 19th Dynasty refurbished a well and a compound there in response to pleas from the local miners. A temple at the site commemorated his achievements and generosity. (See BARRAMIYEH and GEBEL ZEBARA.)

Wadi Qash a site near Coptos on the main Egyptian trade route to the Red Sea. Inscriptions from the predynastic times and the Early Dynastic Period (2920–2575 B.C.) were discovered there.

Wadi Natron a site near modern Cairo, located on the fringe of the desert, where NATRON was discovered and processed by the ancient Egyptians from predynastic times. Natron, a soda-like substance, was commonly used as a detergent. It also had antiseptic and drying qualities, and in time was incorporated into embalming processes.

Wadi Tumilat a fertile depression north of Bubastis in the eastern Delta that was used by the ancient Egyptians as a path to the Red Sea. The wadi led to the Bitter Lakes, which in turn opened onto the Red Sea. The route was called "Sweet Water" by the Egyptians.

Wadj the third king of the 1st Dynasty (reign dates unknown), who was included in the historian Manetho's KING LIST. Wadj's limestone stela, inscribed with a SEREKH, is preserved in the Louvre. The stela was discovered at ABYDOS, where Wadj built his mortuary complex. An inscription bearing his name was also discovered near EDFU. His wife was probably queen Mereneith, who served as regent for his heir, Den.

Wadjet a goddess of ancient Egypt, the protector of the northern territories, Lower Egypt, called Buto in Greek texts. Wadjet was associated at times with the goddess HATHOR. NEKHEBET was her sister goddess, the patron of Upper Egypt. Wadjet was also associated with the Osirian cult, and was believed to have helped the goddess ISIS keep watch over the infant deity HORUS on Chemmis in the Delta. Wadjet arranged the reeds and foliage to hide the divine mother and son from all enemies so that Horus could mature to strike down his father's assassin, SETH. Wadjet was depicted as a cobra or as a woman. As a woman holding the crown of Lower Egypt, with an entwined papyrus scepter and a serpent, she was included in the coronation ceremonies of the kings. This goddess offered the crown of Lower Egypt to each new ruler in the rituals.

Wadjmose a prince of the 18th Dynasty, the son of TUTHMOSIS I (1504–1492 B.C.) and Queen 'AHMOSE. He died young or was set aside for TUTHMOSIS II. Wadjmose was a brother of HATSHEPSUT.

Wall of the Prince a series of fortresses and garrisons along the eastern boundary of Egypt, with a corresponding number probably erected on its western borders. AMENEMHET I (1991–1962 B.C.) of the 12th Dynasty is credited with the first of these garrisons, which were continued by his successors. There were similar fortresses at the cataracts in NUBIA. The Wall of the Prince was mentioned in the prophecies of NEFERTI.

Waret the ancient Egyptian name for the watery abyss or chaos which preceded the moment of creation in the cosmogonic mythology. (See COSMOGONY and PRIMEVAL MOUND.)

warfare See MILITARY.

Waset See THEBES.

Waters of Re' a branch of the Nile that stemmed from the river at Heliopolis and flowed northeast to enrich the agricultural area termed Goshen in the bible. The stream was referred to as the Waters of Avaris during the 19th Dynasty. At el-Qantara the stream became the "Waters of Horus" and then emptied into the sea near Sinu, later called Pelusium by the Greeks.

Wawat an area south of Aswan and the First Cataract, that was easily subdued and settled by the ancient EGYPTIANS. It is called Lower NUBIA in some records. The capital of the territory was Aniba, called

Miam in various lists. The Viceroy of Nubia resided in Wawat in some eras. (See VIZIER.)

Way of Horus   an ancient Egyptian road of strategic importance, linking the eastern bordertown of modern el-Qantara to Gaza in southern Palestine. The road was kept under guard by the Egyptians to protect the caravans that traveled it, and garrisons were built at various locations to repel nomad and Bedouin attacks. The road ran directly across the Isthmus of Suez, also secured by a series of fortified wells dug by the Egyptians to accommodate caravans and military forces on the move. (See TJEL.)

Wegaf (Khutawyre')   the first king (1783–1779 B.C.) of the 13th Dynasty. Little is known of his reign.

Wenamon   a real or fictional official of RAMESSES XI (1100–1070 B.C.) and the protagonist of the Report of Wenamon, which serves as an important account of the customs, traditions and political realities of the time. Wenamon was sent on an expedition to the Mediterranean coast for timber, a vital resource rare in Egypt in that period. On his return home he reported his trials and tribulations to the king. The text of his report depicts Egyptian life and the loss of prestige and military power. The nation was no longer a world leader, and the king was a recluse, kept in ignorance by his ambitious officials. (See HERIHOR and SMENDES.)

Weni   an official of the 6th Dynasty initially serving PEPI I (2289–2255 B.C.). Weni was a military commander and an innovator in tactics and defense. He fought the Sinai Bedouins in one campaign, chasing them all the way to Mount Carmel. Other campaigns followed, and Weni displayed remarkable cunning. His abilities renewed and altered the Egyptian military spirit. He demanded aggressive behavior on the part of his troops, instead of the usual defensive posture, and he incorporated Nubian warriors into his armies. Under Pepi I's successor, NEMTYEMZAF, Weni became the governor of Upper Egypt. He cut a series of channels alongside the Nile at the First Cataract and made other military improvements.

Weni was also asked by the king to investigate a harem plot involving a royal wife (called Amtes or Yamtisy in some lists). Weni gave an account of his investigation of the plot and the subsequent trial on a stela but did not include the verdict or the fate of any involved. His tomb at Abydos had a beautiful poem describing the return of the Egyptian army safely under his command after having defeated the enemy in the face of many dangers inscribed on a stela.

Wenis (Unas in some lists.)   the ninth king of the 5th Dynasty (2356–2323 B.C.). Trade expeditions were conducted during his reign, and he had an inscription raised at the Elephantine, showing a giraffe being brought into Egypt, obviously a rare creature at the time. Battle scenes appear on a vase bearing his name, discovered in Byblos. Accounts of a famine during his reign were also found. His wife was Queen Nebet, the mother of Prince Wenisankh (or Unasankh). Another wife was Khenut. Wenis' tomb at Saqqara is famous for the PYRAMID TEXTS inscribed on its walls.

Wepwawet   the jackal (sometimes called a wolf) god of ancient Egypt, assimilated into the cult of ANUBIS. Wepwawet was a friend of the god OSIRIS and was called the "Opener of the Ways." In some myths Wepwawet piloted the sun boat as it traveled through the chambers of the night. He was honored in many NOMES.

Wereret   See CROWNS.

Weret   called Wer in some records, an ancient Egyptian god of the sky, referred to as the "Great One" in hymns and litanies. He was identified with the cults of THOTH and HORUS in various regions. The sun and the moon were traditionally held to be his eyes, and on moonless nights he was thought to be blinded. In this blinded state Weret was the protector of priest-physicians who treated diseases of the eyes and the patron of blind musicians. In some reliefs he was depicted as a harp-playing god.

Wersu   called Worsu in some records, an official of the 18th Dynasty, serving in the reign of AMENHOTEP II (1427–1401 B.C.). Wersu was the superintendent of the gold-mining operations in the southern domains any may have served as Viceroy of Nubia as well. Statues of him and his wife were discovered in Coptos.

Weshptah   an official of the 5th Dynasty, serving in the reigns of SAHURE' (2458–2446 B.C.) and KAKAI (2446–2426 B.C.). He began his career during the reign of Sahure' and later became the VIZIER of Egypt under Kakai. A noted architect and the chief justice of the nation, Weshptah fell ill while attending the king. The court physician was summoned but could not save the aged official. When Weshptah died,

Kakai was supposedly inconsolable. He arranged for the ritual purification of the body in his presence and then commanded that an ebony coffin be made for Weshptah. The vizier's son, Mernuterseteni, was ordered by the king to bury his father with special tomb endowments and rituals. Weshptah was given a grave site near the pyramid of Sahure' in return for his services. The tomb contained a touching description of the honors.

Westcar Papyrus a document in the Egyptian Museum of Berlin. The Tale of Khufu and the Magicians and other texts concerning that era were discovered in the papyrus.

Western Waters also the Western River in some records, the Canopic arm of the Nile in the Delta. This great branch of the Nile was noted for its vineyards and fine wines. In some eras there were royal residences built along its banks.

White Chapel small structure with fine reliefs, erected by SENWOSRET I (c. 1971–1926 B.C.) of the 12th Dynasty discovered at KARNAK. Restored, the chapel is now on the grounds of Karnak and is a masterpiece of Egyptian architecture of the Middle Kingdom, a period considered by later generations of Egyptians as the golden age of the nation. The carved wall reliefs depict Senwosret I being embraced by Ptah, Amon, Atum and Horus, each god placed at the cardinal points of the earth.

Window of Appearance a station incorporated into the design of New Kingdom palaces, and perhaps earlier, where the king could show himself to the people and could dispense honors to worthy recipients. The most famous Window of Appearance was in el'-AMARNA, where AKHENATEN (Amenhotep IV) and Queen NEFERTITI appeared before the faithful of ATEN.

women the role of women is difficult to assess because of the absence of extant records about their activities and legal status. Royal women and those of non-royal status seldom had records attesting to their duties or rights, and in almost every case (with the exception of the queen-pharaohs) they were considered for the most part in terms of their relationships or services to males. Even the mortuary stelae, the tablets erected for women as commemoratives, equated them with their husbands, fathers or sons. Their depictions in tombs always portray them in a secondary position, if they are shown at all. In some eras women were shown the same size as their husbands, but in most instances they were smaller and placed in a peripheral area. Men never listed their mothers or their wives in their tombs, and children were described as their fathers'. As the mortuary depictions are the basis of much of the available information about women, their roles and achievements are left obscured.

The royal women are the best documented, but even they are only cursorily mentioned in dynastic records. In the nomes, however, many women, such as Princess NEBT, did maintain their own estates and held ranks personally or as regents for their minor sons.

Legally, the women of ancient Egypt were the equals of men, and they are mentioned frequently in regulations concerning the proper attitudes of officials. Some didactic literature warns young men against frivolous or flirtatious women, but there is also a text that admonishes young men to think about the travails and sufferings their mothers endured for their sake. Women depicted in the mortuary reliefs and paintings are shown conducting the normal household tasks, although women of higher status no doubt had household servants to attend to these chores. Women are also presented as young and beautiful in most tomb scenes, whether they are the wives or mothers of the men buried there. Such idealization was part of the mortuary or funerary art and did not represent the actual age or physical condition of the women portrayed.

No women are recorded as having excelled in the various arts. Few government positions were held by women, except regent in the royal households or in the nomes, and even the role of women in the temples became peripheral. The early priestesses, if they were priestesses in truth, were relegated to songstresses in the New Kingdom. In the 18th Dynasty, queens held the rank of "Wives of Amon," but that title was honorary and accorded little authority. They served only as escorts or as welcoming committees when the god was paraded on festivals. It appears that the home was truly the domain of the woman, a situation that lasted only until the death of the husband or divorce. (See QUEENS.)

writing materials See SCRIBES.

"writing from the god himself" a term used by the ancient Egyptians for any document from early eras of the nation. Any source from the past was revered and considered a holy text to be obeyed and imitated.

XYZ

Xois the modern Sakha, located in the central Delta, a city of ancient Egypt. During the Second Intermediate Period the nobles from this region began the Xoite Dynasty (14th Dynasty), which ruled contemporaneously with the HYKSOS and Asiatic line and with the Theban dynasty in the south. Manetho listed 76 Xoite kings and 72 of the names were confirmed by the TURIN PAYRUS. During the 20th Dynasty, in the reign of RAMESSES III (1194–1163 B.C.), Xois was one of the towns overrun by the Libyan forces under the command of the MESHWESH. Ramesses III defeated the Libyans and set Xois and its neighboring communities free of the foreign domination.

Yam a region of ancient Nubia, visited by the Egyptians of the 6th Dynasty. HARKHAF, on an expedition under PEPI II (2246–2152 B.C.) was reported as having been befriended by the people of Yam.

Yuf an official of the 18th Dynasty, in the reign of 'AHMOSE I (c. 1550–1525 B.C.). Yuf served as the steward of Queens AHHOTEP and 'AHMOSE. A stela discovered in Edfu gives an account of Yuf's career. He also served the temple on that site.

Yuia an official of the 18th Dynasty, serving in the reigns of TUTHMOSIS IV (1401–1391 B.C.) and AMENHOTEP III (1391–1353 B.C.). Yuia was the father of Queen TIY, the wife of Amenhotep III. He was also a Master of Horse, a title which carried the name "Father of the God." Yuia served as chancellor of the North and as a priest of Hermonthis and Amon during his career. His wife, TUIA, was of Egyptian descent. His mummified remains indicate that Yuia was of Indo-European stock, probably a Hurrian. That particular ethnic group served in the cavalry units of the Egyptians.

Yuny an official of the 19th Dynasty, serving in the reign of RAMESSES II (1290–1224 B.C.). Yuny was the chief scribe of the court, the overseer of priests and the royal steward. His tomb at Deir Durunka, south of Assiut, portrays Yuny as an hereditary prince and count. A life-size statue of him was discovered in the tomb.

Zanakht (Nebka) the first king (2649–2630 B.C.), of the 3rd Dynasty believed to have been an older brother of DJOSER. He was listed in the Turin Canon and in the Abydos KING LIST. His tomb at Saqqara was incorporated into the STEP PYRAMID. Zanakht is also mentioned in the Westcar Papyrus.

Zannanza a prince of the Hittites, sent to Egypt by his father, King Shuppiluliumash, at the request of Queen ANKHESENAMON, the window of TUT'ANKHAMUN (1333–1323 B.C.). Ankhesenamon offered herself and the throne of Egypt to the prince. He was slain at the border of Egypt, probably by the agents of HOREMHAB.

Zawiet el-Amwat a site on the eastern desert of Egypt, northeast of BENI HASAN, where a step pyramid was discovered. The pyramid was designed as a trapezoid, covered with masonry. The structure dates to the Old Kingdom (2575–2134 B.C.).

Zawiet el-Aryan the modern name for the necropolis just south of Giza, where two pyramids have been discovered. One, the "Layer Pyramid" was erected by KHA'BA of the 3rd Dynasty (2603–2599 B.C.). Alabaster vases found nearby provide the only information about this pyramid, which was not finished. The second pyramid, whose owner is unknown, probably from the 4th Dynasty, is called the

"Unfinished Pyramid." Only the subterranean levels were begun, but a sarcophagus was discovered embedded in the floor of the burial chamber.

Zekhen See SCORPION KING.

Zerukha the site of MALKATA on the western shore of the Nile opposite Thebes, where AMENHOTEP III (1391–1353 B.C.) of the 18th Dynasty built his vast complex of pleasure palaces.

Zoser See DJOSER.

SUGGESTED READING LIST

Adams, Barbara. *Ancient Hierakonpolis*. Warminster, England: Aris & Phillips, Ltd., 1974.

Adams, Barbara. *Egyptian Mummies*. Aylesbury, England: Shire Publications, Ltd., 1984.

Albright, W.F. "The Amarna Letters from Palestine." In *Cambridge Ancient History*, 3rd ed., vol. 2, 98–116. Cambridge: Cambridge University Press, 1975.

Aldred, Cyril. *The Development of Ancient Egyptian Art from 3200–315 B.C.* London: Alec Tiranti, 1962.

Aldred, Cyril. *Egypt to the End of the Old Kingdom*. New York: McGraw Hill, 1965.

Aldred, Cyril. *Jewels of the Pharoahs: Egyptian Jewelry of the Dynastic Period*. New York: Praeger Publication, 1971.

Aldred, Cyril. *Akhenaten and Nefertiti*. Exhibition Catalog, The Brooklyn Museum. New York: Viking Press, 1973.

Aldred, Cyril. "Egypt: The Amarna Period and the End of the Eighteenth Dynasty." In *Cambridge Ancient History*, 3rd ed., vol. 2, 49–97. Cambridge: Cambridge University Press, 1975.

Aldred, Cyril. *Egyptian Art in the Days of the Pharoahs*. New York: Oxford University Press, 1980.

Aldred, Cyril. *The Egyptians*. rev. ed. London: Thames and Hudson, 1984.

Aldred, Cyril. *Akhenaten: King of Egypt*. London: Thames and Hudson, 1988.

Allen, Thomas G. *The Egyptian Book of the Dead: Documents in the Oriental Institute Museum at the University of Chicago*. Chicago: University of Chicago Press, 1960.

Andrews, Carol. *The Rosetta Stone*. London: British Museum Publications, 1988.

Baines, John and Malek, Jaromir. *Atlas of Ancient Egypt*. New York: Facts On File, Inc., 1980.

Barnett, R.D. "The Sea Peoples." In *Cambride Ancient History*, 3rd ed., vol. 2, 359–378. Cambridge: Cambridge University Press, 1975.

Baumgartel, Elise J. "Predynastic Egypt." In *Cambridge Ancient History*, 3rd ed., vol. 1, 463–498. Cambridge: Cambridge University Press, 1970.

Bianchi, Robert S. et al. *Cleopatra's Egypt: Age of the Ptolemies*. Exhibition Catalogue. Brooklyn: The Brooklyn Museum, 1988.

Berbrier, Morris. *Tomb-Builders of the Pharoahs*. New York: Charles Scribner's Sons, 1984.

Bjorkman, G. *Kings at Karnak: A Study of the Treatment of Royal Predecessors in the Early New Kingdom*. Boreas: Uppsala Studies in Ancient Mediterranean and Near Eastern Civilizations, 2. Uppsala: Alumqvist & Wisell, 1971.

Bowman, Alan K. *Egypt after the Pharoahs, 332 BC-AD 642*. Berkeley: University of California Press, 1986.

Braun, T.F.R.C. "The Greeks in Egpt." In *Cambridge Ancient History*, 2nd ed., vol. 3, 32–56. Cambridge: Cambridge University Press, 1982.

Butzer, Karl W. "Physical Conditions in Eastern Europe, Western Asia, and Egypt Before the Period of Agricultural Settlement." In *Cambridge Ancient History*, 3rd ed., vol. 1, 62–69. Cambridge: Cambridge University Press, 1970.

De Cenival, Jean-Louis. *Living Architecture: Egyptian*. New York: Grosset and Dunlap, 1964.

Cerny, Jaroslav. "Egypt From the Death of Ramesses III to the End of the Twenty-First Dynasty." In *Cambridge Ancient History*, 3rd ed., vol. 2, 606–657. Cambridge: Cambridge University Press, 1975.

Cerny, Jaroslav. *Paper and Books in Ancient Egypt*. London: H.K. Lewis & Co., Ltd., 1952.

Clarke, Somers, and Engelbach, Reginald. *Ancient Egyptian Masonry: The Building Craft*. London: Oxford University Press, 1930.

Cockburn, Aidan, and Cockburn, Eva, eds. *Mummies, Disease, and Ancient Cultues*. Cambridge: Cambridge University Press, 1980.

Davies, W.V. *Egyptian Hieroglyphs*. London: British Museum Publications, 1987.

Dawson, Warren R., and Uphill, Eric P. *Who Was Who in Egyptology*. 2nd ed. London: Egypt Exploration Society, 1972.

Edwards, I.E.S. "Early Dynastic Period in Egypt." In *Cambridge Ancient History*, 3rd ed., vol. 1, 1–70. Cambridge: Cambridge University Press, 1971.

Edwards, I.E.S. "Egypt: From the Twenty-Second to the Twenty-Fourth Dynasty." In *Cambridge Ancient History*, 2nd ed., vol 3, 534–581. Cambridge: Cambridge University Press, 1982.

Faulkner, Raymond O. *The Ancient Egyptian Book of the Dead*. London: British Museum Publications, 1985.

Faulkner, Raymond O. "Egypt: From the Inception of the Nineteenth Dynasty to the Death of Ramesses III." In *Cambridge Ancient History*, 3rd ed., vol. 2, 217–251. Cambridge: Cambridge University Press, 1975.

Fischer, Henry G. *Ancient Egypt Calligraphy: A Beginner's Guide to Writing Hieroglyphs*. New York: Metropolitan Museum of Art, 1979.

Fischer, Henry G., and Caminos, R. *Ancient Egyptian Epigraphy and Palaeography*. New York: Metropolitan Museum of Art, 1976.

Garrod, D.A.E. "Primitive Man in Egypt, Western Asia, and Europe in Paleolithic Times." In *Cambridge Ancient History*, 3rd ed., vol.1, 70–77. Cambridge: Cambridge University Press, 1970.

Ghalioungui, Paul. *The Physicians of Pharaonic Egypt*. Deutsches Archaologisches Institut, Abteilung Kairo, Sonderschrift 10. Mainz am Rhein: Verlag Philipp von Zabern, 1983.

Harris, James E., and Wente, E.F. *An X-Ray Atlas of the Royal Mummies*. Chicago: University of Chicago Press, 1980.

Hayes, William C. "Egypt: From the Death of Ammenemes III to Seqenenre II." In *Cambridge Ancient History*, 3rd ed., vol. 2, 42–76. Cambridge: Cambridge University Press, 1973.

Hayes, William C. "Egypt: Internal Affairs from Tuthmosis I to the Death of Amenophis III." In *Cambridge Ancient History*, 3rd ed., vol. 2, 313–416. Cambridge: Cambridge University Press, 1973.

Hayes, William C. "The Middle Kingdom in Egypt: Internal History from the Rise of the Heracleopolitans to the Death of Ammenemes III." In *Cambridge Ancient History*, 3rd. ed., vol.1, 464–531. Cambridge: Cambridge University Press, 1971.

Hayward, R. *Cleopatra's Needles*. Buxton, England: Moorland, Publishing Co., 1978.

Heinen, H. "The Syrian Egyptian Wars and the New Kingdoms of Asia Minor." In *Cambridge Ancient History*, 2nd. ed., vol. 7, 412–445. Cambridge: Cambridge University Press, 1984.

Hobson, Christine. *The World of the Pharoahs: A Complete Guide to Ancient Egypt*. New York: Thames and Hudson, 1987.

Hoffman, Michael A. et al. *The First Egyptians*. Exhibition catoloque. The McKissick Museum and the Earth Sciences and Resources Institute of the University of South Carolina.

Columbia, South Carolina: The McKissick Museum, University of South Carolina, 1988.

Hornung, Erik. *Conceptions of God in Ancient Egypt: The One and the Many*. Ithaca: Cornell University Press, 1982.

James, T.G.H. *Ancient Egypt: The Land and Its Legacy*. London: British Museum Publications, 1988.

Kaczmarczyck, A., and Hedges, R.E.M. *Ancient Egyptian Faience: An Analytical Survey of Egyptian Faience from Predynastic to Roman Times*. Warminster, England: Aris and Phillips, Ltd., 1983.

Kees, Hermann. *Ancient Egypt: A Cultural Topography*. Chicago: University of Chicago Press, 1977.

Kemp, Barry J. *Ancient Egypt: Anatomy of a Civilization*. London and New York: Routledge, 1989.

Kischkewitz, H. *Egyptian Drawings*. London: Octopus Books, 1972.

Kitchen, Kenneth A. *The Third Intermediate Period in Egypt (1100–650 B.C.)*. 2nd ed., rev. Warminster, England: Aris and Phillips, Ltd., 1986.

Lewis, Napthali. *Life in Egypt under Roman Rule*. Oxford: Clarendon Press, 1983.

Lloyd, Alan B. *Herodotus, Book II*. 3 vols. Etudes Preliminaires aux Religions Oientales dans l'Empire Romain, vol. 47, parts 1–3. Leiden: E.J. Brill, 1975–1988.

Manetho. *Aegyptiaca*. Trans. W.G. Waddell. Cambridge, Mass.: Harvard University Press, 1940.

Manniche, Lise. *Sexual Life in Ancient Egypt*. London: KPI, 1987.

Maragioglio, V., and Tinaldi, C.A. *L'Architettura delle Piramidi Menfite*. Translated by Ernest Howell. Vols. 2-8. Turin, Italy: Centro per la Antichita e la Storia delli Arte de Vicino Egizio di Torinao, 1963–1977.

Museum of Fine Arts, Boston. *Egypt's Golden Age: The Art of Living in the New Kingdom, 1558–1085 B.C.* Exhibition catalogue. Boston: Museum of Fine Arts, 1982.

Peck, William H., and Ross, John G. *Egyptian Drawings*. New York: E.P. Dutton, 1978.

Pomeroy, S. *Women in Hellenistic Egypt from Alexander to Cleopatra*. New York: Schocken Books, 1984.

Porter, Bertha, and Moss, R.L.B. *Topographical Bibliography of Ancient Egyptian Hieroglyphic Texts, Reliefs, and Paintings*. 7 vols. Oxford: Oxford University Press for the Griffith Institute, Ashmolean Museum, Oxford, 1927–1981.

Ray, John D. "Egypt, 525–404 B.C." *The Cambridge Ancient History*, 2nd. ed., vol. 4, 254–286. Cambridge: Cambridge University Press, 1988.

Saleh, Mohammed, and Sourouzian, Hourig. *Egyptian Museum, Cairo: Official Catoloque*. Mainz am Rhein: Verlag Phillip von Zabern, 1987.

Schaefer, J. Heinrich. *Principles of Egyptian Art*. Oxford: Clarendon Press, 1974.

Smith, William S. *A History of Egyptian Sculpture and Painting in the Old Kingdom*. 2nd ed. London: Oxford University Press for the Museum of Fine Arts, Boston, 1948.

Smith, William S. "The Old Kingdom in Egypt and the Beginning of the First Intermediate Period." In *Cambridge Ancient History*, 3rd ed., vol. 1, 145–207. Cambridge: Cambridge University Press, 1971.

Spencer, A.J. *Brick Architecture in Ancient Egypt*. Warminster, England: Aris and Phillips, Ltd., 1979.

Taylor, John H. *Egyptian Coffins*. Shire Egyptology, 11. Aylesbury, England: Shire Publications, 1989.

Thomas, Angela P. *Egyptian Gods and Myths*. Shire Egyptology, 2. Aylesbury, England: Shire Publications, 1986.

Turner, Eric G. "Ptolemaic Egypt." In *Cambridge Ancient History*, 2nd ed., vol. 7, 118–174. Cambridge: Cambridge University Press, 1984.

Watterson, Barbara. *Introducing Egyptian Hieroglyphs*. Edingburgh: Scottish Academic Press, 1981.

Winlock, H.E. *The Rise and Fall of the Middle Kingdom in Thebes*. New York: Macmillan and Co., 1947.

INDEX

The following entries have been grouped to lead the reader to related sources of information on specific topics covered in this volume. The reader should consult the entry corresponding to the subject listing first, and then see the entries that follow for additional information.

GOVERNMENT

LITERATURE

LAWS AND COURTS

MORTUARY RITUALS AND CULTS

─────────── **WARFARE** ───────────
see details of this subject under Military; see also: